To my parents

Contents

Preface

This book, based on the author's PhD thesis, attempts to integrate and interpret the vast corpus of existing research evidence on social class, slums and crime. The goal is to seek answers to two policy questions. First, will policies to redistribute wealth and power within capitalist societies have effects upon crime? Second, will policies to overcome the residential segregation of social classes have effects on crime?

To attempt to answer these questions research evidence from various capitalist societies is jointly overviewed, with particular emphasis upon evidence from the United States, Great Britain and Australia. A basic assumption of the book is that the crime problems of differing capitalist societies have a similar class basis. It will be seen that in very few cases have cross-national differences emerged from empirical criminology with regard to variables which connect class to crime. Nevertheless, where there are problems in extrapolating findings from one nation to others, an attempt is made to discuss these difficulties.

There has been so much empirical research and theorizing on class, slums and crime that an attempt to pull it all together into a framework which makes it possible for policy-makers to make judgments on what kinds of egalitarian reforms within capitalism might reduce crime is long overdue. The reader will discover that when all of the evidence is assembled there are a number of surprises in store. These surprises have regrettably remained submerged because criminologists have in the past shown scant interest in systematic reviews of the evidence on egalitarian reform as a solution to crime. The protagonists—conservatives, social democratic reformers, and Marxists—have preferred to snipe at each other's work from entrenched ideological positions. The question of whether a more equal society would be a less criminal society is resolved to everyone's satisfaction at an ideological level. All parties selectively use data supportive of their position as a tactical tool in the ideological battle. The author is not immune from an ideological commitment. He is a socialist. But an attempt has been made in this book to review non-selectively all the evidence on key empirical questions in the policy analysis.

Part I of the book defines the problems to be tackled and reviews the current standing of theory and empirical research on the relationship between class and crime. Part II analyses whether greater residential mixing of classes might have efficacy for crime reduction, while Part III examines the value for crime reduction of policies to equalize wealth and power.

The first chapter defines the main constructs of concern and discusses the problems of operationalizing these constructs. Chapter 2 reviews the evidence on whether lower-class people, and people who live in lower-class areas, exhibit higher crime and delinquency rates than the remainder of the population. Various theoretical explanations of the findings in chapter 2 (theories which predict greater criminality among the lower class and among people living in lower-class areas) are evaluated in chapter 3. The implications of these theories for the effect on crime of egalitarian policies are also explored.

Chapter 4 elaborates the findings and the theory from Part I on the relationship between crime and social class of area into theories which predict that greater residential mixing of classes would reduce crime. Alternative theories which predict that greater residential mixing of classes would increase crime are also discussed. Chapters 5 to 8 investigate the association between class-mix and crime by analysing, in turn, existing data in the literature (chapter 5), self-report juvenile-crime data from a Brisbane survey (chapter 6), court records of juvenile crime in Brisbane (chapter 7), and inter-city comparisons of crime rates from the United States (chapter 8). Chapter 9 summarizes the conclusions of Part II on the effect of the residential segregation of classes on crime, and discusses the policy options available to social planners who might set out to reduce crime through fostering class-mix.

Chapter 10 refocuses upon the traditional conceptions of the social-class distribution of crime discussed in chapters 2 and 3, and calls into question these traditional conceptions when white-collar and corporate crime are taken into account. A new theory of class and crime is presented which incorporates white-collar crime. Chapter 11 considers various alternative levels of analysis for ascertaining whether greater equality is associated with lower crime-rates. Do nations with a high degree of economic inequality have higher crime-rates than more egalitarian societies? Within nations, do cities which have a wide gap between the rich and the poor have higher crime-rates than cities with a more equal income structure? As the degree of inequality in cities or nations increases and decreases across time (e.g. with recessions), does the crime-rate concomitantly increase and decrease? Have anti-poverty programmes been shown to reduce crime and delinquency? Finally chapter 12 draws together conclusions about the efficacy of greater equality as a policy for crime reduction.

Acknowledgments

Many people have offered criticism on the ideas expressed in this book. However, special recognition is due to my PhD supervisor, Paul Wilson, who has always been critical, but always encouraging.

Other people who deserve special mention for reading and criticizing earlier drafts of the work are Gilbert Geis, Duncan Chappell, John Western, Henry Law, Kay Bussey, Boris Crassini, June Fielding, Greg Smith, Mike Emmison, Diane Gibson, Richard Gaven, Bill Gibson and Jake Najman. My most painstaking and constructive critic has been my wife, Valerie.

I am indebted to the YMCA for allowing me to include in this book data which I collected while employed by them at the University of Queensland. Officers of the Department of Children's Services also gave great assistance in the compiling of data on court-recorded delinquency.

I would like to thank Annette Waters and Jenny McDowall for their patience and hard work in typing the manuscript.

Acknowledgments

Part I

Chapter 1

Defining the problem

The research goals

For many years criminologists have been preoccupied with social inequality as an explanation of crime. The emphasis in this preoccupation has shifted from an early stress upon ecological (or inter-area) inequality to inequality among individuals. Discussions of the slum as a cause of crime and individual poverty as a cause of crime have usually been intertwined, often in a confusing way. It is important that confounding between the two levels of analysis be untangled, because policies which are appropriate for tackling the problem of ecological inequality are quite different from policies to reduce inequalities among individuals. Part II of this book is devoted exclusively to a public-policy analysis of ecological inequality, and Part III to an analysis of inequalities among individuals.

There is a variety of individual and ecological inequalities. In the case of the former, the focus of this work is restricted to a discussion of policies to create greater equality of wealth and power among individuals. Other inequalities, such as in prestige, or in educational opportunity, are considered only in so far as they are relevant to the impact of policies to equalize wealth and power. At the ecological level, the focus is entirely upon policies to create greater social class-mix; that is, on policies to reverse the tendency for lower-class people to be segregated into slums. To be more explicit, the goals of this book are in Part II to analyse whether policies to create greater class-mix might have any efficacy for reducing crimes against persons and property, and in Part III to analyse whether policies to change the distribution of wealth and power in society might have any efficacy for reducing crimes against persons and property.

No attempt is made here to analyse the desirable and undesirable

3

effects of greater class-mix and equality on other goals of public policy besides crime reduction. Moreover, in no sense can it be argued that an examination of the data logically impels the criminologist to opt for the kind of policy analysis chosen for this book. If, for example, the data leads one to conclude that poor people are more criminal than others, why not study the efficacy of assigning more police to surveillance of the behaviour of the poor, or more social workers to help the poor, rather than study the efficacy of reducing poverty? To opt for these approaches would be, perhaps, neither more nor less an arbitrary and value-laden choice than the choice I have made.

The call for class-mix as a solution to crime

The slum has long been regarded as the breeding ground for crime and delinquency. Historically, the most favoured solution to the problem of the slum has been slum clearance or urban renewal. In recent years, however, this solution has fallen out of favour because of a belief that the criminality of the slum is more the product of its social and economic conditions than of its physical character. Urban renewal is felt simply to 'shift the location of the [criminal] subculture from one part of a city to another'.[1] Moreover, it is widely believed that in the long run urban renewal makes things financially more difficult for the poor by depleting the stock of cheap rental housing.[2] Baldwin, Bottoms and Walker's review of studies shows that slum clearance programmes may be just as likely to increase the criminality of its beneficiaries as to reduce it.[3]

The most fundamental objection to urban renewal, however, has been that forced residential mobility disrupts the lives of people, fragmenting cohesive bonds which control deviant behaviour. Once a person is removed from the stable environment to which he is accustomed, his standards can become relativistic in response to the clash of old and new social expectations, and he begins to play the game of life by ear instead of by clearly defined rules. There is now a great volume of evidence to show that the experience of residential mobility is associated with delinquent behaviour by juveniles.[4]

As alternatives to attempting to solve the problems of the slum by slum clearance, a variety of policies have been suggested to encourage greater class-mix—scattering the sites of public housing, modifying local-government zoning regulations which encourage class segregation, providing facilities which will encourage middle-class people to return to lower-class areas, legislating to combat discrimination in housing. These policies seek to destroy the slum by dispersion, where urban renewal sought to do so by knocking it down and rebuilding it. Of course urban renewal could be used to produce greater class-mix if the dislocated lower-class residents of the slum were rehoused in middle-class areas. In practice, however, urban renewal has tended to result in the replacement of deteriorated homogeneous lower-class areas with shiny new homogeneous lower-class areas. If urban renewal were used as a means for creating greater class-mix, it would suffer the important disadvantage that it would involve the forceful relocation of people.

Writing in the United States President's Commission report on Juvenile Delinquency and Youth Crime, Rodman and Grams[5] suggested that to create a low-crime environment, new towns should be designed so as to foster 'balanced communities' in racial and economic terms. The report of a working party entitled *Planning a Low Crime Social Environment for Albury-Wodonga* concluded that class-mix should be encouraged in the new growth centre to keep down crime.[6]

> The group considered that care must be taken to prevent the development of deprived neighbourhoods where services are limited and there are pockets of low standard housing leading to a potential slum area.
>
> The group was informed and accepted that the housing policy for the new growth areas was designed so that there was a 'mix' of housing styles. For a given tract of land, the Housing Commissions of Victoria and New South Wales, the Development Corporation and private enterprise, would each develop a proportionate share of the housing in the area.

The United States National Advisory Commission on Criminal Justice Standards and Goals has also suggested that increased class-mix would reduce crime.[7]

> The Commission recommends that State and local governments break down patterns of racial and economic segregation in housing through such measures as planning scatter site construction of public housing, providing rent supplements to eligible individuals, and enacting and aggressively enforcing fair housing laws, which should provide for legal penalties as a deterrent to future discrimination.

Similarly, Moynihan in the introduction to the report of the National Commission on the Causes and Prevention of Violence asserts that

5

'Efforts to improve the conditions of life in the present caste-created slums must never take precedence over efforts to enable the slum population to disperse throughout the metropolitan areas involved.'[8]

Although this kind of policy recommendation has frequently been made by influential commissions, there has been little critical analysis of its efficacy and, in particular, there has been no investigation of the empirical basis for having confidence in such a policy. The purpose of Part II is to help remedy this deficiency in the literature.

The call for a reduction in inequality as a solution to crime

There is no shortage of academics and politicians who regard the abolition of poverty as not only a way of reducing crime, but as *the main solution* to crime. Burgess is not atypical when he lists it number one on his agenda for delinquency prevention.[9]

An adequate and complete program for juvenile delinquency prevention should combine the following factors:
1. Assured family income to provide for a minimum American standard of living.

Jordan, the executive director of the National Urban League in the United States, says that 'The most powerful anti-crime measure would be a National Full Employment Policy that guarantees decent jobs for all',[10] and the President's Commission on Law Enforcement and Administration of Justice took a similar position.[11]

What is imperative is for this Commission to make clear its strong conviction that, before this Nation can hope to reduce crime significantly or lastingly, it must mount and maintain a massive attack against the conditions of life that underlie it (p. 60).

Warring on poverty, inadequate housing and unemployment, is warring on crime (p. 6).

The Commission has no doubt whatever that the most significant action that can be taken against crime is action designed to eliminate slums and ghettos, to improve education, to provide jobs, to make sure every American is given the opportunities that will enable him to assume his responsibilities (p. 15).

Perhaps the most extreme statement of this point of view has been Brady's recent assertion: 'poverty, discrimination, and human exploitation. Nearly all brands of criminologists will now argue that these conditions are the underlying causes of crime.'[12]

This belief in the centrality of egalitarian policies in a strategy to reduce crime has included inequality of power as well as inequality of wealth. Gordon says, 'It seems unlikely that we shall be able to solve the problem of crime in this country without first effecting a radical redistribution of power in our basic institutions.'[13]

Part III of this book is an evaluation of whether there is justification for this boundless confidence in the efficacy for crime reduction of policies to equalize wealth and power. Emphasis will be upon a review of existing empirical evidence rather than upon generating new data. In the past few decades there has been a monumental accumulation of empirical studies on social class, social inequality and criminal behaviour in the United States and Great Britain. Yet there has been no systematic effort to integrate these findings into a coherent policy analysis. This tendency for research on inequality to continue churning out more data, while rarely stopping to assess what it all means for public policy, has been criticized by Rein.

> In the course of examining the literature related to poverty, it became evident that . . . there is little attempt to bring together or acknowledge contradictory evidence, let alone an attempt to reconcile differences in fact and interpretation. Moreover, there are few efforts made to explore the implications for social policy of what is known and accepted.[14]

Before embarking on an analysis of the implications for crime-control policy of what is known about the relationship between class and crime, key concepts in the analysis must be defined.

Definitions

Wealth is defined as 'an abundance of costly material possessions and/or a large and stable monetary income'.[15] *Poverty* is then defined as a condition of having a relatively low level of wealth compared to others living in the same nation at the same point of time. In this book, a 'relative' rather than an 'absolute' definition of poverty will be adopted. Absolute poverty is measured against certain physical standards (such as capacity to purchase a minimum amount of food, clothing, and housing), whereas relative poverty is measured against the standards of certain groups of people. Thus an increase in economic growth which benefits all sections of the community equally reduces absolute poverty but does not affect relative poverty. The choice of a relative conception of poverty is based on the (untested) assumption that how a person compares with those around him is more likely to affect his chances of criminality than how he measures up in terms of some absolute standard.

A likely criticism of the definition of poverty adopted here is that it is based on a 'nominalist' rather than a 'realist' conception of poverty.[16] Nominal definitions consist of objective indicators (in this case, wealth), whereas realist definitions incorporate the meaning of the definition for those to whom it is applied. The use of a nominal definition sidesteps the issue of whether 'the poor' really 'exist', in the sense that they:

1 act as a social group demarcated by patterns of interaction and barriers to interaction with members of other groups; rather than stand only as an aggregate or category of individuals;
2 perceive themselves as being 'poor';
3 are perceived by others as being 'poor';
4 have a distinctive 'culture of poverty'.

Undoubtedly a realist definition, where it can be operationalized, depicts a more meaningful sociological category, and thus facilitates a clearer understanding of the phenomenon. But one's definition must be related to one's purposes. In this work the *ultimate* goal is not to obtain a maximum understanding of the phenomenon, but to evaluate whether a specific type of policy will have a specific effect. Poverty is defined as a low level of wealth because level of wealth is what we are concerned with changing in the policy analysis. Within limitations of empirical meaningfulness, the choice of definitions must be subservient to the goals of the research. Thus, under the nominalist perspective, patterns of interaction and consciousness are relegated to the status of intervening variables between poverty and crime.

Tawney defines *power* as 'the capacity of an individual, or group of individuals, to modify the conduct of other individuals or groups in the manner which he desires, and to prevent his own conduct being modified in the manner in which he does not.'[17] This is the basic definition of power adopted by most sociologists since Weber. It is rather too broad a definition, however, for the purposes of this book. As Tawney defines power, the mugger could be said to be exerting power over his victim, or a person could be said to have great power over his best friend because the friend respects his opinion. There is no concern in this study with power in the sense of interpersonal coercion or influence.

The definition of power is therefore restricted here to the capacity to modify the conduct of others in the manner desired, and to prevent the modification of one's conduct in a manner not desired, *which is legitimated by society, and which is exerted in the enactment of institutional roles.* Since institutions are defined as associations which are organized, systematized and stable,[18] we are concerned with power as defined by Tawney, which is also legitimate, organized, systematized, and stable. This is similar to that kind of power which Weber called authority.[19] Put another way, the focus is upon power which is equalizable by changes in the social structure rather than by changes in individuals or in culture. More than anywhere else, this kind of power exists in the institutionalized roles of the workplace.

The degree of *inequality* of wealth and power is the extent to which some people have more wealth and power than others. Inequality can be reduced by changing the distribution of wealth and power in two conceptually different ways. Reducing poverty can mean either reducing the wealth gap between the poor and the remainder of the population, or it can mean moving selected individuals across this gap and out of poverty. This conceptual distinction becomes important later in this book and is discussed in greater detail in chapter 11.

Usage of the term 'social class'

It is essential to state explicitly that this work is not concerned with social class as it has been traditionally defined by most sociologists, but rather is concerned with inequality in the distribution of wealth and power. The terms *lower class* and *middle class* are used respectively as convenience expressions to. denote those relatively low in wealth and power and those relatively high in wealth and power. Given the variety of ways in which social class traditionally has been defined, it is perhaps unfortunate that lower class and middle class are used as shorthand convenience terms in this way. Short of coining a neologism, however, there is little choice but to refer to those relatively low on the continuum of wealth and power as lower class, and those relatively high on the continuum as middle class.

But, it cannot be stated too strongly that there is no intent in this book of drawing fine distinctions among categories called upper class, middle class, working class, and lower class. The analysis is concerned with wealth and power as continua, not with some sociological conception of class.

For the sake of consistency with the above use of class, *class-mix* is defined as the probability that, in a geographical area, those low in wealth and power will live in close proximity to those high in wealth and power.

Defining crime

Crime is defined as behaviour which is in violation of the law. It is behaviour which is punishable by law, though not necessarily punished. That is, one does not have to be caught by the official agents of social control for one's behaviour to be classified as criminal. It should be noted that the law under which the behaviour is punishable need not necessarily be in the Criminal Code: it can appear in various civil codes such as the Income Tax Act or the Consumer Affairs Act.[20]

Delinquency or juvenile crime, when used in this book means crime committed by people who have not yet attained adulthood. For the most part, a special distinction is not made between crimes committed by juveniles and crimes committed by adults. The dichotomy between juvenile and adult crime does not distinguish especially distinct patterns of behaviour, so that data on one help to complement understanding on the other. Nevertheless, care has been taken to indicate the approximate age group involved in each study discussed. For certain special problems where it is likely that considerations which apply to juvenile crime do not apply in quite the same way to adult crime, studies on juvenile and adult crime are reviewed separately. The conclusions of these separate reviews will then normally be drawn together so that generalizations can be made which hold for crime among all age groups.

Many criminologists object to a definition of crime based on a legalistic criterion. The objection is often ideological—the law as it stands is seen as a tool in the hands of the ruling class for the purpose of protecting ruling-class interests. But the most common objection is methodological—the behaviours defined as criminal are not so defined because of any inherent homogeneity in the structure of the behaviours themselves, but because some external authority decrees that they should all be illegal. Third, the traditional definition of crime is attacked because it is said to assume a societal consensus about what should be illegal, when this consensus does not in fact exist.[21]

Does the law serve ruling-class interests?
The ideological objection to the legalistic definition may be based on a

false premise. The law as it stands has more protection to offer to the lower class than it does to the ruling class. Proveda points out that lower-class people are more often the victims of crime, particularly violent crime, than are other groups in the community.[22]

> Another surprising statistic to middle class citizens is that a Negro male (in Chicago) runs the risk of being a victim six times as often as a white male in crimes against the person. A Negro woman is likely to be a victim eight times as often as a white woman.

Consequently, lower-class people fall back on the law for protection much more so than do the ruling class, who also generally have at their disposal more effective means for protecting their interests.

The ruling-class interest argument also ignores the great proliferation of laws geared explicitly to protecting the powerless from the powerful (e.g. consumer affairs, trade practice, pollution control, pure food and drugs, labour relations, and industrial-safety legislation). Nevertheless, to say that the law as it is defined in books has more protection to offer the powerless than the powerful is not to deny that the law is more often implemented in practice in a way that is extremely biased against lower-class interests. This should give rise to an ideological objection to the way the law is implemented, not to the way it is defined in the statute books.

There is an important feature of the power relationships in a parliamentary democracy which explains why the law in the books has more protection to offer the powerless than the powerful, while the law in action does not. This feature has been alluded to by a number of radical criminologists, including David Gordon.

> Latent opposition to the practices of corporations may be forestalled, to pick several examples, by token public efforts to enact and enforce anti-trust, truth-in-lending, antipollution, industrial safety, and auto safety legislation. As James Ridgeway has most clearly shown in the case of pollution, however, the gap between enactment of the statutes and their effective enforcement seems quite cavernous.[23]

Similarly, Chambliss and Seidman have shown that 'The anti-trust laws illustrate nicely how laws may emerge which appear to conflict with the interests of those in power without actually doing so.'[24] They demonstrate how it was 'commonly agreed that these laws should never be *enforced* (God forbid!) but should only be enacted to cool down the temper of the "radicals".'[25] The suggestion is that it is in the

11

nature of a parliamentary democracy, where powerful financial interests also control the reins of political power, that the clamorings of the powerless for legal protection are defused by the enactment of legislation which is almost never enforced. So that while the democratic process allows many laws protective of the powerless to get on to the books at the legislative stage, the summoning-up of the real power of the elite at the executive stage ensures that enforcement does not proceed.

There is another way in which the process of parliamentary democracy has produced a situation in which the law in the books has more protection to offer the powerless than the powerful—one that has operated in Australia at least. Throughout this century the Australian Labor Party, during its periodic spells in government, claims to have been in the business of enacting laws to protect the powerless. For example, the last Labor Attorney-General proclaimed that his goal was to change the principle of consumer affairs legislation from *caveat emptor* to *caveat vendor*, and he achieved some success to that end. Upon the demise of Labor governments, the situation historically has been that the conservative parties have been loath to repeal such legislation for fear of an electoral backlash from the people the laws serve to protect. Instead the response has been to keep the legislation on the books, but to *tone down enforcement*.

Of course there are laws enacted by the powerful against the interests of the powerless. As Anatole France pointed out, 'The law in its majestic equality forbids the rich as well as the poor to sleep under bridges, to beg in the street and to steal bread.'[26] In the 1970s, however, there are probably fewer laws of this kind than there are laws (albeit unenforced) designed to protect the powerless from the powerful. If this is the case, it impoverishes the argument of most radical criminologists that a study such as this should investigate the way inequality and capitalism lead to the creation of legal norms, as well as the way inequality leads to the violation of such norms once created.[27]

Increasingly the notion that laws in a capitalist state fulfil the teleologically inferred 'fundamental interests' of an ambiguously defined ruling class has come under attack.[28] As Greenber points out, the ruling-class interest argument too often portrays powerful groups as 'operating virtually without restraint, never as being forced to make concessions to challenging groups or as being forced to act contrary to short-run interests so as to maintain legitimacy by responding to the expectations of a public. The role of law in regulating conflicts among members of the propertied class is ignored just as completely as the problem of crime within the working class.'[29] In reality the law, being

12

the complex outcome of a long history of forgotten compromises, is often as much a mystery to present-day members of the ruling class as it is to the proletariat.

The taken-for-granted approach to the definition of crime adopted here does not treat official reaction to crime as unproblematic. Indeed, it deals as intensively as possible with the problem of selective enforcement of the law in the books. It does, however, assume that the law in the books is, by and large, morally defensible and worthy of being taken for granted.

Be that as it may, many criminologists may find that the legalistic definition of crime encompasses behaviour which they consider should not be criminal. Each researcher must apply his/her own ethics to the solution of this problem. For my part, I accept the prime function of the law to be the protection of our persons and our property. Even though Morris and Hawkins's analysis evades the issue of whose property is to be protected, I am in accord with their contention that 'man has an inalienable right to go to hell in his own fashion, provided he does not directly injure the person or property of another on the way.'[30] This is one of the several reasons for *the focus of this research being limited to crimes which involve actual injury to persons or loss of property* (so that offences such as homosexuality, promiscuity, drug offences, obscene language, and vagrancy are excluded from the analysis).

Limitation of the scope of the book to crimes against persons and property does create practical difficulties when one is confronted with studies in which the measure of crime includes both offences with and without victims. In many studies of this kind, the offences which involve no injury to persons or property are in a very small minority, so their conclusions are useful for our purposes. Studies in which this is blatantly not the case are excluded from consideration in this book; and for studies in which caution is merited about relevance to an analysis of crimes against persons and property, a cautionary note appears in the text or footnote.[31]

Is crime a unidimensional construct?
To consider the second major objection to the legalistic definition of crime—the objection that there is no homogeneity in the behaviours subsumed under the rubric—we must look to the data. It is an empirical question whether the universe of behaviours defined as criminal are in any sense homogeneous. Is participation in one form of crime highly correlated with participation in other forms of crime? In chapter 6 the evidence on this question from the analysis of self-reported juvenile

13

crime data is reviewed. On the basis of such multivariate studies of self-reported delinquency, the best conclusion seems to be that there is a general delinquency factor, but that much of the variance is accounted for by a number of specific factors.

A further important finding of the multivariate analysis undertaken by Braithwaite and Law was that drinking and drug-taking items were relatively unrelated to the general delinquency factor.[32] The fact that such crimes without victims are empirically relatively unrelated to offences against persons and property is further justification for limiting the scope of the study of crime to crimes against persons and property, while treating crimes without victims as separate phenomena. Kraus[33] has reached the same conclusion in his recent analysis of official records of juvenile crime. He found that while there were strong positive inter-correlations among a variety of offences against persons and property, 'carnal knowledge', and various other 'sexual offences' were, if anything, slightly negatively correlated with other juvenile crime.

Is there societal consensus about crime?

A further criticism of adopting the legal *status quo* as a basis for defining delinquency has been that such a position generally involves the background assumption of a consensus model of society.[34] Positivist sociologists generally define crime as behaviour in violation of those societal norms which are enforced by the official agents of social control in the society (the police, courts, etc.). But radical criminologists correctly point out that the assumption that there is consensus in the society about such norms is problematic. They point out that there is dissensus about the rightness or wrongness of such offences as marijuana use, vagrancy, public drunkenness, and various sexual offences. Nevertheless, if such crimes without victims are eliminated from the analysis, people are generally in agreement about the remaining legal norms.[35] It is widely agreed that theft, burglary, fraud, assault, and murder should be illegal. One of the most prominent figures in the new radical criminology, Jock Young, has been prepared to concede this.

> However much the new deviancy theorist talked of diversity and dissensus in society, the ineluctable reality of a considerable consensus over certain matters could not be wished away. This was particularly noticeable, moreover, in the widespread and uniform social reaction against various forms of deviancy (and, especially, against crimes against the person and certain crimes against property).[36]

The lack-of-consensus argument can be construed as an argument for limiting the scope of positivist criminology to those legal norms about which there is consensus—namely offences which involve direct harm to persons or their property. For the positivist criminologist, it is a fundamental assumption that a unifying theme among the diversity of behaviours labelled criminal is that they are all violations of norms. Thus, it is best that the positivist realize the limitations of his approach and eliminate from his analysis that area of crime in which this assumption cannot be sustained.

Defining crime—conclusions

The literature is replete with critiques of traditional definitions of crime by liberal and radical criminologists alike, but notably absent have been formulations of alternative definitions. Exceptions have been Sellin's[37] attempt at a redefinition based on 'conduct norms' and the Schwendingers'[38] attempt based on politically defined human rights. Neither of these definitions has been operationalized in any empirical research work, not even by their own creators. In the absence of credible alternatives, the positivist criminologist has little choice but to persevere with the *status quo*.

It cannot be denied that crime, traditionally defined as behaviour punishable by law, is a weak construct. The construct does not arise from the intrinsic nature of the subject matter at hand; crime is not an attribute strongly inherent in certain forms of behaviour; it is an attribute conferred upon these forms by external authority. Without a more coherent alternative construct being forthcoming, the traditional legalistic definition at least has the strength that it is a construct which is understood and regarded as important by ordinary people and policymakers alike.

Moreover, it is contended that the inevitable weaknesses of the legalistic definition can be ameliorated by limiting the focus of the definition to offences which involve injury to persons or property. By excluding from the analysis offences which do not involve injury to other persons or loss of property, the crime construct is strengthened in terms of unidimensionality and societal consensus that the crimes constitute norm infractions which should be sanctioned. The resulting definition also better coincides with the author's personal ideological position on the proper function of the law. In the next section it will be seen that by excluding offences without victims, the rate for the reporting of offences to the police is improved dramatically. Thus, crime is hereafter defined as *offences which are punishable by law and which involve injury to persons other than the offender or loss of property.*

Operationalizing crime

Official records

The most common way of operationalizing crime is to define persons who appear in official records of crime from the courts, the police, the prisons, or institutions for juvenile delinquents as relatively more criminal than other people. This approach has come in for consistent criticism in the literature.[39] The major problem with official records of crime is that they include only a fraction of the criminal activity which takes place in the community. The most thorough study of unrecorded crime was the Cambridge-Somerville Youth Study in which caseworkers maintained records of observed and admitted crimes by 114 'underprivileged' boys from their eleventh to their sixteenth years.[40] Of these 114, 101 had been more-or-less serious offenders, but only 40 of them were ever taken to court. Conservatively it was estimated that the total group had committed a minimum of 6,416 infractions of the law during the 5-year period, but only 95 (about 1.5 per cent) of these infractions resulted in court action. Nevertheless, it is notable that those who became 'officially delinquent' were the more persistent unofficial offenders. The official delinquents committed from 5 to 323 violations each, with a median of 79 offences, whereas the unofficial delinquents averaged only 30 offences each. Official delinquents are partly selected on the basis of the gravity and the frequency of their offending. Indeed this is the main advantage of official sources of data—they can provide a measure of serious crime which is relatively uncluttered by trivial offences.

Official criminals are selected, however, on a variety of other criteria besides the frequency and seriousness of their criminality. Various biases operate to select out those offences which are reported officially: whether the rate of reporting offences to the police is high in a particular suburb; whether a policeman decides that a particular offender 'deserves a break'; whether the offender is clever enough to avoid detection; the agreement between a policeman and an offender that he will be let off if he 'squeals' on one of his mates; plea-bargaining; and so on. The most important possibility of bias for the purposes of this thesis is that lower-class criminals are more likely than middle-class criminals to be selected for official labelling. This possibility will be discussed in detail in the next chapter.

The fundamental problem arising from the fact that most crime is not officially recorded is that in comparing the crime rates for different groups, one must assume that the selectivity operates in the same way for the different groups. That is, one must assume that officially recorded crime is a constant proportion of real crime for all groups compared.

These problems can be attenuated by concentrating on crimes which have the least proportions of unrecorded offences. Clearly homicide is the best example here: comparatively few homicides occur without being noted in police records, and the sheer gravity of the offence invokes extra checks and balances in the system which put limitations on the extent to which considerations such as class bias can operate. A sample of homicide offenders would normally be a very small sample, however, so that some broader basis for including offences with acceptable reportability must be suggested. Sellin and Wolfgang[41] have reviewed a deal of empirical evidence to show that crimes without victims, or what they call 'consensual offences' (e.g. abortion, gambling, drug offences, most sex offences) and 'offences against public order' (vagrancy, public drunkenness, prostitution) are the offences with by far the lowest reportability. They argue the case that 'reportability is a function of the presence of injury to the victim'.[42] Their evidence is a further argument for restricting the focus of positivist criminological research to crimes with victims.

Nevertheless, even after limiting the analysis of official records to offences of maximum reportability and minimum bias, there remains the problem of interpreting what the official records mean in the context of the informal negotiation processes used to constitute official designations out of complex social situations. As Cicourel says: 'The set of meanings produced by ex post facto readings of statistical records cannot be identical to the situational meanings integral to the various stages in the assembly of the official statistics.'[43]

Self-reports

Many researchers disenchanted with the validity of official statistics have turned to self-report measures of criminality. Under this method respondents (usually juveniles) are asked to indicate which of a number of offences in a questionnaire or interview schedule they have committed, and how many times they have committed each one. This method rises or falls on the question of whether respondents will give honest answers about their delinquent involvement. Some may tend to hide their delinquency, others may tend to exaggerate it.

17

Concurrent validity of self-report measures has been established by a large number of studies which have found either a significant correlation between official and self-report measures, or that on self-report schedules official delinquents were highly likely to report specific offences which appeared in official records.[44] However, this high admission rate may not apply to offences which have not been detected by the police, as such offences will not be so memorable. Furthermore, respondents may feel they have nothing to lose by reporting an offence which the police already know about. More importantly, Nettler has questioned the rationality of validating the measure against the very criterion on which it is supposed to be an improvement.

Suppose that students interested in the fruitfulness (*criminality*) of different regions (*classes, nations*) doubt whether counting oranges (*crimes known to the police*) provides a fair tally of fruitfulness. The skeptics propose that counting apples (*confessions*) may yield a more accurate estimate of fruitfulness. To prove their case they compare the distribution of apples and oranges in regions that produce both. Assume, now, that the different regions are found to contribute different proportions of apples and oranges. What has the exercise demonstrated?[45]

There have been other tests of concurrent validity, however, which have used as criterion variables the reports of peers on the delinquent behaviour of their friends,[46] the ratings of misconduct by schoolteachers and counsellors,[47] polygraph ('lie-detector') readings while being interviewed,[48] and a chemical analysis of a urine specimen to test for opiate use.[49] In addition to concurrent validity, Farrington[50] has demonstrated the predictive validity of self-reports. Self-reports at age 14–15 were significantly associated with officially recorded delinquency over the next three years.

Validation studies thus provide reasonable support for the validity of self-report measures. The percentage of respondents who admit to specific known offences is typically very high—the lowest reported confession rate among juveniles being 70 per cent in the McCandless study.[51] When the total number of officially recorded acts is correlated with the total number of self-reported delinquent acts, the correlation is typically low, though significant.[52] But it is important to remember that the validation studies concentrate on offences which are memorable because the offence resulted in apprehension by the police, or because acts are selected which are sufficiently memorable to be mentioned by other people, or because of the selection of unusual offences such as heroin use. In view of this inherent bias in validation studies, more attention than normal might be given to reliability as opposed to validity in assessing the adequacy of this technique.

Clark[53] reported at the Syracuse conference on self-report measures of delinquency that he had obtained test–retest reliability coefficients on several instruments of approximately ·80. Dentler and Monroe[54] found that each of five items was given the same response by at least 92 per cent of subjects in a test and retest two weeks apart, while Belson[55] obtained an average figure of 88 per cent with a larger questionnaire and a one-week interval. Kulik and Sabin[56] achieved the impressive reliability coefficient of ·98 with a two-hour test–retest interval. Undoubtedly these studies underestimate the measurement error, since over such short time intervals, and particularly with short questionnaires, subjects are likely to recall their previous responses. Over a two-year test–retest interval on a 38-item schedule Farrington[57] produced very discouraging results indeed. The measure of reliability used here was the percentage of those admitting to an act at age 14–15 who denied it at age 16–17. For example 54 per cent of those who admitted to car theft at the first age denied ever having stolen a car two years later. Over the thirty-eight offences, the median percentage of admissions which were followed by denials two years later was 43 per cent. Although the majority of validation and reliability studies have supported the adequacy of self-report measures, the fact that the only long-term reliability study found a well-constructed self-report measure to be characterized by considerable error must cast some doubt upon their use. Another interesting piece of evidence on reliability, which highlights the seriousness of the problems of consistency of response with self-reported deviance, appears in James Coleman's *Adolescent Society*.

> A high school junior distributed short questionnaires on drinking and smoking in a Baltimore girls' high school, and found that 58 per cent of the girls reported that they smoked (compared to 23 per cent in the study), and 30 per cent reported that they drank, (compared to less than 15 per cent in the study). [The original study was administered by an adult male.] [58]

A further weakness of self-report measures has been that they have concentrated on relatively trivial offences which often are not even illegal (offences such as 'defied parents' authority', 'had sexual intercourse', 'ran away from home', and even 'masturbated'). The reason for this is that the more serious the offence, the less the likelihood that there will be obtained a sufficient number of respondents admitting to the offence to justify its inclusion in the study. Clearly it would be a waste of research resources to ask 'Have you ever committed murder?' because positive responses would be so rare. But the inclusion of even a small number of items of too low a level of seriousness can totally destroy the validity of a self-report measure.

As previously noted, a general delinquency factor emerged from the self-report items analysed by Braithwaite and Law,[59] but the items tapping delinquency of a trivial nature (e.g. 'sneaking into the movies without paying') and the items tapping delinquency without victims (e.g. drinking beer) were relatively unrelated to this general factor. Yet it is the trivial items, the very items which do not measure general delinquency, which account for most of the variance in self-report measures. That is, if there are mostly serious delinquent acts in a scale, with only small percentages of the sample admitting to each one, and one trivial delinquent act to which 50 per cent of the sample confess, then whether one scores high or low on the overall measure of delinquency will be determined more by the trivial item than by any other item.

Engaging in various trivial delinquencies seems to be a normal activity for adolescent males in Western cultures. Yet when most of the variance in self-report measures is accounted for by such activities, we are investigating trivial delinquency, something which seems to be empirically unrelated to general delinquency. This raises the issue of the scaling procedures which have been used in the literature to justify the inclusion of trivial crime and victimless crime together with more serious offences. The problem of the use of abysmally inappropriate scaling procedures in the self-report literature has been reviewed by Braithwaite and Law.[60]

The assorted problems of acquiescence bias, faulty memory, interviewer bias, and failure to understand the meaning of the criminal categories as they are worded in the schedule have been reviewed elsewhere.[61] Perhaps the most fundamental of these problems is the varying meanings which different cultural and subcultural groups place on delinquent acts. A curious example appears in Gould's[62] study, in which he compares the self-reported delinquency of Caucasians, Negroes, and Orientals. A larger percentage of Orientals than of either Negroes or Caucasians admitted to the offence 'defying parents' authority'. But this very likely means something quite different to Orientals than it does to the other cultural groups.

This section opened with the assertion that self-report measures of crime rise or fall depending on the honesty of respondents. But validity is not simply a matter of honesty combined with good memory. Even when respondents are recalling accurately and honestly, what are they being honest about? When Gold probed the responses to his self-report schedule he found that 'some concealed weapons, upon questioning, turned out to be boy scout pocket knives; gang fights shrank to minor playground scuffles; and instances of auto theft were exposed as quick spins around the block in the family car.'[63] A further problem with self-report schedules, therefore, is that one does not know how much of the data from them actually constitutes criminal behaviour.

In view of these considerable difficulties, the present author is inclined to agree with Nettler's judgment.

> The hope that asking people about their crimes would provide criminologists with better data than official figures cannot be said to have been fulfilled. . . . This is so because *asking people questions about their behaviour is a poor way of observing it.* Sociologists, this one included, continue to ask people questions. It is one thing, however, to ask people their opinions about a matter. It is quite another task to ask people to recall *what they have done*, and it is particularly ticklish to ask people to recall their 'bad' behaviour.
> Confessional data are at least as weak as the official statistics they were supposed to improve upon.[64]

Conclusion

It has been pointed out that the problems associated with a legal definition of crime at the theoretical level are compounded by the unreliability of both official and self-report data at the operationalization level. Nevertheless, in the absence of an alternative construct capable of being operationalized, it is argued that the use of a legal definition of crime can be justified, particularly if the definition excludes those offences which do not involve injury to other persons or loss of property. Thus defined, the crime construct gains strength in relation to all three common objections raised in this chapter. That is, the more limited definition meets with greater ideological acceptance on the part of the present author, the offences included exhibit greater unidimensionality, and there is greater consensus that the crimes constitute norm violations which should be sanctioned. Finally, it has been shown that the more restricted definition of crime proposed in this chapter serves to increase the reliability of the construct through excluding offences of low reportability.

As to the unreliability associated with both methods of operation-alizing the construct, we can hope that when hypotheses survive confrontation with these two totally disparate methods, each with its very different kind of error, they have a validity which transcends that obtainable from confirmation within the constricted framework of a single method. Sheehan,[65] opening with a quotation from Webb *et al.*,[66] argues the case cogently.

'If a proposition can survive the onslaught of a series of imperfect measures, with all their irrelevant error, confidence should be placed in it.' If the restraints on accuracy of inference appear overwhelming, they remain so only as long as one set of data, one methodology, is considered, separately. Taken in conjunction with other procedures and matched against the one concept under scrutiny, there is strength in the converging of weaknesses.

In the next chapter we shall see how there may be 'strength in the converging of the weaknesses' of self-reported and officially reported crime, arising from the probability that the class biases operating within one method are quite the opposite of those at work in the other.

Chapter 2

The class-crime relationship

Introduction

Is the lower class more criminal than the rest of the population? Do people who live in lower-class areas engage in more crime than people who live in middle-class areas? These questions have dominated modern criminology, and have stimulated more empirical research than any other criminological hypotheses. They are central questions for this thesis, because if the poor and powerless are indeed the most criminal, and if those living in slums are the most criminal, then eliminating these underlying conditions of poverty might well be relevant to the reduction of crime.

This chapter is directed toward examining whether lower-class people, and people who live in lower-class areas, exhibit higher crime rates than the remainder of the population. Evidence from official records of crime and delinquency from throughout the world will firstly be reviewed. Then follows a discussion of class bias in official records, and finally a review of evidence on the class–crime relationship from self-report studies.

Although social class has been *defined* in a variety of ways, in the literature on the class–crime relationship these various definitions have almost always been *operationalized* in the same way. Those relatively low on the social-class continuum (sometimes referred to as the lower class, sometimes as the working class, sometimes as the low socio-economic status group) are those who have unskilled or semi-skilled occupations; or, in some cases, are the unemployed. In the case of juveniles, the operationalization of social class is almost always based on the occupation of the father. Thus, studies based on disparate definitions of class are comparable at the operationalized level.

The predominance of occupation as an index of social class is justifiable both theoretically and empirically. Occupational status correlates more highly with alternative indices of social class than does any other index.[1] Those with low occupational status are assumed to have less wealth and power than most of those with high occupational status. Indeed it is probable that of all personal characteristics, occupation has more effect than any other in determining levels of wealth and power.[2]

The second variant of the class–crime relationship is concerned with social class of area. The social class of an area is most frequently operationalized as the percentage of the adult male population of the area who are in lower-class occupations, the percentage unemployed, the percentage on welfare, the percentage below some poverty line, or some combination of these. It is also common for composite indices of social class of area to include variables such as the proportion of houses which are substandard, or of below-average value, and the proportion of the population which has a below-average educational attainment. Social class of area is a highly robust and empirically meaningful construct. In numerous factorial ecologies of cities throughout the world, social class of area has consistently emerged as a stable underlying factor in the ecology of these cities,[3] and in most of these studies social class of area has accounted for more of the variance than any other factor in the ecology of the city. Moreover, Sweetster[4] and also Schmid and Tagashira[5] have shown that the emergence of a factor representing social class of area is invariant under substitution of measures. These studies found that a social class of area factor consistently emerged from correlation matrices of 42, 21, 12, and 10 ecological variables.

The majority of studies on the class–crime relationship has been based on official records of crime. The results of these studies, separately for social class and social class of area, and for juvenile and adult crime, are presented in Tables 2.1 to 2.4.

Summary of the review of studies of officially recorded crime

The review in Tables 2.1 to 2.4 is, no doubt, incomplete. In particular, there has been little mention of the work on the class–crime relationship carried out in developing countries. This has already been covered in an excellent review by Clinard and Abbott of studies from Manila, Kuala Lumpur, Bombay, Kanpur, Lucknow, Kampala, Lima, Mexico City, Caracas, and Puerto Rico.[6] These studies seem to show unanimously that lower-class people and people from lower-class areas appear

Table 2.1 *Studies of the relationship between social class and officially recorded juvenile crime*

Author/s[1]	Location of study	Sample size	Lower-class juveniles more criminal?
Allen & Sandhu (1968)	Florida, US	179	Yes
Burt (1944)	London	Unknown	Yes
Canadian Govt (1951)	Canada	6,198	Yes
Cardarelli (1974)	Unnamed US city	975	Yes
Conger & Miller (1966)	Denver, US	2,348	Yes
Connor (1970)	Sverdlovsk, USSR	Unknown	Yes
De Fleur (1969)	Cordoba, Argentina	273	Yes
Douglas *et al.* (1966)	Great Britain, national sample	2,402	Yes
Empey *et al.* (1971)	Los Angeles	262	No
Empey & Lubeck (1971)	Utah and Los Angeles	667	No
Engstad & Hackler (1971)	Seattle, US	200	Yes
Erickson (1973)	Rural Utah	336	No
Farrington (1973)	London	405	Yes
Frease (1973)	Marion County, Oregon	1,232	No
Garrett & Short (1975)	3 US cities	2,711	Yes[2]
Gibson (1971)	Cambridge, Great Britain	402	Yes
Glueck & Glueck (1966)	Boston	1,000	Yes
Gould (1969a)	Seattle	217	Yes
Havighurst (1962)	'River City'	238	Yes
Kelly & Balch (1971)	Unnamed US county	1,227	Yes
Kvaraceus (1945)	Passaic, US	533	Yes
Levy & Castets (1971)	Paris	Unknown	Yes
Little & Ntsekhe (1959)	London	381	Yes

The class–crime relationship

Author/s[1]	Location of study	Sample size	Lower-class juveniles more criminal?
Lunden (1964)	Canada	4,949	Yes
McClintock (1976a)	NE England	Unknown	Yes
McClintock (1976b)	Dover, England	302	Yes
McDonald (1968)	London & SE England	851	Yes
Ibid.	Another London sample	126	No
Mannheim (1948)	Cambridge & Lincoln	166	Yes
Mannheim, Spencer & Lynch (1957)	London	400	Yes
Matsumoto (1970)	Tokyo	6,172	Yes
Meade (1973)	Unnamed US city	439	No
Merril (1959)	Boston	300	Yes
Morris (1957)	Croydon, Great Britain	79	Yes
Mugishima & Matsumoto (1970)	Tokyo	11,931	Yes
Palmai (1971)	London	453	No
Piliavin (1969)	Madrid, Spain	447	Yes
Polk & Halferty (1966)	Unnamed US city	410	Yes
Polk, Frease & Richmond (1974)	Pacific NW county, US	265	No
Reiss & Rhodes (1961)	Nashville, US	9,238	Yes
Rhodes & Reiss (1969)	Davidson County, Tennessee	Unknown	Yes
Robins, Gyman, & O'Neal (1962)	Unnamed US city	450	Yes
Shoham & Shaskolsky (1960)	Tel Aviv, Israel	100	Yes
Spadijir-Dzinic (1968)	Yugoslavia	Unknown	Yes
Sullenger (1936)	Omaha, US	500	Yes

Author/s[1]	Location of study	Sample size	Lower-class juveniles more criminal?
Toro-Calder (1970)	San Juan, Puerto Rico	1,051	Yes
Vedder & Somerville (1970)	California	837	Yes
Wadsworth (1975)	England and Wales, national sample	2,196	Yes
Warner & Lunt (1941)	'Yankee City'	Unknown	Yes
Wattenberg & Balistrieri (1952)	Detroit	2,774	Yes
Williams & Gold (1972)	US national sample	847	No

[1] See Bibliography for the full references of all articles in Tables 2.1 to 2.6.
[2] 'Lower class' in all three cities had highest police-contact rate, but in one city the 'upper class' had a higher rate than the 'middle class' and 'working class', and in another city the 'middle class' had a higher rate than the 'working class'.

Table 2.2 *Studies of the relationship between social class and officially recorded adult crime*

Author/s	Location of study	Sample size	Lower-class adults more criminal?
Amir (1971)	Philadelphia	1,292	Yes
Asunti (1969)	Western Nigeria	53	Yes
Baldwin, Bottoms & Walker (1976)	Sheffield, England	1,225	Yes
Bannister (1976)	Scotland	102	Yes
Barber (1973)	Queensland, Australia	248	Yes
Cameron (1964)	Chicago	443	Yes
Cardarelli (1974)	Unnamed US city	975	Yes
Chimbos (1973)	Ontario, Canada	446	Yes
Clinard & Abbott (1973)	Kampala, Uganda	5,812	Yes
Cormack (1976)	Scotland	1,891	Yes

The class–crime relationship

Author/s	Location of study	Sample size	Lower-class adults more criminal?
District of Columbia Crime Commission (1969)	Major violent-crime offenders known to the police in Columbia		Yes
Dunlop & McCabe (1965)	London and Warrington	107	Yes
Gil (1970)	National US sample of perpetrators of physical child abuse	1,380	Yes
Glueck & Glueck (1930)	Massachusetts	500	Yes
Glueck & Glueck (1934)	Massachusetts	500	Yes
Green (1970)	Ypsilanti, US	3,156	Yes
Hollingshead (1947)	'Elmtown'	Unknown	Yes
Lalli & Turner (1968)	US national sample	5,183	Yes
New South Wales Bureau of Crime Statistics and Research (1974)	New South Wales, Australia	1,000	Yes
Nixon (1974)	All offenders convicted in New Zealand magistrates' courts in one year		Yes
Palmer (1960)	New England, US	51	Yes
Pownall (1969)	All US Federal-prison releases in June 1964		Yes
President's Commission (1967)	All persons committed to State and Federal prisons and reformatories in the US in 1960		Yes
Robins, Gyman & O'Neal (1962)	Unnamed US city	503 (Sample I) 409 (Sample II)	Yes Yes
Simondi (1970)	Florence, Italy	80	Yes
Smith, Hanson & Noble (1973)	Birmingham, England	214	Yes
United States Bureau of the Census (1923)	All persons committed to State and Federal prisons and reformatories in the US in 1923		Yes

Author/s	Location of study	Sample size	Lower-class adults more criminal?
University of Pennsylvania (1969)	Homicide, rape and robbery offenders on Philadelphia police records		Yes
Warner & Lunt (1941)	'Yankee City'	705	Yes
Willett (1971)	England	599	Yes
Wolf (1962)	Denmark	3,032	Yes
Wolfgang & Ferracuti (1967)	Reviews 13 studies of homicide in the US, Italy, Great Britain, Denmark, Finland, Ceylon, Mexico, South Africa		All Yes
Wood (1961)	Ceylon	777	Yes

Table 2.3 *Studies of the relationship between social class of area and officially recorded juvenile crime*

Author/s	Location of study	Sample size	Juveniles from lower-class areas more criminal?
Baldwin, Bottoms & Walker (1976)	All juveniles appearing before Sheffield courts for four months in 1966		Yes
Bates (1962)	St Louis US	Unknown	Yes
Bloom (1966)	Unamed US city	Unknown	Yes
Bordua (1958)	Detroit	748	Yes
Burt (1944)	London	About 2,000	Yes
Carr (1950)	Detroit, Toledo, Flint, Jackson, Dearborn, Ann Arbor, Monroe	All unknown	All Yes
Cartwright & Howard (1966)	Chicago	16 gangs	Yes
Cherchi *et al.* (1972)	Sardinia	Unknown	Yes
Chilton (1964)	Indianapolis, US	1,649	Yes

The class–crime relationship

Author/s	Location of study	Sample size	Juveniles from lower-class areas more criminal?
Chilton (1967)	Indianapolis, US	5,507	Yes
Conlen (1971)	Baltimore, US	Unknown	Yes
De Fleur (1971)	Cordoba, Argentina	5,453	Yes
Dirksen (1948)	Hammond, Gary, East Chicago, US	All unknown	All Yes
Dunstan & Roberts (1977)	Melbourne	Unknown	Yes
Galle, Gove & McPherson (1972)	Chicago	Unknown	Yes
Garrett & Short (1975)	Three US cities	Unknown	Yes
Glueck & Glueck (1966)	Boston	1,000	Yes
Gold (1963)	Flint, US	Unknown	Yes
Hardt (1968)	Middle Atlantic State, US	814	Yes
Kvaraceus (1945)	Passaic, US	533	Yes
Lander (1954)	Baltimore, US	8,646	Yes
Mannheim, Spencer & Lynch (1957)	London	400	Yes
Martin (1961)	New York	6,808	Yes
Matsumoto (1970)	Tokyo	6,172	Yes
Olds (1941)	Pittsburg, US	Unknown	Yes
Polk (1958)	San Diego, US	Unknown	Yes
Polk (1967)	All males appearing before Portland Juvenile Court in 1960		Yes
Quinney (1971)	All juvenile arrests by Lexington (US) police in 1960		Yes
Reiss & Rhodes (1961)	Nashville, US	9,238	Yes
Rhodes & Reiss (1969)	Davidson County, Tennessee	Unknown	Yes

Author/s	Location of study	Sample size	Juveniles from lower-class areas more criminal?
Rosen & Turner (1967)	Philadelphia	504	Yes
Shaw & McKay (1969)	Chicago, 1900–6	8,506	Yes
Ibid.	Chicago, 1917–23	8,141	Yes
Ibid.	Chicago, 1927–33	8,411	Yes
Ibid.	Philadelphia	5,859	Yes
Ibid.	Boston	4,917	Yes
Ibid.	Cincinnati	3,829	Yes
Ibid.	Cleveland	6,876	Yes
Ibid.	Richmond	1,238	Yes
Sheth (1961)	Bombay	Unknown	Yes
Singell (1967)	Detroit	Unknown	Yes
Spady (1972)	Baltimore, Portland, & San Diego	All unknown	All Yes
Timms (1971)	All juvenile court cases in Luton, England, for 1958–60		Yes
Vinson & Homel (1972)	All juvenile offenders in Newcastle, Australia, known to the police in 1971		Yes
Wallis & Maliphant (1967)	London	Unknown	Yes
Willie (1967)	Washington, DC	6,269	Yes
Wolfgang *et al.* (1972)	Philadelphia	9,945	Yes

in disproportionately large numbers in the official records of crime and delinquency in these countries.

Of the 51 studies of class and juvenile crime which have been reviewed here, 42 showed lower-class juveniles to have substantially higher offence rates than middle-class juveniles. Among adults, all 46 studies found lower-class people to have higher crime rates. Juveniles who lived in lower-class areas were found to have higher juvenile crime rates in all 57 studies; and for adults this was the case in all 13 studies.

Table 2.4 *Studies of the relationship between social class of area and officially recorded adult crime*

Author/s	Location of study	Sample size	Adults from lower-class areas more criminal?
Baldwin, Bottoms & Walker (1976)	All adults appearing before Sheffield courts for four months in 1966		Yes
Bechdolt (1975)	Los Angeles & Chicago	Unknown	Yes
Brown, McCulloch & Hiscox (1972)	Northern England	Unknown	Yes
Clinard & Abbott (1973)	Kampala, Uganda	5,812	Yes
Moran (1971)	Boston	258	Yes
Porterfield (1952)	Fort Worth, US	Unknown	Yes
Quinney (1971)	All arrests by Lexington, Kentucky, police in 1960		Yes
Shaw & McKay (1969)	Results of a number of studies in US cities (see Table 2.3)		All Yes
Timms (1971)	All court cases in Luton, England, 1958–60		Yes

Thus it has been demonstrated, with a degree of consistency which is unusual in social science, that lower-class people, and people living in lower-class areas, have higher official crime rates than other groups. The problem, of course, is whether this reflects a greater real criminality on the part of the lower class, or a higher probability for its members to be caught in the criminal-justice net.

Class bias in official records

It is common for modern criminologists to accept the proposition that pervasive class bias operates at all levels in the compilation of official records of crime. Such confidence is placed in this proposition that, for many authors, it is not even considered necessary to cite empirical evidence to support it. The following statement by Chambliss is typical.

Persons are arrested, tried, and sentenced who can offer the fewest rewards for nonenforcement of the laws and who can be processed without creating any undue strain for the organizations which comprise the legal system. . . . The lower class person is (i) more likely to be scrutinized and therefore to be observed in any violation of the law, (ii) more likely to be arrested if discovered under suspicious circumstances, (iii) more likely to spend the time between arrest and trial in jail, (iv) more likely to come to trial, (v) more likely to be found guilty, and (vi) if found guilty more likely to receive harsh punishment than his middle or upper class counterpart.[7]

A central role is normally assigned to the attitudes and behaviour of the police in the implementation of this bias. Especially with the less-serious forms of juvenile crime, the policeman has available to him a range of interpretations which he can confer upon behaviour which he observes. Different policemen might regard the same behaviour as an amusing prank, high-spiritedness, juvenile crime, or mental disturbance. In addition to the imputation of meaning to behaviour, the policeman has to play the legal expert in deciding whether the behaviour fits the fuzzy definition of some legal prescription, and whether a charge under that definition can be made to stick without too much inconvenience to himself. Box explores some implications of this.

In this negotiation process of 'What really happened?' and 'Was it illegal?' the interactants, including the suspect, may be differentially endowed with dramaturgical skills. In the social construction of reality, the suspect may sometimes be better able to manipulate the symbolic meaning of behaviour and the situational context so as to persuade the police that nothing really wrong occurred, or, even if it did, that it was accidental and reflected little about his character. Furthermore, if the suspect is able only to maintain the ambiguity of the situation, the police may refrain from proceeding because the chances of getting a good clean pitch may appear comparatively poor.[8]

Middle-class people, it is suggested, have more highly developed skills in manipulating such negotiation processes than do the lower classes. The Myerhoffs tell us that the former manage to stay out of official records because 'techniques of smooth relations are the bread and butter of the middle classes'.[9] Hence, through the sincere affirmation of repentance (admitting that 'he had made a mistake'); through a dazzling display of middle-class propriety; through flattering deference to the policeman's authority; or through other dramaturgical manipulations, the middle-class suspect wriggles out of official recognition for his offence.

In addition, the middle-class suspect is likely to pose more of a threat to the career interests of the policeman than his lower-class counterpart. The influential middle-class offender can kick up a fuss, the upshot of which may be a dressing down of the policeman by his superior officer for heavy-handedness. Bayley and Mendelsohn report that the reply to a question about which kinds of people pose the greatest threat of appeal over the patrolman's head to a superior was 'the wealthy section . . . associated in the public mind with a relatively high concentration of . . . professional people'.[10] This may be another reason for the policeman to take more care in handling the middle-class suspect.

With respect to middle-class juvenile crime, parents often come to the rescue to prevent their children from being officially labelled. West suggests that 'middle class parents are more likely to protect their children by making good loss or damage so as to forestall complaints or prosecution.'[11] In a similar vein, Gibbens and Ahrenfeldt argue that '[middle class] parents know how to enlist the help of other community resources: the boy is taken to a child guidance clinic for advice; if necessary, he is sent to a residential school for maladjusted children. Understandably, the police may not proceed with a case which is clearly being dealt with vigorously by the family.'[12] Although the hypothesis that middle-class parents exert more efforts and use more ploys to get their delinquent children off the hook enjoys a great deal of support among criminologists, the only empirical study on this question lends no support to the hypothesis. In a study of 120 alleged delinquents, Ashpole found no class differences in the parental utilization of strategies and resources to influence the juvenile court, so as not to have their children adjudged delinquent.[13]

The predisposing factor which has been most frequently put forward to explain an overrepresentation of lower-class people in official records has been a belief among policemen that lower-class people are more criminal. This belief becomes a self-fulfilling prophecy via increased vigilance when observing the behaviour of lower-class people, a more pronounced assumption of guilt when lower-class suspects are being dealt with, and more concentrated surveillance in lower-class areas. Cicourel[14] suggests that the 'delinquency theories in the mind' have more to do with who ends up in official records than the delinquency theories which are in fact valid. In his observational study of a police department in a United States city, he found that one of the key 'delinquency theories in the mind' of policemen was the theory that lower-class youth is more delinquent. Moreover, policemen divided the city into ecological areas according to their deviant status—'good' areas and 'bad' areas.[15]

There is an alternative common-sense typification, however. The policeman who apprehends a teenager from a wealthy family might be more harsh on him than on the disadvantaged youth, because the former is perceived as having done the wrong thing even though he has been given every chance in life. In contrast, the delinquency of a youth from a poverty-stricken family may seem more excusable.

Which view predominates varies from police department to police department. In James Q. Wilson's[16] study of eight American police departments he found that in what he called 'legalistic departments' there was a strong commitment to prosecuting all-comers, and to equality before the law. Policemen in these departments at times even took pride in prosecuting powerful people or the offspring of powerful people, as indicative of their impartiality and of the integrity of the justice they administered. In contrast, 'watchdog departments' were loath to prosecute, and exhibited a preference for the metaphorical 'kick in the pants'. In these departments, the wide discretion over the decision to prosecute resulted in proportionately more middle-class people being 'kicked in the pants', and proportionately more lower-class people being prosecuted.

One suspects that the view that regards the delinquency of youths from poor families as more excusable is a minority view among policemen. Indeed, O'Connor and Watson found that a majority of policemen agreed with the statement that 'In most cases involving lower class, underprivileged, slum type juveniles, strong police and court action are necessary because the families of these offenders are incapable of exercising proper control.'[17]

The empirical support for the hypothesis that policemen believe that crime and delinquency emanates disproportionately from the disadvantaged is quite strong.[18] How frequently this 'delinquency theory in the mind' is translated into harsher treatment of lower-class suspects, and how frequently into more lenient treatment of them is an empirical question which merits further investigation. Nevertheless, one can fairly safely assume that it will be translated into greater surveillance of lower-class behaviour by the police.

Surveillance is critical to arrest and eventual official labelling. Chapman[19] makes the point that the extent to which one's behaviour is exposed to surveillance by the official agents of social control depends upon what proportion of one's time is spent in public rather than private space. The proportion of time spent in public space varies from about 95 per cent in the case of a person of 'no fixed abode' to perhaps 5 per cent in the case of a very wealthy person who has access to private transport on all occasions, who conducts all of his business in privacy, and who can purchase private space in hotels, restaurants and theatres. In general, the lower-class person spends a greater proportion of his time in public space, thus making his behaviour more available for police surveillance.

Police persecution of the lower class may go beyond heightened surveillance. A variety of kinds of evidence suggests that the police have a greater antipathy towards the lower class (particularly towards lower-class members of racial minorities) than towards other groups. For example, Box and Russell found that complaints *against* the police for misconduct were more likely to go unheeded when they came from a lower-class person.[20] Similarly, Black,[21] and Black and Reiss[22] discovered that complaints *to* the police about crimes were less likely to be taken seriously and accepted as genuine when they came from lower-status complainants. Interestingly, the latter could be a countervailing factor making for underrepresentation of lower-class offenders in official records because the lower the status of the victim, the greater the probability that the offender is of lower status.[23]

Police antagonism towards blacks can be self-reinforcing. Blacks who resentfully hit back at police antipathy towards them confirm police stereotypes about blacks, and encourage further antipathy. James Q. Wilson quotes a senior police officer who expresses this view.

> [The police have to] associate with lower-class people, slobs, drunks, criminals, riff-raff of the worst sort. Most of these . . . now in [this city] are Negroes. The police officer sees these people through middle-class or lower-middle-class eyeballs, he can't go on the street . . . and take this night after night. When some Negro criminal says to you a few times, 'You white motherfucker, take that badge off and I'll shove it up your ass', well, it's bound to affect you after a while. Pretty soon you decide that they're all just niggers and they'll never be anything else but niggers. It would take not just an average man to resist it, and there are very few ways by which the police department can attract extraordinary men to join it.[24]

It is common in the criminological literature for scholars to point to one or two of the above class-bias theories, and assume that the case for class bias in the compilation of official records is proven. As Terry has stated, this assumption is made 'even though empirical research dealing with these issues is relatively sparse and poorly conceived'.[25]

Review of evidence on class bias — juvenile crime

A number of early American studies found that Negro juvenile offenders receive harsher penalties, or are more likely to be processed further in the system, when compared with whites.[26] Similarly, a number of studies have shown that lower-class juvenile offenders are treated more harshly than middle-class offenders.[27] Such studies suffer from a major methodological weakness. The fact that Negroes and lower-class offenders are more likely to be recidivists and to commit more serious offences[28] implies that these variables should be controlled in an examination of the effect of race and class. Otherwise, a finding that more severe dispositions are meted out to low-status groups may merely reflect the fact that those groups are indeed more serious offenders.

A few studies on the effect of race on dispositions have taken this precaution to varying degrees. Goldman[29] found that whereas a Negro child arrested for a minor offence had a greater chance of being taken to the juvenile court than a white child, this difference disappeared with arrests for serious offences. McEachern and Bauzer[30] set out to test the effect of race on referral to the juvenile court, while controlling for legal variables. However, they found no need to introduce these controls because there was no tendency for a greater proportion of apprehended Negroes to be sent to court compared to whites. Similarly, an analysis of 500 cases in the Juvenile Aid Division of the Philadelphia Police Department by Hohenstein[31] found that an offender's race played a virtually insignificant part in determining dispositions.

However, Arnold[32] found that white youths were slightly less likely than minorities to be referred by probation officers to court, even after seriousness of offence and previous record had been controlled and were considerably more likely to be sent by the judge to an institution after seriousness of offence and previous record were controlled. Ferdinand and Luchterhand[33] also found black youth to be disproportionately labelled as delinquent and referred to the juvenile court after controlling for these variables. After appropriate controls, Thornberry[34] found blacks to receive more severe dispositions. However, contradictory results are reported by Terry,[35] and Weiner and Willie.[36] Terry found that severity of treatment by the court, the police, and the probation department did not vary by race after the gravity of offences and recidivism were controlled; while Weiner and Willie found no racial bias in the decisions of juvenile officers in Washington DC and Syracuse after appropriate controls had been introduced.

Thus studies designed to ascertain the existence of racial bias in the handling of suspects have produced contradictory results. Such contradictions may accurately represent the reality that, while courts in some parts of the United States show significant racial bias, in other geographical areas bias is non-existent. Of course, studies of racial bias may not be directly relevant to class bias. Nevertheless, one feels impelled to include a review of the former because research bearing directly on class bias is so scarce, and it seems to be assumed in the literature that class bias and racial bias in the juvenile justice system exist for exactly the same reasons.

Both the studies by Terry[37] and Weiner and Willie[38] cited above uncovered no tendencies for lower-class juveniles to receive harsher dispositions, after controlling for legal variables. Similarly, Shannon,[39] in a comparison of juvenile-court referral rates for three areas of different class composition, found the tendency for the lower-class areas to have a higher court referral rate to disappear after controlling for the seriousness of the offences committed. In the face of this evidence, Bordua[40] concluded from his review that there was 'little or no evidence' to support the claim that police discretion disfavoured the lower classes. Thornberry was also forced to conclude from his review that 'Given the findings of the research reported to date, blacks and low SES subjects are not more likely than their counterparts to be treated more severely in the juvenile justice system when recidivism and the seriousness of the offence are held constant.'[41] Nevertheless, Thornberry went on to discover that in his sample of 9,601 cases severity of disposition was greater for lower-class offenders, even after controlling for recidivism and seriousness.

The evidence is riddled with inconsistencies, and findings continue to emerge which challenge existing assumptions. For example, there is Black and Reiss's startling finding, replicated by Lundman *et al.*,[42] that the tendency for Negroes to be arrested more frequently than whites for offences of equal seriousness could be totally explained by the insistence of complainants (especially Negro complainants) that arrests be made in cases where the offender is a Negro. They found that the arrest differential between races disappeared for offences where there was no complainant (that is, police-initiated investigations). So Black and Reiss suggest that it is the general public rather than the policeman who introduces bias. Apparently in contradiction to this, White recently found no effect of the offender's occupational status on the public's punitive reaction to crimes.[43]

The Black and Reiss study also called into question the results of a well-known study by Piliavin and Briar,[44] who showed that youths who signified to the police that they were 'tough guys' by being disrespectful were more likely to be arrested than boys displaying a more respectful demeanour to the police. However, Black and Reiss found that arrest was most likely when bearing was either unusually disrespectful to the police or *unusually respectful*. Reviewers often cite the Piliavin and Briar study as empirical evidence for the existence of class bias. This is unjustifiable, first because it needs to be demonstrated that lower-class youth are less respectful towards the police than middle-class youth, and second because the Black and Reiss study has called the original finding into doubt.

Apologists for the failure of the empirical evidence to uncover consistent support for the class-bias hypothesis argue that this research looks in the wrong place for class bias. For example, Matza convincingly explains:

> Most discussions of police bias or abuse of discretionary power miss the main point. Beginning too late in the process of investigation, these analyses point to the least consequential forms of bias. Moreover, having selected the wrong section of police work for observation and scrutiny, some writers even conclude that claims regarding police bias are exaggerated. Small wonder: the main bias. . . follows from how and where the police look when *no one* has fallen under incidental suspicion.[45]

One can only accept Matza's assertion that what happens before a suspect is found is a critical possible source of class bias. However, participant observation studies in lower-class areas such as Whyte's[46] and Suttles's[47] have taught us that conventions often develop whereby people in lower-class areas do not report illegal behaviour to the police;[48] and because of the volume of delinquency going on, the police ignore it, adopting the role of controlling the consequences of crime rather than punishing or preventing it. Although there have been no comparable studies in middle-class areas, it is perhaps unlikely that such large-scale turning of the blind eye would be tolerated in these areas. So there are some grounds for suspecting that at Matza's pre-suspect stage some forces may be at work to deflate the degree of exposure to legal sanction of lower-class people when compared to middle-class people. Of course other forces may be at work to exaggerate the exposure of lower-class people (more police patrols in lower-class areas, for example). The point being made is simply that at all levels in the analysis of the legal process, existing and well-known pieces of evidence inconsistent with the class-bias hypothesis have been conveniently ignored. This has meant that the extent of class bias in official records of juvenile crime has been exaggerated.

Nevertheless, such a belief is based upon research evidence tainted by an important methodological deficiency. Box has expressed this deficiency as follows.

> However, a criticism that plunges like a stake into the heart of these studies is that they have, in all innocence, taken objectively relevant criteria, such as type of offence and prior record, at their face value. What such an acceptance implies is a failure to consider that the offence with which an individual is charged may bear slight relation to his actual behaviour, and that prior record is, in many respects, the sedimentation of previous deployment, detection and dispositional decisions, all of which were influenced by social considerations.[49]

To control for number of previous offences may be to control effectively for the amount of class bias which the subject has been exposed to in the past. If the hypothesis that class bias exists is true, then to test this hypothesis while partially controlling for how much class bias the subject has been exposed to in the past is to increase the chances of rejecting the hypothesis. Thus the studies comprise a conservative test of whether class bias exists.

Review of evidence on class bias — adult crime

Most of the early empirical investigations of the class-bias hypothesis on adult crime data have led to less ambigious conclusions. A Dutch survey of 1,455 cases of theft found that lower-class offenders suffered higher chances of prosecution.[50] This study, and one by Cameron[51] of shoplifters, partially controlled for seriousness of offence by concentrating on only one type of offence. Cameron found that Negro shoplifters were more likely to be prosecuted than whites; if prosecuted, were more likely to be found guilty; if found guilty, were more likely to be sent to jail; and if sent to jail, were more likely to receive a longer sentence. Bullock[52] was able to show, while controlling for type of offence and previous criminal record, that Negroes were likely to receive a longer prison sentence than whites. A recent study by Marshall and Purdy[53] found that conviction for known drunk-driving offences was related to lower-class status when the frequency and seriousness of offences were controlled.

An analysis of the files of a private-detective agency employed by American industrial and commercial enterprises also yielded consistent results.[54] Robin's examination of these files revealed that public prosecution was instigated against a third of the executives apprehended for illegal conduct whilst at work; but for cleaners, public prosecution was the fate of two-thirds of offenders. Even when length of service and value of property involved were controlled, the higher-status offenders remained more protected from public prosecution.

Another American study by Nagel[55] found that the poor were less likely than other groups to negotiate successfully for release from custody on bail; more likely to be found guilty; more likely to be sent to prison; and less likely to be recommended for probation or granted a suspended sentence. The latter difference persisted when previous records were taken into account.

Two studies by Green[56] found a relationship to exist between sentence severity and race. However, unlike the above studies, the tendency for blacks to be treated more severely disappeared after controls for seriousness of the offence and prior record were introduced.

In a study of rape in Georgia, Wolfgang and Riedel[57] found, using a stepwise multidiscriminant analysis, that while the race of the offender did not on its own affect the probability of a death sentence, the combination of the offender being black and the victim white did significantly increase the chances of a death sentence.

An important work is Garfinkel's[58] analysis of official records of homicide offences in North Carolina between 1930 and 1940. He found that almost twice as many white males indicted for killing Negroes won a not-guilty judgment when compared to Negroes indicted for killing a white person. Moreover, Garfinkel discovered that whereas 70 per cent of Negroes initially indicted for first-degree murder were finally charged with that offence, the figure was only 40 per cent for whites. The probable reason for this was that whites, through plea-bargaining, managed to have murder allegations reduced to lesser charges, such as negligent manslaughter. Plea-bargaining is a crucial factor in class bias. The poor are less able to retain a private lawyer than the wealthy.

Newman[59] has shown that those with a lawyer were more likely to win a guilty plea to a lesser charge; and were also more likely to win the concession of a prosecution promise to press for a lighter sentence.

Wolfgang and his colleagues,[60] in an examination of death sentences in Pennsylvania between 1914 and 1958, found that twice as many whites as Negroes had their sentences commuted. The critical factor seemed to be the type of lawyer representing the prisoner. Two-thirds of the whites had private counsel, compared with 10 per cent of the blacks. Private counsel was more successful in securing a commuted verdict than court-appointed counsel. In another study, Eggleston[61] has shown that legal representation for poor Australian Aborigines results in more lenient treatment by the courts than otherwise occurs. However, class bias arising from the inadequate legal representation of the poor is not likely to disappear with the more widespread availability of legal aid throughout the Western world. The legal-aid officer is usually less experienced, with less time to devote to his client, and less incentive to succeed, compared to his private practice counterpart. Oaks and Lehman[62] found that whereas 29 per cent of defendants who retained private counsel secured dismissal of their case before trial, this was the case for only 8 per cent represented by the public defender.

The previously mentioned studies of homicide sentences by Garfinkel, and Wolfgang *et al.* suffer from the weakness that they do not control for the seriousness of the offence and prior criminal history. Controlling for seriousness of offence, Bensing and Schroeder[63] studied 662 homicides in Cleveland between 1947 and 1954. No evidence of racial discrimination emerged. While blacks who killed whites were generally sentenced more severely than whites who killed blacks, the former group were more likely to have faced more serious charges, such as homicide while committing robbery or rape.

Recently Pope[64] has produced perhaps the most thorough analysis to date of racial bias in the handling of adult offenders. This study of California felony offenders found no variation by race in the decision to hold or release suspects prior to trial. After Pope controlled for prior record and seriousness of offence, he found that rural courts tended to sentence blacks to a more severe type of sentence (e.g. jail rather than probation) than whites at both lower- and superior-court levels. This racial bias existed in neither the lower nor the superior urban courts. No racial differences were found in either urban or rural courts in sentence lengths brought down by the court.

Evidence for the existence of bias against blacks and/or lower-class adults in the administration of justice, based mainly on American studies, is not nearly as strong as conflict theorists would have us believe. Some of the more recent studies cast serious doubt as to whether there is significant bias against lower-status groups in many urban courts and police agencies in the United States in the 1970s.

For example, two recent studies of decisions to prosecute shoplifting offenders contradict Cameron's[65] finding of bias in the handling of shoplifters. Hindelang[66] used data on over 6,000 cases of shoplifting from a large number of southern Californian stores to show that there was virtually no relationship between race and the probability of being prosecuted, after a control for the retail value of items stolen was introduced. Cohen and Stark[67] also found that, when the value of goods stolen was taken into account, store detectives showed no tendency to disfavour blacks or lower-class offenders, except that unemployed offenders were somewhat more likely to be referred to the police than offenders who had jobs.

In a study of the length of prison sentences given to 10,488 offenders in North Carolina, South Carolina and Florida, Chiricos and Waldo[68] found no evidence of an effect of class on sentence after controlling for legally relevant variables. Other recent American studies on the effect of class on severity of sentence by Willick *et al.*[69] and Lotz and Hewitt[70] have repeated this finding.

A review by Hagan[71] of seventeen studies of racial and class bias in sentencing has cast further doubt upon the assumption of widespread bias. Hagan's review is important because it re-analyses the results of studies which have never been reviewed previously, mostly because they appear in relatively obscure law journals. Hagan concluded that knowledge of the race and social class of offenders contributes very little to our ability to predict judicial dispositions.

In conclusion, the tide of evidence is turning against the assumption that there is all-pervasive bias against the lower-class offender in the criminal-justice system. Nevertheless, many specific police departments and many specific judges undoubtedly continue to perpetrate class bias. Furthermore, while the courts might be more impartial than we give them credit for, we must not lose sight of Matza's claim that the most important kinds of bias may take place long before a case comes to court.[72]

More fundamental issues in class bias

Many radical criminologists tell us that the real issue with respect to class bias is that 'law is a tool of the ruling class'.[73] Official records are biased against the lower class because they represent the enforcement of laws which are antithetical to lower-class interests. Hirschi has echoed the argument cogently:

> The beliefs of a group foster obedience to law insofar as the group in question makes the law. If a group has little or no say in the making of law, its beliefs may be favourable to violation of law, not because the members of the group are amoral or immoral, but because their morality is not that embodied in law.[74]

As has been argued in chapter 1, however, the lower class do accept the morality embodied in the law, are more often the victims of crime, and more crave the protection of the law than do the powerful. Congalton and Najman[75] showed that, while the lower class regarded poverty and crime as the two problems they were most concerned about, the middle class rated inflation and education as the two major problems of concern facing Australia. If anything, the evidence suggests that the lower class are more rigidly intolerant of certain forms of deviance than the middle class: 'A growing body of research has documented the higher degree of intolerance for deviant behaviour among those of low education and socio-economic position.'[76]

This conclusion is confirmed by a study by Faust[77], which showed that lower-class adults were less tolerant of delinquent behaviour than middle-class adults, and Negroes less tolerant than whites. Whether or not the Marxist criminologists choose to dismiss this (tautologically) as 'false consciousness' is beside the point. The point is that a greater tendency for the lower class not to comply with the law cannot be explained away as a widespread moral rejection of the law by the lower class.

Inequalities do exist in the administration of justice, and the conflict criminologists have made great theoretical contributions to understanding these inequalities. However, it is totally mislocating the source of inequality to suggest that the only crimes likely to get on to the statute books are those typically perpetrated by the lower class. There are more offences on the statute books typically committed by the powerful than offences typically committed by the powerless. The real source of inequality is that the former offences are rarely prosecuted and that often they are legally defined as civil offences rather than criminal offences. Jock Young[78] has grasped the point that it is *not* at the stage of defining what is punishable by law that equality before the law is corrupted.

To argue that the law is a weapon constructed by the powerful in its own interests (that it solves problems confronted by the powerful), hardly enables explanation of the widespread law-breaking currently exposed, and normally institutionalized, in the activities of powerful corporations and political men—law-breaking which, according to Gordon (1971), Pearce (1973), and even Ramsay Clark (1970), is carried out on a scale that makes Al Capone and the Great Train Robbers look like novices. The rule-makers comprise the most ardent of rule-breakers; and, for the new deviancy theorist sensitized to the inequality of the wider society, the problem is that there is far too much rule-breaking amongst the powerful for his simple conception of law to make sense.

Young has raised another fundamental issue, not touched on so far in this review of the evidence, on class bias in official records. The review has been restricted to studies of crimes handled by the police. Yet this is a selective bias in itself because the crimes not handled by the police are crimes which are predominantly perpetrated by middle-class people. Tax evasion, misrepresentation in advertising, restrictive trade-practice violations, use of defective building materials, illegal pollution, civil fraud, industrial-safety violations, and similar occupational offences are not police matters. If they are handled at all, it is by civil authorities, such as the Taxation Department, the Air Pollution Control Council, or the Industrial Affairs Department. These offences fit the definition of crime adopted in this work as offences against persons or property punishable by law. In chapter 10 the evidence is reviewed to show that these occupational offences, commonly known as white-collar crimes, are disproportionately committed by higher-status persons, and occur in such volume as to reverse traditional conceptions about the social-class distribution of adult crime.

The distinction between those occupational crimes handled by the police and those which are not is unclear and arbitrary. In Queensland, for example, criminal fraud is handled mostly by the Police Department, civil fraud mainly by the Department of Consumer Affairs. But in reality, if the Department of Consumer Affairs decided to be more punitive, most of the civil fraud which it handles could be prosecuted as criminal fraud. Conversely, most of the criminal fraud handled by the police could be prosecuted as civil fraud.

This section has discussed class bias in the official recording of those types of offences handled by the police. It is recognized that the restriction of the focus to offences handled by the police is, in itself, an important class bias with respect to adult crime. The latter bias is not critical with respect to juvenile crime, because middle-class juveniles are too young to fill the occupational roles which provide the opportunity for their parents to engage in white-collar crime.

Conclusion – class bias in official records

The empirical studies on the processing of juvenile offenders by the juvenile justice system have reached inconsistent conclusions on the existence of class bias. Faced with this evidence, the widespread claims in the literature that official records drastically overstate the proportion of delinquency committed by the lower class seem exaggerated.

A similar conclusion is warranted for adult crime. While a number of studies have shown that black and lower-class offenders do receive harsher treatment by the criminal-justice system, other studies have found no evidence of this. The safest conclusion would seem to be that, in some courts and some police departments, class bias is considerable, and in others it is minimal or non-existent. If this is correct, then the unanimous finding, from all courts and all police departments, that lower-class people have higher rates for those types of crime handled by the police, cannot be totally explained away as a manifestation of class bias.

Finally, it has been pointed out that official-record data exclude those behaviours defined as criminal which are not typically dealt with by the police. Inclusion of these predominantly white-collar crimes drastically alters the nature of the class–crime relationship—an issue which will be taken up in chapter 10.

Self-report studies on the class–crime relationship

If class bias renders official records of limited value in determining the distribution of crime across classes, then we must look to other sources of data. Table 2.5 reviews studies on the relationship between self-reported juvenile crime and class, while Table 2.6 provides a summary of findings on the relationship between self-reported juvenile crime and the social class of the area in which respondents live. There has been only one self-report study of adult crime which has investigated the question of class distribution. On a sample of American adults, Tittle and Villemez[79] found, after controlling for race, no evidence for a

Table 2.5 *Studies on the relationship between social class and self-reported juvenile crime*

Author/s	Location of study	Sample size	Inter-view or question-naire?	No. of items	Lower-class juveniles more criminal?
Akers (1964)	Washington	836	Q	7	No
Allen & Sandhu (1968)	Tampa, Florida	198	Q	6	Yes[1]
Arnold (1965)	Unnamed US city	180	Q	32	No
Belson (1969)	London	1,425	I	44	Yes
Belson (1978)	London	1,565	I	53	Yes
Braithwaite & Braithwaite	Brisbane, Melbourne, Ipswich, Australia	422	Q	32	No
Casparis & Vaz (1973)	Rural Switzerland	489	Q	23	No
Cernkovich (1978)	Midwestern US city	412	Q	30	Yes
Christie, Andenaes, & Skirbekk (1965)	Oslo, Bergen, & rural areas of Norway	3,372	Q	25	No
Clark & Wenninger (1962)	4 US communities	1,154	Q	38	Yes & No[2]
Dentler & Monroe (1961)	3 rural US communities	912	Q	5	No
Elliott & Voss (1974)	California	2,617	Q	12	Yes & No[3]
Elmhorn (1965)	Stockholm	950	Q	21	Yes
Empey & Erickson (1966)	Utah, US	180	I	22	Yes & No[4]
Engstad & Hackler (1971)	Seattle	200	Q	Unknown (Nye-Short scale)	Yes
Epps (1950)	Seattle	356	Q	11	Yes & No[5]
Erickson (1973)	Rural Utah	336	I	14	No[6]

The class–crime relationship

Author/s	Location of study	Sample size	Inter-view or question-naire?	No. of items	Lower-class juveniles more criminal?
Gold (1970)	Flint, Michigan	522	I	51	Yes & No[7]
Hassall (1974)	Christchurch, New Zealand	872	Q	Unknown (Hirschi & Nye–Short scales)	No
Himelhoch (1965)	Rural Vermont, US	Unknown	Q	Unknown (Nye–Short scale)	No
Hirschi (1969)	Richmond, US	1,121	Q	6	Yes & No[8]
Johnson (1969)	Baton Rouge, US	Unknown	Q	Unknown	No
Kelly (1974)	2 small towns in New York State	173	Q	25	No
Kelly & Pink (1975)	Unnamed US county	284	I	2	Yes
Kratcoski & Kratcoski (1975)	Unnamed US city	Unknown	Q	25	No
Lanphier & Faulkner (1970)	Small US town	739	Q	6	Yes
McDonald (1968)	London & SE England	851	Q	44	Yes
Nye, Short, & Olson (1958)	6 small Ohio communities	2,350	Q	18	No
Phillips (1974)	Unnamed US city	469	Q	Unknown	Yes
Quensel (1971)	Cologne, Germany	599	Q	16	Yes
Reiss & Rhodes (1961)	Nashville, US	158	I	Unknown	Yes
Sherwin (1968)	Middletown, Ohio	280	Q	20	Yes & No[9]
Slocum & Stone (1963)	Washington	3,242	Q	5	Yes
Vaz (1966)	Canada	1,639	Q	21	No

Author/s	Location of study	Sample size	Inter- view or question- naire?	No. of items	Lower- class juveniles more criminal?
Voss (1966)	Honolulu	620	Q	16	No
Walberg, Yeh, & Paton (1974)	Chicago	430	Q	13	Yes[10]
West (1973)	London	411	I	38	Yes
Wilcox (1969)	Rocky Mountains Area	403	Q	Un- known	No
Williams & Gold (1972)	National sample, US	847	I	16	No
Wilson, Braithwaite, Guthrie & Smith (1975)	Brisbane	129	I	8	No
Winslow (1967)	Los Angeles	259	Q	9	No

[1] Allen & Sandhu seem to misinterpret their data at one point in their paper as showing that adolescents from high-income families are more delinquent than those from low-income families. Why they do this is puzzling. From Table 2, p. 265, it is quite clear that while 46 per cent of those in the low-family-income category are high on self-reported delinquency, only 37 per cent of those in the higher-income category are high on self-reported delinquency.

Calculated from Table 2 (Allen & Sandhu)

		Delinquency		
		Low	High	TOTAL
Family Income	Low	54% (57)	46% (48)	100% (105)
	High	63% (59)	37% (34)	100% (93)

[2] 'Yes' for the 'Industrial city' sample, 'No' for other areas. There is an association between social class and the more serious self-report delinquency items, even in the latter areas.

[3] This is a longitudinal study in which the relationship between class and crime is examined at two time periods – junior and senior high school. For neither time period were the Nye–Short items classified as non-serious, significantly related to social class. Serious delinquency was significantly associated with social class at the junior-high-school level, but not at the senior-high-school level.

[4] This study is based on an unusual non-random sample of 50 high-school boys, 30 boys with one court appearance, 50 boys on probation and 50 incarcerated offenders. Three subscales, 'general theft', 'serious theft', and 'common delinquency' showed correlations of $-.20$, $-.17$ and $-.17$ respectively with social class. But when these results were broken down into more detail the correlations were the result of middle- and lower-status respondents reporting more delinquency than those in the upper-status category, while there were no differences between middle- and lower-status boys.

Footnotes for Table 2.5 (continued)

[5] 'Yes' for females, 'No' for males. A number of items in this study represent crimes without victims.

[6] This study is based on an unusual non-random sample. The sample consisted of 100 incarcerated offenders, 136 'Provo Experiment' offenders, and 100 youths who were officially non-delinquent.

[7] 'Yes' for males, 'No' for females.

[8] See the discussion of this study in the text.

[9] Lower-class youth did not admit to committing a greater number of different offences. However, they admitted to committing most offences with greater *frequency* than middle-class youth.

[10] The independent variable here is 'family background' rather than social class as such. 'Family background' is indexed by the number of middle-class, school-relevant objects in the home (telephone, dictionary, encyclopaedia, etc.) and the nature of the psychological relationship between parent and child, particularly with regard to school expectations. That is, the independent variable purports to be an index of the existence of a middle-class ethos in the family situation.

Table 2.6 *Studies on the relationship between social class of area and self-reported juvenile crime*

Author/s	Location of study	Sample size	Interview or questionnaire?	No. of items	Juveniles from lower-class areas more criminal?
Braithwaite & Braithwaite	Brisbane, Melbourne, Ipswich, Australia	422	Q	32	Yes
Clark & Wenninger (1962)	4 US communities	1,154	Q	38	Yes[1]
Elmhorn (1965)	Stockholm	950	Q	21	No
Hardt (1968)	Middle Atlantic state, US	814	Q	19	Yes & No[2]
Johnson (1969)	Baton Rouge, US	Unknown	Q	Unknown	No
McDonald (1968)	London & SE England	851	Q	44	Yes
Smith (1975)	Brisbane, Australia	184	Q	17	Yes

[1] Basically 'Yes', although in a low-income rural area less delinquency was reported than in a high-income urban area.

[2] 'Yes' for 14–15-year olds, 'No' for 12–13-year olds.

negative correlation between class and the self-reporting of theft, gambling, cheating on tax, assault, and marijuana use. With the exception of the male reporting of cheating on tax, the Tittle and Ville-mez data do show that non-whites (male and female) reported higher levels of involvement than whites in all other comparisons. In Tables 2.5 and 2.6, studies which find the lower class to admit to more delinquency, but where this difference is not statistically significant, are recorded as 'No' (lower-class juveniles not more criminal).[80]

Of the 41 self-report studies reviewed in Table 2.5, 15 found lower-class adolescents to report significantly higher levels of involvement in delinquent behaviour than middle-class youth. Seven studies provided qualified support for this hypothesis, and 19 found no significant differences in reported delinquent involvement among classes. While a greater proportion of the studies have found a significant difference than would be expected on the basis of chance, the fact that almost half of the studies have failed to uncover a statistically significant difference must leave serious doubt about the relationship.

The review of research on the question of whether adolescents living in lower-class areas report more delinquency than those living in middle-class areas (Table 2.6) yields more consistent support for the class–crime relationship. Four studies supported the hypothesis, one provided qualified support, and two found no significant difference. One other self-report study by Pine[81] has not been included in this review so far because it could not be placed into either Table 2.5 or Table 2.6. In this study Pine used a composite index of social class, which incorporated *both* the socioeconomic status of the area in which the individual lived and the socioeconomic status of his family. In his New England sample of 683, he found no significant relationship between questionnaire-reported delinquency and this index.

Earlier reviews have pointed out that a number of the studies which have failed to find a relationship between class and self-reported delinquency were conducted in rural areas.[82] It is suggested that testing the class–crime association in urban areas is more pertinent because 'In non-urban areas class differentiation may not have developed sufficiently for it to result in distinctive ways of acting, thinking and feeling.[83] This proposition seems to be corroborated by the studies of officially recorded delinquency by Erickson, Frease, Polk *et al.* (see Table 2.1), which found no class differences among rural youth.

More important, a number of the studies which have found no significant relationship are particularly susceptible to methodological criticism. The pioneering work of Nye *et al.* has been criticized for

51

internal inconsistency,[84] and Gold's recomputation of the published data leads him to conclude that the data *do* support the class–juvenile delinquency relationship anyway.[85] The inappropriate use of Guttman scaling in this study[86] has resulted in a requirement for boys to admit to either drinking or to drinking and heterosexual relationships in order to get into the most delinquent category. Both of these 'offences' are treated as more serious than 'stealing a car'. The study by Akers is probably also best dismissed because the small number of items are dominated by crimes without victims and very petty forms of delinquency.[87] McDonald also points out that the significance test in the Akers study is based on a sample with only thirteen cases in the lowest (unskilled) category.[88]

Hirschi has argued that an underrepresentation of the very lowest in the social-class continuum has been a fundamental weakness of self-report studies.[89] 'The *class* model implicit in most theories of delinquency is a peculiarly top-heavy, two-class model made up of the overwhelming majority of respectable people on the one hand and the lumpenproletariat on the other.'[90] Hirschi's data supports the efficacy of such a model. Between father's occupation and self-reported delinquency he finds only 'a very small relation that could easily be upset by random disturbances of sampling or definition'.[91] However, when he looks at the very lowest on the social-class continuum (the 'lumpenproletariat'), he finds a clear association. 'Boys whose fathers have been unemployed and/or whose families are on welfare are more likely than children from fully employed, self-sufficient families to commit delinquent acts.'[92] Spady[93] has also shown with official records that, as the bottom cutting point is moved toward the lower end of the social-class distribution, the obtained association between social class and delinquency tends to be strengthened.

In common with most other self-report studies, Hirschi included items such as 'Have you ever taken little things (worth less than $2) that did not belong to you?' and 'Have you ever banged up something that did not belong to you on purpose?' It has been pointed out that the angry school child who takes another student's pencil and breaks it is guilty of both of these offences. In Hirschi's study a child who admits to both of these offences would be placed with the 20 per cent in the highest delinquent category. It is fairly safe to assume that anyone who denies ever having 'taken little things' is lying. Who has not stolen a rubber or a paper clip? Clark and Tifft, in their validation with a lie detector, found that, while only 32·5 per cent admitted to this offence in the first administration, 87·5 per cent admitted to it in the final administration.[94] If this item is treated as a lie item rather than as a measure of delinquency, the results of studies such as those of Hirschi and Dentler and Monroe can be shown to provide statistically significant support for the class–crime association. The failure of both of these works to show a significant relationship largely reflects the fact that there were no class differences between those who admitted to no offence and those who admitted to only one offence.[95]

Gold[96] has pointed out that many of the offences in the original Nye, Short, and Olson scale (the scale which most subsequent researchers have adopted or modified) are not really violations of the law. 'Disobeyed your parents', 'had a fist fight with another person', 'told a lie', 'ran away from home' and 'defied your parents' authority' are not forms of misbehaviour specifically proscribed as punishable by law. Clark and Wenninger, after having found no class differences in the reporting of so-called 'nuisance offences' but clear class differences on the more serious offences, concluded that 'Perhaps the failure of some researchers to find differences among the social classes in their misconduct rates can be attributed to the relatively less serious offences included in their questionnaires or scales.'[97] Box considers that the Akers, Voss and Vaz studies in Table 2.5 should be ignored because their 'delinquency' items are so contaminated with adolescent-status offences and bad manners.[98] All of these are studies which report no relationship between class and self-reported crime. The Voss study is also particularly weak in that it is based on a sample which is half Japanese, yet there is no control for race. Slocum and Stone's study, which supports the class-delinquency relationship, should also be ignored because of the inclusion of items on drinking, truancy, and parental defiance, which account for most of the variation of scores on the delinquency measure.

The majority of the studies labelled 'No' in Table 2.5 report a very slight (non-significant) tendency for the lower class to admit to more delinquency. Bytheway[99] has demonstrated the importance of these slight trends by pooling the data from three studies often cited as evidence against the class-delinquency association. The increased sample size, through pooling the data from the Nye *et al.*, Akers, and Hirschi studies, results in a statistically significant tendency for the children from low-occupational-status families in the three studies to report more delinquent involvement.

The studies by Erickson, and Williams and Gold, which found no class differences in self-reported delinquency, must also be called into question because both of these studies failed to find class differences in *officially* recorded delinquency on their samples. Since a finding of no class differences in officially recorded delinquency is extremely un-usual, one can only assume that sampling error has resulted in rather atypical delinquents being included in these samples.

In short, the findings of seven studies can be questioned—six of which find no significant relationship between class and crime (the studies by Akers, Dentler and Monroe, Erickson, Nye *et al.*, Vaz, Voss, and Williams and Gold). If these studies are ignored, there remain in Table 2.4 14 studies which support the hypothesis, 7 which partially support it, and 13 which find no significant difference. If studies based on rural or small-town samples were also excluded, the ratio of signifi-cant to non-significant findings would increase further. The number of studies which have uncovered a significant relationship is clearly greater than would be expected on the basis of chance. It is possible that the failure to find significance in a large number of studies is the result of the contamination of measures with items measuring misbehaviour not normally punishable by law, the setting of lower-class cutting points too high, or the choice of a sample which is disproportionately middle class to the exclusion of the very lowest social-class groups.

Class bias in self-reported delinquency

Another possible explanation of the failure of many self-report studies to show a class–crime association is that the self-report methodology tends to exaggerate the proportion of delinquency perpetrated by the middle class. It has been suggested that, when confronted with the un-familiar white middle-class researcher with his probing questions, the lower-class respondent may be more suspicious and defensive than his middle-class counterpart. Rather than focusing upon guardedness with the middle-class interviewer or researcher, Gold has suggested that class bias arises from cultural differences in the interpretation of questions.[100]

> But it might be expected that items such as 'purposely damaged or destroyed public or private property' would have different meaning for youngsters in different social strata; lower class boys and girls might minimize, even forget, acts of property damage which would be reported by their middle class peers for whom the sanctity of property may be a more salient attitude.

Christie *et al.* have also suggested some reasons for class bias.[101]

A further possibility could be that the more educated and higher-class subjects are revealing relatively more of their crimes than the less-educated and lower-class ones. They are more trained in using paper and pencil, and thereby have more time to think through each question. They have probably also more self-confidence in this situation, and therefore do not hesitate to reveal their murky past. Furthermore, they are according to common stereotypes brought up in a climate where norm-infractions are considered more serious. They will forever remember that terrible day when they, at the age of seven years, stole an apple from the corner shop, while youngsters with another background will concentrate on reporting more serious activities.

However, Box[102] has been quick to point out that there is an alternative typification which views the lower-class respondent as more prone to boasting and bragging about delinquent involvement, while the middle-class respondent is more concerned with preserving respectability by denying delinquent behaviour. This typification predicts just the opposite kind of class bias. However, while a certain amount of evidence can be gleaned from the literature to support the assertion of the former typifications—that self-reports exaggerate the proportion of delinquency committed by the middle class—there seems to be no available evidence for the contrary hypothesis.

The existence of class bias in self-report measures can be demonstrated by looking at the way officially recorded offences are self-reported. From the data in chapter 8 of this book it is known that in Queensland, lower-class youth are more than four times as likely as middle-class youth to have a conviction in the children's court. Yet a Queensland study by Carter[103] found no significant class differences for a random sample of youth in response to the question, 'Have you ever been found guilty by a Children's Court?'

Braithwaite and Braithwaite[104] found no significant differences by social class or by social class of area in self-reporting of the following items:

In the last year have you ever been roused at by a policeman for something you did?

In the last year have you ever been taken to the police station for something you did?

In the last year have the police ever come to see your parents for something you did?

In the last year have you ever been to the Children's Court for something you did?

It is a fact that these things do happen to lower-class youth more than to middle-class youth. So why are there no class differences in the self-reporting of them? The conclusion must be that lower-class youth are more defensive in reporting delinquent behaviour, or possibly that middle-class youth are more prone to exaggerate their delinquent involvement.

This conclusion is further supported by Hardt's[105] finding that the percentage of boys self-reporting police questioning showed no variation by social class of area.[106] This was in a study which found that 14–15-year-old boys from lower-class areas did self-report higher overall delinquency rates than their counterparts from middle-class areas.

Smith[107] has compared the delinquent involvement of adolescent males from a lower-class Brisbane suburb with adolescents from a middle-class suburb. The frequency with which youngsters from the lower-class area were picked up by the police was many times higher than in the middle-class area. Yet when, on a self-report questionnaire, respondents were asked 'Have you ever been picked up by the police?' the class difference shrank to a matter of only 10 percentage points. Thirty per cent of respondents from the lower-class area admitted to being picked up by the police compared to 20 per cent from the middle-class area. This 10 per cent difference is exactly the same as the average percentage class difference over all other self-report items in the schedule. Such a 10 per cent difference would normally be taken as indicative of minimal class differences. However, when a 10 per cent difference is also reported on behaviour for which we know (objectively) there to be class differences of some hundreds of per cent, then it must be concluded that self-reporting is contracting real class differences.

Thus evidence from the self-reporting of officially recorded offences points to the existence of class bias in self-report measures. While it is known that lower-class youth are much more likely than middle-class youth to get into trouble with the police and the courts, a number of studies have shown that lower-class youth do not *report* that they have been in trouble with the police or the courts more frequently than do middle-class youth.

The first systematic study of bias in self-reports of delinquency was undertaken by Hackler and Lautt.[108] They found that against the criterion variables of police records, court records, teachers' reports, and official school-misconduct records, underreporting of self-reported delinquency was greater for Negroes than whites among seventh grade boys, but that this difference did not hold for ninth grade boys.

Martin Gold in *Delinquent Behaviour in an American City*[109] reports evidence both for and against the class-bias hypothesis. Gold notes that he found it more common for middle-class respondents to interpret the meaning of questions so that very minor transgressions or non-delinquent behaviour were reported as delinquency.

> Such over-reporting was sometimes related to other variables in which we were interested; for example, the proportion of accidental or trivial acts of property destruction was significantly higher among wealthier white boys than among poorer ones.[110]

Although middle-class delinquency may be inflated by a rather broad middle-class interpretation of what constitutes delinquency, Gold found no evidence, on a sub-sample of 125, that middle-class respondents were any more honest in reporting known offences. He shows that, against the criterion of reports of peers on delinquent behaviour, there were no class differences in the proportion of offenders who were 'truthtellers'. The validation study is rather questionable because of the sweepingly broad definition of 'truthteller'. A 'truthteller' was one who 'confessed to everything which informants had told us *or to more recent or more serious offences*' (my emphasis).

An important technique for testing out class bias is the use of 'lie' items. The present author, together with Paul Wilson and Greg Smith, has experimented in two self-report studies with the 'lie' item, 'Have you ever done anything which would have got you into trouble with your parents or teachers if it were found out?' On both occasions a higher percentage of middle-class than lower-class respondents admitted to the 'offence'. The only published self-report delinquency study using lie items replicates our finding. Hardt and Peterson-Hardt[111] found that more boys from a white middle-income neighbourhood scored low on a five-item lie scale than boys from lower-income white or non-white neighbourhoods. They also found that boys from the white middle-income neighbourhood were more honest in admitting (on the self-report instrument) to offences which had been officially recorded.

In summary, the greatest weight of evidence supports the hypothesis that the self-report methodology exaggerates the proportion of delinquency perpetrated by the middle class. However, some evidence also exists to favour the null hypothesis that no class bias operates in the administration of self-report measures. There is no evidence whatsoever to support the hypothesis that self-reports exaggerate the proportion of delinquency committed by the lower class.

In many of the studies in Table 2.5, class bias may have also been introduced by the sampling procedure. The vast majority of self-report studies have been conducted on high-school samples. This biases the sample toward including the successful upwardly mobile lower-class youth who stay in school, and excluding the large numbers of stable or downwardly mobile lower-class youth who drop out of school. This may be a critical source of bias, since it has been well documented that school drop-outs are disproportionately lower class;[112] and Hirschi[113] has shown that it is delinquent youth who are most likely to drop out of school.

Other studies on the class–crime relationship

A number of studies have used sources of data other than official records or self-reports to investigate the class–crime relationship. One rather telling study by Hindelang[114] avoids the biases of both official records and self-reports by analysing the results of the National Crime Panel victimization survey. Whereas only 11 per cent of the American population are black, Hindelang found that 39 per cent of rape victims in the survey reported their assailant to be black. Similarly, 62 per cent of robbery victims, 30 per cent of aggravated assault victims, and 29 per cent of simple assault victims reported their assailant to be black. Woods[115] used reports of pack rape in newspapers to establish an association between lower-class areas and the incidence of pack rape. Congalton and Najman[116] report that residents of lower-class areas are less likely than residents of middle-class areas to regard it as safe to walk in the area both at night and during the day. In response to the question 'Is there much crime or delinquency committed by young people (in their teens or below) in your community?' Smith[117] found that 40 per cent of respondents in a lower-class suburb said 'very much', compared to 15 per cent in a middle-class suburb.

Not only is there evidence showing that people *living* in lower-class areas commit more crime than people living in middle-class areas, but also there is quite a large body of evidence that, for most types of crime, offences *occur* disproportionately in lower-class areas.[118] If it is assumed that the majority of crimes which occur in an area are committed by people who live in that area, then this evidence can be interpreted as support for the hypothesis that people living in lower-class areas are more criminal. Another source of support for the association between class of area and crime comes from observational studies of delinquent gangs. These have found that gang areas are mostly in lower-class sections of the city.[119] Evidence which contradicts the class-of-area hypothesis has been reported by Won and Yamamoto.[120] From an analysis of 493 cases of shoplifting apprehended by the security firm for a chain of supermarkets in Honolulu, it was found that shoplifters came disproportionately from middle-class areas, and that people from low-income areas were underrepresented. Unfortunately, Won and Yamamoto do not report whether the stores were *located* predominantly in middle-class or lower-class areas.

Studies on behaviour regarded as related to criminality are often cited in the literature as evidence that lower-class people are more criminal. Hartshorne and May's[121] experiment, which found that poor children were more prone than others to lie, cheat, and steal, is sometimes cited. West[122] found that lower-class children were more guilty of misbehaviour at school and were more frequently rated by psychiatric social workers as suffering from conduct disorders. However, using a self-report measure of school misbehaviour, Stinchcombe[123] uncovered no class differences. Lerman[124] found that lower-class boys are more familiar with argot terms or criminal slang than boys from the middle class; and Lovegrove[125] reports that lower-class youths score higher on the Delinquency Proneness Scale of the California Psychological Inventory. The Gluecks[126] discovered that among 1,000 delinquents, those from poor backgrounds were somewhat less likely to reform over the next fifteen years (by not falling into adult crime). In *The Changing American Parent*, Miller and Swanson[127] report that lower-class Detroit boys more often expressed aggressive impulses directly, while middle-class boys tended to block aggressive expression. However, in a questionnaire study of a United States national sample of 1,176 adults, Stark and McEvoy[128] question the view that lower-class people are more violent. They maintain, on the basis of their data, that different class groups simply have different ideas about what kinds of situations are appropriate for the expression of violence. For example, while lower-class people were more inclined to agree that 'When a boy is growing up, it is very important for him to have a few fist fights', middle-class people were more inclined to say that they would 'participate in physical assault or armed action' against 'a group of people who are deliberately blocking rush-hour traffic to protest the war in Vietnam'.

The foregoing review of studies which do not fit into the framework of Tables 2.1 to 2.6 provides some extra weight of evidence moderately consistent with the view that lower-class people commit more criminal acts. Needless to say, most of this evidence is tainted with the same methodological problems which were confronted in the discussion of either self-reports or official records. A type of study which does not fall within the official records or self-report framework, and which adds considerably to our knowledge, is the direct observational study. Systematic observational data on the class distribution of crime is scarce in the literature. One could perhaps point to Short and Strodt-beck's[129] study in which lower-class youth were observed to be more often present in delinquent gangs than middle-class youth. However, the only genuinely systematic study is that of W.B. Miller.[130] Miller's work is based on direct observation by several fieldworkers of a large number of instances of theft by gang members over a two-year period. His findings were clear cut in the direction of lower status being associated with higher crime rates.

> On the basis of contact period theft involvement, lower class 3 groups [lower lower class] engaged in theft three times as frequently as groups from lower class 2 [middle lower class] (p. 34).

> Its patterning was so decisively related to social status that status differences as small as those between lower class 2 and 3 had marked influence on its frequency (p. 37).

Direct observational studies of the class distribution of crime are rare because it is logistically very difficult to mount a research effort which systematically observes enough crime to calculate rates for different groups. Yet direct observation clearly is the best source of data, because it is the very second-hand and third-hand nature of self-report and official-record compilation which permits bias to enter into measures. Thus the confirmation of the class–crime relationship by direct observational data is crucially important.

Summary and conclusions

The evidence is far from consistent in supporting the existence of class bias in the compilation of official records of both juvenile and adult crime. The most reasonable conclusion is that official records of crime often exaggerate the proportion of crime committed by the lower class, but that for many courts and police departments this bias may be minimal or non-existent. Therefore the finding that the records of *virtually all* courts and police departments show the lower class as committing more criminal acts cannot be explained away by the existence of monumental class bias in *all* of these statistics.

Most theorists have certainly exaggerated the magnitude of the class differential in treatment by the police and the courts. Even the studies which have provided the strongest indications of class bias do not demonstrate a degree of bias which could explain away findings that lower-class people can have official crime rates five and six times as high as those of the middle class. Class-bias theories are particularly incapable of totally explaining away the class distribution of more serious crimes such as murder, for which checks and balances against bias in the system are maximal.

Scattered evidence suggests that self-reports of juvenile crime contain an opposite class bias. That is, it is likely that self-report measures of criminality exaggerate the proportion of crime perpetrated by the middle class. Self-report studies show fairly consistently that juveniles living in lower-class *areas* commit more crime. However, support for the hypothesis that juveniles from lower-class *families* commit more crime has not been consistent in self-report studies. Such studies typically report a slight tendency for the lower class to admit to more delinquency, and more often than not this tendency fails to reach statistical significance. Nevertheless, the number of studies which do find a significant difference in this direction is substantially higher than would be expected on the basis of chance.

Only one study has systematically calculated class differences on the basis of direct observation. This study supports the hypothesis that lower-status people commit more crime than those of higher status.

The hypothesis that criminality is negatively related to social class is therefore strongly supported by a large number of studies which use a measure probably biased in favour of the hypothesis; weakly supported by a large number of studies which use a measure probably biased against the hypothesis; and strongly supported by one study which uses a measure which avoids the systematic class bias of the other two. It therefore seems reasonable to accept the hypothesis.

One important qualification must be made, however. Almost all of the studies reviewed here have totally ignored corporate crime and crimes handled by civil authorities. To restrict the focus to those types of crimes handled by the police is to exclude from consideration that area of crime which is disproportionately middle class—the area of

61

white-collar crime. It will be shown in chapter 10 how, when this restriction is lifted, conclusions about the class distribution of crime can be completely reversed. Nevertheless, as noted earlier, ignoring white-collar crime does not change our conclusions about the class distribution of *juvenile* crime, since juveniles do not normally occupy any of the occupational roles which would give them the opportunity to indulge in white-collar crimes.

The best conclusions which can be reached on the basis of almost 300 studies on the class distribution of crime reviewed in this chapter seem to be as follows.

1 Lower-class adults commit those types of crime which are handled by the police at a higher rate than middle-class adults.
2 Adults living in lower-class areas commit those types of crime which are handled by the police at a higher rate than adults who live in middle-class areas.
3 Lower-class juveniles commit crime at a higher rate than middle-class juveniles.
4 Juveniles living in lower-class areas commit crime at a higher rate than juveniles living in middle-class areas.

Postscript

Subsequent to the writing of this chapter another review article in the long tradition of attempting to demonstrate the 'myth' of the class–crime relationship has appeared. Tittle and Villemez[131] conclude that 'of 49 research reports we were able to locate, only 24 (49%) report a general negative relationship between socioeconomic status and crime/delinquency, while 19 (39%) find no class gradient, and 6 (12%) report an inverse association only for some specific subcategory of individuals within a sample.' These forty-nine include both self-report and official-records studies. Furthermore, we are told that

> those studies based on official police or court data are less con-
> sistent than has usually been assumed. For one thing, such studies
> are actually not very numerous. Despite frequent reference (with-
> out citation) in the literature to 'many studies', we were able to find
> only 16 investigations that used official police or court delinquency
> figures and only 7 studies examining official arrest or conviction
> data for adults.

All we can say is that if this was all that Tittle and Villemez were able to find, then they did not look very hard. In the class–crime literature we must be wary of reviews which pretend to be exhaustive but are in fact quite selective.

Chapter 3

Theories of lower-class criminality

Introduction

A great number of theories have been put forward to explain the relationships between social class and crime, and social class of area and crime. In this chapter a review of these theories and an assessment of the degree of empirical support which each theory enjoys is undertaken. Each theory is evaluated in the light of the hypothesis that a reduction in inequality will reduce crime. Policy implications of the theories for the class-mix hypothesis will be discussed in the next chapter.

No attempt is made in the present chapter to provide a well-rounded evaluation of the contribution which each of the major theories of lower-class criminality has made to explaining the crime phenomenon. Nor is there any attempt at a critical account of the historical development of class-based criminology. The only concern is with the implications of the major theories for the policy question of whether greater equality will reduce crime.

Engels, Bonger, and Marxist theory

The earliest influential theorist on lower-class criminality was Frederick Engels.[1] A central position is ascribed by Engels to the 'brutishness' inflicted on lower-class people in so many spheres of their lives. In their education, lower-class people are treated 'like the dullest of brutes'— they are educated by physical force, intimidation, and humiliation. In their contacts with employers and the law they are treated as 'brutes'.

> There is therefore no cause for surprise if the workers, treated as brutes, actually become such; or if they maintain their consciousness of manhood only by cherishing the most glowing hatred, the

most unbroken inward rebellion against the bourgeoisie in power.[2]

The latter part of this statement must be rejected because of the evidence that most of the 'brutishness' of the lower class is not directed at the bourgeoisie. 'It is a simple fact that the majority of working-class crime is *intra-* and not *inter-*class in its choice of target.'[3] But for Engels crime was only one of a number of possible reactions available to the lower class. In response to their brutalization they could engage in crime, struggle for socialism, collapse into a demoralized heap, or finally, give in to the competitive values of capitalist society, and enter into a war of all against all.

Engels suggests that the lower class engage in so much crime not only because they are brutalized, but also because their poverty leaves them disillusioned about the 'sacredness of property'.

> What inducement has the proletariat not to steal? It is all very pretty and very agreeable to the ear of the bourgeois to hear the 'sacredness of property' asserted; but for him who has none, the sacredness of property dies out of itself. Money is the god of this world. The bourgeois takes the proletarian's money from him and so makes a practical atheist of him.[4]

> It was not clear to his mind why he, who did more for society than the rich idler, should be the one to suffer under these conditions. Want conquered his inherited respect for the sacredness of property, and he stole.[5]

Consequently, Engels would agree that greater equality would be conducive to less crime. However, economic inequality is less important as a cause of crime than the war of all against all, which arises from capitalist relations of production.

> In this country, social war is under full headway, everyone stands for himself, and fights for himself against all comers, and whether or not he shall injure all the others who are his declared foes, depends upon a cynical calculation as to what is most advantageous to himself. It no longer occurs to anyone to come to a peaceful understanding with his fellow-man; all differences are settled by threats, violence, or in a law-court. In short, everyone sees in his neighbour an enemy to be got out of the way, or, at best, a tool to be used for his own advantage.[6]

Some decades later, another Marxist scholar, Willem Bonger, in his *Criminality and Economic Conditions* (1916) developed a similar analysis.[7] Cupidity, and exploitativeness in interpersonal relations emerge in the capitalist transformation of work from its value for use to its value for exchange.

As soon as productivity has increased to such an extent that the producer can regularly produce more than he needs, and the division of labour puts him in a position to exchange his surplus for things that he could not produce himself, at this moment there arises in man the notion of no longer giving to his comrades what they need, but of keeping for himself the surplus of what his labour produces, and exchanging it. Then it is that the mode of production begins to run counter to the social instincts of man instead of favouring it as heretofore.[8]

Notwithstanding the ambiguous teleology of his 'social instincts', the seminal thrust of Bonger's argument is that capitalism 'has developed egoism at the expense of altruism'.[9] In one crucially important respect Bonger's is a more sophisticated theory than anything produced since. The theory is not confined to explaining the widespread criminality of the lower class: it also offers an explanation of the widespread criminality of a different kind, among the industrial bourgeoisie (what is now called white-collar crime). Firstly, a criminal attitude is engendered by the conditions of misery inflicted upon many of the lower class under capitalism, and secondly, a similar criminal attitude among the bourgeoisie arises from the avarice fostered when capitalism thrives. Unlike Bonger's, all the more recent influential theories are limited to explaining why the lower class are more criminal, without countenancing the possibility that for certain types of crime (white-collar crime) the middle class clock up a track record which leaves the lower class for dead.

In broad terms, the theories of Engels and Bonger both depict two main causes of the widespread criminality of the lower class. Primarily, the structure of capitalism is said to create a criminogenic quality of social life, characterized by exploitativeness and avarice. In addition, crime is caused by the economic misery and brutalization of the lower class, and the engendered sense of having had a raw deal out of life. Clearly, Engels and Bonger see the overthrow of capitalist relations of production as the ultimate solution to crime. However, the brutalization argument also implies that alleviating the conditions of deprivation of the lower class would have some efficacy for crime reduction, even in the absence of the dismantling of capitalist production.

The brutalization argument really amounts to a crude frustration-aggression hypothesis as later described by Dollard *et al.* in their classic *Frustration and Aggression.*[10]

That certain types of occupation are more arduous, disagreeable, or dangerous than others is obvious; by implication, persons who are forced into these intrinsically less desirable kinds of work will experience, other things being equal, a higher-than-average amount of frustration and will therefore show a heightened tendency towards criminality.[11]

However, the Engels and Bonger hypothesis could be more adequately described as oppression–aggression than frustration–aggression, because critically the frustration is introduced by the exploitative exercise of power.

Modern-day proponents of the oppression–aggression hypothesis are rare,[12] though some rekindling of interest has been demonstrated by economists who have recently displayed a concern with redressing what they regard as the 'sociological' and 'psychological' dominance in criminology. For example, Feldman and Weisfeld quote at length from an interview with a 24-year-old gang leader to illustrate the hypothesis.[13]

Interviewer: What about what Roger said earlier, about whether they think they're getting back at the people in the suburbs, when they rip them off?
Gang leader: Every kid that lives in this neighbourhood hates people that live in the suburbs. . . . They hate anybody that got more than they do.
Interviewer: You could hate them because they're better off or you could hate them because they took it from you.
Gang leader: No, we hate them because—like me, I'm a roofer, but when I go out there to do one of the roofs, you know, they sit there on the patio or something and drink Pepsi-Cola, Jack, when you're sweating your ass off, man, and they look at you like you're some kind of creep, man, and they stick their nose up in the air. . . . I don't like nobody with money anyway. Because they don't get money. Most of them own businesses, like Breits–Breits supermarket. Leslies department store, all them, right? The way they got up there, man, they robbed people, right? But they robbed them in a way where they couldn't get arrested for it. Only they're good people. To society they're good people.

Apart from such selected personal accounts, empirical testing of the generality of a relationship between subjectively perceived relative deprivation, frustration, or oppression, and crime has been almost non-existent.[14] Moreover, it is probable that many lower-class people do not perceive themselves as having been oppressed, because they see a very real distinction between what is an equal distribution of wealth and what is a just distribution of wealth. As J. Stacy Adams says:

> Many men, when comparing their rewards to those of another, will perceive that their rewards are smaller, and yet they will not feel that this state of affairs is unjust. The reason is that persons obtaining the higher rewards are perceived as deserving them.[15]

Thus, objective poverty does not always result in a subjective sense of economic injustice.[16] This is one possible explanation for why some poor people commit crime and some do not.

Powerlessness

Redistribution of power as a solution to crime has gained widespread respectability during the 1960s and 1970s. The National Advisory Commission on Criminal Justice Standards and Goals recommends that 'Individuals who have been on the outside looking in, who have experienced the helpless feeling of inability to exert power within the system, must be given a participatory role.'[17] However the theory is taken to imply only a very limited kind of redistribution of power—participation by lower-class people in decision-making at a local community level.

> Citizen participation, in and of itself, is the active expression of faith in the dignity and worth of the individual in promoting creativity, initiative, self-reliance, and leadership; to deny effective participation, including the opportunity to choose, to be heard, to discuss, to criticize, to protest, and to challenge decisions regarding the most fundamental conditions of existence, is to confirm the individual's sense of impotence and subservience.[18]

The theory of powerlessness and crime posits that many delinquent and criminal acts are an attempt to make a mark on the world, to be noticed, to get identity feedback, and that 'one way to get society to pay more attention is to muss it up a little'.[19] Matza is a pre-eminent theorist of this view in his *Delinquency and Drift:*[20] 'Being "pushed around" puts the delinquent in a mood of fatalism. He experiences himself as effect. In that condition, he is rendered irresponsible.'

Powerlessness is particularly critical when the youth is 'pushed around' in a way he perceives as unjust or oppressive, because a sense of

injustice can abrogate the moral bind of law: 'The subculture of delinquency is, among other things, a memory file that collects injustices.'[21]
While rejecting the subjectivism of Matza's approach, the authors of
The New Criminology concur with the critical assertion that delinquency
is a desperate effort to 'make things happen'.[22]

> We believe that it is true that delinquency is in part the result of
> an external situation of inequality, poverty and powerlessness and
> can be seen as an attempt to assert control and thereby re-establish
> some sense of self.

The re-establishment of a sense of self—the need to 'be somebody' in
the face of this powerlessness—is echoed in the work of Rainwater.[23]
Since the poor person is powerless to achieve a definition of self-worth
on the ubiquitous goals of 'occupational success' or the 'good American
life', he must internalize other criteria of self-worth. He must seek in
other ways to construct a self which provides some measure of gratification of needs and earns some recognition of himself as a social being.
Deviant behaviour can be an effort to attain some sense of valid identity.

It is implicit in these latter formulations that a wounded self-concept
is an intervening variable between powerlessness and the decision to
'make things happen' through crime or delinquency. There is consistent
empirical support for an association between delinquency and low self-
esteem.[24] However, there are more studies which have failed to establish association between lower-class status (powerlessness) and low self-
esteem,[25] than there are studies which have supported this
relationship.[26]

In spite of the ambiguous evidence on the effect of self-concept as
an intervening variable, the empirical backing for the more direct relationship between powerlessness and crime is reasonably strong. The
review by Allen reports fairly consistent support from studies using
various scales to measure powerlessness for the hypothesis that lower-
class people experience greater subjective feelings of powerlessness than
do the middle class.[27] Jaffe[28] found that junior high-school boys who
scored as more delinquency-prone on the Gough Delinquency-Proneness
Scale also scored as feeling more powerless on the Rotter and Seeman
Powerlessness Scale. Of course 'delinquency-proneness' is not delinquency, but Jaffe does show that 70 per cent of his delinquent-prone
boys had been involved in court cases, compared to none of his controls.
Gold reports on research by Bachman and Kahn, which included a
cross-section of more than 2,000 American tenth-grade boys.[29] They
established a reliable but slight correlation between a self-report

delinquency measure and the Srole Anomie Scale. Great significance cannot be attached to this evidence, however, because the Srole scale measures other dimensions of alienation besides powerlessness. Moreover, a later study by Engstad and Hackler, using the Srole scale on a much smaller sample of 183, failed to produce a positive correlation.[30] Another study by Dorn[31] found delinquents to be more 'alienated' than non-delinquents. But again, because the author does not list the items in his 'alienation' scale, we have no idea as to what extent this scale might reasonably be regarded as an index of powerlessness.

Merton, Cloward and Ohlin, and opportunity theory

In *Social Theory and Social Structure*, Merton[32] presents a general theory of deviance, the greatest application of which has been in the areas of crime and delinquency. Merton says that in any society there are a number of important cultural goals which provide a frame of aspirational reference. The most important of these goals in America, and the goal which is relevant for this thesis, is this-worldly material success. In addition to cultural goals held up as 'worth striving for', there are defined legitimate institutionalized means for achieving the cultural goals. The legitimate means for achieving the cultural goal of material success are a good education, a good job, investment, and so on.

Merton asserts that when an individual has internalized a certain goal, and when the legitimate means for achieving that goal are blocked, the individual is under pressure to resort to illegitimate means to achieve the goal. The lower-class child learns that he should strive for the cultural goal of material success, but legitimate means for achieving that goal are closed to him because he cannot do well at school, he does not have the 'connections', the 'polish', or the 'presentability' to swing a good job, and he has no capital for investment. He is therefore in the market for an illegitimate means of achieving the cultural goal he has been taught to value so highly.

The important assumption is that for crime to ensue, the success-goal must be internalized by all classes in the society.

It is only when a system of cultural values extols, virtually above all else, certain *common* success-goals for the population at large while the social structure rigorously restricts or completely closes access to approved modes of reaching these goals *for a considerable part of the same population,* that deviant behaviour ensues on a large scale.[33]

In modern capitalist societies the mass media play an important role in ensuring this widespread diffusion throughout the class structure of the material-success goal. Phillip Adams explains:[34]

Telly is the most egalitarian of mediums, in that it transmits its plastic dreams to rich and poor alike. Thus admass fantasies intended for the penthouse finish up in the slums, and Raquel Welch works herself into a lather over Lux in houses that don't run to hot water. Glittering models ooze out of luxury limousines in homes where the kids' shoes don't fit. And airlines offer the world to viewers who've forgotten their last holiday.

Merton suggests that American society is characterized by an obsession with the overriding goal of material success, without an equal emphasis on the proper way to achieve it. 'The morality of such a society is summed up by the expression, "it's winning that matters, not how you play the game." '[35] In this kind of society, the Mertonian explanation for the greater criminality of the lower class is that while all classes are attracted towards the material-success goal, for the lower class legitimate access to this goal is less readily available, and thus its members are more likely to resort to illegitimate means for achieving the goal.

Cloward and Ohlin have been responsible for an important development on the work of Merton in the area of juvenile delinquency.[36] They maintain that if delinquency is to result from the desire to achieve a cultural goal then *two* things are necessary. First, like Merton, they say legitimate means for achieving the goal must be blocked; but second, illegitimate means for achieving the goal must be open. Within any given community there may or may not be a system of illegitimate opportunities (a criminal subculture). If, for instance, a lower-class adolescent who does not have legitimate access to success goals available to him is sent to live in a very respectable middle-class suburb, he may find that no illegitimate opportunities are available either. There will be no criminal-role models and criminal-learning structures, no delinquent gangs to provide social support for delinquency, and tight informal social control operating within the community. Thus having either legitimate paths to success goals open or illegitimate paths closed may be enough to prevent an adolescent from becoming delinquent.

Nevertheless, having legitimate paths to success blocked and

71

illegitimate paths open does not inevitably lead to delinquency. Cloward and Ohlin suggest that delinquency is more probable under certain conditions. The most important of these 'is the attribution of the cause of failure to the social order rather than to oneself, for the way in which a person explains his failure largely determines what he will do about it'. Belief that one is the victim of an unjust system will result in alienation from that system, and withdrawal of attributions of legitimacy from official norms. Belief that failure is the result of one's personal deficiency results in pressures to improve oneself, and leaves the legitimacy of established norms intact.

Cloward and Ohlin cite two main factors that determine attributions of blame to internal or external causes. First is the perception of discrepancies between official criteria of achievement (hard work, ability, perseverance, etc.) and pragmatic criteria ('connections', familial ties, luck, etc.). Second is the perception of systematized prejudices in conferring success, prejudices against people of a given race, class, place of residence, or other visible group. Failures become angry when they perceive themselves to be equally endowed in those criteria which are institutionally and normatively stated to be relevant, but are unjustly deprived because of visible barriers.

Cloward and Ohlin therefore see greater equality of opportunity as a means of attenuating some of these barriers, thereby reducing system-blame and delinquency. Moreover, equality of opportunity will give the poor *hope* that they will lift themselves out of poverty, perhaps in the next generation at least.[37] Thus the theory is taken as implying a policy of *equality of opportunity* rather than *equality of results*.[38] Indeed Cloward and Ohlin's work was one of the major theoretical underpinnings of the equality of opportunity programs of the 'War on Poverty' of the late 1960s in the United States.

The evidence that blaming the system for personal failure correlates with delinquency is not strong. Rosenberg and Silverstein[39] report that their 130 very poor lower-class and mostly quite delinquent youth reported feelings of 'deep resignation' rather than 'relative deprivation', and were prone to explain their predicament in terms of personal inadequacy rather than system-blame. Gold found no differences between the responses of repeated official delinquents and non-delinquents to the question, 'Do you feel that every boy in this country has as good a chance as every other boy?'[40] Quicker[41] concludes from his review that the evidence is conflicting and inconclusive on the question of whether system-blame rather than self-blame leads to delinquency. Since that review a study by Picou *et al.* has been published which found that lower class Negro delinquents were more likely than lower-class non-delinquents to believe that opportunities for the attainment of occupational goals were blocked *both* because of 'my race', and because they were 'not smart enough'.[42] Another review by Elliott and Voss,[43] mainly of studies using Rosenweig's measure of punitiveness, also concluded that there is little evidence that blaming the system is associated with delinquency. Contrary to Cloward and Ohlin, it is reasonable to hypothesize that if one fails in a system, one will withdraw attributions of legitimacy to that system, irrespective of the reasons for failure.

Even though delinquents are not very clear as to who or what is to blame, they do believe (more so than non-delinquents) that opportunity for educational and occupational advancement is relatively closed to them. While there is not consistent evidence to support the hypothesis that delinquents are more prone to view 'the system as rotten', and while there is not consistent evidence to show that there are differences between delinquents and non-delinquents in *what* they perceive as blocking their opportunities, delinquents are more inclined to feel that *something* is blocking their opportunities. A large number of studies using various awareness of limited opportunity measures have consistently found delinquents to perceive their opportunities as more limited compared to non-delinquents.[44] Short and Strodtbeck found that members of delinquent gangs both perceived their legitimate opportunities to be lower than did a sample of non-gang members, and perceived their illegitimate opportunities to be greater compared with the non-gang boys.[45]

It is scarcely necessary to demonstrate that delinquents objectively suffer from limited legitimate opportunities to achieve success goals. In chapter 2 it was shown that delinquents are disproportionately lower class, and lower-class youth clearly have fewer legitimate opportunities than middle-class youth. Hence we know that people who have legitimate means blocked are more likely to opt for illegitimate means (crime). To confirm this, Tallman[46] set up an experimental situation in which he demonstrated that when legitimate means to achieving a success goal were blocked, subjects resorted increasingly to illegitimate means.

The major assumption of Merton's formulation, that lower-class as well as middle-class people subscribe to the cultural goal of material success, is undoubtedly supported by the evidence. Both lower-class and middle-class people aspire to educational and occupational success,[47] and although middle-class people aspire to positions which are somewhat higher in absolute terms than the positions aspired to by

73

lower-class people, it is doubtful whether lower-class people have lower aspirations *relative to their present position.*[48] Moreover, there is some evidence to suggest that class differences in absolute terms are the result of the realistic downgrading of aspirations by lower-class people in response to blocked opportunity.[49]

Even so, on the basis of their data, Picou *et al.*[50] argue that the job aspirations of lower-class youth, both delinquent and non-delinquent, are best described as 'unrealistically high'. Picou *et al.* show that most of them have no likelihood of achieving what they aspire to. If not delinquency and rebellion, at least dejection and depression must ensue when expectations begin to fall below aspirations. The possibility that delinquency is a common response to this situation is attested by some studies which have found an association between delinquency and the degree of discrepancy between aspirations and expectations.[51]

There have been two main threads to criticism of Merton's opportunity theory. Researchers such as Mizruchi[52] and Winslow[53] point to their findings that the *absolute* aspirations of lower-class youth are lower than those of middle-class youth, as if this is disconfirmation of Merton's assumption that lower-class people share material-success goals. Merton's theory depends only on the assumption that lower-class people aspire to greater material success, and it does not deny the possibility that the intensity of these aspirations may be greater for the middle class. Indeed, as Merton himself has rebutted: 'It is sufficient. . . that a *sizable minority* of the lower strata assimilate this goal for them to be differentially subject to this pressure as a result of their relatively smaller opportunities to achieve monetary success.'[54]

The second major criticism of Merton's theory has been that it is capable only of explaining why lower-class people should engage in higher rates of acquisitive offences against property. Why do lower-class youth engage in non-utilitarian acts of vandalism, and non-utilitarian crimes against persons at a higher rate than middle-class youth? Merton's theory has no answer because it conceives of crime as a compensatory utilitarian means of achieving monetary goals. To explain non-utilitarian crime, the criminologist must turn to other theories.

Cohen and the school

Albert Cohen,[55] like Merton, prefaces his theory of delinquency with the assumption that both lower-class and middle-class boys begin their school careers with a commitment to traditional success goals. But because lower-class socialization equips lower-class boys less adequately than their middle-class counterparts for success at school, more of the lower-class boys become failures in the status system of the school. This failure initially engenders shame and guilt, and perhaps some resentment and bitterness as well. A sense of inferiority and lack of personal worth is intensified by teachers who withhold various privileges and opportunities from unsuccessful boys, by other students who label the failures as 'dumb' or 'stupid', and by the realization that future job prospects are dimmed by poor school performance.

Having failed in the status system of the school, the student has a status problem and is in the market for a solution. He solves it collectively with other students who have been similarly rejected by the school. The outcasts band together and set up their own status system with values the exact inverse of those of the school—contempt for property and authority instead of respect for property and authority, immediate impulse gratification instead of impulse control, apathy instead of ambition, toughness instead of control of aggression. The delinquent's conduct is right by the standards of his subculture precisely because it is wrong by the standards of the school. By participating in this subculture, the poor academic performer can enhance his self-image by rejecting his rejectors. The boy's status problem is solved by the collective creation of a new status system in which he is guaranteed some success.

The first proposition of Cohen's theory, that lower-class boys are more likely to fail at school than middle-class boys, is clearly confirmed by a wealth of evidence.[56] It is also beyond doubt that those who fail at school are more likely to engage in delinquent behaviour.[57] Moreover, Toby and Toby[58] have shown longitudinally that poor academic performance precedes delinquency, rather than vice versa. This is important because it is plausible that the reverse direction of causality to that posited by Cohen applies—poor performance results from participation in a delinquent subculture.

Although the most fundamental propositions survive confrontation with empirical evidence, Cohen's theory is weak at a number of points. For example, Downes[59] has concluded from his study of delinquents in Stepney and Poplar that the typical response to failure is not Cohen's 'reaction formation' but 'dissociation'. Rather than rebelliously turning the values of the school upside down, it is more typical for the delinquent to simply withdraw interest from the work world of the school. Box[60] also suggests that there is no 'reaction formation' because the lower-class boys do not 'internalize' the status criteria of the school in the first place; it is simply that the boys 'can't be indifferent to' the status criteria of the school.

These are intrinsically important issues. But irrespective of whether lower-class boys 'internalize' or 'can't be indifferent to' the status criteria of the school; irrespective of whether the response to failure is guilt and shame, or resentment and rebellion; irrespective of whether there is a 'reaction formation' or a 'dissociation'; irrespective of whether differential association with delinquent peers following rejection by the school is critical or not;[61] it is the fact that school failure ultimately encourages the delinquency which is essential to this policy analysis.

For the point of discussion let us assume that Cohen's theory, or one of the above variants thereof, is true, such that the *only* reason that lower-class children are more delinquent than middle-class children is that they are more prone to school failure. It is then the case that policies to create greater equality would reduce school failure. If more resources are put at the disposal of the lower class, they should be able to use these resources to create better educational opportunities for their children, so that fewer will fail. This may be so. But to create fewer school failures among the lower class will not reduce delinquency if this means creating more failures among the middle class. This possibility is now briefly considered.

In most schools throughout the Western world, the status system of the school approximates a hierarchy, with all children being given a ranking. The hierarchy need not be an explicit 'top of the class, second, third, . . . down to bottom'; it may be less quantitatively 'one of the better students', 'an average student', 'a poor student'. Educational opportunities for lower-class children achieve only a reordering of children in the hierarchy. For example, if we increase educational opportunities for blacks, we do not change the fact that there will still be someone who comes bottom of the class at school—except that he might be white instead of black. If educational failure is the cause of delinquency, then the way to reduce delinquency is to change the nature of the education system so that failure is less a feature of the system—that is, to make education less competitive.[62] Greater equality may affect *who* fails, but not *how many* fail.

It must therefore be concluded that to the extent that the greater delinquency (and adult crime) of the lower class is caused by school failure, the less effective will be greater equality in reducing delinquency. Several studies have found that school failure was more strongly related to delinquency than was social class but that, controlling for school failure, there still existed a slight correlation between social class and delinquency.[63] A study by McDonald[64] has shown that social class was more strongly correlated with self-reported delinquency than was school performance. On the basis of these studies, there can be some confidence that the relationship between social class and delinquency is not totally explained by the fact that school failure is more common among the lower class. Some of the common variance between class and delinquency remains available for explanation by other theories which predict that greater equality will reduce delinquency.

Lower-class values

Cohen's is one of a number of theories which has regarded the rejection of middle-class values and their replacement with antithetical values as critical in the causation of delinquency. These theories are, in part, inconsistent with the Mertonian view, which assumes that lower-class people embrace middle-class success values.[65]

The most influential of the value theorists has been Walter Miller.[66] From his observations of lower-class gang behaviour, Miller identified 'trouble', 'toughness', 'smartness', 'excitement', 'fate', and 'autonomy' as the key 'focal concerns' of lower-class culture. The primary motivation of gang delinquency is the attempt to act out these lower-class focal concerns.

Miller's methodology is open to the criticism of shallowness and circularity. He infers the lower-class focal concerns from observations of lower-class behaviour, and then proceeds to explain that behaviour by using the focal concerns.[67] Miller and other theorists of his ilk glibly assume that there is one monolithic set of middle-class values, and another monolithic but separate consensus about values among the lower class. Matza and Sykes[68] point out that many of Miller's lower-class focal concerns are almost identical to respectable middle-class goals. Courage, easy money, and adventure, are respectable values which are equivalent to Miller's 'toughness', 'smartness', and 'excitement'. 'Toughness' can save lives or it can kill people, as Sutherland and Cressey point out:[69] 'Though criminal behaviour is an expression of general needs and values, it is not explained by those general needs and values, since non-criminal behaviour is an expression of the same needs and values.'

The only rigorous test of Miller's theory has been by Sherwin.[70] Sherwin tested whether each of Miller's focal concerns was endorsed by the majority of lower-class boys; more often endorsed by lower-class than middle-class boys; and more often endorsed by delinquents than non-delinquents, where delinquency was operationalized by a combination of self-reports and official records. The average percentage endorsement for Miller's focal concerns was:

Lower-class delinquents	48 per cent
Middle-class delinquents	41 per cent
Middle-class non-delinquents	31 per cent
Lower-class non-delinquents	31 per cent

The prediction from Miller's theory that lower-class delinquents would show the strongest commitment to the focal concerns was confirmed. However, even among this group, it can be seen that the majority did not endorse most of the focal concerns. More damaging is the finding that middle-class delinquents are more committed to lower-class focal concerns than are lower-class non-delinquents, and that there are no differences between the two social-class groups among the non-delinquents. As Sherwin says:

> Since Miller does tend to maximize cultural contrasts between the middle and lower class, the fact that a group of middle-class youths have provided a heavier endorsement of lower-class values than another group of lower-class youths, irrespective of which group is delinquent and which non-delinquent, seems to undermine the autonomy which he ascribes to lower-class culture.[71]

In summary, while there is a significant difference in commitment to the focal concerns between delinquents and non-delinquents, there is no evidence to suggest that this difference is related to class in any way. This should hardly be surprising, since Miller's conclusions about *lower-class culture* were induced from observations of *lower-class delinquents*.

Sherwin also measured endorsement of middle-class values, operationalized from the descriptions of middle-class values provided in the writings of Albert Cohen. He found that average endorsement of all middle-class value items was as follows:

Middle-class non-delinquents	82 per cent
Lower-class non-delinquents	78 per cent
Middle-class delinquents	74 per cent
Lower-class delinquents	62 per cent

As the theories predict, the middle-class non-delinquents have the strongest endorsement of middle-class values. However, a clear majority of even the lower-class delinquents also endorse these values. So Cohen's anti-middle-class 'reaction formation' is certainly not a characteristic of lower-class delinquents. Indeed, it can be seen by comparing the above two sets of figures that lower-class delinquents are less likely to endorse lower-class focal concerns than they are to endorse middle-class values. Again there is an inversion situation, with one lower-class group being more committed to middle-class values than one middle-class group. While non-delinquents are consistently more committed to middle-class values than delinquents, there is not a consistent tendency for middle-class boys to be more committed to middle-class values.

The other major study of values and delinquency was undertaken by Short and Strodtbeck.[72] They found no significant differences between members of delinquent gangs and non-members, and between middle-class and lower-class boys, on endorsement of middle-class prescriptive norms. However, on middle-class proscriptive norms, gang boys were more tolerant of infractions than non-gang boys, and lower-class boys were more tolerant of infractions than middle-class boys.

There have been other smaller studies. Landis *et al.*, after discovering minimal class differences in values, concluded from their study that:[73]

The differences in value and awareness perceptions between lower and middle class children, even when treated as poles on a socio-economic continuum are, in all probability, slight at the present time in American urban society and should be expected to decrease even further with time. A leveling effect, brought about by mass communication and other factors is at work in our society, narrowing and eradicating the attitudinal gulf between the social classes.

Specifically on the value of 'toughness', Fannin and Clinard[74] found that lower-class boys had a conception of self which was tougher, more powerful, fierce, fearless, and dangerous, when compared with middle-class boys. But Erlanger,[75] on the basis of his own data and findings from previous studies, concludes that there is more evidence inconsistent with the hypothesis that lower-class people have values more favourable to the use of violence than there is evidence consistent with it.

Interest in values as a cause of delinquency has come in bursts throughout the history of criminology. Barron summarizes the results of a spate of studies from the 1930s on value differences between delinquents and non-delinquents as follows:[76] 'For the most part these revealed either insignificant or contradictory evidence of value differences between the compared groups.'

79

Very recent studies using the Rokeach Value Survey also provide discouraging results for the class–values–crime formulation. Feather[77] found that of the 36 values in the survey, only 6 were significantly related to delinquency. Delinquents ranked 'an exciting life', 'national security', and being 'clean' more highly than did boys in the control group; and 'happiness', 'wisdom', and being 'responsible' were ranked as relatively less important by delinquents when compared with controls. Cochrane[78] found none of these values to be related to male delinquency in another study using the Rokeach Value Survey. Moreover, in two separate surveys, Feather[79] found that of the six values only 'clean' was significantly related to income in both surveys, with lower-income groups ranking being 'clean' as more important. Findings supported in one survey but not the other were no more encouraging. 'National security' was ranked as more important by lower-income earners, and 'an exciting life' was ranked as *less* important by the lowest income group.

Yet another study using the Rokeach Value Survey by Ball-Rokeach[80] found virtually no relationship between values and interpersonal violence and violent crime. Moreover, not one of the few values which were weakly related to violent behaviour was significantly associated with social class.

Cernkovich[81] has published a study which does show that subjects who evidenced a weak commitment to 'conventional values' and a strong commitment to 'subterranean values' were somewhat more likely to self-report heavy involvement in delinquency. Unfortunately, 'conventional' and 'subterranean' are ill-defined and there is no evidence that Cernkovich has used any multivariate scaling technique in developing these indices. The findings are interesting, however, because controlling for socioeconomic status did not reduce the strength of the relationship between conventional value orientation and delinquency involvement, and partialling out the effect of socioeconomic status actually *increased* the correlation between subterranean-value orientation and delinquency. If values did have an effect on delinquency, then it was certainly not because of class factors.

Using a semantic differential, Siegel *et al.*[82] found that delinquents had somewhat less positive attitudes than non-delinquents to 'police', 'law', 'saving money', and 'education'; and more positive attitudes to 'crime' and 'work'. Similarly Chapman[83] found that the 'person who is in trouble with the law' was more positively evaluated by delinquents than by non-delinquents. The data from these studies are consistent with Short and Strodtbeck's finding that delinquents are more tolerant of violations of middle-class proscriptive norms. Also consistent with this conclusion is Hindelang's[84] finding that delinquents approve more of delinquent behaviour than do non-delinquents.

Of course, such studies do not tell us whether delinquent attitudes cause delinquent behaviour or whether involvement in delinquency engenders delinquent attitudes. Studies by Hackler and Liska[85] used path analysis to try to resolve this dilemma, but results from both were equivocal.

Sykes and Matza[86] assert that delinquents do not righteously avow the morality of their behaviour; in fact they express disapproval and guilt. They accept conventional moral standards, but use various 'techniques of neutralization' to justify the suspension of these moral standards in certain situations. The five major techniques of neutralization are (1) *denial of responsibility*, e.g. 'I was drunk'; (2) *denial of injury*, e.g. 'they can afford it'; (3) *denial of victim*, e.g. 'we weren't hurting anyone'; (4) *condemnation of the condemners*, e.g. 'they're crooks themselves'; (5) *appeal to higher loyalties*, e.g. 'I had to stick by my mates'. Richard Ball[87] has shown empirically that when specific situations of delinquency are described to adolescents, both officially recorded and self-reported delinquents are more likely than non-delinquents to agree to techniques of neutralization as acceptable defences for the behaviour. Sykes and Matza disavow lower-class-values theory when they say: 'It is by learning these techniques that the juveniles become delinquent, rather than by learning moral imperatives, values or attitudes standing in direct contradiction to those of the dominant society' (p. 668).

However Sykes and Matza's neutralization theory is just an elaborated version of the general hypothesis that delinquents have a greater capacity for tolerance of delinquent behaviour than non-delinquents. Considering all of the above, this hypothesis has a fair degree of empirical support. However, the complementary hypothesis that lower-class people have a greater capacity for tolerance of delinquent behaviour than middle-class people, does not.[88] Nor do other versions of the theory that lower-class values are related to delinquency enjoy empirical support. This is because the values which have been inferred from *ex post facto* interpretations of the behaviour of delinquent gangs are not endorsed by a majority of either lower-class people or delinquents; nor are they consistently more often endorsed by lower-class than middle-class people. When values supported by a larger minority of delinquents than of non-delinquents have been isolated, commitment to these values is not related to class. Thus class differences in criminogenic values cannot be invoked as an explanation for the greater criminality of the lower class.

The reward–cost model

Criminologists who adopt a reward–cost model claim that the conventional approaches of explaining crime in terms of personality, cultural, or social structural variables are unnecessarily complicated. Most criminals, they argue, decide whether to commit crime on the basis of a rational weighing-up of the rewards to be gained from the successful completion of the crime against the costs entailed in detection.

Recently, David Gordon has employed a reward–cost model to explain the widespread criminality of the lower class.[89]

> The 'legitimate' jobs available to many ghetto residents, especially to young black males, typically pay low wages, offer relatively demeaning assignments, and carry the constant risk of layoff. In contrast, many kinds of crime 'available' in the ghetto often bring higher monetary return, offer even higher social status, and—at least in some cases like numbers running—sometimes carry relatively low risk of arrest and punishment (p. 175).

Moreover, says Gordon, a rational assessment of the costs of being arrested must lead the slum-dweller to conclude that they are fairly low, because life seems almost as dismal outside of prison as it is inside. He quotes a black hustler from Harlem:

> It is not a matter of a guy saying, 'I want to go to jail [or] I am afraid of jail.' Jail is on the street just like it is on the inside. The same as, like when you are in jail, they tell you 'Look, if you do something wrong you are going to be put in the hole.' You are still in jail, in the hole or out of the hole. You are in jail in the street or behind bars. It is the same thing.[90]

Conversely, for the affluent person, the comparison between his present life-style and prison is striking; and the rewards of crime seem small compared to what he can earn legitimately. So the reward–cost ratio of traditional crime is much higher for the lower-class than for the middle-class person.[91] Consistent with this formulation, Ehrlich[92] found that the deterrent effect on violent crime of an increased probability of a prison sentence was significantly less for blacks than for whites.

The reward–cost model is said to be particularly applicable to juvenile delinquency. Middle-class adolescents beginning on the path to building a professional or managerial career have a particularly great deal to lose from damaging their reputation by getting into trouble with the law. Toby has expressed this argument clearly:[93]

> Youngsters vary in the extent to which they feel a stake in American
> society. For those with social honor, disgrace is a powerful sanction.
> For a boy disapproved of already, there is less incentive to resist
> the temptation to do what he wants when he wants to do it.
> Usually, the higher the socioeconomic status of the family, the more
> the youngster feels he has to lose by delinquent behaviour.

The only test of this hypothesis seems to be in the work of Martin Gold.[94] Gold's data showed no tendency for middle-class youth to be more inclined to agree that getting into trouble with the police would harm a boy's future. Even though it is possible that this question means different things to different classes, the finding is a blow to the reward–cost formulation. However, what is true of the calculations of the costs of delinquency in terms of the future success of adolescents, may not be true of the calculation of the immediate financial rewards and costs in the here and now for adult crime.

Criminologists such as Gordon take the policy implication of the reward–cost model to be clearly radical. The poor commit crime because the rewards of legitimate work are small compared to the rewards of crime—so increase their legitimate rewards. The poor commit crime because the cost of dropping from their present condition to that of a convict is small—so improve their present condition and make the cost greater.

This policy analysis, however, expresses only one side of the reward–cost coin. If we redistribute income from the wealthy to the poor, this makes crime relatively less rewarding for the poor, but relatively more rewarding for the wealthy. Increasing the income of the poor, increases the cost of crime for the poor; decreasing the income of the wealthy, decreases the cost of crime for the wealthy. While the poor become less criminal, the rich become more so. Nevertheless, a marginal increase in the income of the lower class may be more intensely felt than the same marginal decrease for the wealthy. To increase the income of the poor by $50 a week might give them a future, while a decrease of $50 a week in the income of the wealthy might not change the fact that the wealthy still have a future. Thus a redistribution of wealth from the wealthy to the poor might produce a reduction for the poor in the reward–cost ratio of traditional crime far greater than the increase in the reward–cost ratio of crime for the wealthy.

Labelling

Being labelled as delinquent or criminal causes a drop in social class— this is one hypothesis which has received little systematic attention in the literature. This inverted assertion that crime causes class rather than class causing crime is not so implausible as it might at first seem.

Going to jail does cause a person's economic position to worsen. Release does not necessarily relieve this situation because arrest records often rule out legitimate employment. The United States Department of Labor has discovered that an arrest record is an absolute bar to public employment in almost 20 per cent of the jurisdictions and public agencies surveyed. Over 50 per cent of jurisdictions barred employment on less specific grounds—poor moral character, for example—in which arrest records were frequently taken into consideration.[95]

Often the economic exclusion is of a more subtle nature. Work done by Buikhuisen and Dijksterhuis[96] in the Netherlands, and Boshier and Johnson[97] in Britain, has shown that when a variety of employers are sent letters of application identical except for the admission or non-admission of a conviction for theft, the applications which admit to the conviction draw a much less favourable response.

In a thirty-year longitudinal study, Robins *et al.*[98] have uncovered evidence consistent with the hypothesis that getting into trouble with the law contributes to economic failure. They compared intergenerational social mobility for delinquent patients at a child-guidance clinic, non-delinquent (mainly neurotic) patients at the same clinic, and a control group from the general population. Over the thirty-year period the delinquents were more downwardly mobile than the other two groups. Robins *et al.* suggest that the criminality of the lower class at all generational levels can be partially explained by the economic consequences of deviance: 'The disproportionate incidence of anti-social children in the lower classes apparently can be partially explained by their high rate of anti-social fathers, whose own deviance has determined their low occupational status.'[99]

Another recently completed longitudinal study by Noblit[100] produced the same result. Youths who got into trouble with the law were less likely than others to be educationally and occupationally successful as adults. However, the results of these two studies need not necessarily mean that delinquency causes downward mobility. It may be that delinquent youth become delinquent because they (realistically) anticipate that they will be failures as adults.

Nevertheless, it is indisputable that apprehension for crime has adverse consequences for occupational futures in many cases. Some part of the negative correlation between class and crime must be explained by this effect.

There is a very different way in which labelling may play a part in explaining the class–crime relationship. More lower-class than middle-class people are labelled as criminal, if only because of class bias in assigning official designations of criminality. The fact that lower-class people are more often labelled as criminal may cause them actually to become more criminal. An adolescent's delinquency may start out as pranks and idle mischief, but a severe labelling response from institutions of social control, or the general public, may lead the adolescent to act and become the way he is defined. To some extent, every individual takes as his definition of himself the way he is seen by others.[101]

Schur is one who has alluded to labelling as a factor pushing lower-class people into crime:[102] 'The conscious or unconscious tendency amongst middle class whites to equate Negroes with crime has given the latter a final shove into total degradation and alienation, providing a powerful nothing-to-lose incentive to criminal acts.'

Schur's formulation is interesting in that it posits a reward–cost calculation as intervening between labelling and crime. There is evidence consistent with the assumption that this widespread stigmatization of the lower class does influence the thinking of lower-class youth. Frease[103] reports that youths from blue-collar families are more likely than those from white-collar families to agree that 'Lots of people think I am delinquent.' The earliest evidence comes from Hackler's[104] path analysis. He found some support for a causal chain whereby an individual's low status results in people expecting delinquency from him; this, in turn, results in his perceiving that others expect delinquency of him; and this ultimately results in delinquency.

The differential labelling applies at an institutional level as well. Chiricos *et al.*[105] have found that, compared with lower-class offenders, extra effort is made to avoid criminal labelling for middle-class offenders in Florida courts. For offenders who are being placed on probation, the middle class more often have stigmatization averted by the withholding of an adjudication of guilt.

The stigmatization and criminalizing effects of imprisonment and participation in the criminal subculture of the prison have been frequently voiced. David Gordon is but one example:[106]

> As for those whom it [the prison] releases, it tends to drive them
> deeper into criminality, intensifying their criminal and violent
> behaviour, filling their heads with paranoia and hatred, keeping
> them perpetually on the run and unable, ultimately, to organize
> with others to change the institutions which pursue them. Finally,
> it blots their records with the stigma of criminality and, by denying
> them many decent employment opportunities, effectively precludes
> the reform of even those who vow to escape the system and go
> 'straight'.

The class biases of the criminal-justice system can become a self-fulfilling prophecy. With lower-class suspects there is a greater propensity to assume guilt, so more of them are thrown into jail. Because so many lower-class people are thrown into jail, lower-class people do in fact become more criminal.

Wilkins[107] has described labelling as a 'deviance-amplifying system'. An initial deviation results in a punitive reaction and labelling; this results in the development of a deviant self-identity and behaviour appropriate to that identity; resulting in further punitive reaction and labelling and so on. In this way a small initial deviation arising from any cause is amplified into a very large deviation. This has dramatic implications for the present policy analysis. Even if the initial deviation were directly caused by poverty, if that deviation has set in train a process which results in the internalization of a deviant self-identity, then the belated removal of the initial cause will have little or no impact. Once the deviance time-bomb mechanism has been set in motion there may be no turning it off. For a man who steals his first loaf of bread because he is hungry, giving him all the bread he needs later on will not reform him as a thief, if in the intervening period he has learnt to derive satisfaction from being a thief. This intriguing problem of the policy analysis will be discussed in more detail in chapter 13.

Gordon[108] has suggested that not only are lower-class people labelled as more dangerous, but crimes which are typically lower class are labelled as more dangerous crimes. Crimes which are typically lower class are severely sanctioned, and the police are prepared to use force to effect arrests. For these types of crime, the criminal is at risk so he must rely on the threat of or commission of violence to protect himself. If prosecutions were equally severe for white-collar criminals, and if police were prepared to engage in shoot-outs with white-collar criminals, these types of criminals would be prepared to use the threat of harm to those who would betray them. Lower-class crime is more violent, therefore, because of the selective attention paid to lower-class crimes. Gordon supports this argument by pointing out that lower-class offences which *are* largely ignored by the police in the United States (such as the numbers racket) rarely involve violence.

The policy implication of the view that lower-class people are more criminal because their behaviour is subjected to more adverse labelling is essentially conservative. The solution does not lie in changing the objective conditions confronting lower-class people, but in changing how people think about lower-class people. The answer is to get inside the heads of people to make them have less stigmatizing attitudes, and choose less stigmatizing means for dealing with the lower class.

Lower-class pathology

Poor control over the bladder, inability to budget expenditure, and spontaneous pilfering from the employer are all parts of the same culture.[109]

The view that both crime and poverty are the effect of some lower-class pathology has been declining in popularity. There are a number of versions of the pathology theory. Lower-class people more often suffer from mental illness or personality defect, and this causes both their poverty and their excessive crime. Lower-class people are of lower intelligence, and this explains both their poverty and criminality. Lower-class people are immersed in a culture of poverty which brings together a wide range of debilitating pathologies. Lower-class people come from disorganized, ineffective families.

The tying together of class and crime with personality defect rests on a weak empirical foundation. There have been vast research efforts to try to establish relationships between personality defect and crime, and personality defect and poverty. Neither have uncovered any clearly known and consistently supported facts about personality and these two variables. Schuessler and Cressey's[110] review of 113 studies of the personality characteristics of criminals reveals that the monumental mobilization of research resources with regard to this question has, in effect, drawn a blank. Allen concluded from his review of poverty and personality that 'for many widely quoted personality correlates of poverty, data are ambiguous at best and overwhelmingly nonsupportive at worst.'[111] The bringing together of these two areas of weak explanatory power to jointly explain the relationship between crime and class is therefore bound for failure. The only attempt has been Conger and Miller's exhaustive work *Personality, Social Class and Delinquency*.[112] While a factor analysis of personality-test items isolated six factors significantly related to delinquency, none of these was in turn correlated with class.

A number of studies have found that delinquents score lower on IQ tests than non-delinquents.[113] One cannot, however, attribute greater inherent stupidity to delinquents on the basis of such findings. IQ tests are measures of the kinds of achievement which are valued in one particular cultural milieu. As Cohen has argued, intelligence tests measure abilities 'that are prized by middle class people, that are fostered by middle-class socialization, and that are especially important for achievement . . . in middle class society'.[114] Delinquents may perform poorly on IQ tests because they are people who have become alienated from the dominant middle-class milieu. Moreover, efforts to measure culture-free intelligence have cast increasing doubt upon the hypothesis that lower-class people are less intelligent.[115] Finally, the notion that stupidity causes crime is theoretically weak because there is no explanation for why it is stupid to commit crime, especially in those cases where crime is quite profitable compared with other available avenues of income, and where the probability of apprehension is minimal.

In a previous section, the question of whether distinctively lower-class values are responsible for the criminality of the lower class was discussed. We must now deal with the related notion that lower-class culture is a cause of crime. Allen[116] has described the cognitive features of the culture of poverty.

> The most frequently mentioned psychological themes referred to
> by the culture of poverty concept are: strong feelings of fatalism
> and belief in chance, strong present time orientation and short time
> perspective, impulsiveness or inability to delay present gratification
> or plan for the future, concrete rather than abstract thinking pro-
> cesses and concrete verbal behaviour, feelings of inferiority, accept-
> ance of aggression and illegitimacy, and authoritarianism.

Recent years have seen scathing critiques of the culture-of-poverty concept by Rodman, Valentine, Roach and Gursslin, and Leacock,[117] and a rash of qualitative studies which fail to find this culture of poverty among the poor.[118] Evidence that the themes of the culture of poverty are in fact more common among the lower class than the middle class is typically weak. It has already been shown that there are more studies failing to establish a relationship between feelings of inferiority and class than there are studies which do (footnotes 25 and 26). Allen has summarized the results of his exhaustive review as follows.[119]

> A review of relevant research leads to the conclusion that: the hypothesis of shorter time perspective among the poor has *not* been demonstrated;[120] the poor are *not* less inclined to delay immediate, less-valued goals for the sake of greater future gains;[121] the poor are *not* more responsive to concrete (material) incentives than the non-poor; systematic data are inadequate concerning differences in self-concept between lower- and middle-class groups.

There is not space here for an exhaustive review of the literature on the culture of poverty. Suffice it to say that the culture of poverty is not a conception which has attracted a great deal of empirical support. Nevertheless, after more research has been undertaken, some of the characteristics of the culture of poverty will possibly be found to be more common among the poor than the non-poor. But such isolated findings need not imply even the partial validity of the culture-of-poverty theory. If we find, as Johnson and Sanday have,[122] that the poor are more fatalistic than the non-poor, does that mean that fatalism causes poverty, or that fatalism is a pragmatic adjustment to poverty? The culture of poverty (if it exists) may be an independent entity that causes a variety of pathologies, including poverty itself, or it may be an adaptive response to a state of want. Liebow, in his participant-observation in *Tally's Corner* found the latter to be the case.[123]

> When Richard squanders a week's pay in two days it is not because, like an animal or a child, he is 'present-time oriented', unaware of or unconcerned with his failure. He does so precisely because he is aware of the failure and the hopelessness of it all.

Hence, the argument that, for example, impulsiveness or inability to delay gratification causes both crime and poverty, and thus explains the association between crime and poverty, is open to attack on three grounds. First, impulsiveness is probably not more characteristic of the poor than the non-poor. Second, even if it is, it may be an adaptive response to poverty rather than a cause of it. Third, impulsiveness is probably not related to crime.[124] The theory does not seem robust enough to survive this triple confrontation.

Finally, the notion that there is a distinct lower-class culture which causes pathology is too riddled with inconsistencies to be of any value.

At one point its proponents talk about the *culture* of poverty; at another point they speak of lower-class life as being totally disorganized —the epitome of *non-culture*. On the one hand they say that the lower class are lazy,[125] therefore they pursue easy money through crime. On the other hand they are stupid, they cannot see that crime doesn't pay.

The belief that the culture of poverty causes delinquency partially motivated many of the community-action programmes of the United States War on Poverty of the 1960s. The evidence is overwhelmingly discouraging to the effect that these massive onslaughts of many and varied kinds upon the culture of poverty, costing hundreds of millions of dollars, had no impact upon delinquency.[126]

However, there is one part of the culture of poverty argument which is deserving of particular attention in relation to crime. This is the suggestion that the weak structure of the lower-class family causes delinquency and also serves to perpetuate the cycle of poverty. There are a great number of studies to show that children from broken homes have heightened chances of delinquency[127] and some evidence that lower-class families are more likely than others to become broken.[128] However, a recent review by Wilkinson[129] suggests that the relationship between the broken family and delinquency is tenuous because, when appropriate controls are introduced, a number of studies find no relationship.

Willie has reported that controlling for broken homes does not make the relationship between class and delinquency disappear.[130] The policy implication of the broken-home argument depends on what it is that causes lower-class families more often to become broken. If it is the stresses associated with economic hardship, then the implication is that greater equality will reduce delinquency. There is certainly evidence that economic failure during the depression had a serious disorganizing impact upon many families.[131]

Gold has concluded that lower-class families encourage delinquency because fathers who are economic failures lose the respect of their sons and consequently become impotent as socializing agents. He set up the following hypotheses, all of which were clearly supported by his data.[132]

The status of a man's job in his society will be related to the amount of influence he wields in his family, so that lower status men are less influential. A son's attraction to his father is related to the influence the father wields in his family, so that the less influential boys perceive their fathers to be, the less they will be attracted to them.

A son's attraction to his father is related directly to the status of his father's job in his society, so that the lower the status of fathers' jobs, the less attractive fathers will be to their sons.

Since attraction is the primary basis of social control, and since fathers are primary sources of social control for adolescent boys: the less boys are attracted to their fathers, the more likely they will be delinquent.

McKinley[133] has confirmed that lower-class youths are less inclined to view their parents as legitimate authorities. The policy implication of Gold's family theory is that the economic success of lower-class fathers must be improved so that they might enjoy respect from, and influence over, their sons.

Bronfenbrenner,[134] in his summary of evidence to that time (1958), concluded that discipline in lower-class families was more often physical, while in middle-class families love withdrawal was the dominant technique; and that the former is less effective in socialization than the latter. Rodman and Grams agree that 'These differences in child rearing practices by social class . . . undoubtedly account for a significant amount of the variance in delinquency rates between social classes.'[135] A more recent review by Erlanger[136] concludes that the tendency for lower-class parents to use physical punishment more than middle-class parents is only weak. Nevertheless, the Bronfenbrenner formulation is consistent with considerable evidence, even if it shows only a weak relationship; and the theory implies that it is changing lower-class child-rearing practices that will affect delinquency, rather than reducing inequality.

Social class of area

The number of theories which have been put forward to explain why lower-class areas have higher crime rates than middle-class areas is far more limited than the number suggested for the relationship between crime and social class of the family.

The physical undesirability of the slum, contrasted with the superior environment of surrounding suburbs, is frequently suggested as contributing to a feeling of being poor, rejected, or the victim of an unjust social system. Rainwater, for example, says:[137]

The physical evidence of trash, poor plumbing and the stink that goes with it, rats, and other vermin deepen their feeling of being moral outcasts. Their physical world is telling them that they are

inferior and bad just as effectively perhaps as do their human interactions. Their inability to control the depredation of rats, hot steam
pipes, balky stoves, and poorly fused electrical circuits tells them
that they are failures as autonomous individuals.

Another theory cites high population density and overcrowding as
the causes of crime in the slum.[138] Impetus has been given to this
theory by the findings of Calhoun and others that population density
causes pathological behaviour among animals.[139] All of the arguments
for density and overcrowding causing crime have been well summarized
by Mays.[140]

(a) Cramped living quarters and overcrowding are likely to cause
tensions and conflicts inside the household, especially if there is
more than one generation cohabiting.
(b) Lack of essential privacy can have an influence on sexual ideas
and behaviour and produce anxieties.
(c) Recreative and leisure time activities become quite impossible
in overcrowded homes and therefore young and old are obliged to
seek their amusements on the streets or in the various kinds of
commercial entertainments available. Lack of room space and
amenity hence engenders inadequate home life and fosters the conditions of delinquent association on the streets.

Impressive reviews by Roncek[141] and Kvalseth[142] found that while
a number of studies have established simple correlations between density and crime, where sophisticated multivariate techniques or appropriate controls have been employed, almost no studies have established
a relationship. However, for overcrowding and crime, Roncek concludes
that regression coefficients have been consistently high over a number
of studies in demonstrating a positive relationship.[143]

Mintburn and Lambert[144] have produced evidence consistent with
the view that the latter relationship arises because overcrowding creates
family friction and consequent diminution of primary social control.
Their finding was that mothers exhibit less affection and warmth towards their children when the number of persons per living unit is high.

The most influential work on lower-class areas and crime has been
Shaw and McKay's *Juvenile Delinquency and Urban Areas.*[145] They
argued that a number of the features of lower-class areas contribute to
their high delinquency rates. The first of these was a high degree of
residential mobility in and out of the area—something which they
found empirically to be a feature of lower-class areas in a number of

American cities. In chapter 1 reference was made to the considerable evidence which supports the view that residential mobility encourages delinquency by creating social disorganization and breaking down informal social control.

That informal social control is crucial to crime control has been repeatedly argued since Shaw and McKay, by people such as Jane Jacobs.[146]

> The first thing to understand is that the public peace—the sidewalk and street peace—of cities is not kept primarily by the police, necessary as police are. It is kept primarily by an intricate, almost unconscious, network of voluntary controls and standards among the people themselves, and enforced by the people themselves. In some city areas—older public housing projects and streets with very high population turnover are often conspicuous examples—the keeping of public sidewalk law and order is left almost entirely to the police and special guards. Such places are jungles.

Shaw and McKay make the point that the mobile individual who is liable to move away at any time does not feel concerned about enforcing informal social control in the neighbourhood.[147] Anonymity and social disorganization become features of areas with mobile and uncommitted residents. Shaw and McKay also argue that social disorganization arises from the lack of consensus over values in lower-class areas, particularly where such areas have a diverse ethnic composition. The question of ethnic composition aside, the evidence in the earlier section of this chapter on class differences in values offers little encouragement to the view that consensus over values would be any less in lower-class than in middle-class areas.

Another thread through Shaw and McKay's discussion is that the adults of lower-class areas, brought up in the same kind of environment themselves, are tolerant of delinquent behaviour. Thus, instead of social control being exerted, a blind eye is turned to much illegal activity. It was concluded earlier in this chapter, however, that lower-class adults do not have more tolerant attitudes towards delinquency than middle-class adults.[148] Even though such attitudinal differences might not exist, it is possible that for other reasons, such as apathy, people in lower-class areas are less inclined to exert social control. This view is supported by the findings of a study by Maccoby *et al.*[149], which compared a high- and a low-delinquency area matched on several other variables. No difference was found between the two areas in the tolerance of attitudes toward delinquency. However, there was some tendency for residents in the low-delinquency area to be more inclined to take some action (e.g. intervene themselves, or inform parents or police) when they observed delinquent behaviour.

Shaw and McKay also point to the presence of plentiful criminal role models in lower-class areas as contributing to delinquency. Adult criminals are often big shots and enjoy a certain amount of admiration from youngsters. Mays[150] has confirmed in his study of the Liverpool docklands that the presence of adults who encouraged or condoned minor offences was an important factor in subcultural delinquency. Illegitimate opportunities for crime are made available in lower-class areas through the presence of fences, pushers, hustlers, junk dealers, and 'no-questions-asked' buyers of consumer durables. Whyte has shown in *Street Corner Society*[151] how racketeers can become very influential role models because they are 'free spenders and liberal patrons of local enterprises'. Popularity with adolescent corner boys is important to the racketeers for recruitment and information. To sustain popularity they help boys to get jobs (legitimate and illegitimate) and lend money to local people and struggling local businesses.

But the influence of adult criminals is not always criminogenic. Kobrin[152] has pointed out that adult criminals will often use their influence to control some of the excesses of delinquency. Violent or disruptive delinquency is controlled by the racketeers in a well-organized criminal area to prevent the area from becoming 'hot'.

The lower-class area also puts in close proximity large numbers of people who have similar adjustment problems arising from their common plight of economic and/or educational failure. The sheer ecological accessibility of other people with kindred problems may facilitate the kind of group delinquent solution to these problems which Albert Cohen[153] has described. In sum, the lower-class area throws together delinquent groups or gangs, and these gangs foster further delinquency through providing social support for delinquent behaviour.

A dramatic development on the social disorganization theme came with Lander's *Towards an Understanding of Juvenile Delinquency*.[154] Lander purported to show that delinquency rates are not related to social class of area at all, but rather to the variables: percentage of homes owner-occupied, and percentage non-white. For reasons that are not very clear he interprets these two variables as not at all indicative of socioeconomic status, but of anomie. The relationship between social class and delinquency is not 'real' but only 'statistical'. The 'real' relationship is between anomie and delinquency.

Lander's conclusion has been shown not to be consistent with the results of his own multivariate analysis. Moreover, he is guilty of a multitude of methodological sins including the atheoretical abuse of factor analysis and partial correlation, and downright calculation error.[155] Gordon[156] has shown that the construct validity on the Campbell and Fiske criteria[157] of Lander's anomie is inadequate compared to that of socioeconomic status. Lander's work does not deserve to be taken seriously today.

Gold has suggested that the reason that lower-class areas have high delinquency rates is the inadequacy of recreational and educational facilities in such areas. In the lower-class area 'excitement has to be made, not queued up for.'[158] Gold has stated his theory as follows.[159]

Hypothesis 1: Recreational and educational facilities will be differentially distributed in a community so that lower status boys have poorer facilities available to them.

Hypothesis 2: The quality of recreational and educational facilities in different neighbourhoods of the community will be related to the attitudes toward the community of boys living in different neighbourhoods, so that boys with poorer facilities available to them will be less attracted to the community.

Hypothesis 3: Since attraction is the primary basis of social control, boys who are less attracted to their community will more likely be delinquent.

Hypotheses 1 and 3 were supported by Gold's data, but not hypothesis 2. While recreational and educational resources were distributed differentially by social class of area, this had no clear effect on boys' attraction to their communities. Thus the theory breaks down. The empirical evidence on the whole question of whether the provision of traditional recreational facilities in areas affects delinquency is quite conflicting.[160]

Labelling theory, as outlined in this chapter, can be applied to lower-class areas as well as lower-class people. Residence in a lower-class area is stigmatized as indicative of social pathology by a wide range of institutions and people, including social scientists. Participant observation studies have testified to the impact of such stigmatization. Armston and Wilson[161] have shown how, in a lower-class area of Glasgow, delinquent labelling became a self-fulfilling prophecy by the usual labelling mechanisms. In particular, they have documented how the vigorous intervention of the police into the area, which accompanied the stigmatization, produced a backlash. Tough policemen put into a 'trouble-spot', who felt a responsibility to crack down on the suburb, and who had a negative attitude towards its people, were hated by the local youth. They used the neutralization technique of accusing the accusers, and the moral bind of law was weakened.

Suttles has found that the tendency to label the residents of a lower-class area as undesirables is even followed by the people of the area themselves with criminogenic consequences.[162]

> It is fairly easy to steal from or molest people in these neighbour-hoods simply because the residents frequently assume that their victims are not crowning examples of virtue themselves. Our economic, ethnic and racial stereotypes give even the worst of us an easy conscience.

The causes of crime in lower-class areas are exceedingly complex phenomena. Different areas adapt to local crime and delinquency in different ways. Sometimes very successful adaptations are evolved which serve to limit crime and delinquency effectively. Suttles's[163] study of the Addams area of Chicago found that reciprocal obligations not to engage in crimes against one another emerged between various individuals and groups. Established mechanisms existed for the intervention of older gangs to quell disturbances involving younger gangs. Individuals who had overlapping connections with two warring factions would use the mutual respect and influence they enjoyed in both groups to defuse trouble. In fact, there was created a 'safe little moral world that is based on private understandings rather than public rulings',[164] and severe sanctions were invoked against those who violated private understandings.

In a later work, Suttles has attacked those who seek to romanticize his position by claiming that all is well in the slum because of its functional social order.[165] Suttles's findings do not imply that slum-dwellers themselves are doing so well at solving the crime problems of the slum that other solutions are not needed. Nevertheless, they do imply that any effort to intervene to remove the conditions which cause the tremendous crime problems of slums, runs the risk of simultaneously interfering with adaptive responses to crime problems which have evolved. Intervention efforts which only partly remove the initial problem, but at the same time totally wipe out the adaptive solutions to that problem, are hardly productive. This is why catastrophic solutions to the criminality of the slum, such as urban renewal, are risky. They run the risk of tearing down the delicate social fabric which keeps crime within reasonable limits.

We cannot hope for a magical formula to solve this problem, since the social order of one lower-class community is uniquely different from that of another. All that we can seek to do is to avoid those ham-fisted methods which maximize the risk of throwing out the baby with the bath water.

Summary

Engels, Bonger, and Marxist theory

The Marxist theories of Engels and Bonger depict two main causes of crime. Primarily, the structure of capitalism creates a criminogenic quality in social life, characterized by exploitativeness and avarice. Second, crime is caused by the economic misery and brutalization of the lower class. The ultimate solution to crime is seen as the overthrow of capitalist relations of production. However, the second cause implies that Engels and Bonger would grant some efficacy for crime reduction to improving the conditions of deprivation of the lower class, even in the absence of the dismantling of capitalist production. The only evidence to support or refute their formulations is anecdotal.

Powerlessness

A number of theorists have suggested that, for the powerless, crime and delinquency are a desperate effort to make things happen, to assert control. The evidence does show that lower-class people experience greater subjective feelings of powerlessness, and that youths who feel powerless are more likely than others to engage in delinquency. However, the evidence does not provide clear support for a wounded self-concept as an intervening variable between powerlessness and crime. The theory predicts that a redistribution of power will reduce crime.

Merton, Cloward and Ohlin and opportunity theory

Building upon Merton's work, Cloward and Ohlin propose that delinquency arises when legitimate means to achieve success goals are blocked and illegitimate means open. Lower-class youths are more likely than middle-class youths to find themselves in this situation. The evidence is clear that delinquents, both objectively and subjectively, have legitimate opportunities more closed and illegitimate opportunities more open than non-delinquents. Moreover, Merton's assumption that most lower-class people aspire to middle-class success goals is justified. Although delinquents perceive legitimate opportunities as closed, the evidence is not clear that they are more inclined than other groups to 'blame the system' for this limitation. The theory predicts that creating greater legitimate opportunities for lower-class people through egalitarian measures will reduce crime.

Cohen and the school

Cohen's theory is based on the well-supported propositions that lower-class youths have relatively high chances of failing at school, and that school failure is followed by increased delinquency. To the extent that the greater delinquency and adult crime of the lower classes are caused by school failure, the less effective will be greater equality in reducing crime and delinquency. Increased equality will affect *who* fails at school but not *how many* fail, because education is almost totally a zero-sum game. A slight relationship between class and delinquency remains when school failure is controlled for, so that the class–delinquency association is not totally explained by the fact that school failure is more common among the lower class.

Lower-class values

The empirical evidence is not consistent with the proposition that lower-class people are more criminal because distinctively lower-class values encourage delinquency, or because adherence to distinctively middle-class values discourages delinquency. The values which have been inferred by sociologists such as Miller from *ex post facto* interpretations of the behaviour of delinquent gangs are not endorsed by a majority either of lower-class people or of delinquents; nor are they consistently more often endorsed by lower-class than middle-class people. Where values which are supported by a larger minority of delinquents than of non-delinquents have been isolated, a class basis for this difference has not been demonstrated. For instance, delinquents have more tolerant attitudes toward delinquency than non-delinquents, but lower-class people do not have more tolerant attitudes toward delinquency than middle-class people.

The reward–cost model

The reward–cost model suggests that the lower class engage in more of those kinds of crime usually handled by the police because the rewards of such crime are greater, and the costs less, than they are for middle-class people. One study of adolescents fails to support the reward–cost formulation. More empirical studies are required. The model has ambiguous implications for the impact of egalitarian policies on crime.

Redistributing wealth from the wealthy to the poor reduces the reward–cost ratio of crime for the poor, but increases it for the wealthy. Nevertheless, it is possible that a marginal increase in the income of the poor would have a greater impact upon their reward–cost ratio for crime, than would an identical marginal decrease in the income of the wealthy have on *their* reward–cost ratio for crime.

Labelling

There is some evidence that being labelled as criminal results in downward mobility. This must account for part of the class–crime relationship. To the extent that crime causes class rather than vice versa, policies designed to narrow class differences will not have an impact on crime.

It is clear that lower-class people are subjected to more criminal labelling than middle-class people. And on the basis of the evidence, it seems likely that criminal labelling encourages criminal behaviour. Thus lower-class people may become more criminal because they are labelled as such. The policy implication of this formulation is to change the way people think about the lower class, rather than to change the objective conditions confronting the lower class.

Lower-class pathology

The evidence enables us to discount most variants of the argument that crime is caused by lower-class pathologies such as low intelligence, shorter time perspective, inability to delay gratification, weak self-concept, and a variety of other suggested personality defects. Where personality factors have been found to be related to delinquency, these are not in turn related to class.

There is some (disputed) evidence, however, that broken homes are associated with both delinquency and class. Although a relationship between class and delinquency remains after controlling for broken homes, part of the class–delinquency relationship might be explained by the effect of broken homes. The policy implication would then be to strengthen the family rather than reduce inequality. However, it is likely that one of the most important reasons for the high incidence of broken homes among the lower class is the stress brought about by economic hardship.

There is evidence to support Gold's theory that lower-class families encourage delinquency because fathers who are economic failures lose the respect of their sons and consequently become impotent as socializing agents. The policy implication is that the economic success of lower-class fathers must be improved so that they might enjoy respect from, and influence over, their sons.

There is also some evidence to confirm Bronfenbrenner's conclusion that lower-class families socialize children more often with physical force, whereas the middle-class technique of love withdrawal is normally more effective for inducing conformity. This formulation predicts that rather than a reduction of inequality, it is changes in lower-class child-rearing practices which will affect delinquency.

Social class of area

Common features of lower-class areas with high crime and delinquency rates are overcrowding, high geographical mobility, breakdown of informal social control, the existence of criminal-role models and criminal-learning structures, and the existence of gangs which provide social support for delinquency. The evidence fails to support the hypothesis that high density, and unattractive recreational and educational facilities are intervening variables between social class of area and crime rates. Some observational studies have concluded that the stigmatization of lower-class areas often operates to increase crime.

Conclusion

The concern in this chapter has been with a social structural variable—inequality—as a predisposing factor to crime. The positivistic preoccupation of this chapter with the effects on crime of changing a structural variable has tended to preclude an appreciation of the processual nature of criminal behaviour. The kinds of theories selected for attention present an 'oversocialized' or mechanistic view of man which can never adequately explain the diversity of criminal behaviour. The purpose of this book is not to foster a well-rounded understanding of deviant behaviour in all of its richness, with its diversity of individual experience, with the groping, backtracking, interpersonal gestures from which it is constituted. Rather, the concern of the book is limited to that proportion of the variance in criminal behaviour which is structurally determined.

Although the theories reviewed generate some conflicting propositions, they are all partial theories, with the validity of one theory not totally precluding the validity of others. It would be naive to believe that any one or two theories encompass the total explanation for the class–crime relationship. Some theories have been ruled out as untenable.

No theories have predicted that a reduction of inequality would *increase* crime. A number of theories, which are consistent with what inadequate evidence is available, predict that reducing inequality would reduce crime. Other theories, also consistent with the evidence, do not make a prediction about the effect of greater equality, but predict that a change in child-rearing practices, school failure, labelling, or broken homes would reduce crime.

It would be wrong to say that a number of separate causal chains of variables linking inequality of wealth and power to crime have been established. While the evidence is consistent with propositions and corollaries from a number of theories, explicit causal connections have rarely been demonstrated. Nevertheless, the evidence seems sufficient for a cautious assertion that inequality is connected to crime through a number of very different sets of intervening variables. This has desirable implications for policy intervention.

The effects of policy intervention are often confounded by a complex of extraneous variables which have unpredictable feedbacks. If there are a number of disparate sets of intervening variables connecting inequality to crime, then the social planner does not have all of his eggs in one basket. If his intervention strategy 'messes things up' so that the desired effect on crime is not produced through one set of intervening variables, the strategy still may have the desired impact through other intervening variables.

In conclusion, there is a reasonable basis in partially tested theory for predicting that a reduction of inequality of wealth and power would reduce the rate of those types of crimes typically handled by the police.

Part II

Chapter 4

The class-mix hypothesis

False Starts

What would be the effect on delinquency of greater residential mixing of classes? Morris[1] subscribes to the theory of 'the bad apple spoiling the case'. He suggests that if lower-class are mixed in with middle-class children, these 'respectable' children will be dragged down into delinquency. However, the more popular argument among town planners has been that greater class-mix will reduce delinquency, because lower-class youth will be 'culturally uplifted' through their contact with the middle-class community.[2]

Of course both arguments involve the dubious assumption of middle-class cultural superiority of some kind. But the most fundamental weakness of both arguments is that although they are based on the same assumption, each ignores the other. To be consistent these theorists must be prepared to concede the possibility of a two-sided effect. As 'bad' boys infiltrate 'good' areas, the probability of the corruption of the 'good' boys by the new arrivals might increase, as might the probability of the reformation of the 'bad' boys under the wholesome influence of their new environment. A similar two-sided effect would be expected from a movement of 'good' boys into 'bad' areas.

Consequently, any prediction that these simplistic theories based on differential association make about the effect of class-mix on delinquency must be equivocal and confused.

Albert Cohen, Cloward and Ohlin, and others among the major theorists have agreed on the criminogenic consequences of the fact that lower-class areas facilitate the juxtaposition of youth with similar status problems. Before a group delinquent solution to status problems can emerge, there must be a sufficiently high density of people with the status problem in a given area. It has often been assumed that a corollary of this position is that a greater dispersal of people with status problems (mostly lower-class people) will hinder the emergence of delinquent subcultures.

But again there are two sides to the story. If lower-class people with status problems are interspersed into middle-class areas, this should reduce the extent to which group delinquent solutions to status problems emerge in lower-class areas. Nevertheless, surely it might also increase the likelihood of the emergence of group delinquent solutions to status problems in *middle-class areas*.

However, it may be that group delinquent solutions are only highly probable when the density of people with status problems passes a certain threshold level. The emergence of delinquent subcultures might not be a linear function of the areal concentration of people with status problems. An increase in the number of people with status problems in an area which previously had few such people may have minimal impact on subculture formation. However, a decrease in the density of people with status problems in an area with a very high density of such people may have a considerable impact on subculture formation. Wolfgang and Ferracuti seem to be arguing for such a non-linear relationship where they assert that 'It is in homogeneity that the subculture has strength and durability.'[3]

The same problems befall the argument that by dispersing the people of the slum, we can destroy the criminogenic consequences of the stigmatization of slums. Labelling by the community and the mass media may be facilitated by the poor being clearly segregated, since areal demarcation makes the poor peculiarly visible. This argument depends on the assumption that moving more poor people into middle-class areas will not result in an increase in the stigmatization of these areas commensurate with the reduction in stigma in the areas from whence they came. This assumption may be justified since it seems only to be very poor areas which suffer from really debilitating stigmatization. Nevertheless, it needs to be demonstrated empirically that stigma is more than a simple linear function of the number of people in the area who are lower class.

Social class and social class of area

In chapter 2 it was shown that both social class and social class of area are related to crime and delinquency. By definition, lower-class areas are populated mainly by lower-class people. Thus, any finding that lower-class people are more criminal may be explained by the proposition that lower-class people mostly live in areas which are conducive to crime. Conversely, any finding that residents of lower-class areas have high crime rates may be explained by the greater numbers of criminally inclined people in these areas.

Key empirical questions to be answered in Part II of this book are whether social class is related to crime after social class of area is controlled, and whether social class of area is related to crime after social class is controlled. On the basis of the theory in chapter 3, it is hypothesized that the answer to both of these questions is Yes: that social class and social class of area both make a unique contribution to explaining criminal behaviour. It will be seen in the next section that through elaborating the theory of Cloward and Ohlin, the interaction between class and class of area can become the basis for predicting that an increase in class-mix will reduce delinquency.

Cloward and Ohlin and the class–class of area interaction

In their theory of delinquency, Cloward and Ohlin[4] proposed that there are two necessary conditions for an adolescent to become delinquent. First, his access to legitimate means of achieving success goals must be blocked. Second, his access to illegitimate means of achieving success goals must be open. In logical terms, there are two necessary conditions for delinquency; if either legitimate opportunities are open or illegitimate opportunities closed, then delinquency will not ensue.

However, speaking in terms of necessary conditions grossly simplifies Cloward and Ohlin's thesis. Their propositions are framed in terms of probabilities rather than certainties. Translating the above proposition into probabilistic terms, Cloward and Ohlin's thesis becomes:

Delinquency is most likely when the two conditions (absence of legitimate opportunities, presence of illegitimate opportunities) apply, but it is unlikely when either condition does not apply.

Further elaboration is required since the necessary conditions are continuous rather than dichotomous variables. Thus the proposition becomes:

Delinquency is most likely when both exposure to legitimate opportunities is low and exposure to illegitimate opportunities is high; but it is unlikely either when legitimate opportunities are high, or when illegitimate opportunities are low.

107

Mathematically, delinquency is a multiplicative rather than an additive function of the blockage of legitimate opportunities and access to illegitimate opportunities. That is, the cumulative effect on delinquency of the blockage of legitimate opportunities and access to illegitimate opportunities is far greater than the sum of their individual effects.

To simplify the argument, let us consider that there are two necessary conditions for delinquency. If so, then *delinquency can be reduced by increasing the extent to which one necessary condition applies while the other necessary condition does not apply*. Consider Table 4.1. To minimize delinquency, policies should be adopted which keep as many people as possible out of cell *A*, and as many people as possible in cells *B, C,* and *D*. The representation in Table 4.1 can be elaborated from one of the necessary conditions to one of non-additive effects, simply by substituting 'high' and 'low' for 'present' and 'absent'.

Table 4.1 *Representation of four contingencies for two necessary conditions*

		Necessary condition 1	
		Present	Absent
Necessary condition 2	Present	A	B
	Absent	C	D

Thus, assuming that the number of people in the community who have each necessary condition is constant, delinquency can be reduced by spreading the necessary conditions thinly, so that many people satisfy one condition but very few satisfy both.

In other words, if the Cloward–Ohlin proposition is valid, it would be better to have *large* numbers of people who have either legitimate opportunities blocked only, or illegitimate opportunities open only; and *small* numbers of people who satisfy both conditions (rather than the converse).

Cloward and Ohlin indicate that the people who have legitimate opportunities closed—those who do poorly at school, are unable to get good jobs, and so on—are the lower class. Cloward and Ohlin also make it clear that the people who have illegitimate opportunities open—those who are exposed to criminal-role models, criminal-learning structures, the social support of delinquent gangs, weak community control, etc. —are people who live in lower-class areas.

Now if, as Cloward and Ohlin suggest,[5] it is being lower class that causes legitimate opportunities to be closed, and it is a characteristic of lower-class *areas* for illegitimate opportunities to be open, *then a reduced coincidence of the necessary conditions for delinquency might be achieved by having fewer lower-class people living in lower-class areas.* This policy inference has not been made, either explicitly or implicitly, by Cloward and Ohlin themselves. Nevertheless, the inference is based on propositions from their theory.

It is possible to propose a more general theory of the same form as that based on Cloward and Ohlin, which replaces blocked legitimate opportunities with a broader construct—delinquent predisposition. Having a delinquent predisposition is one necessary condition for delinquency, and having the illegitimate opportunities to express that predisposition is another necessary condition. Components of the delinquent predisposition related to class are a feeling of relative deprivation, a feeling of powerlessness, school failure, a higher reward–cost ratio for delinquency, delinquent labelling, family disorganization, ineffective socialization, and blockage of legitimate opportunities.

If the combined effect of a strong predisposition to delinquency and access to illegitimate opportunities is greater than the sum of their individual effects, then delinquency can be reduced by having fewer youths with a strong predisposition to delinquency exposed to great illegitimate opportunities. That is, delinquency can be reduced by having fewer lower-class youths living in lower-class areas.

McDonald[6] has suggested another reason why the illegitimate opportunities of the lower-class area may have less impact upon middle-class youth than lower-class youth. The former, she suggests, are partially sheltered from the temptations of illegitimate opportunity.

> A middle-class family in a working-class area can do a lot to isolate the child from working-class influences. The family may manage to stimulate and supervise the child into a grammar school. It may enrol the child in constructive leisure pursuits. It may attend a predominantly middle-class church, and participate in organized activities there that implicitly strengthen middle-class attitudes and abilities. The child may be kept home to study in the evening. He may be sent to camp in the summer.[7]

The only empirical investigation of the Cloward–Ohlin hypothesis that delinquency is a multiplicative function of barriers to legitimate opportunities and degree of exposure to illegitimate opportunities is by Palmore and Hammond.[8] In this study, race, sex, and success at school were taken as causal determinants of access to legitimate opportunities. Family deviance and neighbourhood deviance were conceived as indices of the degree to which young people were exposed to illegitimate opportunities. This causal model is represented in Figure 4.1.

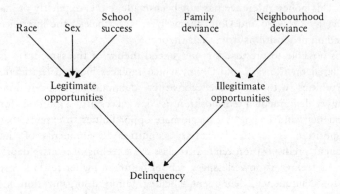

Figure 4.1 *Causal model for the Palmore–Hammond study*

Legitimate and illegitimate opportunities were measured only indirectly through race, sex, school success, family deviance, and neighbourhood deviance. The simultaneous effect on delinquency of all paired combinations of these five variables was examined. The model predicts no interaction (simple additive effects) for the following pairs: race and sex, race and success, sex and success, and family and neighbourhood deviance. The remaining six pairs should show interaction such that when legitimate opportunities are low, the effects of illegitimate opportunities on delinquency will be far greater than when legitimate opportunities are high. Eight of these ten predictions were reasonably well confirmed. For example, neighbourhood deviance increased delinquency more among those failing in school than among those succeeding. The Palmore and Hammond study therefore provides support for the hypothesis that the combined effect on delinquency of legitimate and illegitimate opportunities is a multiplicative rather than an additive function.

Predictions from the theory

The theory of the differential impact on delinquency of exposure to illegitimate opportunity, as outlined in the previous section, makes two clear predictions.

1 Being lower class has more effect in increasing delinquency for youth living in lower-class areas than for youth living in middle-class areas.

or

Living in a lower-class area has more effect in increasing delinquency for lower-class youth than for middle-class youth.[9]

consequently

2 Cities with relatively large numbers of lower-class people living in predominantly middle-class areas of the city, and relatively large numbers of middle-class people living in predominantly lower-class areas of the city, have relatively low delinquency rates.

The theory does *not* predict that areas with a more heterogeneous mix of classes will have lower delinquency rates than homogeneous areas. It is not the fact of living in a more *heterogeneous class* environment *per se* which makes lower-class youth less delinquent, it is the fact of living in a more *middle-class* environment. The theory predicts that the delinquency rate of a heterogeneous class area, other things being equal, will be lower than that of a homogeneous lower-class area, but higher than that of a homogeneous middle-class area. The delinquency rate of an area does not depend on the extent to which its class composition is heterogeneous, but on the extent to which it is lower class. Figure 4.2 represents the prediction of the theory, not Figure 4.3.

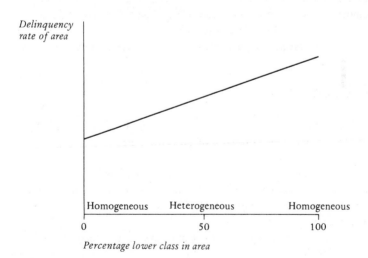

Figure 4.2   *True prediction*

The class-mix hypothesis

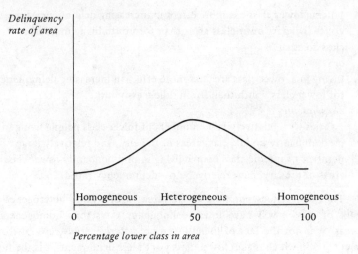

Figure 4.3   *False prediction*

Consequently, it is not possible to test this class-mix theory by comparing the delinquency rates of areas which are heterogeneous and homogeneous. Finally, it should be pointed out that although the original formulation of opportunity theory by Cloward and Ohlin referred to juvenile delinquency, there is no reason to expect that what applies to the effect of opportunities on juvenile crime would not also apply to adult crime. Therefore opportunity theory can be used as a basis for predicting that greater class-mix will reduce adult crime as well.

Norm-conflict theories

It frequently has been argued in the sociological literature that when an area is populated by a diversity of subcultural or ethnic groups, conflict arises over norms which the groups do not share in common. When there is disagreement over norms, the moral force of all norms is weakened; children become confused about which of the conflicting standards are appropriate, and this moral confusion contributes to delinquency.

While it has been argued in the last chapter that value differences between classes are not great, it is still possible for conflict to arise over class differences in behaviour or behavioural expectations. Bohlke has

112

suggested that lower-class boys in middle-class areas are rejected by their middle-class peers. This rejection results in the lower-class boys ganging together to form anti-middle-class subcultures.[10]

> The boy of working class background who has moved to the middle class neighbourhood or suburb behaves in a way that affronts those youth who are middle class in attitudes and values, and the social rejection employed by the latter simply serves as a stimulus to evoke further working class behaviour.

Clearly, if this kind of class conflict does exist, it would undermine community cohesion. If there is no community cohesion, there is no basis for the establishment of social-control norms, surveillance norms, and procedures for monitoring the behaviour of suspicious strangers.

Greenbie argues against class-mix on the grounds that the preservation of cultural continuity is the best protection against the ravages of man's self-interest. He maintains that social stress is least harmful to all classes when familiar group support is present, and that:[11] 'Where a strange population is introduced into the territory of an indigenous one, social health and stability require protection of the cultural integrity of both groups.'

Although such views undoubtedly exaggerate cultural differences between classes, there is evidence that when lower-status people are thrown into middle-class areas, inter-class relationships are rather frigid. Perhaps the most thorough study was by Goldthorpe *et al., The Affluent Worker in the Class Structure.*[12] They found very little interaction between the middle-class residents of a mixed residential area and highly paid workers living in the area. Similarly Gans[13] claims that lower-status people in Levittown rarely formed friendships with middle-class neighbours. Gutman[14] also reports that working-class wives were isolated from middle-class women in a mixed-class suburb because of their supposed lack of middle-class social skills. In contrast, Morris and Mogey found that when people differing in class (among other things) were placed on opposite ends of the same block, interaction levels declined compared with when they were completely intermixed.[15] Nevertheless, after reviewing research studies on this question, Keller concludes:[16]

> The evidence as gathered from new towns and housing estates throughout the world suggests that mixing groups may actually lead to hostility and conflict rather than to a more interesting and varied communal life; that the better off, no matter how defined or

measured, refuse to live side by side, not to say co-operate in community clubs and projects, with those they consider inferior to them; and that those whose conceptions of privacy and friendship, sociability and neighboring are opposed will soon find themselves pitted against each other in resentment or withdrawing into loneliness.

Even though there is evidence that, at least in certain circumstances, residential intermixing between whites and Negroes reduces racial prejudice,[17] the broad conclusion of Keller's review seems justified. This conclusion implies that putting more lower-class people into middle-class areas should not only diminish the neighbourly contacts of middle-class people in these areas, it should also increase the neighbourly contacts of that lower-class minority already living in the area and supposedly so deprived of neighbourly contact.

In one sense, the logic of those who argue against class-mix by pointing to norm conflict as a criminogenic consequence of class-mix is self-defeating. They say that middle- and lower-class people will form more cohesive communities if they live apart, because they have been brought up in a different way, and therefore do not understand each other. Yet, it is implied that one of the reasons that they do not understand each other is that they have been brought up apart.

The norm-conflict position has been taken by the throat by Richard Sennett in *The Uses of Disorder*.[18] Sennett argues that increasing norm conflict is desirable, and in the end will reduce crime. A community order based on community sameness is a powder keg which is bound to explode when that community sameness is threatened. An ordered existence which protects the insularity of groups creates people unable to cope with disorder when it occurs, except by escalating that disorder into violence between polarized groups.

Having, therefore, so little tolerance of disorder in their own lives, and having shut themselves off so that they have little experience of disorder as well, the eruption of social tension becomes a situation in which the ultimate methods of aggression, violent force and reprisal, seem to become not only justified, but life-preserving. . . . This kind of reaction, this inability to deal with disorder without raising it to the scale of mortal combat, is inevitable when men shape their common lives so that their only sense of relatedness is the sense in which they feel themselves to be the same.[19]

Sennett wants to create disorder not only through class- and racial mix, but through almost total urban anarchy—no police, no zoning.

114

His hope is that by increasing the complexity of conflict in the city, instead of polarizing it, people would be forced to confront one another and solve their common problems.

> By restructuring the power of city bureaucracies so that they leave to the hostile groups themselves the *need* to create some truce, in order for chaos to be prevented, hostility can take more open and less violent forms.[20]

In summary, Sennett suggests three reasons why forced interaction between groups with conflicting interests would reduce violence in the long run, even though increasing conflict in the short term. Firstly, people would be forced to learn to express conflict openly and constructively, rather than bottling up conflict until a violent expression of it ultimately erupts. Secondly, stereotypes of other groups and 'us–them' attitudes would be broken down ('The enemies lose their clear image, because every day one sees so many people who are alien but who are not all alien in the same way'[21]). Thirdly, one has no choice but to try to understand the problems of others.

Whether one finds more convincing the conservative functionalism of Gans and Keller or the radical anarchism of Sennett, the question of the impact of culture conflict on delinquency can be resolved only empirically. Nettler[22] has discussed a considerable number of American studies which indicate that the breaking-up of ghettos of Oriental or European immigrants results in a loss of ethnic identity and concomitant delinquency. 'Melting pots' appear to be more criminogenic than ghettoes.

> American studies are particularly rich in reporting the effects of the meeting of cultures upon crime rates. These investigations indicate that migrants, and more specifically their children, are relatively immune to the configurations of crime about them as long as a ghetto is intact.[23]

However, studies on the effect of the homogeneity of Negro communities in the United States have produced somewhat more conflicting results. The research bureau of the Houston Council of Social Agencies conducted the first of these studies on the impact of ethnic congregation, by comparing Negro delinquency rates in areas where the races live apart with those in which they live together.[24] Consistent with predictions about the effect of norm conflict on crime, it was found that the higher the Negro proportion of the population of a census tract, the lower the Negro delinquency rate. The more the Negro child was surrounded by people of his own kind, the lower his chances of becoming officially delinquent.

Another early study by Lander[25] reported that whenever either Negroes or whites predominated in the populations of Baltimore census tracts, delinquency rates (black and white combined) were low. As the black–white ratio approached 50:50, delinquency rates increased. Willie and Gershenovitz[26] also partially supported the finding that ethnic concentration is associated with low levels of delinquency.

(1) In higher socio-economic areas, there are no differences in juvenile delinquency rates between neighbourhoods of homogeneous and heterogeneous racial composition.

(2) In lower socio-economic areas, juvenile delinquency rates tend to be higher in racially heterogeneous than in racially homogeneous neighbourhoods.[27]

However, Bordua[28] in Detroit, and Chilton[29] in Indianapolis failed to confirm Lander's 'parabolic' association between delinquency and the proportion non-white in census tracts. Conlen,[30] in a Baltimore retest more than a decade after Lander's initial Baltimore study, found that delinquency rates continued to be positively correlated with percentage non-white, even after neighbourhoods passed the 50 per cent mark for non-white residents.

In conclusion, there is evidence both consistent and inconsistent with the proposition that ethnic-mix encourages crime. Unfortunately, there are no comparable studies on the relationships among *class*-mix, norm conflict, and crime.

Temptation and relative deprivation

Tobias's[31] observation that in nineteenth-century England domestic servants were overrepresented in records of most kinds of crime, including theft, is frequently commented on in the literature. It has been instanced as evidence that the poor suffer from criminogenic relative deprivation when they are in daily contact with the affluence of the wealthy. Or it is used as evidence that, if the poor find themselves close enough to the possessions of the wealthy, they will not be able to resist the temptation to pilfer them. Fleisher[32] has taken up the latter point with his hypothesis that the number of wealthy people in an area determines the 'supply' of precious goods available to meet the 'demand' of the criminal poor for them. Class-mix, it is suggested, permits a better match of supply with demand. If class-mix does have this effect, or if it increases feelings of relative deprivation, then it would be predicted that class-mix would increase criminal acts against property.

Summary

A variety of theories have been reviewed, some of which predict that greater class-mix would reduce delinquency, others an increase in delinquency with greater class-mix.

Arguments that greater class-mix would reduce delinquency either because 'bad boys' would be reformed by 'good areas', or because the likelihood of delinquent subcultures forming would be reduced if the lower class were dispersed, or because the dispersion of slums would eliminate the criminogenic stigmatization associated with slums, are normally presented in an overly simplistic way. For all of the predicted reductions in delinquent differential association, delinquent subculture formation, and stigmatization, there is the possibility of counter-balancing increases in these variables appearing in other areas as a result of greater class-mix. Nevertheless, if differential association, subculture formation, and stigmatization increase as non-linear accelerating functions of lower-class residential concentration, then these arguments can be used to predict that dispersion of the lower class would reduce delinquency.

A clearer prediction can be made on the basis of Cloward and Ohlin's opportunity theory. It is suggested that lower-class youth have a greater predisposition to delinquency than middle-class. It is also suggested that in lower-class areas there are greater illegitimate opportunities to express a predisposition toward delinquency than in middle-class areas. Both a predisposition to delinquency and illegitimate opportunities to express the predisposition are necessary conditions for delinquency. Delinquency is unlikely to occur if either factor is absent. By encouraging lower-class youth to live in middle-class areas, one is encouraging youth with a predisposition to delinquency to live in an area where it would be difficult for them to find illegitimate opportunities for the expression of the predisposition. Therefore, it is predicted that greater class-mix would reduce delinquency.

Another body of theory suggests that greater intermingling of classes would result in normative conflict between classes, break down community cohesion, and thereby undermine the basis of effective social control. This body of theory therefore predicts that greater class-mix

117

would increase delinquency. This prediction has also been made on the basis of less influential theories which suggest that exposing the poor to the affluence of the rich would put great temptation in the path of the poor, and would intensify their feeling of relative deprivation.

The prediction that greater class-mix would reduce delinquency will be called the *opportunity-theory prediction*, and the prediction that greater class-mix would increase delinquency will be called the *norm-conflict prediction*.

There are two variants of the opportunity-theory prediction, depending on the level of analysis adopted. They are:

1 Being lower class has more effect in increasing delinquency for youth living in lower-class areas than for youth living in middle-class areas.

or the corollary

Living in a lower-class area has more effect in increasing delinquency for lower-class youth than for middle-class youth.

consequently

2 Cities with relatively large numbers of lower-class people living in predominantly middle-class areas of the city, and relatively large numbers of middle-class people living in predominantly lower-class areas of the city, have relatively low delinquency rates.

The remainder of Part II of this book is devoted to testing empirically whether these predictions, or whether the converse norm-conflict predictions, enjoy more support. Chapters 5 to 8 are short chapters devoted to separate tests of the first prediction, and chapter 9 tests the second, or inter-city prediction.

Chapter 5

Testing the class-mix hypothesis on data in the literature

Introduction

The purpose of this chapter is to examine whether data in the published literature can be used to test the opportunity-theory prediction.

McDonald's[1] analysis of self-reported delinquency is one study which enables a test of the hypothesis that *living in a lower-class area has more effect in increasing delinquency for lower-class youth than for middle-class youth*. Her results were consistent with the opportunity-theory hypothesis. She found social class of area to have a stronger negative effect on the delinquency of lower-class boys than on middle-class boys. Of the 44 self-report items, there were 17 significant differences by area for lower-class boys, but only 10 such significant differences for middle-class boys.[2]

Contrary to the McDonald finding, Baldwin, Bottoms and Walker's[3] data from Sheffield shows that while adult conviction rates increased as social class of area declined, this increase was no greater for employed semi-skilled and unskilled males than it was for skilled manual males. This class comparison is clearly an extremely limited one since both non-manual workers, at one end of the class continuum, and the unemployed, at the other, are excluded from the analysis.

Unfortunately, this is the total extent of the evidence to test the opportunity-theory prediction available from a reading of the literature. Nevertheless, other data have been published which can be used, though to date they have not been, to test the prediction. These data were gathered for purposes other than testing the opportunity-theory prediction. Consequently, a re-analysis is necessary.

The most notable of these sources is the study by Reiss and Rhodes, 'The Distribution of Juvenile Delinquency in the Social Class Structure'.[4] The next section contains a re-analysis of the published

Reiss and Rhodes results to test the prediction that *being lower class has more effect in increasing delinquency for youth living in lower-class areas than for youth living in middle-class areas.*

Re-analysis of the Reiss and Rhodes study

Reiss and Rhodes searched court records to ascertain the delinquency of 9,238 white boys, 12 years and more, registered at one of the public, private, or parochial junior or senior high schools of Davidson County, Tennessee. Social class was measured by dividing fathers' occupations into low, medium, and high status. Social class of area was measured by dividing schools into high, medium, and low status on the basis of the percentages of fathers of students having occupations of different status levels.[5] Reiss and Rhodes assumed that the social-class composition of the school, and the social-class composition of the area surrounding the school, would be very similar. The original study contained data on traffic and non-traffic offences. Because of the limitation of the focus of the present work to offences against persons or property, the former are excluded from the re-analysis.

The cross-tabulation of delinquency by social class and school status is presented in Table 5.1, which is presented graphically in Figure 5.1. From Table 5.1 it is clear that both social class and social class of area (school status) were related to delinquency, even after the other was controlled.

Table 5.1 *Delinquency rate per 100 against social class and status-structure of school* (Reiss and Rhodes, 1961)

Status structure of school	Social class			
	High	*Medium*	*Low*	Total
High	2·72 (1,248)[1]	3·01 (1,458)	3·87 (413)	3·01 (3,119)
Medium	3·61 (277)	5·71 (892)	6·45 (511)	5·60 (1,680)
Low	3·80 (289)	9·24 (1,449)	10·10 (1,267)	9·08 (3,005)
Total	3·03 (1,814)	6·03 (3,799)	8·08 (2,191)	5·91 (7,804)

[1] The number in brackets refers to the total number of cases in the cell, not the number of delinquent cases.

It can be seen from Figure 5.1 that for boys who lived in low-status areas (low-school status) delinquency rates jumped dramatically as we moved from high- to medium- to low-status families. Among boys who lived in medium-status areas the jump in delinquency rates was much smaller. And for boys in high-status areas there was hardly any jump in delinquency rates at all. It made little difference whether boys came from a high-, medium-, or low-status family; if they lived in a high-status area, they were unlikely to be delinquent.

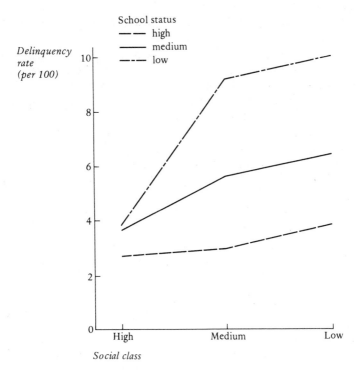

Figure 5.1 The relationship between social class and delinquency rate for different school-status structures

These data clearly refute the prediction of norm-conflict theorists that lower-class boys who live in middle-class areas will have higher delinquency rates than lower-class boys who live in lower-class areas. Indeed the latter had delinquency rates two to three times as high as lower-class boys who lived in middle-class areas.

Thus it is reasonable to expect from this study that policies which result in more lower-class boys living in middle-class areas will result in less delinquency. The data also suggest that the counterbalancing effect of having more middle-class boys living in lower-class areas should have only minimal impact upon delinquency. Delinquency rates for middle-class boys were only marginally higher in lower-class areas than they were in middle-class areas.

In other words, policies which result in more middle-class people living in lower-class areas, and more lower-class people living in middle-class areas, might result in only a slight increase in the delinquency of middle-class youth, but a dramatic decrease in the delinquency of lower-class youth.

However, before any confidence can be placed in this conclusion, it would be wise to test the statistical significance of the data trend on which it is based. A statistical test is required which tests interaction effects on non-parametric data. Lancaster's[6] method of partitioning χ^2, which has been detailed by Lewis,[7] meets this requirement. In essence, this method partitions the total χ^2 for the three-way cross-tabulation (class $\times$ school status $\times$ delinquency) into component χ^2 for each of the three two-variable relationships, and for the three-variable interaction. These component χ^2 values are listed in Table 5.2.

Table 5.2 *Summary of component* χ^2

Comparison	Value of χ^2	Degrees of freedom
Class $\times$ school status	1,119·8[1]	4
Class $\times$ delinquency	46·2[1]	2
School status $\times$ delinquency	101·9[1]	2
Class $\times$ school status $\times$ delinquency	47·2[1]	4
Total	1,315·1[1]	12

[1] Significant at ·001 level.

Table 5.2 shows that the class–delinquency relationship, the school-status–delinquency relationship, and the class–school-status interaction on delinquency were all significant at the ·001 level of significance.

The significant-interaction effect is ambiguous in that it could mean that the relationship between class and school status was different for delinquents than for non-delinquents; and not the relevant hypothesis that the relationship between class and delinquency was different for

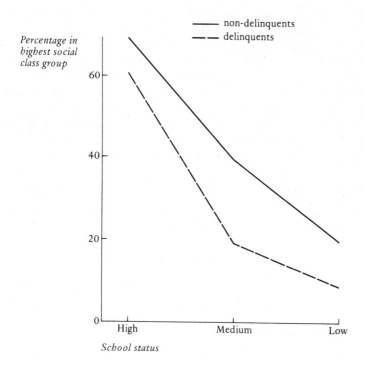

Figure 5.2 *The relationship between school status and percentage in highest social-class group for delinquents and non-delinquents*

different levels of school status.[8] From Figure 5.2 it is clear that the relationship between class and school status was very similar for both delinquents and non-delinquents. Thus the significant-interaction effect can be interpreted as the kind of interaction hypothesized in the present research (represented in Figure 5.1).

Thus, the data from the Reiss and Rhodes study support the prediction that the impact on delinquency of being lower class is significantly greater for youth living in lower-class areas than for youth living in middle-class areas.

Matsumoto's replication

The only replication of the Reiss and Rhodes study has been by

Matsumoto[9] in Japan.[10] Matsumoto used variables and categories identical with those employed by Reiss and Rhodes in a study of 6,172 boys from 30 public junior high schools in Tokyo. His findings, summarized in Table 5.3, were very different from the Nashville findings. In Table 5.3, school status has not been collapsed into the three categories used in the re-analysis of the Reiss and Rhodes data, partly because the numbers of subjects falling into each category were very different in Tokyo. Also the presentation of results for the original seven categories of school status shows the invariance of the delinquency rate of the lowest social-class group for all levels of school status.

Table 5.3 *Delinquency rate per 100 against social class and status structure of school* (Matsumoto)

Status structure of school	Social class			
	High	*Medium*	*Low*	*Total*
High I	1·5 (392)	4·3 (138)	10·2 (61)	3·2 (596)
II	3·5 (692)	5·2 (396)	10·0 (190)	5·2 (1,417)
III	4·6 (549)	6·5 (261)	11·9 (270)	6·9 (1,210)
IV	6·8 (292)	6·5 (231)	8·9 (270)	7·5 (894)
V	6·0 (151)	5·0 (242)	9·8 (123)	7·1 (593)
VI	6·1 (179)	6·4 (330)	9·8 (418)	7·8 (1,017)
Low VII	6·3 (48)	13·7 (95)	10·6 (254)	11·7 (445)
Total	4·3 (2,240)	6·3 (1,693)	10·0 (1,583)	6·7 (6,172)

Matsumoto's findings were strikingly inconsistent with those of Reiss and Rhodes. The impact of social class of area (school status) upon delinquency was greatest for the highest social-class group and least for the lowest social-class group. Indeed there was no tendency whatsoever for the lowest social-class group to have different delinquency rates when they lived in areas of different class composition. This means that not only are the Matsumoto results inconsistent with the opportunity-theory hypothesis, they are also inconsistent with the norm-conflict hypothesis that lower-class boys living in middle-class areas will have higher delinquency rates than lower-class boys living in lower-class areas.

Gross cultural differences between Tokyo and Tennessee could explain the divergent results. Personal communications between the present author and Matsumoto, however, failed to uncover any specific cultural interpretations of obvious potency.

Summary

Data from an American study have been found to be totally consistent, and data from a Japanese study have been found to be totally inconsistent with the opportunity-theory prediction that *being lower class has more effect in increasing delinquency for youth living in lower-class areas than for youth living in middle-class areas.* Less systematic results from a British study by McDonald tended to be consistent with the opportunity-theory prediction, while a very truncated class comparison in Baldwin, Bottoms and Walker's data tends to be inconsistent with it.

This is hardly an adequate basis for either confirming or disconfirming the prediction. Clearly more data are needed. In chapter 6, self-report delinquency data from Brisbane, Australia, are used in a further test of the hypothesis that the combined effect on delinquency of being lower class and living in a lower-class area is greater than the sum of their individual effects.

Chapter 6

Testing the class-mix hypothesis on self-report data

Introduction

The measurement of self-reported juvenile crime is one of the most difficult problem areas in criminology, yet it is one of the most neglected. Before we can proceed to an empirical test of the class-mix hypothesis on self-report data we must have confidence in our measuring instrument.

Normally researchers involved in both theoretical and empirical work implicitly assume delinquency to be a unidimensional construct. This assumption has come under continued attack from labelling theorists, who argue that the universe of behaviours defined as delinquent are not so defined because of any inherent homogeneity in the structure of the behaviours, but because official agencies of social control respond to them in the same way.[1] It is therefore necessary to explore empirically the extent and nature of the homogeneity of acts subsumed under the delinquency rubric.

The scaling of delinquency

The general weaknesses of the self-report method for measuring delinquency with respect to validity, reliability, and systematic bias have been reviewed in chapters 1 and 2. Perhaps the greatest shortcoming in the application of the method has been with respect to scaling procedures. Elsewhere[2] the present author has provided a detailed critique of these shortcomings. Common practices in the literature include:

1 Forming an *ad hoc* scale without any empirical investigation of the way the items in the scale intercorrelate. Unidimensionality is

126

implicitly assumed by the blind adding-up of the number of offences which have been committed by each respondent in the *ad hoc* scale.
2 Forcing unidimensionality upon the data by the uncritical use of Guttman scalogram analysis.
3 Assuming delinquency to be multidimensional without any empirical investigation of the structure of item sets. Such studies simply define a number of supposedly independent scales on theoretical or *ad hoc* grounds, without checking the dimensionality of individual scales or the nature of the relationships between items in different scales.
4 The use of parametric statistical procedures such as cluster analysis and principal-component analysis to test dimensionality.

Studies which use the latter multivariate procedures seem to be making a more serious attempt to explore the structure of their item sets. However, the value of these analyses is also questionable since self-report delinquency data is such that it grossly abuses the metric and distributional assumptions of these parametric techniques. They assume interval scaling, yet it is unreasonable to assume, for example, that the difference between not committing an offence and committing it once is the same as the difference between committing it once and committing it two or three times, and that this equals the difference between committing it two or three times and committing it more than three times. The best that can be assumed is an ordinal scaling of frequency of delinquent response.

When product-moment correlations are calculated between all pairs of items and the resulting matrix of correlations analysed by cluster analysis or factor analysis, there is an implicit assumption that the items are approximately equivalent with respect to their extremeness. Variations in extremeness are likely to produce 'difficulty factors' directly related not to the item content but to the extremeness of the items.[3] Self-report delinquency schedules are characterized by a wide variation in the extremeness of items. This makes it likely that extreme items will fall together along artifactual difficulty dimensions.

What is needed then is a procedure which does not make unwarranted metric and distributional assumptions about the data. The analyses used to form the measures of self-reported delinquency for the present research were non-metric factor analysis, multidimensional scaling, hierarchical clustering analysis, and multidimensional scalogram analysis, all of which satisfy these two conditions to varying degrees. More detailed justification for why conventional models, such as principal component analysis, are inappropriate for dealing with the J-shaped distribution of deviant behaviour will not be presented here, nor will the details of the non-metric analyses which were conducted to form the measures. Such information is fairly technical and has already been published by Braithwaite and Law elsewhere.[4] Before we can proceed to present the result of these analyses, however, details of the sample, items and interviews from which the data were generated must be presented.

The sample

For the present study interviews were conducted with 358 males aged between 15 and 20 years, selected by randomized multiphase sampling procedures.[5]

First, statistical areas (census tracts) within the Brisbane metropolitan area were sampled. Census estimates of the number of 15–20 year olds in each area were used to calculate the proportion of the total Brisbane 15–20-year-old population found in each area. These proportions were then summed to form a cumulative percentage. Random-number tables were used to select 30 of the 51 areas for inclusion in the final sample. Thus the areas with greater 15–20-year-old populations were more likely to be sampled.

Each statistical area is divided into census collector's districts (CDs). The number of CDs sampled from each statistical area was in proportion to the number of 15–20 year olds living in the statistical area. The probability of a CD being sampled increased in direct proportion to its total population.

Streets within CDs were selected by simple random sampling, and interviewers were required to obtain interviews from houses which contained a 2 or a 9 in their number (e.g. 2, 20, 9, 19).

Of course the majority of houses sampled contained no 15–20-year olds. An average of four houses were door-knocked for each interview obtained. When a house with a 15–20-year-old was found, interviewers were required to call back if he was not at home.

The items

The items in the self-report interview schedule were a modified version of Elmhorn's[6] item set. Elmhorn obtained a split-half reliability of 0·86 on a sample of 950, and reported strong concurrent validation against a criterion of official records. Items on marijuana use and alcohol consumption were added to the pool. Thus, seventeen items were included in the study (Table 6.1). However, after the hierarchical-clustering and multidimensional-scaling analyses, it was apparent that items 1 and 8 were behaving rather erratically, and in a way that suggested that much of their variance was measurement error. This prompted a check back on the way several respondents were reacting to the items. Considerable ambiguity was revealed in that some respondents were endorsing the items for instances of borrowing rather than theft. Items 1 and 8 were therefore eliminated from subsequent analyses.

Table 6.1 *Self-report items*

1	Taken money from home without your parents knowing.
2	Sneaked into a cinema or sports ground without paying.
3	Taken fruit from a shop or orchard.
4	Broken street lamps or windows deliberately.
5	Taken part in damaging or destroying park benches, telephone boxes, or other property.
6	Ridden on a motor bike or in a car you knew or believed was stolen.
7	Removed things from cars, motor cycles or bicycles to sell or use them.
8	Taken things or money in a shop or from someone.
9	Taken a bicycle or motor bike which wasn't yours.
10	Taken a car which wasn't yours.
11	Broken into a flat, house, bookstall or slot-machine and taken something.
12	Broken into an attic, cellar or shed and taken something.
13	Threatened or forced someone to give you money, cigarettes or something else.
14	Deliberately lit fires which you knew would damage property.
15	How many bottles of beer would you drink in an average week?
16	How often would you have spirits or hard liquor?
17	Marijuana use.

Clearly, items 15, 16, and 17 are not offences against persons or property, and therefore fall outside of the focus of this book. Indeed, among the principal reasons for the decision to limit the focus of the book to offences against persons or property, were the findings from our multivariate analyses—that these offences without victims (15, 16, and 17) were only weakly related with other forms of delinquency.

In the selection of items there has been no attempt at a representative sampling of the facets of the domain of delinquent behaviours subsumed under the definition. The items were taken more or less *in toto* from another study. Nevertheless, the item pool does have an advantage over those of most previous studies, in that it is not dominated by trivial offences which are not even against the law (items such as 'defying parents' authority', 'gambling', 'running away from home', and 'having sexual intercourse').

The interview

The boy's home was considered a better interview setting than the most commonly used setting of the school. In addition to the likelihood that the authoritarian situation of the school inhibits candour, school samples are biased against drop-outs, truants, boys who skip classes, and boys suspended from school. Moreover, the sampling of schools is inevitably non-random because of the frequent refusal of principals to co-operate in delinquency studies.

One disadvantage associated with interviews in boys' homes is that parents are always eager to hear what questions are being asked of their children, and what answers given. Interviewers were trained to inform parents that confidentiality was important to them for reasons of professional ethics, and that therefore parents were not to be present during interviewing. The fact that the survey was being conducted by the YMCA, with the stated purpose being to assess the need for a youth club locally, meant that parents were generally very co-operative. For 70 per cent of interviews, the interviewer was able to report that a third person was not present for any of the interview. In two-thirds of those cases where there was a third person listening, it was only for part of the interview. Respondents were assured of confidentiality and anonymity at more than one point during the interview.[7]

In order to provide further safeguards with respect to the delinquency items, respondents were handed cards with the items written on them. They were asked whether they had done each one. If the answer was 'Yes', they were then asked if they had done it 'once', 'two or three times', or 'more than three times'.[8]

The interviews were conducted by trained interviewers, most of whom were young sociology undergraduates.

Findings on the structure of self-reported delinquency

In the analysis of the above data by Braithwaite and Law[9] four procedures were applied which represent the similarities among delinquent respondents, variables, and categories in very different ways. All, however, share the common advantage of making few, if any, of the metric and distributional assumptions grossly violated by self-report delinquency data. The fact that the same general structure emerged under these four rather different techniques gave confidence that the result was not the artifactual product of any single approach.

The series of analyses provided fairly strong support for the existence of a general delinquency factor, with a number of specific factors. By a general factor interpretation I mean that after the substantial variance accounted for by the first general factor is extracted from the item pool, significant unexplained variance remains, which is accounted for by a number of specific factors: at the same time, however, the majority of the items are strongly correlated with the general factor. Homogeneous clusters of items which were consistently supported across the non-metric factor analysis, multidimensional scaling, hierarchical-cluster analysis, and multidimensional-scalogram analysis were 'trivial delinquency' (2, 3), 'drug use' (15, 16, 17) 'vehicle theft' (6, 9, 10), and 'vandalism' (4, 5, 14). Other items did not form into specific clusters but typically showed considerable saturation with the general factor. The multidimensional-scalogram-analysis results, by taking frequency into account, strongly suggested that an even more homogeneous cluster than 'trivial delinquency' would be 'frequent involvement in trivial delinquency'. Similarly, 'drug use' would be more homogeneous as '*heavy* drinking and marijuana use'.

While there was strong support for a general-factor interpretation of delinquency, there was evidence to suggest that the items classified as 'trivial delinquency' and 'drug use' may not be strongly related to this general factor. In particular, moderate drinking, which accounts for much of the variance in many measures of self-reported delinquency in the literature, proved to be useless in the present research for discriminating between those high and low in general delinquency.

Consistent with the above, the multidimensional-scalogram analysis yielded three distinct types of respondents: *delinquents, non-delinquents,* and *trivial or drinking delinquents.* The latter were no more nor less involved in the more serious delinquent acts than the non-delinquents. It would seem unwise, then, to include very trivial offences or offences without victims in a measure of self-reported delinquency which is assumed to be unidimensional.

In the multidimensional-scalogram-analysis solution, a comparison among categories within items, among items within similar categories, and among respondents, revealed that the points defined a general 'degree of delinquency' dimension, in which number of different acts committed, the frequency with which these acts were committed, and the seriousness of the acts were all relevant to the dimension. That is, the results are strongly suggestive that people who engage in a greater number of delinquent acts are more likely to engage in those acts more frequently, and more likely to engage in more serious offences. Thus number, frequency, and seriousness may be empirically all part of the same single dimension representing 'degree of delinquency'. Forcing the three on to the same metric may not be reason for methodologists throwing up their arms in horror after all.

Forming measures of self-reported delinquency

Now that an understanding of the structure underlying the items in this study has been attained, it should be possible to combine them to form measures of self-reported delinquency.

Following the discovery of a general-delinquency factor, and the emergence of three distinct clusters of respondents in the multi-dimensional-scalogram analysis, the principal measure of self-reported delinquency in this chapter will be a classification of respondents into *non-delinquents, trivial or drinking delinquents*, and *serious delinquents*. Consistent with the findings about the clustering of respondents in the multidimensional-scalogram solution, the classification will be as follows:

> *Non-delinquents:* none, one or two offences (except where both offences are 'trivial or drinking' offences, in which case the respondent is classified as a 'trivial or drinking delinquent').
> *Trivial or drinking delinquents:* at least two out of the four trivial and drinking items (items 2, 3, 15, 16) and no more than one serious item (items 4–14).
> *Serious delinquents:* at least four offences (except where there are only four offences and at least three of them are 'trivial or drinking' offences, in which case the respondent is classified as a 'trivial or drinking delinquent').

To obtain more detailed information of specific-delinquency clusters, the following measures were formed on the basis of clusters obtained consistently across the four multivariate analyses.

> *Frequent involvement in trivial delinquency:* number of different trivial offences committed at least twice (items 2 and 3).
> *Heavy drinking and marijuana use:* number of different heavy-drinking (at least three bottles of beer a week, or drinking spirits at least once a week) and marijuana-use offences committed (items 15–17).
> *Vehicle theft:* number of different vehicle-theft offences committed (items 6, 9, 10).

Vandalism: number of different vandalism offences committed (items 4, 5, 14).

Operationalizing class

In testing the class-mix hypothesis against self-report delinquency measures, social class and social class of area were operationalized in the ways justified in chapter 2. Social class was indexed by father's occupation as classified by the Australian National University code.[10] The ANU code was collapsed into three social class categories as follows:

High: father in professional or managerial occupation.
Medium: father in skilled, clerical, or sales occupation.
Low: father in unskilled or semi-skilled occupation.

Social class of area was indexed, for the census statistical areas in which respondents lived, as the percentage of males in the workforce in unskilled or semi-skilled occupations.[11] This variable has been found to have the highest loading on the socioeconomic-status factor in a factorial ecology of Brisbane.[12] Social class of area was collapsed into three categories as follows:

High: less than 25 per cent unskilled or semi-skilled.
Medium: more than 25 per cent but less than 35 per cent unskilled or semi-skilled.
Low: more than 35 per cent unskilled or semi-skilled.

Controls

It is normally considered desirable to control for age and sex when examining the relationship between self-reported delinquency and an independent variable. A control for sex was not necessary here, since only males were in the sample. Unfortunately, there could be no control for age because the large number of cells in the three-way cross-tabulations meant that cell sizes would have become too small if a control for age had been included. This should not be reason for great concern, however, since for this sample there was no association between age and either of the independent variables (social class and social class of area).[13]

Serious, trivial and non-delinquents

It will be recalled that the random sample of 358 Brisbane males have been categorized into three types of persons—serious delinquents, trivial or drinking delinquents, and non-delinquents. The most important relationship in this chapter is the interaction between social class and social class of area for serious delinquents. The percentages of respondents who were serious self-reported delinquents from the three class groups, living in the three classes of area, are presented in Table 6.2.

It can be seen from the column totals in Table 6.2 that there was a clear tendency for the percentage of respondents who were serious delinquents to increase with decreasing social class. Although those living in the highest-class areas had the lowest percentage of serious delinquents, the relationship between social class of area and serious delinquency was not so clear cut. The interaction between social class and social class of area for serious delinquents is illustrated in Figure 6.1.

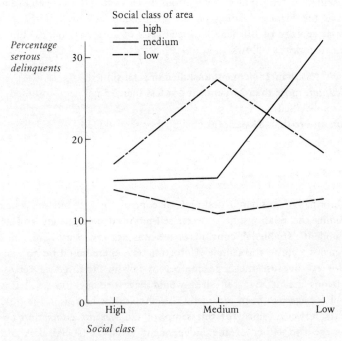

Figure 6.1 *Interaction between social class and social class of area for per cent serious delinquents*

Table 6.2 *Percentage of respondents serious delinquents by social class and social class of area*

Social class of area	Social class			
	High	*Medium*	*Low*	Total
High	13·8 (29)	10·8 (37)	12·5 (24)	14·7 (102)
Medium	14·8 (27)	15·3 (59)	31·9 (47)	22·8 (145)
Low	16·7 (18)	27·3 (33)	18·2 (33)	19·6 (92)
Total	14·7 (75)	16·5 (133)	22·6 (106)	19·5 (339)

The number in brackets refers to the total number of cases in the cell, not to the number of delinquent cases.
Column totals come from a cross-tabulation that excludes cases where information about father's occupation was not known. Row totals come from another cross-tabulation that excludes cases where information about area of residence was not known. All other cells come from a cross-tabulation that excludes cases where information *either* about father's occupation or about area were not known. Consequently, the totals are somewhat larger than the sum of cell samples. This applies to all Tables in this Chapter. It is done simply to make best use of the data by minimizing the exclusion of respondents because of missing data on either occupation or area.

Were it not for the lower-than-predicted delinquency of the lowest-class boys living in the lowest-class areas, the data trend in Figure 6.1 and Table 6.2 would have been totally consistent with the opportunity-theory prediction. For those living in high-class areas, social class had no effect on serious delinquency. For those living in medium-class areas, serious delinquency jumped dramatically with decreasing social class. Finally, for boys living in lower-class areas, the difference in serious delinquency between high- and medium-class boys was greater than for boys living in medium-class areas. However, this trend was not continued for the lowest-social-class boys.

Since the interaction was, apart from this important exception, largely consistent with the opportunity-theory prediction, it was tested for statistical significance (Table 6.3). Neither the relationship between social class and serious delinquency, nor the relationship between social class of area and serious delinquency, nor the class by class-of-area interaction, was statistically significant. It is also worth noting that the tendency for more of the lower-class respondents in the sample to live in lower-class areas did not reach statistical significance. It is perhaps an indication of the relative lack of segregation of the classes in Brisbane

135

that a random sample of more than 300 failed to reveal a statistically significant association between social class and social class of area. Brisbane does have a low degree of class segregation compared to other cities.[14] So one might expect any social-class-of-area effects demonstated in Brisbane to be greater in other cities.

Table 6.3 *Summary of component* χ^2 *for the three-way cross-tabulation among social class, social class of area, and serious delinquency*[1]

Comparison	Value of χ^2	Degrees of freedom
Class × class of area	6·039	4
Class × serious delinquency	2·283	2
Class of area × serious delinquency	2·477	2
Class × class of area × serious delinquency	4·886	4
Total	15·685	12

[1] None significant at ·05 level.

It is clear from Table 6.4 that there was no semblance of an interaction effect between social class and social class of area for the comparison between *trivial or drinking delinquents* and others. For the comparison between *non-delinquents* and others, however, an interaction reappeared (Table 6.5). The result for non-delinquents was, not surprisingly, almost a perfect mirror image of the result for serious delinquents. It can be seen from Figure 6.2 that total consistency of the data trend with the opportunity-theory prediction was again destroyed by the unexpectedly high non-delinquency of the lowest-class group in the lowest-class areas. And again, this data trend, which was mostly consistent with the opportunity-theory prediction, failed to reach statistical significance (Table 6.6).

Specific delinquency clusters

In this section, instead of looking at gross types of persons (in terms of delinquency), we look at the effect of social class and social class of area on the percentages of respondents who admitted to some or all of the items in the four specific delinquency clusters established in the last chapter. The clusters of items are trivial delinquency, heavy drinking and marijuana use, vehicle theft, and vandalism.

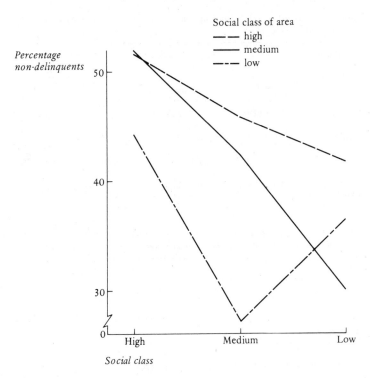

Figure 6.2 *Interaction between social class and social class of area for per cent non-delinquents*

Table 6.4 *Percentage of respondents trivial or drinking delinquents by social class and social class of area*

Social class of area	Social class			
	High	*Medium*	*Low*	Total
High	34·5 (29)	43·2 (37)	45·8 (24)	39·2 (102)
Medium	33·3 (27)	42·4 (59)	38·3 (47)	37·9 (145)
Low	38·9 (18)	45·5 (33)	45·5 (33)	43·5 (92)
Total	34·7 (75)	43·6 (133)	41·5 (106)	39·8 (339)

Table 6.5 *Percentage of respondents non-delinquents by social class and social class of area*

Social class of area	Social class			
	High	*Medium*	*Low*	*Total*
High	51·7 (29)	45·9 (37)	41·7 (24)	46·1 (102)
Medium	51·9 (27)	42·4 (59)	29·8 (47)	39·3 (145)
Low	44·4 (18)	27·3 (33)	36·4 (33)	37·0 (92)
Total	50·7 (75)	39·8 (133)	35·8 (106)	40·7 (339)

Table 6.6 *Summary of component χ^2 for the three-way cross-tabulation among social class, social class of area, and non-delinquency*[1]

Comparison	Value of χ^2 ·	Degrees of freedom
Class × class of area	6·040	4
Class × non-delinquency	4·129	2
Class of area × non-delinquency	1·873	2
Class × class of area × non-delinquency	5·488	4
Total	17·530	12

[1] None significant at ·05 level.

Table 6.7 presents the percentages of respondents who reported frequent involvement in *one* out of the two trivial-delinquency items, and Table 6.8 the percentages who reported frequent involvement in *both* trivial offences. There is no indication of class by class-of-area interaction in Table 6.7. However, from Table 6.8 and Figure 6.3, it can be seen that for respondents living in high-class areas, social class had little effect on the frequency of commission of both trivial offences. On the other hand, for those living in medium- and low-class areas, the social-class effect was considerable. The relationship between social class and frequent involvement for both trivial-delinquency items, and the social-class by social-class-of-area interaction for this variable, were both significant at the ·05 level (Table 6.9). Moreover, the relationship between class and class of area was not different for those who had committed both trivial offences and those who had not. Thus, the significant-interaction effect can be interpreted as lending some support for the opportunity-theory prediction.

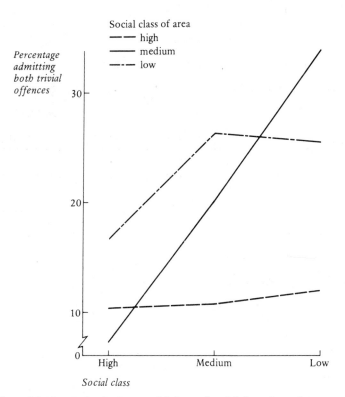

Figure 6.3 *Interaction between social class and social class of area for percentage admitting frequent involvement for both trivial items*

Table 6.7 *Percentage of respondents reporting frequent involvement for one out of the two trivial delinquency items by social class and social class of area*

Social class of area	Social class			
	High	*Medium*	*Low*	Total
High	37·9 (29)	35·1 (37)	40·0 (25)	34·0 (103)
Medium	35·7 (28)	30·5 (59)	29·8 (47)	30·1 (146)
Low	38·9 (18)	32·4 (34)	31·4 (35)	30·5 (95)
Total	38·2 (76)	32·1 (134)	33·0 (109)	31·4 (344)

Table 6.8 *Percentage of respondents reporting frequent involvement for both trivial delinquency items by social class and social class of area*

Social class of area	Social class			
	High	*Medium*	*Low*	*Total*
High	10·3 (29)	10·8 (37)	12·0 (25)	16·5 (103)
Medium	7·1 (28)	20·3 (59)	34·0 (47)	21·2 (146)
Low	16·7 (18)	26·5 (34)	25·7 (35)	24·2 (95)
Total	10·5 (76)	18·7 (134)	25·7 (109)	20·6 (344)

Table 6.9 *Summary of component χ^2 for the three-way cross-tabulation among social class, social class of area, and frequent involvement for both trivial delinquency items*

Comparison	Value of χ^2	Degrees of freedom
Class × class of area	5·771	4
Class × frequent involvement for both trivial delinquency items	6·256[1]	2
Class of area × frequent involvement for both trivial delinquency items	1·846	2
Class × class of area × frequent involvement for both trivial delinquency items	11·529[1]	4
Total	25·402[1]	12

[1] Significant at ·05 level.

Table 6.10 *Percentage of respondents admitting to one of the three heavy-drinking and marijuana-use offences by social class and social class of area*

Social class of area	Social class			
	High	*Medium*	*Low*	*Total*
High	24·1 (29)	27·0 (37)	28·0 (25)	25·2 (103)
Medium	28·6 (28)	25·4 (59)	23·4 (47)	24·7 (146)
Low	11·1 (18)	14·7 (34)	17·1 (35)	15·8 (95)
Total	22·4 (76)	23·1 (134)	22·0 (109)	22·4 (344)

From Tables 6.10 and 6.11, it is clear that there was no interaction between social class and social class of area for the heavy-drinking and marijuana-use cluster.

Table 6.11 *Percentage of respondents admitting to two or three of the heavy-drinking and marijuana-use offences by social class and social class of area*

Social class of area	Social class			
	High	*Medium*	*Low*	Total
High	6·9 (29)	16·2 (37)	16·0 (25)	13·6 (103)
Medium	0·0 (28)	17·0 (59)	14·9 (47)	14·4 (146)
Low	11·2 (18)	14·7 (34)	14·3 (35)	12·6 (95)
Total	5·2 (76)	16·4 (134)	14·7 (109)	13·7 (344)

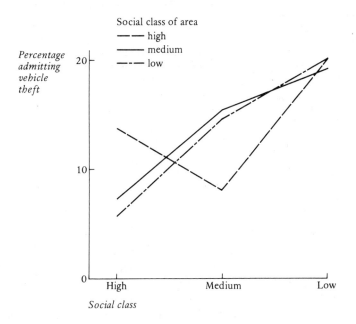

Figure 6.4 *Interaction between social class and social class of area for percentage admitting to at least one of the vehicle-theft offences*

For the vehicle-theft cluster, the effect of decreasing social class in increasing delinquency was greatest for those living in the lowest-class areas, slightly less for those living in medium-class areas, and least for those in the highest-class areas (see Table 6.12 and Figure 6.4). This is consistent with the opportunity-theory prediction. However, the data trend was so weak that it fell well short of statistical significance (Table 6.13).

Table 6.12 *Percentage of respondents admitting to at least one of the vehicle-theft offences by social class and social class of area*

Social class of area	Social class			
	High	*Medium*	*Low*	Total
High	13·8 (29)	8·1 (37)	20·0 (25)	14·6 (103)
Medium	7·1 (28)	15·3 (59)	19·1 (47)	16·4 (146)
Low	5·6 (18)	14·7 (34)	20·0 (35)	13·7 (95)
Total	9·2 (76)	12·7 (134)	19·3 (109)	15·1 (344)

Table 6.13 *Summary of component χ^2 for the three-way cross-tabulation among social class, social class of area, and admission of vehicle theft*[1]

Comparison	Value of χ^2	Degrees of freedom
Class × class of area	5·771	4
Class × vehicle theft	3·798	2
Class of area × vehicle theft	0·375	2
Class × class of area × vehicle theft	1·444	4
Total	11·379	12

[1] None significant at ·05 level.

The interaction between social class and social class of area for the vandalism cluster was unusual (Table 6.14, Figure 6.5). Social class was strongly negatively related to vandalism in medium-class areas, but was minimally related in both low- and high-class areas. This finding is consistent with neither the opportunity-theory nor the norm-conflict predictions. This unusual interaction effect failed to achieve statistical significance (Table 6.15).

Table 6.14 *Percentage of respondents admitting to at least one of the vandalism offences by social class and social class of area*

Social class of area	Social class			
	High	*Medium*	*Low*	Total
High	13·8 (29)	21·6 (37)	12·0 (25)	17·5 (103)
Medium	17·9 (28)	22·0 (59)	42·6 (47)	30·1 (146)
Low	27·8 (18)	29·4 (34)	31·4 (35)	28·4 (95)
Total	19·7 (76)	23·1 (134)	32·1 (109)	25·9 (344)

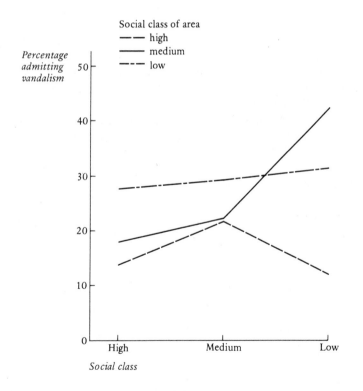

Figure 6.5 *Interaction between social class and social class of area for percentage admitting to at least one of the vandalism offences*

Table 6.15 *Summary of component χ^2 for the three-way cross-tabulation among social class, social class of area, and admission of vandalism*[1]

Comparison	Value of χ^2	Degrees of freedom
Class × class of area	5·771	4
Class × vandalism	4·240	2
Class of area × vandalism	5·493	2
Class × class of area × vandalism	4·805	4
Total	20·309	12

[1] None significant at ·05 level.

Summary and conclusions

'Heavy drinking and marijuana use', a cluster of victimless offences not directly relevant to the goals of this book, was found to be unrelated to either social class or social class of area. However, both clusters of variables and respondent types based on offences against persons or property, provided data trends fairly consistent with greater delinquency on the part of lower-class youth, and, less consistently, with greater delinquency on the part of youth living in lower-class areas. With one exception, however, these trends failed to reach statistical significance.

The interaction between class and class of area tended to be in the direction of the opportunity theory prediction rather than the norm conflict prediction. However, this tendency was neither strong nor consistent, and in only one instance did it attain statistical significance.

This chapter must be concluded in the same way as chapter 5. The data analysed here do not disconfirm the hypothesis that *being lower class has more effect in increasing delinquency for youth living in lower-class areas than for youth living in middle-class areas.* However the support provided for the hypothesis is weak. There is still a need for more data.

Chapter 7

Testing the class-mix hypothesis on official delinquency data

Introduction

It has been argued already that both self-reports and official records provide estimates of delinquency rates which are riddled with error. However, because the sources of error under the two methods are very different, joint confirmation of a hypothesis by both methods may offer reasonable grounds for establishing relationships. Having tested the class-mix hypothesis on self-report data from Brisbane, it is now tested on official records of delinquency from the same city. The official-records method enables a test of the hypothesis on a much larger sample of youths, most of whom have engaged in fairly serious delinquent acts. This is its major advantage over the self-report study, in which cell sizes became small because of the sample size, and in which very few of the respondents were involved in serious delinquency.

Choosing the source of data

There are three sources of official records of delinquency: police records, juvenile-court records, and records of institutions for the care and control of delinquents. The last were totally inappropriate for the present purpose because of the relatively small sample that could be obtained from institutionalized Brisbane delinquents.

The choice between police and court records was, in fact, decided by default owing to the Queensland police commissioner's refusal to allow access to police records. On the other hand, the Department of Children's Services was willing to make available files on all delinquents who appeared before the Children's Court.

The disadvantage of court records over police records is that they are procedurally at a greater distance from the actual crime. The more procedures that intervene between the actual offence and the official recording of the offence, the more opportunities there are for biases to enter into the measure. However, court records enjoy the concomitant advantage that by the time non-prosecuted offences are filtered out, there remains a measure of delinquency which is less cluttered by trivial acts of misbehaviour. Of course court records are also less likely to include many cases in which individuals were in the event innocent of the charges written beside their name.

There were other advantages in the use of court records for the present study. Court records in Queensland on delinquency are maintained much more systematically than police records. A number of different agencies of the Queensland Police Department deal with juvenile crime: the Juvenile Aid Bureau, concentrating on offenders who it is thought would benefit from counselling; the Education Department Liaison Unit, concentrating on offences connected with schools; the local suburban police station—and so on. To a considerable extent, the records of delinquency available from these various sections were not all centrally collected.

On the other hand, all cases appearing before the Children's Court were carefully filed.[1] Because of the greater importance of court files to the state bureaucracy, they are recorded more meticulously than police records. Thus recording of key independent variables such as father's occupation should contain less error. As Phillips[2] has emphasized, the effect of such apparently straightforward errors is considerable, and too often ignored by social scientists. Of particular importance in this study is the recording of false addresses, which is far more likely in police than in court records.

Coding the data

Data were coded from the files of all males appearing before the Children's Court between June 1969 and June 1973. In order to obtain data on all Brisbane offenders who appeared in court during this period, it was necessary to look at the files of courts outside the Brisbane area, so that offences committed in other parts of the state (e.g. at a beach resort) by Brisbane adolescents could be included in the analysis. Offences which did not involve injury to persons or property were excluded from the analysis. Consequently, of the 10,858 files perused, only 2,333 were included in the analysis.

The following official offence types were excluded from the research on the grounds that they did not involve direct injury to persons or property.

Incest
Unlawful carnal knowledge
Unlawful carnal knowledge against the order of nature
Disorderly conduct
Drunkenness
Obscene/insulting behaviour
Indecent behaviour
Wilful exposure
Vagrancy
Unlawfully on enclosed premises
Resisting arrest
Escaping from lawful custody
Possession of dangerous drugs
Breaches of the Liquor Acts
Breaches of the Firearms Act
Breaches of the Customs Act
Breaches of the Railway Acts and Regulations
Breaches of the Racing and Betting Acts
Breaches of the Posts and Telegraph Acts
Breaches of the Marine Acts
Breaches of the Traffic Acts
False representation of a bomb threat
Possession of an offensive weapon
Possession of house-breaking implements
Possession of an instrument for the use of drugs
Likely to lapse into a life of vice or crime or addiction to drugs
Exposed to moral danger
Uncontrollable
Truanting

There were a small number of exceptional cases which fell within the above offence types but which involved a clear injury to a person or loss of property. These offences were classified as either 'other offences against the person' or 'other offences against property'.

Unfortunately, the only kind of offence typology which was possible was one based on the Court's offence categories. Description of the offence was in many cases sketchy and in a number of cases only the legal classification of the offence was stated. The adopted typology of

Table 7.1 *Offence typology*

Number of cases	
	1 Offences against the person
1	Manslaughter
3	Attempted killing
4	Unlawful wounding
4	Bodily harm
3	Robbery with violence
2	Robbery with violence in company
3	Robbery whilst armed
7	Stealing from the person
43	Assault
5	Rape
29	Aggravated assault
6	Indecent dealing[1]
8	Dangerous driving[2]
1	Attempted robbery
1	Indecent assault
	2 Vandalism
5	Attempted arson
11	Arson
120	Wilful destruction of property
83	Wilful damage of property
13	Wilful and unlawful interference of property
	3 Break and enter
9	Burglary
406	Break and enter and steal
22	Attempted break and enter
243	Break and enter with intent
36	Enter with intent
6	Enter and break out
	4 Car theft
434	Unlawful use of a motor vehicle
	5 Stealing and other offences against property
738	Stealing
4	Attempted stealing
41	Receiving
17	Possession of property suspected of being stolen

Number of cases	5 Stealing and other offences against property (continued)
9	False pretences
6	Stealing as a servant
8	Unlawful use of pedal cycle
2	Forgery

[1] Only cases involving violence or force included.

[2] Cases where injury to persons resulted.

offences was formed by combining the Court's offence types as in Table 7.1. In the 20 per cent of cases in which the offender had appeared before the Court for more than one offence, his offender type was based on what the coder considered his most serious offence in the time period under consideration.

The home addresses of offenders were mapped into 1971 Census statistical areas. Social class and social class of area were operationalized as in the last chapter.

Delinquency rates for youths of a certain social class living in areas of a certain social class were calculated by dividing the total number of offenders in that cell, for the period 1969–73, by 1971 Census estimates of the number of 10 to 19-year-old males of that social-class group living in all areas of that social class of area. The 10–19 year olds at the time of the 1971 Census were 8–17 year olds in 1969 and 12–21 year olds in 1973. This seemed the most appropriate age group on which to base delinquency rates for the four-year period, as there were no offenders below 8 years of age, and the age distribution of offenders was severely skewed towards the upper end of the age range (see Table 7.2).

Table 7.2 *Age distribution of offenders at time of Court appearance*

Age	Number	Per cent	Age	Number	Per cent
8	2	0·1	13	301	12·9
9	13	0·6	14	446	19·1
10	19	0·8	15	572	24·5
11	60	2·6	16	785	33·6
12	121	5·2	17	14	0·6

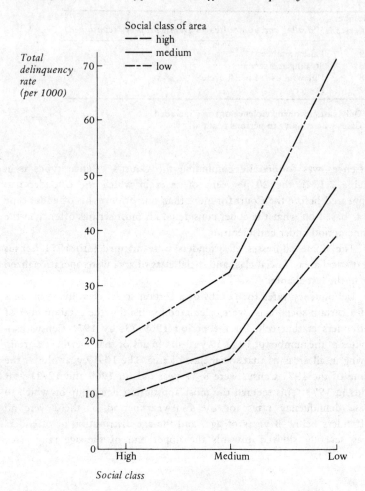

Figure 7.1 *Interaction between social class and social class of area for total delinquency rate (per 1,000)*

Results

Table 7.3 presents total delinquency rates by social class and social class of area for all types of offences combined. The column totals indicate a strong negative correlation between social class and delinquency, and the row totals a strong negative association between social class of area and delinquency. Both relationships remained when the other was controlled for.

The low social class of delinquents was corroborated by the fact that of the 977 delinquents who worked, 562 (58 per cent) were in unskilled jobs. In the random sample of Brisbane 15–20 year olds discussed in the last two chapters, only 20 per cent of those working were in unskilled jobs. Similarly, while 11 per cent of the out-of-school delinquents were unemployed, the figure was 5 per cent for the population sample of 15–20 year olds.

Table 7.3 *Total delinquency rate per 1,000 by social class and social class of area*

Social class of area	Social class			
	High	*Medium*	*Low*	Total
High	9·9 (64)[1]	16·8 (172)	39·0 (168)	19·2 (404)
Medium	12·6 (68)	18·4 (320)	47·9 (456)	26·1 (844)
Low	20·2 (49)	32·3 (358)	72·4 (645)	46·9 (1,052)
Total	12·6 (181)	22·0 (850)	55·8 (1,269)	30·4 (2,300)

[1] Numbers in brackets represent the number of delinquents in each cell.

From the graphic representation of Table 7.3 and Figure 7.1, it is clear that social class has the greatest effect in augmenting the probability of delinquency for youths living in the lowest-class areas. The effect of class on delinquency is also slightly greater for youths living in medium-class areas than for those in the highest-class areas. Thus the data is completely consistent with the opportunity-theory prediction. It is neither necessary nor appropriate to test the statistical significance of this interaction effect because it is based on the ratio of the whole population of Brisbane male Children's Court convictions for a given period to the whole population of Brisbane adolescents, rather than on a random sample of a total population.

Delinquency rates for specific types of offences are now examined. Although both social class and social class of area had negative effects on rates for offences against the person, even when the other was controlled, there was no clear interaction effect (Table 7.4 and Figure 7.2). The small number of 118 offences against the person were not patterned in such a way as to support either the opportunity-theory prediction or the norm-conflict prediction.

151

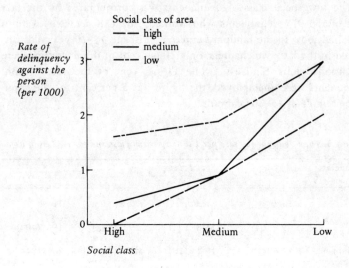

Figure 7.2 *Interaction between social class and social class of area for offences against the person (per 1,000)*

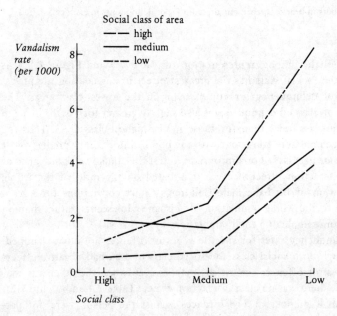

Figure 7.3 *Interaction between social class and social class of area for vandalism (per 1,000)*

Table 7.4 *Offences against the person per 1,000 by social class and social class of area*

Social class of area	Social class			
	High	*Medium*	*Low*	Total
High	0·0 (0)	0·9 (9)	2·3 (10)	0·9 (19)
Medium	0·4 (2)	0·9 (16)	3·0 (29)	1·5 (47)
Low	1·6 (4)	1·9 (21)	3·0 (27)	2·3 (52)
Total	0·4 (6)	1·2 (46)	2·9 (66)	1·6 (118)

Table 7.5 *Vandalism per 1,000 by social class and social class of area*

Social class of area	Social class			
	High	*Medium*	*Low*	Total
High	0·6 (4)	1·8 (18)	4·0 (17)	1·9 (39)
Medium	1·9 (10)	1·7 (30)	4·6 (44)	2·6 (84)
Low	1·2 (3)	2·6 (29)	8·3 (74)	4·7 (106)
Total	1·2 (17)	2·0 (77)	5·9 (135)	3·0 (229)

An examination of vandalism rates revealed that the effect of social class was greatest in augmenting the vandalism of youths living in the lowest-class areas (Table 7.5 and Figure 7.3). This is consistent with the opportunity-theory prediction. However, there was no tendency for the effect of social class to be greater in medium-class areas than in the highest-class areas.

It can be seen from Table 7.6 and Figure 7.4 that the patterning of break-and-enter rates fitted exactly the opportunity-theory prediction. The negative association between social class and the break-and-enter rate was least for boys living in the highest-class areas, greater for boys living in medium-class areas, and greatest for boys living in the lowest-class areas.

As with vandalism, the patterning of car-theft rates was only partially consistent with the opportunity-theory prediction (Table 7.7 and Figure 7.5). While the effect of social class was greatest for those

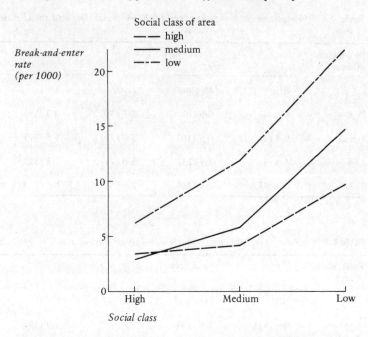

Figure 7.4 *Interaction between social class and social class of area for break and enters (per 1,000)*

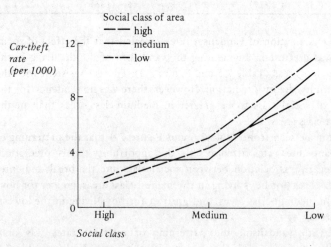

Figure 7.5 *Interaction between social class and social class of area for car theft (per 1,000)*

Table 7.6 *Break and enters per 1,000 by social class and social class of area*

Social class of area	Social class			
	High	*Medium*	*Low*	Total
High	3·2 (21)	4·1 (42)	9·8 (42)	5·0 (105)
Medium	3·0 (16)	5·9 (103)	14·7 (140)	8·0 (259)
Low	6·2 (15)	12·0 (133)	22·1 (197)	15·4 (345)
Total	3·6 (52)	7·2 (278)	16·7 (379)	9·4 (709)

living in the lowest-class areas, there was no clear tendency for the social-class effect to be greater in medium-class areas than in high-class areas.

Table 7.7 *Car theft per 1,000 by social class and social class of area*

Social class of area	Social class			
	High	*Medium*	*Low*	Total
High	1·8 (12)	4·3 (44)	8·4 (36)	4·4 (92)
Medium	3·3 (18)	3·5 (61)	10·0 (100)	5·5 (179)
Low	2·1 (5)	5·0 (55)	11·1 (99)	7·1 (159)
Total	2·4 (35)	4·1 (160)	10·3 (235)	5·7 (430)

The distribution of stealing and other offences against property was moderately consistent with the opportunity-theory prediction (Table 7.8 and Figure 7.6). The social-class effect was clearly greatest for those resident in the lowest-class areas. However, the tendency for there to be a greater social-class effect in medium-class than in high-class areas was so slight as to be almost non-existent.

Summary

Social class and social class of area both had negative effects upon all types of offence rates in an analysis of officially recorded delinquency in Brisbane. This was true even after the effect of one class variable was examined while controlling for the other.

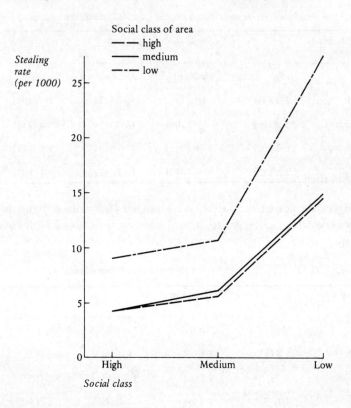

Figure 7.6 *Interaction between social class and social class of area for stealing and other offences against property (per 1,000)*

Table 7.8 *Stealing and other offences against property per 1,000 by social class and social class of area*

Social class of area	Social class			
	High	*Medium*	*Low*	Total
High	4·2 (27)	5·7 (59)	14·6 (63)	7·1 (149)
Medium	4·1 (22)	6·3 (110)	15·0 (143)	8·5 (275)
Low	9·1 (22)	10·8 (120)	27·8 (248)	17·4 (390)
Total	5·0 (71)	7·5 (289)	20·0 (454)	10·7 (814)

For no offence types was there an interaction effect consistent with the norm-conflict prediction that lower-class boys have higher delinquency rates when they live in a community with middle-class rather than lower-class norms.

For all offences combined, the interaction effect was strongly consistent with the prediction that *being lower class has more effect in increasing delinquency for youth living in lower-class areas than for youth living in middle-class areas.* The opportunity-theory prediction was also supported by the interaction effect for the specific offence types of break-and-enter offences, and stealing and other offences against property. Vandalism and car theft were both patterned such as to give only partial support to the opportunity-theory prediction. There was no interaction effect for the very small numbers of offences against persons.

In total, these data give clear support for the hypothesis that the combined effect on delinquency of being lower class and living in a lower-class area is greater than the sum of their individual effects. It is possible, then, that a policy to have fewer lower-class youth living in lower-class areas, and more of them living in middle-class areas might reduce overall delinquency. Perhaps many lower-class youth do have a strong predisposition to delinquency, likely to be realized only under the influence of the illegitimate opportunities of the lower-class area. Before any attempt is made to reach conclusions on these questions, the opportunity-theory prediction will be tested in the next chapter against a totally different level of analysis.

The need for a test of the class-mix hypothesis against an alternative level of analysis should be clear. It is possible, for example, that the relatively low delinquency rate of lower-class youth living in high-class areas is indicative of a kind of social-selection effect. Perhaps the kinds of lower-class people who choose to live in high-class areas are upwardly aspiring lower-class people who are not criminally inclined. What is needed is a test of the hypothesis which does not depend upon comparing categories whose composition is likely to be affected by social selection. Such an alternative test is provided in the next chapter.

Chapter 8

Testing the class-mix hypothesis on inter-city comparisons

Introduction

Thus far we have been concerned only with the first prediction of opportunity theory — that the impact on delinquency of being lower class will be greater for youth living in lower-class areas than for youth living in middle-class areas. This chapter contains a test of the second prediction — that cities with relatively large numbers of lower-class people living in predominantly middle-class areas of the city, and relatively large numbers of middle-class people living in predominantly lower-class areas of the city, will have relatively low delinquency rates. Henceforth, this prediction will be referred to as the *inter-city prediction.*

It was pointed out in chapter 4 that the opportunity-theory predictions about class-mix can be applied to adult as well as to juvenile crime. No distinction is made in this chapter between adult and juvenile offenders because we are working with offences known to the police.[1] For that majority of offences known to the police which are uncleared, there is no way of knowing the age of the offender.

The only existing published study which has undertaken anything approaching a test of the inter-city prediction is Cho's[2] analysis of Uniform Crime Reports. Cho conducted stepwise multiple linear regressions for 35 socioeconomic variables upon crime rates for the 49 largest United States cities, and separately for 40 Ohio cities. One of the 35 socioeconomic variables was a Negro residential-segregation index. Since Negroes are predominantly lower class, Cho's findings might be taken as some indication of the effect of lower-class residential segregation on crime.

Cho found that his Negro residential-segregation index was not significantly related to crime for either the national or the Ohio samples of cities. However, these findings should not be taken too seriously. In the first instance, Cho included in his multiple linear regression almost as many predictors as cases being predicted (35 versus 49 and 40), which was an excessive violation of accepted standards for the required ratio of cases to predictors in multiple-regression analyses.[3] There were clearly severe problems of multicollinearity among Cho's thirty-five predictors, and what the presented jumble of regression coefficients mean, in the context of this multicollinearity, is totally ambiguous. Certainly a correlation matrix is needed to ascertain what common variance among predictors was being partialled out in the stepwise process, but none has been presented.

Operationalizing city crime rates

The first step in designing an adequate test of the inter-city prediction is to find an acceptable measure of city crime rates. The United States is the only country for which uniformly recorded crime statistics are available for a large number of cities, with city boundaries so drawn that crime data is directly compatible with census data. The Uniform Crime Reports (UCR) for the United States give city rates for homicide, rape, robbery, aggravated assault, burglary, and grand larceny ($50 and over). The rates for these seven 'index crimes' are based on all offences known to the police.

In contrast to the analyses of the previous chapters, the test of the inter-city prediction has the advantage that the identity of the offender (his occupation, the suburb in which he lives, etc.) does not need to be known. All crimes known to the police can be used as data, so that biases arising from successive filtering through the various stages of the criminal-justice system are minimized. Nevertheless, important sources of error remain. Principally, these are: failure of victims to report offences;[4] underreporting by the police;[5] variations in legal definitions of crime; variations in police interpretations of legal definitions, and in police decisions to apply these definitions; and variations in crime-recording procedures.[6]

The definitions of the seven index crimes from UCR are outlined below.

Homicide includes murder and non-negligent manslaughter. It excludes deaths caused by negligence, suicide, attempts to kill, and justifiable homicide.
Rape includes assaults to commit rape and attempt rape, but excludes statutory rape without force.

159

Robbery includes all offences which involve stealing from the person by the use of threat or force. Attempted robbery is included.

Aggravated assault means assault or attempted assault with intent to kill or for the purpose of inflicting severe bodily injury by shooting, cutting, stabbing, maiming, poisoning, scalding, or by the use of acids, explosives, or other means. It excludes simple assault, assault and battery, fighting, etc.

Burglary includes house-breaking, safe-cracking, or any unlawful entry to commit a felony or a theft, even if no force is used to gain entrance. It includes attempted burglary. Burglary followed by larceny is not counted again as larceny.

Grand larceny is theft of something valued over $50 without force or violence, and not by fraud. It excludes auto theft.

Auto theft is the stealing or driving away and abandoning of a motor vehicle, including attempts.

These offences are selected for index purposes by the FBI because they are offences with high reportability and high seriousness ratings. The National Opinion Research Center victimization survey for the President's Commission on Law Enforcement and Administration of Justice found, however, that with the exceptions of homicide and auto theft, the index offences were considerably underreported.[7]

Particular emphasis should be placed on findings in relation to homicide because of its extremely high reportability and seriousness. Nevertheless, all of the index offences are high in seriousness compared with other types of crime, and this is an important advantage of the use of UCR.[8] Blumstein[9] has shown that when UCR and Sellin–Wolfgang indices were compared for reported crimes over the 1960–72 period, the two were almost perfectly linearly related. Thus, the explicit incorporation of seriousness into the index contributes no significant additional information.

Skogan[10] has undertaken a thorough investigation of the extent to which measurement error in UCR auto-theft and robbery indices are cause for concern. He compared rates for these offences from UCR with rates calculated from a large victimization survey in ten cities. The correlation between UCR and victimization rates for auto theft was ·94, and for robbery ·39. Skogan concluded:

> The comparison suggests that official figures may be useful indicators of the relative distribution of crime across cities. That is, while they do not specify the exact incidence of crime in a city, they tell us with some accuracy which cities have more crime than

others. The convergence of measures indicates that quantitative studies of inter-city variations in officially measured crime may not be seriously affected by measurement error.[11]

What is more important, Skogan found that the victimization and UCR measures bore almost identical relationships with a variety of demographic and police organization variables. Thus, even though the two measures were only moderately related for robbery, the variance they shared appeared to be that which was systematically related to other variables, so that inferences are not measurement specific.

Even though measurement error did not appear to be systematically related to independent variables at the level of correlations, regression coefficients for the victimization data were as much as three times as high as for the UCR data. This means that regression coefficients from UCR analyses cannot reasonably be used to predict the level of crime in a community, or to predict the impact that given policies or invest-ments will have on crime rates. Applied to the present problem, this means that regressions can be used to determine whether cities with greater segregation of classes have higher crime rates; but regression coefficients cannot be used to predict that an x per cent decrease in class segregation will produce a y per cent decrease in crime rates.

Because of the variation in the reportability of index offences, it was decided to test the inter-city prediction separately for each of the seven offences, rather than form a composite index. This decision was also prompted by the fact that different conclusions have been reached in different studies about the factor structure underlying the seven offences.[12]

Operationalizing lower-class segregation

The theoretical formulations of chapter 4 focus emphasis on the extent to which people at the lower end of the social-class continuum are residentially segregated, as a predisposing factor to crime. The theory assigns to a lesser level of importance the question of whether people of high social class are mixed with people of intermediate levels of social class. Consequently, an index of class segregation which measures the extent to which lower-class people are concentrated into slums is pre-ferred, while putting aside the question of the extent to which people of intermediate status are intermixed with those of higher social class. Most existing indices of residential segregation either measure the extent to which various groups are segregated one from another, or include, in a measure of lower-class segregation, deviations from the expected lower-class populations in intermediate- versus high-social-class areas.[13]

To focus exclusively upon the extent of lower-class segregation into the most lower-class areas of the city, the measure chosen here is the percentage of families who are lower class in that 20 per cent of the city which is most lower class in its composition.

'Lower-class families' is operationalized as those families below the poverty line as defined by the 1970 United States Census.[14] To ascertain which census tracts make up the 20 per cent of the city which is most lower class in its composition, the populations of the census tracts with the highest percentages of families below the poverty line are progressively added, starting from the poorest tract and working upwards, until the total reaches 20 per cent of the total population of the city.[15] These areas then represent the poorest 20 per cent of the city. In most cases, only a fraction of the population of the last tract added was required to make the summated population of the poor tracts up to 20 per cent of the total population. The same fraction of the number of poor families in that tract was used in totalling the number of poor families in the poorest 20 per cent of the city.

Thus the first index of lower-class segregation is *the percentage of families below the poverty line in the poorest 20 per cent of the city*.

However, this is not a totally satisfactory index because a city with a large total proportion of families below the poverty line might have a large percentage below the poverty line in the poorest 20 per cent of the city, even though its poor are highly dispersed geographically relative to the number of poor that exist in the city. An alternative to the above absolute index of class segregation is a relative index of *the ratio of the percentage of families below the poverty line in the poorest 20 per cent of the city to the percentage of families below the poverty line in the whole city*. A ratio of 1 means that there is no residential segregation of poor people at all.

The sample of cities

It was decided to include in the analysis all Standard Metropolitan Statistical Areas (SMSAs) in the United States at the time of the 1970 Census. To qualify as a SMSA, a county or group of counties must contain an urban centre of at least 50,000 inhabitants. Today, UCR are available for all but a few of the smallest SMSAs. Lopez-Rey estimates that UCR coverage increased from 40 per cent of the total United States population living in SMSAs in 1944 to 97 per cent in 1966.[16]

Average annual crime rates for each SMSA were calculated over the seven-year period from 1967 to 1973.[17] It is inadequate to base crime rates only on data from the year of the census since in some of the smaller cities the number of homicides in one year is too small for the calculation of rates. Complete census information on class segregation, complete UCR information on all index offences for each of the seven years, and complete comparability for SMSA boundaries for the two sources of data were available for 167 of the 243 SMSAs. Twenty-six other SMSAs were also included for which crime data was missing for one or two of the seven years on some offences. In these cases crime rates were averaged over five or six years for the offences involved.

The correlation between crime and lower-class segregation

Table 8.1 presents the correlations among UCR-index crime rates and the two alternative indices of lower-class residential segregation for the 193 United States cities. The percentage who were below the poverty line in the poorest 20 per cent of the city was strongly correlated with homicide, rape, aggravated assault and burglary rates. But this relationship did not exist for robbery, grand-larceny and auto-theft rates. All offence rates, including the latter three, were significantly correlated with the ratio of the percentage below the poverty line in the poorest 20 per cent of the city, to the percentage below the poverty line in the whole city.

Thus, the more a city tends to segregate its poor into slums, the higher its crime rate tends to be. Although this conclusion is strongly supported by the correlations, it is possible that these correlations are spuriously high, so appropriate controls must be introduced.

Control variables

There are a variety of interpretations of why lower-class residential segregation is positively correlated with crime rates for cities. It could be argued that class segregation is more pronounced in large cities, and that large cities have high crime rates. Morgan[18] has demonstrated recently that city size was positively correlated with the residential

Table 8.1 *Correlations between UCR index crime rates and two indices of lower-class residential segregation for 193 United States cities*

Segregation index		Homicide	Rape	Robbery	Aggravated assault	Burglary	Grand larceny	Auto theft
% poor in poorest 20% of city	r	·542	·278	·053	·482	·193	·052	·038
	F	80·364[2]	16·153[2]	·540	58·314[2]	7·475[1]	·527	·285
Ratio of % poor in poorest 20% of city to % poor in whole city	r	·254	·333	·419	·247	·252	·250	·315
	F	13·344[2]	24·087[2]	41·003[2]	12·551[2]	13·121[2]	12·823[2]	21·275[2]

[1] p < ·01.
[2] p < ·001.

segregation of classes, and the present data showed a correlation of ·265 between SMSA population and the second of the two segregation indices employed here.[19] And since it is a long-established criminological finding that larger cities have higher crime rates,[20] city size should be controlled in examining the correlation between class segregation and crime.

Another variable which has been found to introduce confounding in analyses of UCR is whether cities are in the South of the United States or not. Cultural traditions which sanction the use of interpersonal violence to settle disputes have been suggested as the reason for the higher homicide and assault rates consistently found in Southern cities.[21] For the present data, not only was violent crime more common in Southern cities, but Southern cities also scored much higher on the first of the two indices of the residential segregation of classes. Consequently a South versus non-South variable was used as a control. Cities were designated as Southern if they were in one of the states defined as Southern by the United States Census.

The percentage of the population of a city which is non-white is the variable which has probably been most consistently found to be strongly related to city crime statistics in the United States.[22] For the present data, per cent white was clearly negatively correlated with all crime indices and both class-segregation indices. It was therefore necessary to control for this variable.

The extent of poverty or income inequality in a city is another variable which has been found by a number of studies to be strongly related to crime.[23] In chapter 11, a study is reported in which four indices of poverty and income inequality are evaluated, in order to determine which is the best predictor of crime rates. The four indices are: percentage below the poverty line in the city, the average income of the poorest 20 per cent of the city's population, the difference between the median income for the city and the average income of the poorest 20 per cent of the city's population, and the percentage of the population earning less than half the median income. The best predictor of crime rates was found to be the difference between the median income and the average income of the poorest 20 per cent. This was therefore used as the income-inequality control.

In summary, on the basis of both the evidence from previous research on inter-city crime-rate comparisons, and the evidence from intercorrelations on the data under discussion here, the variables regarded as most in need of control are city size, the South versus non-South dichotomy, per cent white, and income inequality. It is clearly impossible to control for all possible confounding variables. However, considerable care has been taken in this study to examine the literature to ensure that those variables found most likely to involve a confounding influence are controlled.

Another different kind of variable considered for control was the average population of the census tracts in the poorest 20 per cent of the city. If it is the case that poverty is located in fairly small pockets in the city, a city which has poor census tracts relatively small in size has a greater chance of having poor tracts which are entirely within these small pockets. A city with larger census tracts would have to include wealthier areas surrounding the poor pockets in their poor tracts. Thus an artifactual negative association between the average population of poor tracts and the per cent poor in the poorest 20 per cent of the city is possible. However, when it was found that there was in fact a small *positive* correlation between these two variables (·145), it was considered unnecessary to control for the former.

The regression models

Multiple-linear-regression models were set up to examine the effect of lower-class segregation on crime rates while controlling for SMSA population, South versus non-South, per cent white, and income inequality. For each index crime, a control model was set up with the only predictors being the four control variables. A second model, consisting of the four control variables plus one of the indices of lower-class segregation, was then set up. By subtracting the amount of variance in crime rates explained by the control model, from the amount explained by the second model, we find how much of the variance in crime rates was explained by lower-class segregation, over and above the variance which class segregation shared with the four control variables.

The predictor variables for each of the three regression models being employed here are listed in Table 8.2. The variance explained by each model, for each index crime rate as a criterion, is listed in Table 8.3. F-tests were calculated to ascertain whether the lower-class segregation models explained significantly more variance than the control models.

The complete stepwise multiple-linear-regression results for the control and lower-class segregation models are reproduced in the author's PhD dissertation.

It can be seen from Table 8.3 that lower-class segregation was still

Table 8.2 *Predictors for the three regression models*

Control model	Lower-class segregation Model I	Lower-class segregation Model II
SMSA population	SMSA population	SMSA population
South–non-South	South–non-South	South–non-South
Per cent white	Per cent white	Per cent white
Income inequality	Income inequality	Income inequality
	Per cent below the poverty line in the poorest 20 per cent of the city	Ratio of the per cent below the poverty line in the poorest 20 per cent of the city, to the per cent below the poverty line in the whole city

significantly associated with crime rates for four of the seven index crimes in the case of both of the lower-class segregation indices. All but one of the seven index crime rates—auto theft—were significantly related to at least one of the lower-class segregation indices.

However, even where lower-class segregation accounted for a significant amount of variance over and above that explained by the control variables, the additional variance involved was at most only 4 per cent. This contrasts with as much as 29 per cent explained before the variance accounted for by the control variables was partialled out. Nevertheless, it is still an open question as to how much of the variance partialled out by the control model is attributable to a causal association between lower-class segregation and crime. Introducing the controls may have been justified because the only reason that lower-class segregation bears a strong first-order correlation with crime is that cities with a high degree of lower-class segregation are also large cities, Southern cities, black cities, and cities with an unequal distribution of income. On the other hand, it may be that one of the most important reasons that large, Southern, black cities with an unequal distribution of income have high crime rates is that they tend to be cities which warehouse their poor into slums. As Goldberger points out:

> The whole point of multiple regression . . . is to try to isolate the effects of the individual regressors, by 'controlling' on the others. Still, when orthogonality is absent, the concept of the contribution of an individual regressor remains inherently ambiguous.[24]

Table 8.3 *Variance explained for each index crime rate by control and lower-class segregation models, and F-ratios for the difference between the variance explained by the lower-class segregation models and the control model*

	R^2 control model	R^2 segregation model I	R^2 increase	F for increase	R^2 segregation model II	R^2 increase	F for increase
Homicide	·6685	·6692	·0007	·405	·6789	·0104	6·139[2]
Rape	·2785	·3177	·0392	10·838[2]	·2941	·0156	4·157[1]
Robbery	·5852	·5853	·0001	·042	·6007	·0155	7·347[2]
Aggravated assault	·4137	·4281	·0144	4·766[1]	·4314	·0177	5·898[1]
Burglary	·1345	·1601	·0256	5·768[1]	·1455	·0110	2·425
Grand larceny	·1166	·1562	·0396	8·866[2]	·1240	·0074	1·596
Auto theft	·2365	·2415	·0050	1·246	·2472	·0107	2·702

[1] p < ·05.
[2] p < ·01.

In view of this ambiguity, the finding that all of the crime indices except auto theft were significantly related to at least one of the lower-class-segregation indices, after the variance explained by the control variables had been partialled out, can be interpreted as some support for the inter-city prediction. However, the results do not point to class segregation as the single predictor of note, since the amount of unique variance explained by this variable, over and beyond that explained by the control variables, is small.

One can only speculate as to why auto theft was the odd one out. It is possible that car theft is an offence peculiarly the outcome of an impulsive feeling of relative deprivation through being exposed to the automotive affluence of the middle class. Hence, a situation in which lower-class people live in close proximity to middle-class people driving flashy cars might simultaneously increase the opportunities, and the covetous motivation, for auto theft among the deprived.

Chapter 9

Class-mix: conclusions and policies

Summary of findings

On the basis of opportunity theory, it was hypothesized that to encourage lower-class people to live in lower-class areas is to encourage
people with a strong predisposition to crime to live in areas where
there is every chance that they will have opportunities to express that
predisposition. Thus it was suggested that policies to discourage class
segregation would reduce crime. However, there is an alternative prediction: that when lower-class youth live in middle-class areas, they
experience community tension and norm conflict, which, in fact,
increases their criminality.

To test which prediction is more consistent with the evidence, the
results of seven different studies of class-mix and crime have been
analysed — three studies of officially recorded delinquency, one limited
study of adult crime, two studies of self-reported delinquency, and one
examination of Uniform Crime Reports. From none of these studies
was there any support for the norm-conflict prediction that greater
class-mix would increase crime, and that lower-class youth living in
middle-class areas would have higher delinquency rates than lower-class
youth living in lower-class areas.

The re-analysis of Reiss and Rhodes's study of official delinquency
among 9,238 high-school students in Nashville clearly supported the
contrary hypothesis that the impact on delinquency of being lower class
is greatest for youth living in lower-class areas. The Brisbane study of
Court records, on a much larger sample of serious delinquents, strongly
supported the same conclusion. However, Matsumoto's Tokyo study
supported neither the norm-conflict nor the opportunity-theory predictions. Delinquency rates for lower-class boys did not vary by social
class of area. Further investigation is necessary to establish whether

170

the opportunity-theory prediction applies only in cities with Western class structures.

Consistent with the opportunity-theory prediction, McDonald's self-report study found social class of area to have a stronger negative effect on the delinquency of lower-class boys than on middle-class boys. However, a more adequate test by self-report interviews on a random sample of Brisbane youth provided only weak support for the opportunity-theory prediction. Although there was a tendency for the impact on delinquency of being lower class to be greater for youth living in lower-class areas than for youth living in high- or medium-class areas, this tendency was neither strong nor consistent, and in only one of a number of comparisons did it reach statistical significance.

Baldwin, Bottoms and Walker's examination of adult crime rates in different areas of Sheffield failed to support the opportunity-theory prediction. The study is of limited value for this purpose, however, because it is restricted to a comparison between crime rates for skilled manual workers versus semi- and unskilled workers.

Weak to moderate support was provided for the inter-city prediction of the opportunity-theory formulation by an analysis of United States Uniform Crime Reports. There was a strong tendency for cities with a high degree of segregation of lower-class people into slums to have relatively high crime rates. When this relationship was re-examined controlling for city size, South–non-South, per cent white, and income inequality, eight of the fourteen relationships between lower-class segregation indices and crime rates remained statistically significant. After the variance accounted for by the control variables had been partialled out, only small proportions of the variance in crime rates were explained by lower-class residential segregation. While this constitutes only very moderate support for the inter-city prediction, it is possible, even probable, given the multicollinearity among predictors, that some of the substantial variance in crime rates partialled out by the control variables could be explained by a direct causal relationship between lower-class segregation and city crime rates. Thus, the partialling out of as much as 68 per cent of the variance by the control model makes this a very conservative test of the strength of the relationship between class segregation and crime.

Together, these studies lend some support in Western societies for the predictions that the impact on crime of being lower class is greater for those living in lower-class areas than for the inhabitants of middle-class areas, and that cities which segregate their poor have higher crime rates. Excluding the Japanese study, from Western sources we have two studies which give strong support to the opportunity-theory prediction, one study, rather inadequate for the purpose, which fails to support it and three which give weak to moderate support. Therefore, policies which result in fewer lower-class people living in predominantly lower-class areas might be granted some efficacy for crime reduction.

However, to embark on a crime-reduction strategy of encouraging class-mix on the strength of these findings would be premature. The support found for the association between class-mix and crime is far from unequivocal, and the need for further evidence is obvious.

Class-mix policies

The desirability of greater class-mix, and the most effective policies for achieving it, are issues which are beyond the scope of this book. The decision as to whether greater class-mix would be a worthy goal depends on many more important considerations than crime reduction. This book, however, is limited exclusively to considering the effect of class-mix on crime.

Nevertheless, it must be demonstrated, at least, that policies exist which could be used for reducing crime through overcoming class segregation. It could be contended that even if greater class-mix would reduce crime, there are no feasible ways of achieving greater class-mix other than by forcibly uprooting lower-class people from slum environments. Appendix I is devoted to demonstrating that such a contention is nonsense. It is shown that a wide diversity of policies exist which can be used (and often already are) for fostering class-mix, and which do not involve the forced relocation of people.

If it were the case that forced residential mobility were the only way of overcoming class segregation, then there would be little chance for crime reduction through class-mixing. Certainly, forced residential mobility can itself be a cause of crime.[1] However, it is shown in Appendix I that the factors which maintain lower-class residential segregation involve much more force and limitation of free residential choice for lower-class people than do class-mix policies. Exclusionary practices are used to prevent lower-class people from moving into middle-class areas. The fact is that most lower-class people who live in slums are forced to do so through a variety of circumstances. These circumstances could be attenuated by a strategy for encouraging class-mix, which would widen freedom of residential choice, and decrease residential mobility.

As well as detailing many of the specific policies which would be available to the social planner who wished to undertake such a class-mix strategy, Appendix I demonstrates that governments are continually making decisions which (often unintentionally) have dramatic consequences for the residential mix of classes.

The effect of class-mix is therefore not a question with no practical-policy ramifications. Moreover, even if the effect of class segregation on crime is only moderate, it is important to consider the implications of this for public policy, since there is some evidence which points to the likelihood that class segregation in our cities will increase in decades to come.[2]

The complexity of policy implementation

The relationship between lower-class residential segregation and crime may be particularly intractable because it is partly self-reinforcing. The Griers warn that 'Crime and violence are among the greatest deterrents to affluent families who prefer to live in central areas.'[3] And Bailey[4] has used South Austin in Chicago as a case study to illustrate how there is a downward spiral: as blacks invade the area, crime increases; and as crime increases, 'respectable citizens' are advised by the police to 'move to a safer area'.

To confront the full complexity of class-mix policies is beyond the scope of this book. It should at least be pointed out that there are various levels of class-mix. Apart from total intermixing versus total segregation, there is the possibility of small clusters (say twenty dwellings) of homogeneous class composition being scattered amongst other clusters of different class levels. Thus we have a kind of heterogeneity at a macro level, with homogeneity at a micro level. Jones suggests that 'This may combine some of the benefits of both homogeneity and heterogeneity.'[5] Alternatively, it may give us the worst of both worlds. Certainly the gross analysis of class-mix and crime undertaken in this book needs to be taken to a more advanced stage, in which the effects on crime of different kinds of class-mix are separately analysed.

Showing that greater class-mix is associated with less crime does not necessarily mean that policies to increase class-mix will reduce crime. For one thing, establishing an association is a necessary—but not a sufficient—condition for demonstrating causality. There is no graceful movement from criminological-research findings to policy implications about crime prevention.[6] The social planner must cope with monstrous complexities and a host of specific problems which are unique to each intervention programme.

Of particular concern is how public opinion reacts to the class-mix policy. Gibbens and Ahrenfeldt have outlined just one of many possible adverse public-opinion reactions to a class-mix programme.[7]

> Social class differences and potential animosities may be inflamed
> by building a slum-clearance estate in the midst of a middle-class
> area of a city. The 'estate boys' are blamed for all the delinquency
> in the area, and feel the need to keep up a vendetta of provocation
> against their 'stuffy' neighbours.

As pointed out in chapter 3, many communities which suffer from conditions objectively criminogenic evolve successful adaptations to control crime. Any intervention programme runs the risk of disrupting these evolved social-control mechanisms. It often happens that a programme which sets out to change the objective criminogenic conditions in a community has very little effect in changing those objective conditions, but has considerable effect in tearing down the delicate social fabric of adaptive controls which keeps crime within reasonable limits.

Of special concern with slum dispersal is the question of whether cultural dispersal is being effected as well. As shown in chapter 4, it can often be the case that social cohesion, and therefore social control, is strongest when the integrity of a cultural group is maintained intact. I am not supporting the conspiracy theories of some Negro activists in the United States, who claim that slum dispersal is a conscious plot by whites to divide and rule, which amounts to cultural genocide. However, before slum dispersal is undertaken as a policy to reduce crime in a specific situation, there needs to be a long hard look at whether what is being dispersed is a disorganized slum or a viable ethnic enclave which exercises effective community control.

Conclusion

Firm guidelines cannot be set down as to when class-mix policies will be effective in reducing crime and when not. So many of the complexities are situation-specific. What needs to be carried out is a separate qualitative evaluation of the likely effects of any class-mix policy proposal on social control and public opinion among the people specifically affected by the proposal.

It can be said, however, that class-mix policies are particularly unlikely to reduce crime when they involve force or uprooting people. The violent backlash to the enforced bussing to obtain integrated schools in Boston is an instance of what can happen if unlike groups are forced against their will to integrate.

Finally, if analysis of the relationship between class-mix and crime is to proceed further, what is needed is a longitudinal evaluation of the effects on crime of systematically implementing policies such as those discussed in Appendix I.

Part III

Chapter 10

Rethinking the distribution of crime among classes

Introduction

This chapter moves into that area long ignored by empirical criminologists—white-collar crime. There is little empirical evidence on the nature of white-collar crime because the powerful tend to make it difficult for criminologists to study their abuses. Given this dearth of empirical research, the present chapter is necessarily more speculative than the remainder of the book. However, to ignore white-collar crime in analyses of class and crime, as most criminologists have tended to do, is to submit to class-biased selectivity. In the area of class and crime the scholar must be especially wary of the danger that 'the more measurable tends to drive out the more important.'[1]

On the basis of a vast volume of empirical evidence, the following conclusions were reached at the end of chapter 2.

1 Lower-class adults commit those types of crime which are usually handled by the police at a higher rate than middle-class adults.
2 Adults living in lower-class areas commit those types of crime which are usually handled by the police at a higher rate than adults who live in middle-class areas.
3 Lower-class juveniles commit crime at a higher rate than middle-class juveniles.
4 Juveniles living in lower-class areas commit crime at a higher rate than juveniles living in middle-class areas.

In this chapter, further consideration is given to the first of these four conclusions. Specifically, consideration is given to how this conclusion might change if crimes not usually handled by the police were included. The reader will recall that crimes not normally handled by the police and/or which normally go unpunished are included in the definition of crime adopted throughout this work. Crime refers to any offence against persons or property punishable by law.

In this chapter, through investigating white-collar crime, the paradoxes inherent in traditional criminological theory on class and crime are exposed. After revealing these paradoxes, an attempt is made at a theoretical resolution of them.

The volume of white-collar crime

It is commonplace in criminology to read of how police and criminal-court records of crime, which demonstrate disproportionate lower-class criminality, ignore so much crime committed by middle-class people in the course of their occupations. Sutherland[2] called these offences white-collar crimes. His seminal work on white-collar crime included the startling finding that the 70 largest corporations in the United States had a total of 980 convictions recorded against them in various civil and criminal courts up to 1949. Sutherland cited a great deal of evidence to illustrate the extent of white-collar crime, including the following.

> The financial cost of white-collar crime is probably several times as great as the financial cost of all the crimes which are customarily regarded as the 'crime problem'. An officer of a chain grocery store in one year embezzled $600,000, which was six times as much as the annual losses from five hundred burglaries and robberies of the stores in that chain. Public enemies numbered one to six secured $130,000 by burglary and robbery in 1938, while the sum stolen by Krueger is estimated at $250,000,000, or nearly two thousand times as much. The New York *Times* in 1931 reported four cases of embezzlement in the United States with a loss of more than a million dollars each and a combined loss of nine million dollars. Although a million-dollar burglar or robber is practically unheard of, these million-dollar embezzlers are small-fry among white-collar criminals. The estimated loss to investors in one investment trust from 1929 to 1935 was $580,000,000.[3]

Sutherland was not the first to demonstrate the extent of white-collar crime. As early as 1895 Barrett[4] showed that banks lost more from fraud and embezzlement than from bank robberies. More recently the President's Commission on Law Enforcement and Administration of Justice concluded on the basis of its investigations of white-collar crime that:

180

There is no knowing how much embezzlement, fraud, loan sharking, and other forms of thievery from individuals or commercial institutions there is, or how much price-rigging, tax evasion, bribery, graft, and other forms of thievery from the public at large there is. The Commission's studies indicate that the economic losses those crimes cause are far greater than those caused by the three index crimes against property.[5]

It is not only the amount of money misappropriated in white-collar offences that is so great; it is also the number of white-collar offences, and the number of white-collar offenders, which are so high when compared with the volume of lower-class crime. For example, elsewhere[6] this author has presented the results of a study of used-car fraud in Brisbane in 1974. It was estimated from observations of mileage readings in this study that, on over a third of used cars sold in Brisbane, odometers are tampered with to show a lower mileage reading. Most of these offences involve defrauding the consumer of some hundreds of dollars on the sale price of a used car. Since there are more than 200,000 used cars sold in Queensland each year, one could estimate an annual number of offences in the state of the order of 70,000. This is almost as many as the total number of 80,181 offences of all types[7] reported to the Queensland police during the 1974–5 financial year, with 25,572 arrests. None of these reported offences or arrests was for the turning back of odometer readings. Although there were no prosecutions for criminal fraud, there were seven prosecutions for civil fraud under the Consumer Affairs Act for tampering with odometers.

It is shown in the used-car study that it is mostly proprietors, managers, or other middle-class people, who are responsible for used-car fraud, and there are normally several offenders who break the law for any one offence. Thus, on the basis of this single small area of commercial fraud, one could propose the converse of the conclusion from police statistics that more offences and offenders are lower class than middle class.

Frank Pearce[8] estimates that the $284 million worth of goods burgled in 1965 in the United States represents only 3 per cent of the estimated annual profits of organized crime, and only 3 per cent of the money gained by the tax frauds of the wealthiest 1 per cent of the population in 1957. Pearce claims that officials of the Federal Trade Commission itself have estimated that in 1968, when robbery netted $55 million, *detectable* business fraud netted in excess of $1 billion.[9] The president of the United States Fidelity and Guaranty Co. has written in the *FBI Law Enforcement Bulletin* that the losses to employers from white-collar embezzlement exceed those caused by fire in substantial measure.[10]

One could go on and on detailing this kind of evidence, and more extensive examinations of the evidence are available elsewhere.[11] It is beyond dispute that if all offences punishable by law are included in the analysis, then middle-class adults commit more and bigger offences against property than lower-class adults. The volume of offences such as price-fixing, commercial fraud, misrepresentation in advertising, bribery to get contracts, illegal stock-market manipulations, misapplication of funds, and illegal practices in receiverships and bankruptcies, is so great as to invert traditional conceptions of the social-class distribution of crime.

The relationship between class and adult crimes against the person is perhaps not quite so clear cut. For intentional and direct interpersonal violence (offences such as homicide and assault) lower-class people certainly exhibit higher rates. Nevertheless, many white-collar crimes have the effect of doing injury to persons, but such an effect is not directly intended, nor is it brought about in face-to-face violent encounters. A manufacturer may merchandize a car safety belt or an electric heater which violates statutory safety requirements, and this may be responsible for hundreds of deaths.[12] The manufacturer does not intend to kill hundreds of people by breaking safety laws; he does so to increase his profits.

It is undoubtedly true that more people are killed and injured as a result of law-breaking by middle-class than by lower-class people. In the United States this century, 100,000 men have died in coal mines.[13] Swartz[14] argues that many of these lives could have been saved if mine safety laws were not so flagrantly violated. He points out that in more than half the coal mines in Kentucky, the concentration of coal dust was found to exceed the legal limit, in some cases by a factor of ten.

Carson's[15] analysis of violations of factory legislation by 200 randomly selected firms in England revealed that over the four and a half year period of the study, 3,800 offences were recorded against the firms. The vast majority of these offences involved failure to meet mandatory requirements for the physical safety of workers, including 1,451 offences of 'lack of secure and properly adjusted fencing at dangerous machinery', and 460 offences of 'inadequate precautions against fire and explosion'.

The way large numbers of people are killed and injured by misrepresentation in the advertising of drugs has been well documented.[16]

One could go on to document the thousands of injuries and deaths caused annually by violations of automobile safety standards, pure-food legislation, pollution laws, and various other laws to protect the safety of consumers and workers. Geis concludes, after referring to findings such as those of Ralph Nader on the building of potentially lethal cars, and electrocution deaths caused by the failure to enforce legal safety requirements on electrical equipment, that 'support clearly seems to exist for the view that acts reasonably defined as white-collar crime result in more deaths and physical injuries than acts which have been traditionally defined as murder and manslaughter.'[17]

If violations of international law, such as torture of prisoners of war, illegal acts of aggression, and genocide are counted as crimes,[18] then the extent of crimes against the person by powerful people increases in magnitude to the point at which other crimes pale into insignificance.[19] Since the order-giver rather than the order-taker is generally culpable under international law, most violations are classifiable as white-collar crimes.[20] With genocide we have seen a million Armenians slaughtered by a deliberate policy of the Turkish government for almost five years; a similar number of Biafrans slaughtered in Nigeria; and even a greater number of Jews slaughtered in Europe. Lest we think that Anglo-Saxon stock has not been involved in such slaughter, we should look through history, from the slaughter of 27,000 people by Richard the Lion-hearted at Accra, to the killing of 150,000 Vietnamese civilians in recent times. One is also reminded of the activities of the CIA (such as engineering the 1954 coup in Guatemala)[21] which have been illegal both under national and international law.

Clearly there are considerable qualitative differences among the types of white-collar crime discussed above. Rather than being instigated by a single person, violations of international law can in a sense be socially instigated. Bloch and Geis[22] distinguish among three types of white-collar crime: committed by independent individuals (e.g. lawyers); committed by employees against corporations or governments (e.g. embezzlement); and committed by policy-making officers of corporations (e.g. price-fixing, misrepresentation, labour exploitation). Very different kinds of explanations are required for these differing types of white-collar crime. However, we shall see that one explanation which these disparate types of crime share in common is that they all arise out of the abuse of the power inherent in white-collar occupational roles. Moreover, the fact that diverse types of behaviours punishable by law are included under the white-collar crime rubric should not obscure the fact demonstrated here that middle-class people engage in more acts punishable by law, with more serious consequences, than do lower-class people.

Implications of the extent of white-collar crime

Even excluding violations of international law from the analysis, it is indisputable that middle-class adults perpetrate more crimes than lower-class adults, and engage in crimes that involve larger amounts of money and more widespread injury to persons. By removing the selectivity of examining only those offences usually handled by the police, and examining instead all offences against persons and property punishable by law, the class distribution of adult crime is reversed.

Certainly this conclusion is based on unsystematic evidence, and it could perhaps also be pointed out that there is a great deal of petty occupational crime by blue-collar workers, which is also ignored by the police. Nevertheless, the conclusion that lower-class adults do not engage in more crime than middle-class adults seems inescapable, given the enormous unmeasurable volume of white-collar crimes such as commercial misrepresentation.

The implications of this seem dramatic. How can reducing poverty reduce crime when the evidence is that (for adults at least) poor people are not more criminal? How can reducing powerlessness reduce crime when it is the powerful people, not the powerless, who engage in most crime?

Most traditional criminological theory has been based on the assumption of greater criminality among the lower class. Yet, since Sutherland, there has been a nagging awareness among criminologists that white-collar crime challenges this assumption. The majority have managed to repress the realization that practically the entire elaborate superstructure of criminological theory with which they work could be toppled because it is based on the shaky foundation of greater lower-class criminality. Ignoring this shaky foundation, criminologists continue to produce PhD dissertations on whether the greater criminality of the lower class can be explained by low self-esteem, or whether the greater criminality of the lower class can be explained by labelling and the like.

In chapter 3 of this work, a large number of theories were discussed which attempted to explain why lower-class people engage in more crime than middle-class people. Does the finding that lower-class adults do not engage in more crime than middle-class adults negate everything written in chapter 3 as utter nonsense?

Only the social-class explanations of juvenile crime are spared from this embarrassing confrontation with empirical reality. Since juveniles are too young to occupy white-collar occupational roles, they are not given opportunities to engage in white-collar crime. The conclusion that lower-class juveniles engage in more crime than middle-class juveniles therefore survives unchallenged.

How is white-collar crime different?

Since Sutherland first challenged the assumptions of class-based criminology, various attempts have been made to rationalize why white-collar crime is not 'real' crime.[23] It is pointed out that most so-called white-collar crimes are not prosecuted under the criminal code but under various civil codes — they are torts rather than crimes.

It is argued that civil wrongs are qualitatively different phenomena from crimes, because a demonstration of 'wilful intent' is not normally necessary,[24] defendants are not given the protections built into criminal proceedings, and apprehension is not normally carried out by the police. However, as Newman[25] has pointed out, although most violations of civil regulations are not *tried* in criminal courts, they are mostly *triable* in criminal courts. In Braithwaite's study of used-car fraud[26] it is shown that although the wilful turning-back of mileage readings on used cars could be prosecuted in Queensland as criminal fraud, on the rare occasions when prosecution is invoked, it is for civil fraud under the Consumer Affairs Act.

The decisions to prosecute white-collar crimes as torts rather than crimes are less often a reflection of the legal quality of the act than of the desire not to criminalize the illegal activities of 'respectable citizens'. The fact that decisions to invoke civil rather than criminal sanctions are partly indicative of class bias is reflected in Sutherland's[27] finding that of 438 successful actions under the Sherman Antitrust Law, 27 per cent of business prosecutions were criminal, compared with 71 per cent of trade union prosecutions.

Consequently, to limit the definition of crime to only those offences normally prosecuted under the criminal code and normally handled by the police is to engage in selectivity so contaminated by class bias as to invalidate any analysis of class and crime. It is very difficult to sustain the argument that white-collar crime is different from other crimes on legal grounds. As Newman points out: 'Furthermore, white collar crimes are far from arbitrary; most of them have roots in the common law and merely reflect an application of common law principles regarding theft, fraud, and the like to modern social and economic institutions.'[28]

It has also been argued that white-collar crimes are different because they are not regarded by society as serious crimes. White-collar crimes are serious, if seriousness is measured objectively in terms of the amounts of property lost and the extent of injuries to persons. Nevertheless, there is probably some truth in the assertion that the public are more leniently disposed to a man who embezzles a certain amount of money than to the man who burgles the same amount. Yet this difference in the perception of seriousness is a quantitative rather than a qualitative difference, and could hardly be used to lay the basis for distinguishing the two types of crime.

Moreover, there is some evidence that public disapproval of white-collar crime can be quite strong. Wilson and Brown[29] found that in a list of twenty-five crimes, the seriousness rating of the offence 'A company director fraudulently misappropriates $300,000 from company funds' was exceeded only by murder, rape, armed bank robbery, and pushing drugs. Rated as less serious were assault resulting in hospitalization, unlawful killing through reckless driving, and even 'an adult male sexually assaulting a young child'. Reed and Reed[30] showed empirically that only a very few people felt that any of a wide variety of white-collar crimes should go unpunished.[31]

Burgess suggests that white-collar crimes are not really crimes because white-collar criminals do not think of themselves as criminals — and 'a criminal is a person who regards himself as a criminal.'[32] While it may be true that white-collar criminals are less likely to construe their illegalities as criminal, there are many lower-class offenders who similarly do not regard themselves as criminals, and many white-collar offenders who do, so that subjective perceptions can hardly be used to distinguish white-collar from other kinds of crime.

Having failed to establish a clear basis for differentiating between white-collar and other crimes, we return to Sutherland's original definition of white-collar crime as 'a crime committed by a person of respectability and high social status in the course of his occupation'.[33] This definition is fairly widely accepted, and has been only occasionally modified over the years. The *Dictionary of Criminology* defines a white-collar criminal as 'A person with high socio-economic status who violates the laws designed to regulate his occupational activities.'[34]

From examining these definitions, I propose that the essence of what distinguishes white-collar crime from other crimes is that, unlike other crimes, *white-collar crime involves the illegal abuse of the power inherent in white-collar occupational roles.* If this is taken, by definition, as the key difference between white-collar and other crime, we can begin to make progress in understanding the paradox of the social-class distribution of crime.

Explaining the paradox

White-collar crime is in fact fundamentally different from other crime because it involves the illegal abuse of the power inherent in white-collar occupational roles. One is bound to look for different explanations, on the one hand, for the bank robber who takes the initiative to create a situation where he can rob a bank, and, on the other, for the bank manager who exploits the power inherent in the situation in which he normally finds himself to embezzle from the bank or to defraud customers. White-collar crime is fundamentally different from other crime and requires fundamentally different explanations.

Being incumbent in a position of power in one's occupation opens up a new range of illegitimate opportunities, such as are not available to most people – the power to embezzle, to defraud, to misappropriate, to abuse safety laws, to engage in price-fixing, and so on. It is possible that if lower-class people were exposed to the same vast opportunities for white-collar crime, they too would engage in the large-scale criminality of the powerful.

It is virtually a self-evident proposition that people with power are most likely to commit crimes consisting of the abuse of positions of power. It is therefore suggested that middle-class people commit offences involving the abuse of positions of power at a higher rate than lower-class people; and that lower-class people commit offences which do not involve the abuse of positions of power at a higher rate than middle-class people. The body of theory in chapter 3 can be used to explain why the second proposition should be so, but we need a new body of theory to explain the first proposition.

The theme of the model used here to explain the paradox of the two conflicting social-class distributions of crime is summarized in a somewhat oversimplified way as *too little power and wealth creates problems of living, and this produces crime; too much power corrupts, and this also produces crime.*

Since chapter 3 was devoted to the first half of this proposition, consideration is given in the next section to the theory of how a great deal of power might cause crime. But first we need to summarize and clarify what the new conceptualization of the social-class distribution of crime means in terms of social policy.

The social-class distribution of adult crime is reversed, depending on whether the crime involves the abuse of occupational power or not. Thus to add offences arising, and offences not arising from the exercise of power together, to ascertain an overall distribution of crime across classes, is to calculate a rather meaningless average of two opposite trends. Rendering explicit the interaction in the effect of social class on crime for power versus non-power offences lays the foundation for a clearer policy analysis. If power offences arise because certain people have a great deal of power (trite as that seems), then this kind of crime might be reduced by reducing the power of these people. If non-power offences arise because certain people have so little power and wealth, then this kind of crime might be reduced by increasing their power and wealth. Thus the theory suggests two different solutions for the two different kinds of offences—a more fruitful analysis than that which is built on inducing one solution from a single social-class distribution of crime.

Power and corruption

How does great power predispose people to engage in crime? One answer is simply because great power creates great opportunities to engage in profitable crimes. This is one obvious explanation, and perhaps the one that would be open to least dispute. Indeed, on its own, this simple proposition might be sufficient to sustain the theoretical framework being proposed. Nevertheless, other more elaborate theories have been put forward to explain why power corrupts, and these merit mention.

The assertion that power corrupts has not been solely a radical catch-cry expressed in left-wing journals. The Bible, hardly a left-wing publication, emphasises that 'It is harder for a camel to go through the eye of a needle than for a rich man to enter the Kingdom of God.' When the president of the United States Fidelity and Guaranty Co. writes that a major reason for white-collar crime is that corporations place 'too much trust in key personnel',[35] he is really saying (in jargon acceptable to capitalist ideology) that power corrupts.

Nevertheless, the left-wing proponents of the theory have attracted most attention. Taylor, Walton, and Young, in the first chapter of

Critical Criminology are emphatic about the importance of developing a theory of how power causes crime.

> Radical deviancy theory would not deny the importance of indicating that the rule-makers are consistently the major group of rule-breakers in such a society . . . radical deviancy theory has the task of demonstrating analytically that such rule-breaking is institutionalized, regular and widespread amongst the powerful, that it is a given result of the structural position occupied by powerful men — whether they be Cabinet ministers, judges, captains of industry or policemen.[36]

Curiously, no effort is made in the remainder of the book to undertake the task of demonstrating how crime by the powerful is the 'result of the structural position occupied by powerful men'. Some effort will be made here to rectify this omission by briefly summarizing available theory on the question.

Sorokin and Lunden in *Power and Morality* put forward a rich variety of arguments for how power corrupts. They suggest that power has an 'intoxicating' effect on men, and that holders of positions above the mass of ordinary men come to believe that they are indeed above the moral and legal precepts that govern those beneath them:[37] 'Power generates in them (and in others, too) a belief that they are the chosen and anointed who are far above the ruled population and its common-heard moral and legal precepts of right and wrong, good and evil.'

To those who make the rules, the arbitrariness of the rules is more transparent than it is to ordinary men. The second factor which Sorokin and Lunden emphasize is that control of the means of violence and diplomatic functions demands cynical machinations, lying and killing. Such behaviour, they argue, is inseparable from the business of ruling vast organizations. As the most extreme example they state that 'No war activity can be carried on without throwing to the wind, at least temporarily, all the moral imperatives.'[38] In the diplomatic dealings of powerful people, a great deal is at stake. Inevitably then:

> Diplomatic operations exhibit a peculiar mixture of honest and dishonest techniques of influence by organized spying, skillful lies, hypocritical assurances, false promises, threats and bribes, semi-rational persuasions, limited coercion, cloak and dagger actions, cynical machinations, and other morally doubtful procedures.[39]

A third 'criminalizing element' which Sorokin and Lunden point to is the incessant bombardment of the powerful by a multitude of contradictory interests and pressures. These conflicting pressures, which vary in strength up to the point of bribery, can generate a sense of moral confusion, ambiguity and arbitrariness in ethical thought. To get into positions of power most men depend on the favours of others. Favours given, demand favours returned. When the favour to be returned involves an action which the incumbent of power views as morally wrong, he faces a dilemma — to be a hypocrite or an ingrate.

Finally, Sorokin and Lunden emphasize social selection. The chances of people getting into positions of power are greater if they are 'callous, unsympathetic, aggressively selfish, hypocritical, dishonest, and cynical manipulators of human relations'.[40] There is a little evidence that the kind of social selection to which Sorokin and Lunden refer does operate. Geis[41] indicates that in the General Electric Corporation, the selecting out of people with moral scruples against price-fixing from senior positions where price-fixing was demanded was one factor which made possible the famous heavy-electrical-equipment conspiracy. However, interviews with used-car sales managers conducted by the present author[42] suggested that the social-selection effect operating in their industry may be more complex. While many of those who were 'too soft' or 'too honest' were weeded out in the competitive struggle, there was also some suggestion that used-car dealers who were overly dishonest were ultimately driven out of business by their bad reputation. Perhaps this was because, although relatively powerful, the used-car dealer does not have quite enough power to enable him to cover up his abuses completely.

Michael Maccoby's[43] psychiatric interviews with a sample of senior executives of American corporations led him to a similar conclusion about the effects of social selection. In addition to studying men right at the top, the presidents and vice-presidents, Maccoby tested and interviewed many middle managers. He concluded that those who do not make it to the top often show signs of being either too humanistic to exercise power with sufficient ruthlessness or too sadistic to exercise it with finesse.

It is not unreasonable to propose that the more wealth and power is associated with positions at the top of the social structure, the more likely that men will be tempted to use exploitative, dishonest means to achieve those positions. More adequate empirical evidence is needed to ascertain whether the concentration of power has this criminogenic consequence. Sorokin and Lunden also hint that even when power is inherited, the exploitative personality which resulted in the initial social selection into power is passed on in the socialization of the future generations of inheritors. In this regard, they quote John D. Rockefeller's statement on the education of his sons: 'I cheat my boys every chance I get; I want them sharp. I trade with the boys and skin them and just beat them every time I can. I want to make them sharp.'

Much has been written about the pressures to break the law on powerful people in capitalist enterprises. The author's used-car study includes a lengthy examination of how the competitive struggle to maintain profits in the used-car industry fosters crime. In oligopolistic markets, crime no doubt takes on a different quality from the highly competitive used-car industry—perhaps taking on a more collusive rather than a throat-cutting quality. Both industry structures—the competitive and the oligopolistic—can be corrupting when the commitment to profits (or growth or risk minimization) becomes so strong as to override legal and ethical considerations. Virtue soon evaporates when the new manager in a corporation finds that when a clash arises between the goal of maximum profit and another goal, such as minimizing pollution, standing up for the latter will do harm for his future in the corporation. Through this kind of experience, managers can quickly acquire blunted moral sensibilities, and if they do not, they can be quickly selected out in the race for the most powerful positions.

C. Wright Mills[44] calls it 'structural immorality' when manipulative advertising techniques, creating false needs, cutting corners with the safety of workers, promoting military expenditure to maintain profits, and the like, are part of the normal role enactment of managerial positions. One cannot survive without fading personal integrity.

The empirical evidence that it is overcommitment to the profit motive which is responsible for much white-collar crime is not limited to the author's used-car study. Lane[45] also reports that most of the managers he interviewed suggested the 'fast buck' as the key motivation in the criminality of their peers. Quinney[46] found that pharmacists who had a 'business' rather than a 'professional' role orientation—that is one that placed greatest emphasis on profit-making—were those who committed by far the most violations of prescription laws. Among American college students, Rosenberg[47] found that those most dedicated to 'monetary success' and 'getting ahead in the world' were those most likely to argue that they 'can't afford to be squeamish about the means' they choose. With lower-class crime we were dealing with crime arising from failure to achieve the success goals of the capitalist system; here we are dealing with crime arising from an unprincipled overcommitment to these success goals among people who are in fact successful.

In Spencer's study of thirty imprisoned white-collar offenders, he

191

reported that 'There was, moreover, a kind of ruthless determination in some of the sample to achieve their goal.'[48] Whereas most incarcerated offenders have an occupational history of downward social mobility, Spencer's white-collar offenders were clearly characterized by upward social mobility. One is tempted to go well beyond the data, and suggest that whereas lower-class criminals are the victims of the capitalist system, white-collar criminals are the birds of prey of the capitalist system. Or, in more explicitly polemical terms, crime among the lower class arises partly from the fact that they are exploited; crime among the upper classes arises partly from the fact that they exploit.

The blurred distinction between astute business practice and white-collar crime is a characteristic of capitalist enterprises which fosters those rationalizations of white-collar criminality which Cressey[49] found to be so important. One of Australia's top industrial spies justified his work in a press interview thus: 'But as far as I'm concerned, we don't consider ourselves criminals. We work for businessmen or companies. What goes on in these companies—which is quite legal—is as bad as anything we do.'[50]

In the business world there appears to be so little difference among what is legal and ethical, what is legal but unethical, and what is illegal and unethical, that there is fertile ground for this kind of rationalization.[51]

For the top administrator, it is a habit to do whatever he chooses without limitations being put upon his power. Perhaps unconsciously, he expects that this will continue to be the case when, in the exercise of his power, he crosses the fine line of illegality. Metaphorically, in his role as a top administrator he is a law unto himself, and the metaphor becomes literal when he crosses that indistinct line of illegality.

Studies by Martin,[52] Robin[53] and Feest[54] have shown that only a small proportion of offences committed by people in private enterprise, and discovered by their companies, is reported to the police. Even when offences do great harm to a company, they are likely to be kept quiet for fear that the disclosures would shake the confidence of shareholders, employees and customers. In this way, the nature of the capitalist system makes large-scale white-collar crime a fairly safe activity to engage in. The good name of the firm is worth far more than prosecuting the offender and attracting ugly publicity. Moreover, since every company has something to hide, the danger in prosecuting senior employees is that the offender will 'know where the body is buried' and dig it up in court.

A participant observation study by Campanis[55] of managers in a firm he called 'Expansionetics' generated a number of ideas about the way managerial roles in capitalist enterprises generate normlessness. He argued that managers suffer a kind of exhaustion from continually fighting moral ambiguities.

> Managers are not paid to develop new moral codes, but to make the existing slippery ones work. They are not initiators of norms themselves, but reactors to them. The pure model of the middleman applies; he buys anything from anyone and in turn sells it to any buyer who will pay the price. A spirit of not belonging to oneself is found here, making it hard to live by the motto 'To thine own self be true', because the self is irrelevant. In short, managers are normless in carrying out their official duties as mainsprings, key cogs, and kingpins of the system.[56]

Campanis also argued that capitalism puts managers into a situation in which they are isolated from other managers by a competitive struggle, so that a moral consensus, which is the basis for any form of social control, is not able to develop.

> When managers try to work out moral formulas, they have no models because top management is out of view, because other managers are physically and sentimentally distant from one another, and because no agency exists to enforce moral stances. Sentimental distance is also partly the result of having been trained to value struggling alone in careers.[57]

This view was strongly supported by the results of the used-car study, where it was reported by managers that they did not get together to enforce a code of ethics because they felt so sentimentally isolated from other managers who were engaging in cut-throat competition with them.

Campanis made the further point that the constant change in modern organizations, arising from changing markets, changing technology, and expansion, means that the stable basis for the evolution of a normative structure is lacking. The manager finds himself 'confused and frustrated by situations having no firm precedent' and forever groping in a 'moral fog'. In all of these situations, the manager must confront anew the question of to whom he is responsible – the shareholders, the workers under him, his managerial peers, his superior, the consumer. Campanis concluded that in response to all of these ambiguities, 'The temptation is to suggest that, basically, they feel responsible to no one or no thing.'[58]

193

Summarizing the conclusions of the Campanis study, we may say that capitalism puts the powerful into a position in which they are isolated from other managers so that a moral consensus cannot develop; where they can be true to the system but not to themselves; where placing personal morality above expedience invokes negative sanctions; where the changing situational nature of problems would make the application of absolute ethics problematic anyhow; and where, even if a moral commitment were possible, there would be ambiguity as to whom the commitment should be owed.

Blau, in *Exchange and Power in Social Life*,[59] put forward a theory of power not limited in application to managerial positions in capitalist enterprises. He expressed the point which is most crucial to the present analysis:

> Generally since the significance of social approval for the stable organization of collective effort puts restraints on the exercise of power, exploitation and oppression are less pronounced and less prevalent within the context for organizations than outside them. The power conflicts that are most severe and fought out most ruthlessly are those between groups, organizations, and entire nations. . . .[60]

In other words, Blau says that the closer organizationally the person who exercises power is to the persons over whom he exercises the power, the more he depends upon the social approval and co-operation of those people, and therefore the less likely he will be to do something exploitative, which will endanger that co-operation and approval. For example, the on-site foreman cannot be as exploitative towards his workers as can the general manager, since achieving his goals and maintaining his power depends more on the social approval of the workers than is the case for the general manager. It follows that to the extent that power is exerted by people close to the impact of decisions (that is, to the extent that power is decentralized), the abuse of power will be less frequent.

In societies in which there is great inequality of wealth and power, it is not only the dominance of the powerful which contributes to crime, but also the subordination of the powerless. Scholars who set out to explain why there is so much more government corruption in Third World countries almost always refer to the vast gulf in status, wealth and power between the government official and the people he most typically serves. This, of course, is only one of many reasons for the high levels of corruption in developing economies, but it is one of the more important. When the poverty-stricken peasant approaches a bureaucrat who may be a university graduate, he is suppliant, attempting to appease a powerful man whose ways he cannot fathom. In contrast, the more equal power relationships which apply between public servants and citizens in developed countries often result in interactions with the citizen demanding his rights. The Third World bureaucrat can extort bribes with impunity because of the powerlessness of the people he 'serves'.

The theory of how power corrupts has been neglected in criminology, so it has been possible to present only a limited treatment of isolated explanations. Moreover, empirical investigations of white-collar crime have been so sparse as to render proper evaluations of these explanations impossible.

Too much power, too little power

A deal of theory has now been reviewed which predicts that having a very great amount of power results in high involvement in one kind of crime, while chapter 3 reviewed theories which suggest that having very little power causes crime of another kind. Therefore a redistribution of power, so that there are fewer people at either extreme of the power continuum, would be expected to reduce crime of both types.

The reader may have incorrectly inferred from this that those of intermediate levels of social class are the least criminal of all socialclass groups. The theoretical framework presented here analyses two conceptually and empirically different types of crime — power and non-power offences (or white-collar and other crimes). Those who commit power offences are those least likely to commit non-power offences, so to treat them as both part of the one unidimensional construct would be absurd. Power offences increase as an accelerating function of power, and non-power offences decrease as a function of power.[61] Therefore, the theoretical framework predicts that people of intermediate levels of social class will commit fewer power offences than those of higher social class, but more non-power offences than those of higher social class. Conversely, they will commit more power offences than those of lower social class, and fewer non-power offences than those of lower social class.

Policies to redistribute power

If limiting the power of the powerful will reduce white-collar crime, then how might this be achieved? The purpose of this section is to discuss briefly some of the policies which might be used to achieve a redistribution of power.

Lieberman[62] argues that public bureaucracies are given too much discretionary power. Policies are exposed to wide public scrutiny at the legislative stage but virtually none at the executive stage. And most of the real power resides in the executive, since legislation typically permits the public service unbridled discretion in implementation. Lieberman then argues, that the legislature should draw firm guidelines to limit the ways in which the public service can exercise its power, and that these guidelines should then be open to public scrutiny. He points to vague blank-cheque statutes—such as 'disloyalty to the state', 'immoral behaviour', 'public nuisance', 'suppression of Communism'—as being particularly corrupting of the public service: 'Discretion can, of course, breed contempt for the law directly. Someone long accustomed to having his own way is not often inclined to permit others to test his actions, and malice works best under cover.'[63]

In addition to the above, Lieberman suggests open government, making all government reports open to the public, a Freedom of Information Act, unlimited freedom of the press, Ombudsmen, welfare-rights officers, limitations on police power, and the right for citizens and interest groups to challenge government decisions in court. As a check on the arbitrary exercise of power, he rather idealistically argues that a convention should be established whereby reasons accompany all official decisions. But his principal suggestion is that the government should publish guidelines for the implementation and enforcement of legislation because publication would '(1) force the government to write guidelines, (2) would greatly simplify the task of monitoring the government to see that it abides by its own regulations, and (3) would inform people what the law really is.'[64]

Lieberman also makes the point that dispersal of power can be just as encouraging of crime as concentration of power, if in the dispersion of power there is a diffusion of responsibility. For example, in the way power is decentralized in the armed services, with responsibility running up a chain of command, it is possible to locate part of the blame for a criminal act at every point in the chain, so that the full weight of criminal responsibility never comes down on anyone. On a broader scale, Maddox has made the same criticism of the method of decentralizing

196

governmental power which is Australian Federalism.[65]

> In a federal system of government where people are held in utter confusion as to which Government is responsible for what area of administration, there is ample opportunity for hidden economic interests and local tyrannies to amass and consolidate power almost unnoticed.

The message is that if one wishes to reduce crime by redistributing power, one must do it in a way that incorporates clear and unambiguous rules for determining accountability.

It is notable that the principal suggestions for limiting white-collar crime put forward by people with wide experience investigating business crime often involve limiting the power of those in positions with great illegitimate opportunities. Jeffery, president of the United States Fidelity and Guaranty Co., has made these suggestions about limiting crime against companies by senior employees.

> It is generally good practice not to put one employee in complete charge of any one phase of administration where accounts receivable or payable are involved; for example, a credit manager should not be permitted to receive money and at the same time be in charge of posting and deposits and the preparation, mailing and distribution of monthly statements to clients.
>
> Cashiers or accountants should prepare the reports of receipts, which should be verified by someone else who would be responsible in turn for deposits and the posting of ledgers. Shipping and receiving, whenever possible, should be two completely separate operations and the responsibility of at least two individuals, each having to submit individual returns to the accounting office.
>
> Collection receipts and bank deposits should be verified as to their individual entries and not as to totals only. And this should be done by someone other than the person preparing the statement. Also, the monthly itemized statement should be verified with the bank.
>
> Spot-checks, audits, and inventories should be made at frequent intervals, and on a surprise basis, and the results compared with other results that will corroborate them or prove them in error.[66]

Jaspan and Black, who also draw upon wide practical experience investigating white-collar crime, have made the following suggestions about how the limitation of the power of senior employees is central to a system of preventive management against white-collar crime.

Protection from fraud demands that work be subdivided so that
no employee has complete control over any record or transaction.
Responsibility is allocated so that, without duplicate effort, an
employee verifies the work of others in the normal course of his
duties. This check and review which is inherent in any good system
of control, greatly reduces the possibility that errors or fraud remain undetected for inordinate periods. The following are examples
of how dual responsibility is maintained over typical work functions:

1. The preparation of the payroll and the payment of employees
is handled by two different groups of employees, especially if
employees are paid in cash.
2. Persons who maintain inventory records are not allowed to participate in the actual physical counting of inventory.
3. Persons approving payments on invoices or customers' bills are
not allowed to participate in the actual receiving of supplies or
merchandise.
4. Shipping records are matched against billings to customers by
employees in two different departments.
5. Wrappers in stores compare items and prices on saleschecks made
out by salesclerks with the items to be wrapped.
6. Employees in sensitive positions are rotated from one job to
another. For example, branch managers should be periodically
shifted to different stores, warehouses, sales offices. Truck drivers'
routes can be changed. Factory foremen and supervisors should
be rotated. Payroll and accounts receivable clerks who handle
alphabetical listings should be shifted from say a, b listings to e, f
listings.[67]

Most of these measures are geared to catching people at middle levels
of management, who offend against the company itself. But there is
clear evidence that the amounts of money involved in these kinds of
offences increase dramatically as we move higher up in the status hierarchy of the firm.[68] And what of the corporation men who do not
offend against the corporation, but on behalf of the corporation? The
measures suggested by Jeffery and Jaspan and Black are yet another
illustration, in the area of white-collar crime, of Daniel Drew's cobweb:
'Law is like a cobweb; it's made for flies and the smaller kinds of
insects, so to speak, but lets the big bumblebees break through.'[69]

Writers such as Sharpston[70] have suggested that the real solution to
corruption is to change radically the situation in which power is concentrated in a few hands. Industrial democracy or workers' control is

seen as the ultimate solution. Not only will workers' control structure out of the organization many opportunities for crime formerly enjoyed by managers, it will also increase scrutiny of the behaviour of managers in any areas where the opportunity for illegitimate discretion remains. Coates has expressed this argument clearly.

> If the accounts of every firm are available to the inspection of its shop-stewards, they will pose the constant risk that cheating will be unmasked, as the workmen's inspectorate checks the books against the facts of its daily industrial experience. This is not to say that every shop-steward is an accountant. But every steward can call on the resources of his union and professional advice can be procured. . . . Thus, the union grapevine provides an intelligence network, gratis, which no Government department could possibly begin to rival.[71]

This belief is perhaps one of the reasons why the British Labour government in 1969 announced as part of its industrial policy that workers' councils should have access to company records.

Redistributing power may not be enough. Several of the theories discussed in the last section indicate that it is not simply inequality of power which is criminogenic, but inequality of power in the context of a capitalist system. As Schur said, 'The inclination to try to take advantage of the other party is, in a sense, built into the structure of our kind of social order.'[72] It is when that inclination is combined with a position of power which offers a multitude of lucrative opportunities for putting the inclination into effect that the greatest crime results.

It is also questionable whether the theories presented in the last section about the criminogenic effect of the concentration of power in the hands of a few individuals would apply to companies as well as individuals. Certainly, with the evolution of capitalism, we have seen the emergence of bigger and bigger multinational corporations, and certainly, as corporations have become bigger, spectacular new kinds of crime associated with oligopoly have gained prominence — such as price-fixing, gaining political favours by huge donations to political campaigns, and masterminding coups to overthrow governments. The big-corporation — big-crime theory is also supported by Lane's[73] study of 275 shoe-manufacturing firms in the United States, which found that larger companies were much more likely to be convicted under the trade-practice laws than smaller firms. However, Lane found no clear trend for larger companies to be more frequent violators of labour-relations laws.

The reason one hesitates to suggest that decentralizing power into smaller companies would reduce crime is that when an industry is dominated by large firms, competition does seem to be less intense than in a situation in which there are a large number of small firms. As the used-car study suggests, it is the 'dog-eat-dog' attitude, which the dealers blame on intense competition, that is responsible for so much white-collar crime.

Summary and conclusions

A vast quantity of unsystematic evidence on the widespread nature of white-collar crime, which is not recorded in normal police and court statistics, leads to the rejection of the hypothesis that lower-class adults engage in more law-violating behaviour than middle-class adults.

The only basis on which white-collar crime can be clearly distinguished from other crime is that white-collar crime involves the illegal abuse of the power inherent in white-collar occupational roles. White-collar offences are therefore called power offences, and other offences non-power offences. Power offences are fundamentally different in nature from non-power offences and require fundamentally different explanations. The social-class distribution of crime is reversed depending on whether we are considering offences that involve the abuse of occupational power or not. Theoretical development in criminology can be enhanced by conceiving of the existence of two separate social-class distributions of crime, with two separate sets of explanations for the opposite trends in these distributions.

The body of theory used to explain the paradox of the two conflicting social class distributions of crime is summarized, in a somewhat oversimplified way, as follows: *Too little power and wealth creates problems of living, and this produces crime of one type: too much power corrupts, and this produces crime of another type.*

Most fundamentally, it is hypothesized that being in a position of great power in one's occupation causes crime, because it opens up a new range of illegitimate opportunities such as are not available to ordinary people—the opportunity to embezzle, to defraud, to misappropriate, to abuse safety laws, to engage in price-fixing, and to engage in the whole range of illegalities made possible by participation in complicated paper transactions involving great sums of money.

A variety of other theories as to how power corrupts was presented. Although the proposition that power corrupts has been one that has appealed to conservative and radical thinkers alike, and one that has not attracted counter-theories to retort that power is not corrupting, the theory of power and corruption is not based on a substantial body of empirical evidence. There is a great need for empirical investigation, in so far as it is possible, to compare the extent of white-collar crime in organizations in which power is centralized versus decentralized.

If having extremely little power and wealth explains non-power offences, and having extremely great power explains power offences, then a redistribution of power so that there are fewer people at either extreme would have efficacy for reducing both types of crime.

A variety of policies for the redistribution or limitation of power have been considered, ranging from workers' control of industry to Jaspan and Black's more mundane techniques for preventive management by establishing dual responsibility over work functions. Lieberman has made the important point that dispersion of power can actually encourage crime, if in the dispersion of power there is a diffusion of accountability. Any policy to reduce white-collar crime by dispersing power must incorporate clear and unambiguous rules for determining accountability.

Chapter 11

Alternative levels of analysis for determining whether inequality contributes to crime

Introduction

In exploring the hypothesis that poverty causes crime, most criminologists have examined whether poor people engage in more crime than the non-poor. This chapter considers alternative approaches for investigating the effect of economic inequality on crime.

The last chapter served to demonstrate that inequality may be responsible for more than just the crime of the lower class. This point will now be taken further, by arguing that much of the delinquency committed by middle-class adolescents is explained by the anticipation of economic failure among middle-class adolescents who are doing badly at school. Hirschi has clearly expressed this conclusion.

> For example, children doing well in high school and children who expect to graduate from college are much less likely to be delinquent, regardless of their father's occupation or education. Put another way, the evidence is clear on one point: the lower the social class the child will enter, the more likely he is to be delinquent, regardless of his class of origin.[1]

Stinchcombe[2] has been the dominant advocate of the view that it is the social-class futures of adolescents, rather than their social-class origins, which are most critical to delinquency. In fact, Stinchcombe found that middle-class students who failed at school engaged in more rebellious behaviour at school than lower-class school failures. Studies by Kelly and Balch,[3] Kelly,[4] Frease,[5] and Polk et al.[6] have all provided moderate to weak support for the hypothesis that middle-class school failures engage in more delinquent behaviour than lower-class school failures.[7] However, Polk[8] failed to find any support for the hypothesis — academically unsuccessful lower-class boys were found to be just as delinquent as academically unsuccessful middle-class boys.

It is suggested that since middle-class children have higher aspirations for success, middle-class school failures suffer from a greater discrepancy between aspirations and expectations of occupational success. And it has been shown that children with a great discrepancy between aspirations and expectations are more likely than others to engage in delinquency.[9] Moreover, the middle-class school failure possibly becomes more delinquent because he is under greater pressure to succeed than the lower-class school failure, and because he has further to fall through downward occupational mobility.[10]

Thus we can see how inequality might explain considerable middle-class, as well as lower-class, delinquency. A system which has economic failure built into it fosters crime not only among those who have objectively failed. There are also the pathological consequences of anticipation of failure, fear of failure, and failure to achieve the success aspired to or expected.

Clearly then, there is merit in moving to alternative levels of analysis, where, instead of merely ascertaining whether the lower class are more criminal than the middle class, we examine the effect of conditions of inequality on crime rates for all class groups combined. We could explore whether nations with a high degree of economic inequality have higher crime rates than more egalitarian societies. Within nations, do cities which have a wide gap between the rich and the poor have higher crime rates than cities with a more equal income structure? Instead of this kind of cross-sectional analysis, we could move to a time-series level of analysis. As the degree of inequality in nations or cities increases or decreases, does the crime rate concomitantly increase and decrease? A final level of analysis is to observe directly whether policies to reduce inequality reduce crime.

Each of these alternative levels of analysis will be considered in turn. By adopting ecological levels of analysis, we are not perpetrating the ecological fallacy of inferring individual behaviour from ecological correlations. Ultimately, the theoretical unit of interest in this policy analysis is not individual poverty, but societal inequality.

International comparisons

At the time of this research there had been no international comparisons of crime rates to ascertain whether nations with high levels of income inequality experience high crime rates. The only study approaching this had been Pavin's study of 'Economic Determinants of Political Unrest',[11] in which political unrest was measured by the death rate from violent outbursts such as riots, bombings, and assassinations. Pavin's regression analysis showed that income inequality was a contributor to political unrest.

At first consideration, an international comparison of crime rates seems impossible. The problem is that definitions of crime vary from nation to nation, as do levels of detection and recording procedures. Burglary, assault, rape, larceny, robbery, and even automobile theft all mean different things under different criminal justice systems. Nevertheless, one offence which has a fairly uniform meaning across nations is homicide. And it can probably be safely assumed that the reportability of homicide is fairly uniformly high in all countries. In chapter 8, it was pointed out that, in the United States, homicide had higher reportability and seriousness ratings than any other offence type.

The United Nations records homicide rates for all nations annually in its causes of death statistics.[12] In comparing such rates, some concern is warranted over the way in which unlawful killing by the use of a motor vehicle is classified in different countries. Inconsistent classification of such offences as homicide in some countries, but not in others, would account for the major proportion of variance in homicide rates. However, the chief statistician of the World Health Organization has stated, in a personal communication, that in United Nations statistics, unlawful killing by the use of a motor vehicle is definitely excluded in all cases from homicide rates. He concluded: 'It seems that cross-national comparisons in homicide mortality are relatively reliable.'

Homicide is defined in the United Nations statistics as including 'all injuries inflicted by another person with intent to injure or kill, by any means'. This does leave the grave problem that the homicide statistics include deaths resulting from war. The precaution of excluding nations from the analysis with homicide rates that may include significant numbers of deaths resulting from operations of war is one that has not always been taken in the literature.[13] In the present analysis, the list of nations to be included was submitted independently to two historians, and when there was suspicion that significant numbers of deaths because of operations of war (including civil war) might have occurred in a given nation during the year of concern, then that nation was dropped from the analysis. Three nations were excluded for this reason.

International comparisons of levels of inequality of wealth are also problematic because of the lack of comparability in procedures for the recording of financial data. However, a very thorough study by Lydall[14] was able to derive an ordinal scaling of the twenty-five nations for which adequate records were available on inequality of earnings. The fact that only ordinal scaling, and not interval scaling, was possible is indicative both of the inadequacy of the data, and of the fact that Lydall was not prepared to read more into the data than was reasonable. To obtain even a simple rank ordering of nations on earnings inequality, Lydall had to make a large number of assumptions which he carefully detailed.

Inequality in the distribution of income earned through employment, upon which Lydall's rank ordering is based, is only a part (though a large part) of inequality of wealth. There is also the level of inequality generated by social security transfers, inheritance, land speculation, and so on.

After the exclusion of nations for which inadequate data were available for either homicide rates or earnings inequality, twenty nations remain. These nations are listed in Table 11.1. The year for which Lydall's inequality data are available is matched with the nearest year for which adequate homicide data are available.

A Spearman rank correlation was calculated between the two variables, yielding a coefficient of ·41, which is significant at the ·05 level for a one-tailed test. Thus, nations with high levels of earnings inequality did have higher homicide rates.

Although the relationship seems a clear-cut one, it must be remembered that cross-national comparison is a hazardous business at the best of times. It is anyone's guess as to what extreme differences among nations on cultural, demographic, and economic variables might intervene between earnings inequality and homicide rate. This finding should therefore be interpreted cautiously as a failure to disconfirm the hypothesis that earnings inequality is positively correlated with crime.

It has already been pointed out that earnings data exclude social-security income—such as pensions, unemployment benefits, aid to the handicapped, or to children in low-income families. Since social-security expenditure is so directly the result of government policy, its impact on crime is of special importance. The United States Social Security Administration has collated cross-national comparisons on the ratio of social-security expenditure to gross national product.[15] This permits adequate data on social-security expenditure and homicide rates for twenty-nine nations (see Table 11.2).

The Spearman rank correlation between social-security expenditure (as a percentage of GNP) and homicide rate was —·50, which is significant at the ·005 level. That is, nations which spent the highest proportions

205

Table 11.1 *Rank ordering of 20 nations on earnings inequality and homicide rates*

Nation	Earnings inequality rank	Homicide rate rank	Year of inequality data	Year of homicide data
Mexico	1	1	1960	1960
Chile	2	6	1964	1964
India	3	3·5=	1958-9	1960
Japan	4	5	1955	1955
France	5	15	1963	1963
Finland	6	3·5=	1960	1960
Netherlands	7	20	1959	1959
Austria	8	12=	1957	1959
United States	9	2	1959	1959
Belgium	10	18=	1964	1964
Canada	11	10	1960-1	1961
Germany (FR)	12	14	1957	1958
Poland	13	9	1960	1960
Sweden	14	18=	1959	1960
United Kingdom	15	16	1960-1	1961
Denmark	16	18=	1956	1958
Australia	17	8	1959-60	1960
Hungary	18	7	1964	1964
New Zealand	19	12=	1960-1	1961
Czechoslovakia	20	12=	1964	1964

of their GNP on social security had the lowest homicide rates. Since we are dealing with a somewhat larger sample of nations than was the case with the analysis of earnings inequality, it is possible to introduce one crude control for GNP.

Nations were dichotomized into high GNP and low GNP, in the

Table 11.2 *Rank ordering of 29 nations on the 1960 ratio of social security expenditure to GNP, and homicide rates*

Nation	Social security expenditure rank	Homicide rate rank
West Germany	1	16=
Czechoslovakia	2	16=
Belgium	3·5=	22=
Luxemburg	3·5=	24·5=
Austria	5	14
France	6	10
New Zealand	7	16=
Italy	8	12·5=
Sweden	9	22=
Denmark	10	26·5=
Great Britain	11·5=	22=
Netherlands	11·5=	28
Norway	13	26·5=
Finland	14	7
Ireland	15	29
Poland	16	8
Canada	17	12·5=
Australia	18	11
Switzerland	19	18·5=
Iceland	20	24·5=
United States	21	5
Panama	22	4
Portugal	23	18·5=
Japan	24	9
Ceylon	25	6
Spain	26	20
South Africa	27	2
Guatemala	28	1
Turkey	29	3

same way that Cutwright[16] has done on 1960 figures. The high-GNP nations were Australia, Belgium, Canada, Denmark, France, Great Britain, Luxemburg, Netherlands, New Zealand, Norway, Sweden, Switzerland, United States, and West Germany. The low-GNP nations were Austria, Ceylon, Czechoslovakia, Finland, Guatemala, Iceland, Ireland, Italy, Japan, Panama, Poland, Portugal, South Africa, Spain, and Turkey.

Among the fourteen high-GNP nations, the rank correlation between social security expenditure and homicide rate was —·27, which is not significant at the ·05 level. Among the fifteen low-GNP nations, the rank correlation between social-security expenditure and homicide rate was —·48, which also just fails to attain statistical significance. The reliability of these coefficients is clearly very low because of the small sample sizes when the original sample is split in two. Nevertheless, they suggest the possibility that part of the strong negative correlation between social-security expenditure and homicide rate may be attributable to confounding introduced by GNP.

Subsequent to the completion of the present analysis another investigation of international variations in crime rates has been published. In a comparison of twenty-seven countries, Krohn[17] has confirmed the finding of the present study that homicide rates are positively correlated with levels of income inequality. This remained true, even after controlling for GNP per capita and energy consumption per capita. However, when Interpol statistics were used to make international comparisons among 'property crime rates' and 'total crime rates' negative correlations with inequality emerged both before and after controls were introduced. Suffice it to say that we can have no idea as to what 'total crime rates' and 'property crime rates' mean in countries with vastly disparate cultures, legal codes, attitudes towards property, levels of community reporting of crime, and levels of police efficiency. Cross-national comparisons on such unexplicated indices are worse than meaningless.

International comparisons permit only crude analyses based on small samples of nations, with little scope for entering appropriate controls. It will be seen in the next section how more sophisticated analyses are possible with a shift from the international level of analysis to an intra-national or inter-city level of analysis.

Intranational comparisons

Some of the confounding introduced by comparing crime rates for countries of vastly different cultural backgrounds can be avoided by comparing cities or states within countries. Cultural differences loom less large when comparisons are being made among cities within a single country to ascertain whether those with higher levels of inequality of wealth have higher crime rates.

The earliest attempt at such a comparison was by Wiers,[18] in which delinquency rates for nineteen Michigan counties were compared, mostly on the basis of juvenile-court data from the 1920s. A variety of indices of economic inequality, poverty, and unemployment produced conflicting results on the question of whether counties with a more equal distribution of wealth had lower delinquency rates. Correlations varied from strongly positive to strongly negative, depending on which index was being used.

The next major attempt was Fleisher's[19] widely quoted study. In an analysis of delinquency in 101 United States cities, Fleisher found a strong tendency for cities with high unemployment rates to have high delinquency rates. Unemployment rate could be regarded as a crude index of inequality of wealth, since a high unemployment rate is normally associated with considerable poverty, and therefore economic inequality. Fleisher also found through his regression analysis that income inequality, as measured by the interquartile range of the income distribution, was positively associated with delinquency. These conclusions remain valid, even though much of Fleisher's work has fallen into disrepute because of his misuse of regression coefficients to estimate what percentage reduction in delinquency would result from given economic policies.

Other studies have produced ambiguous results on the effect of unemployment rate on crime. Schuessler and Slatin[20] reported almost zero correlations between rates for UCR-index crimes and unemployment levels for 101 United States cities in 1950. The same analysis for 133 cities on 1960 data produced clear positive correlations only for robbery and auto theft.

On 1960 data for 135 United States cities, Singell[21] established a clear positive association between unemployment rates and total crime rates. A multiple-regression analysis on 1970 violent-crime rates for 103 United States cities by Spector[22] found no association between city violent crime and unemployment rates. However, for 1970 burglary and robbery rates in 222 cities, Danziger found positive correlations with both unemployment levels and degree of income inequality as measured by the Gini coefficient.[23] With respect to unemployment, these results contradict earlier findings on 1960 cross-sectional data by Danziger and Wheeler[24] that unemployment levels showed no significant relationship with US city burglary and robbery rates. Nevertheless, for their 1960 analysis, an income-inequality index still did have the largest positive elasticity in all regressions. Another study by Hemley and McPheters found that while the metropolitan unemployment rate had a pronounced positive effect on the rates of burglary and larceny, it did not significantly affect the robbery rate.[25]

Cho[26] also analysed UCR-index crimes in 1970 for the forty-nine largest cities in the United States. Income inequality was a significant positive predictor only for aggravated assault and grand larceny. However, since there were a large number of predictors in Cho's multiple regression, and a great deal of multicollinearity among economic predictors, this finding does not deserve to be interpreted as failure to support consistently the association between inequality and crime. Similarly, the finding that percentage of the population below the poverty line was significantly positively associated only with rape among the seven index crimes does not permit an unequivocal interpretation. Indeed McCarthy *et al.*[27] reported clear correlations between the percentage of the population of cities below the poverty line and violent crime from both the 1950 and 1970 Uniform Crime Reports. From 1970 UCR for 840 cities, Flango and Sherbenou[28] found a rather vaguely defined 'poverty' factor to be one of the two best predictors of rates for serious crimes, robbery, aggravated assault, burglary, and auto theft. On 1967 UCR for United States cities with a population of over 100,000, Booth *et al.*[29] report positive correlations between the percentage of households earning less than $3,000 a year and murder, manslaughter, assault, and burglary rates. However, there was no relationship for rape, robbery, auto theft, and larceny rates.

In Angell's[30] recent study, 'dwelling value spread' was a variable which was, in part, an index of inequality of wealth. Dwelling-value spread is an index of dispersion in the value of dwellings. Surprisingly, dwelling-value spread is listed as having a negative correlation of $-\cdot 30$ with the total UCR crime index in 1970 for 112 cities.

Another recently published study by Ehrlich[31] measured inequality by the percentage of families in each state receiving less than half the median income for the state. This index of inequality showed a positive regression coefficient with crime rates for US states in 1940, 1950, and 1960. The relationship was particularly strong for UCR crimes against property, but less strong for crimes against persons (especially rape and homicide).

A study of city crime in the United States by the Council on Municipal Performance reached conclusions very similar to those reached through the regression analysis in the next section of this chapter.[32] No relationship was found between a high incidence of poverty and a high city rate for reported property crimes. There were positive relationships between poverty and violent crime, and between unemployment rates and both violent and non-violent crime, but none of these was statistically significant. However, there was a statistically significant correlation between both violent and property crime rates and income inequality, as measured by the Gini coefficient. The greater the income inequality in a city, the higher the crime rate. Unfortunately, this study was conducted on only a small sample of cities—the thirty largest in the United States. Its findings are consistent with those of the Danziger and Wheeler study reported above. A study by Loftin and Hill[33] compared homicide rates for 48 US states, and found *both* the Gini index of income inequality, and a structural-poverty index, to be positively related to homicide.

To further add to the confusion provoked by this review, Eberts and Schwirian[34] have found that cities with 'balanced' ratios of wealthy to poor people had lower crime rates than homogeneously poor or homogeneously wealthy cities. Eberts and Schwirian's curvilinear relationship *between* communities has been refuted by an ecological analysis *within* the Melbourne community by Dunstan and Roberts.[35]

In summary, while the evidence tends to favour the conclusion that cities or states with a high degree of economic inequality and/or unemployment have higher crime rates, there have been a number of dissident findings refuting this conclusion. In particular, there are a substantial minority of studies that have failed to show a positive association between crime and unemployment rates, or crime and proportion of people below the poverty line. Significantly though, the literature shows fairly uniform support for a positive association between inequality and crime among those studies which, instead of using an unemployment or poverty index which focuses upon the bottom tail of the income distribution, use a global index of income dispersion such as the Gini coefficient. Unfortunately, none of the above studies has tested the effects of a variety of indices of inequality, while systematically controlling for key predictors of city crime rates. In the next section an attempt is made to redress this lack of a genuinely systematic analysis of different types of inequality and city crime rates.

211

An analysis of inequality and city crime rates

Chapter 8 contained an analysis of average annual crime rates between 1967 and 1973 for 193 United States Standard Metropolitan Statistical Areas (SMSAs). This data will now be used to test the hypothesis that cities with a high level of income inequality have high crime rates.

The following test of the hypothesis is superior to the studies reviewed above, because: it is based on crimes committed over a seven-year period instead of one; it is based on a much larger sample of cities than in most other studies; several alternative indices of inequality are used; and appropriate controls are introduced. It is hoped that such a more adequate examination of the relationship between income inequality and city crime rates will resolve some of the ambiguities from the above findings.

There are different kinds of inequalities in the distribution of income in cities, and different kinds of policies for reducing inequality. Some policies reduce the gap between the rich and the poor, while other policies move a number of people across the gap, thus reducing the number of people who are poor. Changing the tax structure, or introducing guaranteed minimum income, are examples of policies to reduce the gap between the rich and the poor; retraining schemes for the unemployed exemplify efforts to reduce the number who are poor.

Policies to reduce the number who are poor change the income distribution such that there come to be fewer people in the extremely poor category, and more people in the average-income category. Policies to reduce the gap between the rich and the poor change the income distribution such that the income difference between the extremely poor category and the average category comes to be decreased.

For this analysis, separate indices are used for the number who are poor, and for the income gap between the poor and the average-income earner. It is possible that policies which reduce the number of people who are poor leave behind a smaller but more hard-core and desperate group of poor people, whose sense of deprivation is heightened by the realization that they have become a smaller minority deprived of the financial benefits bestowed upon the vast majority of the population. That is, policies to reduce the number of poor might make those who remain poor feel more deprived because they become more exceptional. Therefore, policies which reduce the number who are poor might conceivably decrease the criminality of those who are lifted out of poverty, but increase the criminality of those who are left behind. For this reason, policies to reduce the number who are poor may do less to reduce the overall crime rate than policies whose effects tend more in the direction of reducing the gap between all poor people and the rest of the population.

The number who are poor is measured by the percentage of families in the city who are below the poverty line as defined by the United States Census.[36] This index is open to the criticism that it is an absolute index of poverty, rather than one relative to the income standards of particular cities. It may be how poor one is, compared to the income of other people living in one's city, which causes crime, rather than whether or not one is below the national poverty line. It was therefore decided to have a second index of the number of poor which adopts the suggestion by Fuchs[37] of using *the percentage of families who receive less than half the median income for the city.*

The gap between the poor and the average-income family is indexed by *the difference between the median income for families in the city and the average income of the poorest 20 per cent of families in the city.*[38]

Table 11.3 presents the correlations between UCR-index crime rates and the three indices of income inequality.

Percentage of families below the poverty line and percentage receiving half the median income or less are both significantly related only to homicide and aggravated assault out of the seven offences. The income gap between the poor and the average-income family is significantly positively associated with rape, robbery, burglary, grand-larceny and auto-theft rates.

These relationships are now examined while controlling for SMSA population and whether the city is in the South or not. These two variables form a control model for the multiple-regression analysis which follows. The purpose of this analysis is to ascertain whether regression models of the two control variables plus each income-inequality index in turn account for significantly more of the variance in crime rates than the control variables alone. The reasons for selecting SMSA population and South–non-South as control variables has already been explained in chapter 9. The results of introducing these controls are summarized in Tables 11.4, 11.5, and 11.6.

The implications of the results presented in Tables 11.4 to 11.6[39] are quite dramatic. After controlling for SMSA size and whether the city is in the South or not, there is no evidence whatsoever of a positive association between either index of the proportion of families who are poor and any of the index-crime rates. Of the fourteen relationships examined in Tables 11.4 and 11.5 only one is significant, and this is a

Table 11.3 *Correlations between UCR index crime rates and three indices of income inequality for 193 United States cities*

		Homicide	Rape	Robbery	Aggravated assault	Burglary	Grand larceny	Auto theft
% below poverty line	r	·351	·087	—·121	·310	·049	—·081	—·158
	F	27·154[2]	1·462	2·882	20·505[2]	·459	1·271	4·961
% receiving half the median income or less	r	·255	·087	—·048	·251	·070	·004	—·043
	F	13·411[2]	1·472	·436	12·999[2]	·942	·003	·358
Difference between median income and average income of the poorest 20% of families	r	—·029	·246	·362	—·035	·203	·321	·347
	F	·165	12·421[2]	29·069[2]	·237	8·287[1]	22·110[2]	26·368[2]

[1] $p < ·01$.
[2] $p < ·001$.

Table 11.4 *Variance explained for each index crime rate by the control model and the control model plus the variable percentage below the poverty line*

	R^2 control model[1]	R^2 control model plus % poor	R^2 increase	F for increase
Homicide	·4739	·4742	·0003	·099
Rape	·1576	·1580	·0004	·081
Robbery	·4952	·5137	·0185	7·272[2]
Aggravated assault	·3542	·3543	·0001	·031
Burglary	·0474	·0475	·0001	·035
Grand larceny	·0120	·0190	·0070	1·352
Auto theft	·1676	·1783	·0106	2·472

[1] SMSA population and South–non-South.
[2] $p < ·0.1$.

Table 11.5 *Variance explained for each index crime rate by the control model and the control model plus the variable percentage receiving half the median income or less*

	R^2 control model[1]	R^2 control model plus % receiving half the median income or less	R^2 increase	F for increase
Homicide	·4739	·4750	·0011	·406
Rape	·1576	·1583	·0007	·154
Robbery.	·4952	·4970	·0018	·685
Aggravated assault	·3542	·3593	·0051	1·500
Burglary	·0474	·0486	·0012	·256
Grand larceny	·0120	·0122	·0002	·037
Auto theft	·1676	·1677	·0001	·004

[1] SMSA population and South–non-South.

Table 11.6 *Variance explained for each index crime rate by the control model and the control model plus the variable difference between the median income and the average income of the poorest 20 per cent of families*

	R^2 control model [1]	R^2 control model plus difference between median income and average income of the poorest 20% of families	R^2 increase	F for increase
Homicide	·4739	·4980	·0241	9·160[2]
Rape	·1576	·2329	·0753	18·752[2]
Robbery	·4952	·5616	·0664	28·927[2]
Aggravated assault	·3542	·3659	·0117	3·503
Burglary	·0474	·0996	·0522	11·069[2]
Grand larceny	·0120	·1165	·1045	22·584[2]
Auto theft	·1676	·2332	·0656	16·329[2]

[1] SMSA population and South–non-South.
[2] $p < ·005$.

significant *negative* association between percentage poor and robbery rate. There is consequently no support at all for the hypothesis that cities in which a high proportion of families are poor, either in absolute or relative terms, have high crime rates.

In contrast, there is strong and consistent support for the hypothesis that cities in which there is a wide income gap between poor and average-income families have high rates for all types of crime. In Table 11.6, only aggravated assault has a non-significant positive association with the difference between the median income and the average income of the poorest 20 per cent of families. Even this association is only slightly short of statistical significance at the ·05 level.

The finding that the size of the gap between the average-income earner and poor families is correlated with crime, but not the number who are poor, is of considerable theoretical importance. It may be that, when there are only a small number of poor families in a city, these families feel a far more acute sense of missing out on the benefits of the Great Society than do poor families who are in cities where they are surrounded by many other families in exactly the same plight. Policies that reduce the number of poor people should certainly reduce the propensity to crime of those people lifted out of poverty, but do they at the same time create even greater despair, frustration and criminality amongst those who remain poor?

Anti-poverty policies in most capitalist countries have not often been geared to reducing the gap between the poor and the rest of the community through means such as restructuring the tax system, guaranteed minimum income, higher welfare benefits, and reducing the cost of housing to lower-class people. More often, anti-poverty programmes in nations such as the United States have aimed at reducing the number of people who are poor by helping selected groups of people to acquire occupational skills, to overcome their sense of powerlessness, to lift themselves out of the 'culture of poverty', and the like. The finding that cities with smaller numbers of poor people do not have lower crime rates after controls are introduced, calls into question the efficacy of strategies of this latter type for crime reduction.

Before it is assumed that strategies to reduce the income gap between the poor and the rest of the population do have efficacy for crime reduction, it would be advisable to establish whether the relationship between the income gap and crime remains, when the variance accounted for by the percentage of the city's population which is non-white is partialled out. It may be that the only reason that cities with a big income gap between the poor and the median income have high crime rates is that such cities have a large black population. Table 11.7 summarizes the variance in city crime rates explained by a control model of SMSA population, South–non-South, and percentage white; and this control model plus the income gap between the poor and the median income.

From Table 11.7[40] it can be seen that the income gap between the poor and the median income is significantly positively associated with rates for five of the seven index crimes, even after the variance accounted for by percentage white is partialled out. Even for the two crimes where the relationship is no longer significant, one cannot rule out the possibility of a causal association between the income gap and crime. It may be that one of the reasons cities with a large black population have a high crime rate is that such cities tend to have a large income gap between the poor and the remainder of the population.

Another dimension of income inequality which has often been alluded to as a factor in crime causation by reports such as that of the National Advisory Commission on Criminal Justice Standards and

Table 11.7 *Variance explained for each index crime rate by a new control model (of SMSA population, South–non-South, and percentage white) and this control model plus the variable difference between the median income of families and the average income of the poorest 20% of families*

	R^2 new control model	R^2 control model plus difference between median income and average income of poorest 20% of families	R^2 increase	F for increase
Homicide	·6684	·6685	·0001	·021
Rape	·2440	·2785	·0345	9·101[2]
Robbery	5489	·5852	·0363	16·624[2]
Aggravated assault	·4129	·4137	·0008	·242
Burglary	·1115	·1345	·0230	5·050[1]
Grand larceny	·0262	·1166	·0904	19·445[2]
Auto theft	·1874	·2365	·0491	12·215[2]

[1] $p < ·0.5$.
[2] $p < ·005$.

Goals[41] is the income gap between whites and blacks. This special kind of income inequality is said to be especially criminogenic through festering the wounds of discrimination and exploitation.

Table 11.8 examines whether the difference between the median income of Negro families and the median income of all families adds significantly to the variance explained by a control model consisting of SMSA population, South–non-South, percentage white, and the income gap between the poor and the average-income earner. Cities were excluded from the analysis for which there were fewer than 500 Negro families. This meant that only 175 cities were included in this analysis.

After the variance in crime rates explained by the income gap between the poor and the average-income earner is partialled out, the income gap between blacks and whites is not positively associated with crime. Indeed, in the case of all index crimes, the regression coefficient is negative for the income gap between blacks and whites. In the case of rape and robbery, this negative association is statistically significant. Thus, if anything, after the income gap between the poor and the average-income earner is controlled, the effect of a large income gap between blacks and whites is to decrease crime rather than increase it. We must therefore totally reject the hypothesis that inequality between the races causes special crime problems over and above those caused by the general level of income inequality in the community.

Table 11.8 *Variance explained for each index crime rate by a control model and this control model plus the variable difference between the median income of Negro families and the median income of all families in the city*

	R^2 control model[1]	R^2 control model plus difference between median income of Negroes and median income for whole city	R^2 increase	F for increase
Homicide	·6685	·6698	·0007	·686
Rape	·2785	·3119	·0334	8·181[3]
Robbery	·5852	·5954	·0102	4·257[2]
Aggravated assault	·4137	·4139	·0002	·064
Burglary	·1345	·1508	·0163	3·237
Grand larceny	·1166	·1175	·0009	·183
Auto theft	·2365	·2376	·0011	·251

[1] Control model consists of SMSA population, South–non–South, percentage white, and the income gap between the poor and average-income earner.
[2] $p < ·05$.
[3] $p < ·005$.

It is possible that in cities with a high general level of income inequality, but relative equality between the races, low-income whites become jealous of the relative success of blacks, who they think should be in an economically inferior position to their own, and that this generates an atmosphere of frustration, racial antagonism, and a climate of violence. This is speculative, but it might explain the negative associations between racial inequality and rape and robbery, after the variance explained by general inequality is partialled out.[42]

Further light is cast on the question of racial income inequality by a report on interregional differences in delinquency rates in New Zealand by Boven and O'Neill.[43] Consistent with the above speculation, Boven and O'Neill found in their path analysis that one of the best predictors of white offending rates was the difference in affluence between the white and Maori populations for the regions. In regions for which the affluence differential between whites and Maoris was small, white offending rates were high. At the level of zero-order correlations, there was no significant relationship between racial inequality and total delinquency rate ($r = \cdot19$), but there was a strong negative association between racial inequality and the white delinquency rate ($r = -\cdot52$). It may well be, then, that both in the United States and New Zealand, when the white man sees the coloured man approaching his level of affluence, his own sense of relative deprivation is intensified.

The time-series level of analysis

People who wish to argue the case that poverty causes crime often point to studies such as those by Ross,[44] Singell,[45] Fleisher,[46] Phillips *et al.*[47] and Brenner,[48] or to earlier studies by Bonger,[49] Thomas,[50] Winslow,[51] Van Kleek,[52] Warner,[53] Wiers,[54] and Phelps,[55] which found that crime and delinquency increased during periods of high unemployment. On the other hand, those who choose to argue that poverty does not cause crime point to studies such as those of Parent[56] and Henry and Short[57] which found that crime decreased during periods of economic recession, or to studies such as those of Bogen,[58] Glaser and Rice,[59] and the review by Carr,[60] which concluded that while adult crime might be positively correlated with unemployment, juvenile crime is negatively correlated.

Typical of the latter point of view is the following statement by Gold: 'If poverty were a major provocation to delinquency, one would expect delinquency rates to go up in times of unemployment and depression and down in times of prosperity. In fact, the opposite is true.'[61]

First, such conclusions are not warranted because the evidence is highly conflicting on the question of whether crime and delinquency rates are positively or negatively correlated with recession.[62] Secondly, and more fundamentally, one does not know whether the measures of recession and prosperity used in these studies are in any sense indices of levels of inequality of wealth. Prosperity is not the same thing as equality, nor is recession synonymous with inequality. The indices used in studies of the economic cycle and crime have included wholesale prices, composite business indices, unemployment rates, poverty indices, cotton prices, real wages indices, retail trade, and cost-of-living indices. It is possible that some of these indices are inversely related one to the other, and that not all are genuinely indices of inequality. Periods of low unemployment are often periods of high inflation, and both of these factors in the economy have consequences for levels of equality. Many of the studies of the economic cycle and crime examine the impact of the 1930 Depression on crime rates. Yet Mendershausen[63] has shown that since the Depression hit the highest income groups hardest in dollar terms, the income distribution became more equal during the Depression years.

In the terms of the previous section, it may be that during most recessions, the number who are poor increases, but the gap between the rich and the poor does not. If there is some evidence that crime can decrease when the number of poor increases, then this might be because the poor come to feel less relatively deprived as more and more of the formerly affluent join their ranks. Henry and Short used this kind of interpretation to explain their finding that while the homicide rate for whites increased during recessions, the homicide rate for Negroes decreased. Negroes, they suggest, may feel less discriminated against, less frustrated, and less relatively deprived when they can see so many whites coming down to their level. The landmark time-series analysis of crime rates undertaken by Gurr, Grabosky and Hula[64] also drew on this kind of interpretation. They found that in London, Stockholm and Sydney, throughout the nineteenth century, economic recession was associated with jumps in crime rates; but that in the twentieth century, this trend was reversed, with short-term increases in affluence being associated with increases in crime. In the terms of the theoretical categories used in this book, Gurr *et al.* explain this reversal as a consequence of economic growth causing a reduction in the explanatory power of the reward–cost model, and an increase in the explanatory power of relative deprivation.

More likely, though, we are faced with evidence of two different socioeconomic processes. In times of want, the people most affected steal out of necessity. In the economic slumps of the nineteenth century, so many people were pushed so close to the margin of sur-

221

vival that the gains of theft frequently outweighed the attendant risks. The other process is one of increased opportunity coupled with increased resentment by the young and the poor of others' affluence. When many are poor and few are rich, it is probably easier to accept one's own poverty and more difficult to alleviate it by theft than when one is a shrinking minority of the poor.[65]

The only methodologically sound time-series study which has con-trasted the effects of clearly defined alternative indices of income inequality on crime rates in the United States is the regression analysis for the period 1949–70 by Danziger and Wheeler.[66] They found, after controlling for several other variables, that during periods when either the absolute or the relative income gap between rich and poor increased crime rates increased. As in many other studies, however, no significant relationship was found over the period between unemployment levels and crime rates. More work such as that of Danziger and Wheeler needs to be done to establish whether the contradictory evidence from time-series studies can be reconciled in the same way as the cross-sectional evidence has been reconciled in this book — that while the number who are poor is not an ecological correlate of crime, the income gap between the rich and poor is.

Studies of the economic cycle and crime must confront major methodological problems. Definitions of crime categories often change over time, as do levels of police surveillance and the punitiveness of the ideologies prevalent in criminal-justice systems. There is the tendency pointed out by Short,[67] for more money to be spent on welfare as unemployment gets worse. There are also questions about the validity of economic statistics, about which major historical variables to control for, and about the time lag to be allowed before changing economic conditions are presumed to have an impact on crime.

For all these reasons, studies of crime and the economic cycle for the time being seem to be of very limited use for confirming or disconfirming the hypothesis that reduced inequality of wealth results in less crime.

The effect of anti-poverty programmes on crime

During the 1960s in the United States, a wide range of anti-poverty programmes were instigated in the so-called 'war on poverty'. A number of these programmes were evaluated for their impact on delinquency. The best review of these evaluation studies has been provided by Burkhardt,[68] who shows that the conclusion has been virtually unanimous that the anti-poverty programmes had no impact whatsoever on delinquency. In some cases, recidivism has even been found to increase amongst the beneficiaries of these programmes.

Burkhardt points out, however, that it is wrong to call the community-action programmes of the 1960s anti-poverty programmes, or even efforts to expand legitimate opportunities. They were, in fact, predominantly counselling programmes designed to attack the so-called 'culture of poverty', rather than poverty itself. In no instance did the programmes effect a direct redistribution of wealth to the poor. Instead, they offered multifaceted programmes incorporating features such as remedial education, individual and family counselling, gang work, community organization, and vocational training.

The ideology of the social workers who ran these programmes was that a multipronged approach was needed to rehabilitate the multiproblem family. This meant that when their programmes did involve components which might have effects on income distribution (such as job training) it was impossible to ascertain whether the overall failure of the project to reduce recidivism was the result of the anti-poverty components, or to one of the social casework or community organization components.

Most evaluation studies of the war on poverty programmes are therefore useless for answering the question of whether a redistribution of wealth would reduce crime, because it is doubtful whether the programmes had any impact whatsoever on the distribution of wealth; and in those cases where they may have, it is often impossible to isolate the effect of the redistribution component of the programme from the effects of the more predominant social-work components. The same point applies to evaluation studies of assaults on the 'culture of poverty' which were attempted prior to the war on poverty — such as Miller's evaluation of the Boston Midcity project of 1954-7.[69]

The most notable recent example of a study purporting to have relevance to the question of the effect on crime of reducing inequality, but which in fact has none, is Cho's[70] multiple-regression analysis. Cho found that the cities with the highest per capita expenditure from the Office of Economic Opportunity, for Headstart, and for similar war on poverty programmes, were the cities with the *highest* crime rates. One can hardly draw any inferences from this finding about the impact of these expenditures on crime, since clearly an effort has been made to concentrate the war on poverty expenditure into those cities with the greatest urban problems of crime and poverty.

Fortunately; there are a few evaluations of programmes which have attempted to benefit the poor directly and financially through job opportunities. Hackler[71] and Hackler and Hagan[72] have followed up over four years the impact on delinquency of the Opportunities for Youth Project in Seattle. This was a project specifically for providing part-time employment to 13 to 15-year-old boys from a lower-class housing project. Compared to a control group, those who obtained the part-time jobs show an *increase* in officially recorded delinquency. A similar programme for providing holiday jobs for poor school children was evaluated by Robin.[73] Over the period of the study, both the control and the experimental group showed a reduction in delinquency. However, the experimental group did not have a significantly greater reduction than the control group.

Similarly, the Lane County Youth Project, a programme which offered alienated youth employment as 'youth consultants' to community agencies, did not reduce delinquent recidivism compared with controls.[74] The San Francisco Youth Opportunities Center managed to bring about a significant increase in employment for its clients through vocational and non-vocational counselling and job-training services.[75] However, the increase in employment was accompanied by an increase in arrest rates.

Jones[76] found that Mobilization for Youth's Reintegration Project, which offered 'intensive family casework' and school and work opportunities for youngsters released from correctional institutions, produced recidivism rates no different from those of control groups. The results of this study undoubtedly confound the effects of the work opportunities with the effects of the intensive family casework. Odell[77] compared the recidivism rates of delinquent boys treated by either traditional casework, intensive casework, or by educational training with job placement. The boys who received job placement and/or educational training for treatment showed significantly lower recidivism rates over nine months than boys in both of the casework groups.

Zivan[78] has reported the results of an ambitious vocational programme at the Children's Village in New York. The in-care component of the programme consisted of an assessment of the vocational needs of the boy, vocational counselling, occupational orientation, and work exposure. The after-care component included supportive counselling and job-replacement aid. No significant impact on recidivism (compared with controls) was produced by the programme. Zivan partially attributed this failure to prejudice in the community against employing Children's Village boys.

A very similar programme for institutionalized delinquents was the

New Start project in Denver, Colorado.[79] The programme consisted of vocational training, including job try-outs, for 17 to 21-year-old males. Although the experimental group had a lower recidivism rate than controls, the difference was not significant at the ·05 level.

While the evidence on the impact of providing jobs for adolescent youth is quite discouraging, some more favourable results have been produced in the case of young adults. The Manhattan Court Employment Project is a pretrial intervention programme in New York which diverts arrested offenders from the criminal-justice system, and gives them vocational counselling and job placement. Richert[80] has shown that the project does succeed in placing offenders into higher-paying jobs, and that a substantially lower percentage of participants in the project recidivate compared with controls. However, since the controls were not matched with the experimental group on key characteristics, one does not know whether this difference resulted from the creaming of less intractable offenders into the experimental group.

Another important pretrial intervention programme is Project Crossroads in Washington DC. Through individual manpower services to lower-class arrested offenders, Project Crossroads both increased the income of offenders and decreased recidivism rates by 10·4 per cent.[81] Although this was not a dramatic decrease, it was sufficient to induce savings in court expenses and the cost of crime, which exceeded the cost of $200 per participant in the programme. Indeed Holahan's[82] careful cost–benefit analysis of the project produced a ratio of benefits to costs of between 1·8 and 2·2.

There is a great deal of empirical evidence that the released prisoners most likely to become recidivists are those who are unsuccessful in getting jobs when released from jail.[83] Realization of this fact has prompted various manpower programmes for prison releases. One of these was the Rikers Island Project in the New York City jail.[84] In this project, 137 16 to 21-year-old males were given occupational training, remedial reading, counselling, rather extensive job-placement assistance, and some cash on release. A matched control group of 127 were given no special assistance.

After two years, 48 per cent of the experimental group had committed crimes which put them back in jail, compared to 66 per cent of controls. Forty-eight per cent of the experimentals ended up in white-collar jobs compared to 18 per cent of controls.

Even though experimentals and controls were carefully matched on a large number of social and economic variables, Taggart[85] points out

225

that there were substantially more drug-users among the control group, and that this could account for their higher recidivism.

Another major study of this kind has been undertaken to evaluate 25 projects (in 30 institutions) funded under the United States Manpower Development and Training Act.[86] The post-release experience of 2,877 who enrolled in the MDTA programme and over 1,000 matched controls were measured three and six months after release. They were given trade training, mainly in welding, auto mechanics, and upholstery, and about half were also given special job-development and placement assistance.

The follow-up indicated that the employment experience of the trainees was little or no better than that of the controls. Trainees were more likely than controls to be employed full time after three months, but less likely to be employed full time after six months. Even though the impact of the programme on employment was minimal, the recidivism of trainees was 3 to 5 per cent lower than that of controls.

Project Develop, a post-release manpower programme of the New York State Division of Parole, has been carefully analysed for its impact on recidivism.[87] Project Develop provided vocational guidance, work orientation, counselling, education, training, support, placement, and follow-up assistance to young (17 to 23-year-old) undereducated and underemployed parolees with above-average intelligence.

The recidivism of the 115 who completed the programme was compared with that of a carefully selected control group. Parole violation or arrest for a new crime within a two to ten-month period happened with 15 per cent of Project Develop completers, and with 23 per cent of the controls. Only 6 per cent of the experimental group were sent back to jail, compared with 12 per cent of the controls. However, these differences were not statistically significant, and Taggart[88] points out that if the control group had been compared with all those who enrolled (including those who dropped out, or were back in jail before the project was completed) instead of only those who completed, it would be the control group which performed better.

Another study by Gearhart *et al.*[89] in two Washington State institutions examined the effect of vocational training in office-machine repair, auto mechanics, barbering, body and fender work, machinist work, carpentry, drafting, dry-cleaning, electronics, shoe-building and machine operation. A follow-up of three years showed no significant effect on recidivism in a comparison with untrained controls. Gearhart did report, however, that when a trainee succeeded in finding a job related to his area of training, his chances of becoming a successful parolee were improved. It is possible, then, that vocational programmes fail because the skills acquired cannot be applied in the employment market.

This review can only reach the same conclusion as the reviews by Taggart,[90] Martinson,[91] and Lipton *et al.*[92]: programmes for increasing income inequality through job training or job placement have had minimal impact on crime and delinquency. One of the main reasons for this is that typically the programmes have had minimal impact on employment prospects. A survey of releasees from United States prisons in June 1964[93] revealed that those who had some vocational training did not have a significantly higher employment rate than those who had no training, unless they had received it over an extensive period. Since most prison stays are short, there is not sufficient time for manpower investment which will have any real impact. This is also confirmed by the review by Lipton *et al.*,[94] which concluded that vocational training for offenders has had no measurable effect upon post-release employment.

The programmes reviewed in this section have attempted to work with extremely disadvantaged subjects, who are alienated, unreceptive, and who often just want to be left alone. Typically, the programmes deal with people who, for a variety of reasons, have already become so demoralized that they are no longer salvageable.

One suspects that many manpower programmes are counterproductive in their effect on crime because they raise expectations they cannot fulfil. They become a tantalizing exercise in disillusionment. Before manpower programmes for criminals can have an effect on crime, they must *motivate* criminals to undertake *adequate* training in *marketable* skills which will not be denied use because of either *prejudice* against ex-convicts, or fears about security risks. Most fundamentally, as Rein has pointed out: 'We seem to have done far better in reorienting, re-habilitating, and retraining individuals [for jobs] than we have at re-educating and reorganizing our economic institutions to receive them when they are ready.'[95]

All of the foregoing anti-poverty programmes have not produced tangible economic benefits for most of the deprived people they were supposedly benefiting. More often, they breed disappointment and cynicism, succeeding only in labelling the beneficiaries as inferior people who need to be helped.

Summary

Inequality as an explanation of middle-class delinquency
Much middle-class delinquency might be explained by the existence of inequality in society. Middle-class children who fail at school exhibit delinquency rates higher, or as high, as lower-class school failures. Much middle-class delinquency might therefore be explained by the anticipation of lower-class futures, instead of by lower-class origins.

International level of analysis
Nations with a high level of earnings inequality have high homicide rates, and nations with a low level of expenditure on social security have high homicide rates. However, we do not know the extent to which these two strong relationships are confounded by gross cultural, demographic, and economic differences among nations.

Inter-city level of analysis
After controlling for city size and geographical region, there is no tendency for United States cities with a large proportion of families in poverty to have higher rates on any index crime. This is true irrespective of whether an absolute or a relative index of poverty is used. In contrast, the hypothesis that cities with a wide income gap between low- and average-income earners have high crime rates is consistently supported, even after controlling for city size, geographical region, and percentage white.

It is therefore concluded that gross economic policies which reduce the gap between all poor people and the average-income earner are likely to reduce crime; but that policies which aim to reduce the number of poor people by concentrating on a limited target group who are lifted out of poverty will not reduce crime. While the latter type of policy might reduce the crime of those who are lifted out of poverty, it might also increase crime among those left behind, because, as they become a more exceptional minority, their sense of relative deprivation becomes more acute. Further research, investigating these two groups separately, is needed to test this hypothesis.

Racial inequality
Income inequality between Negroes and whites does not seem to create special crime problems in United States cities, over and above those explained by the general level of income inequality. It is possible, however, that greater racial equality is associated with heightened relative

deprivation among poor whites, and consequently, higher white crime rates.

The time-series level of analysis

There is little data adequate for the purpose of testing whether crime rates rise during periods when inequality of wealth is increasing, and fall when inequality of wealth is decreasing. Such data as exists tends to be consistent with the view that it is a widening of the income gap between rich and poor which is associated with growth in crime rather than increases in unemployment or in the number of poor.

The effect of anti-poverty programmes on crime

There is very little evidence that policies to reduce poverty among limited target groups have effects even upon the crime or delinquency of these target groups. It is doubtful whether most so-called anti-poverty programmes have had any impact whatsoever on the distribution of wealth; and in those cases where they have, it is often impossible to isolate the effect of the redistribution component of the programme from the effects of the more predominant social-work components. A number of programmes have been explicitly geared to lifting people out of poverty through vocational training and job placement. In a very few cases these have been successful. However, more often they have had minimal effects on crime, because they have had minimal effects on employment. In many cases, they may have been counterproductive because of labelling, and because they raise expectations about occupational futures which they cannot fulfil.

Chapter 12

Inequality: conclusions and policies

Introduction

The purpose of this chapter is to outline the broader conclusions of this book about the effect of inequality on crime, and to expound some of the complications involved in inducing from these conclusions that policies to redistribute wealth and power would reduce crime.

Lower-class people engage in those crimes which do not involve the abuse of occupational power at a higher rate than middle-class people. Conversely, middle-class people engage in crimes which do involve the use of occupational power at a higher rate than lower-class people. Theories based on lower-class deprivation and brutalization, powerlessness, blocked legitimate opportunities, broken homes, eroded respect of sons for fathers who are economic failures, and reward–cost calculations for crime, can be used to predict that the former type of crime will be reduced by greater equality. These theories are not appropriate for explaining offences which involve the abuse of occupational power (white-collar crime). Chapter 10 has put forward a body of theory which suggests that the concentration of power into a few hands encourages white-collar crime.

It is important to emphasize that, in criminology, there has been an absolute dearth of counter-theories predicting that poverty and power-lessness do *not* encourage crime; and a dearth of suggestions as to why excessive power also does *not* encourage crime. Thus there seem to be reasonable theoretical grounds, in some cases supported by a substantial body of empirical evidence, for predicting that a redistribution of wealth and power, from those who have much to those who have little, would simultaneously diminish the crimes of the powerful and the crimes of the powerless. Confidence in this prediction is increased by findings that cities and nations with more egalitarian distributions of wealth have lower official crime rates. Nevertheless, the purpose of this chapter is to detail some of the factors which might shake this confidence.

Will anti-poverty programmes work?

Anti-poverty programmes are defined here as programmes which aim to reduce the number of poor people by lifting a target group out of poverty. All of the strategies of the United States war on poverty were of this kind — programmes such as Headstart, the community-action programmes, the manpower-training programmes, and the small-business programmes. It is a conclusion of this book that such programmes, which aim to lift a target group out of poverty, will not reduce crime. In contrast, it is predicted that gross economic measures to reduce the gap between the poor and the rest of the population will reduce crime.

This conclusion flies in the face of much of the conventional wisdom of criminology. Gross economic measures are regarded as shot-gun approaches which are unlikely to yield a high proportion of hits if the target is crime. They do not concentrate all resources on high-risk individuals. For this reason, anti-poverty programmes which select for special attention a high-risk target group are favoured.[1]

This argument ignores the fact that when we select out a group for special attention, we are engaging in a labelling process. In contrast, gross economic measures avoid the counter-productive consequences of labelling, and in the case of measures such as the restructuring of income tax and guaranteed minimum income, the stigma of welfare hand-outs and degradation by social welfare bureaucracies are also avoided.

But the most fundamental reason for predicting that policies to reduce the number of people who are poor will not reduce crime is the evidence from the last chapter that cities with smaller numbers of poor people do not have lower crime rates. This, and other evidence, has led to the hypothesis that when the number of people who are poor is decreased, those who remain poor become more atypical, and therefore suffer greater relative deprivation.

In any case, it was shown in the last chapter that programmes which set out to lift target groups out of poverty do not normally succeed in doing so. More often, they raise expectations which they cannot fulfil, adding yet another disappointment to the long line of disappointments inflicted upon the people they set out to help.

But even if reducing the number of poor would reduce crime, and even if there were anti-poverty programmes which would succeed in lifting people out of poverty, it is still doubtful whether such programmes would lower the crime rate. All of the programmes of the war on poverty *ultimately* sought to reduce poverty through employment — either by equipping people to get jobs where they could not get them before, or by equipping them for better-paid jobs. The point is that, in the context of a capitalist system, expanding the opportunities of one person contracts the opportunities of others. So in a slum, where there is always a lot of unemployment, upgrading the educational standard of one person, so that he/she can get a job, will normally mean putting another person, who has not upgraded his educational standard, out of a job. Perhaps the only way to increase opportunities for everyone is to change the structure of the capitalist system which depends for its survival on maintaining a pool of unemployed labour.

In summary, it is concluded that anti-poverty policies which seek to lift selected groups of poor people out of poverty will not reduce crime because:

1 They will not normally succeed in lifting people out of poverty.
2 They foster cynicism and disappointment by raising expectations which they cannot fulfil.
3 They label people as disreputable and inferior.
4 Even if they do succeed in lifting people out of poverty, in a capitalist economy they typically do so at the expense of other people who are thrust into poverty.
5 Even if they do reduce the total number of poor people in a city, this is unlikely to reduce crime because cities with smaller numbers of poor people do not have lower crime rates.

An optimum level of inequality?

Oughton[2] has argued that a major factor which drives middle-class people to white-collar crime is a belief that, with increasing equality in British society, they are not getting the share of the nation's wealth which they deserve, considering their superior training and responsibility. They decide to rectify this economic injustice perpetrated against them through white-collar crime.

> Many of the highly skilled men are the disgruntled men of our time, and this applies particularly to chartered engineers, research and development personnel, industrial chemists. Under a socialist

government they found themselves less well paid than, say, ordinary shopfloor operatives, who have no real skills and have not spent years studying for professional qualifications.[3]

One is tempted to dismiss Oughton as an apologist for the twisted rationalizations of the privileged for their crimes. However, in support of Oughton, my own interviews with businessmen on reasons for engaging in tax fraud[4] evoked consistent references to 'supporting dole bludgers through taxes', 'We work hard while they bludge on welfare', and rewards which were not in proportion to the amount of work put into their businesses. In so far as one could judge, these seemed to be not mere rationalizations, but genuinely part of the vocabulary of motives which led to law violation.

Pavin, in his influential research on 'Economic Determinants of Political Unrest',[5] argued that whereas greater equality relieves the frustration of the lower orders, it also increases the insecurities of persons of privilege, who perceive their privilege as being threatened. Both factors, he argued, predispose people to political violence. When the level of inequality decreases past a certain point, further reductions of inequality produce absolutely minimal diminutions of lower-class frustrations, but monumental increases in middle-class status threat. Further reductions of inequality will then increase the overall propensity to political violence, rather than decrease it. Pavin suggests then that there is an optimum level of income inequality for minimizing political violence, but hastens to add that we need to reach a much lower level of inequality before that optimum point is passed in modern societies.

Similar considerations might apply to crime generally.[6] While there are good reasons for predicting that, given the present circumstances in Western capitalist societies, greater equality would reduce crime, there are also good reasons for suspecting that progressive reductions of inequality would eventually result in a point being reached beyond which this prediction would no longer hold.[7]

Some further complications

If poverty causes some types of crime, is that effect reversible? Or does the fact that a person has been poor scar him for life as it were, so that a belated alleviation of his poverty makes little difference? Rosenfeld has made this point succinctly.

Knowing the forces that *contribute* to a social evil tells us nothing about how to eradicate the evil. In fact, why should it? There is no logical reason why the weapon most effective in destroying a social phenomenon should be in a direct way related to the forces that make it grow.[8]

With regard to the reversibility of the effect of poverty on crime, Lemert's[9] seminal distinction between primary and secondary deviation is especially relevant. Box[10] has illustrated how, even though primary deviation might be caused by poverty, alleviating poverty might not affect the more pervasive secondary deviation.

> If an adolescent is hungry and poor, and steals, we may well feel we can explain his behaviour by reference to his deprived condition. But if he is caught and punished more severely than he considers just, and if the policeman also taught him a sharp lesson which he remembers — but not in the way the policeman intended — then he might, at some later date, engage in further acts of deviance. That he is poor and hungry may now no longer be as important in explaining his behaviour (both conditions may in the meantime have been ameliorated) as is his resentment at the treatment he received, and his perception that further law-violating behaviour is retaliation against those who abused him.[11]

If, in fact, the effect of poverty on crime is not reversible, then reducing inequality will not 'cure' the crime of the present generation of poor people, but will succeed only in preventing the crime of the on-coming generation. There would be, then, a time-lag before the effect of the egalitarian policy was felt.

There are other complications, of a more macrosociological nature, which could subvert any attempt to reduce crime through reducing inequality. Consider the four possibilities briefly outlined in the next four paragraphs.

Might a gradual improvement in the conditions of the poor result in a revolution of rising expectations, when these expectations by far exceed the capacity of the capitalist economy to meet them? Small improvements can exacerbate frustrations by creating more demands, rather than satisfying existing ones. As de Tocqueville has argued:

> Nations that have endured patiently and almost unconsciously the most overwhelming repression often burst into rebellion against the

yoke the moment it begins to grow lighter.... Evils which are patiently endured when they seem inevitable become intolerable when once the idea of escape from them is suggested.[12]

Will the mobilization of that political unrest among the poor which is a necessary precondition to egalitarian social change engender feelings of subjective deprivation which create more crime problems than are relieved by the lessening of objective deprivation? Egalitarian political programmes are often more successful in whipping up discontent about injustice than in eliminating injustice itself. One of the explanations suggested by Adler[13] for the apparent rise in female crime in recent years is that the women's liberation movement has succeeded in heightening discontent among women, but has achieved little in removing the objective causes of that discontent.[14]

Might a steady reduction of inequality be counterproductive in the long run if it is ultimately followed by a reversal of the improvement? This is the proposition which is central to the theory of relative deprivation and revolution proposed by Davies.[15] 'Revolutions', he claims, 'are most likely to occur when a prolonged period of objective economic and social development is followed by a short period of sharp reversal.'[16]

Will the reduction of inequalities in wealth and power result in the emergence of new criteria for signifying superiority and inferiority which are equally criminogenic? One might expect this to happen if one subscribed to Alfred Adler's theory that man is inevitably conditioned from infancy to strive for superiority over other men, by one means or another.[17] Or one might expect new criteria of superiority to emerge if one subscribed to Dahrendorf's theory that because there are norms, and because sanctions are necessary to enforce conformity to these norms, it follows that some form of inequality of rank among men is inevitable.[18]

These are grand theories which are, by and large, untestable. They are the more dramatic among the infinite range of potential 'unanticipated consequences of purposive social action', as Merton calls them.[19] Consider the following two possibilities, as an illustration of how difficult it is to anticipate the consequences of egalitarian policies. A reduction in poverty may attenuate the labelling of poor people as disreputable, and this may unexpectedly give the poor a new self-confidence which helps to lift them further out of poverty, and so on in a cumulative process. Or alternatively, people may respond to a planned reduction in poverty by believing that poor people are getting soft treatment, of which they are undeserving because of their inveterate laziness. This conservative backlash results in poor people being even more intensively labelled as disreputable.

The range of unintended consequences of planned social change is indeed infinite and unpredictable. The only way to cope with this unpredictability is to monitor the effects of policy implementation as an ongoing process. Prolonged arm-chair stargazing about what could go wrong serves little purpose. What is needed is a thoroughly empirical evaluation of the impact of policy as it is gradually introduced.

A strong *prima facie* case has been made in this study for the proposition that reducing inequality of wealth and power will reduce crime. Nevertheless, to show, for example, that cities with a high level of inequality have a high crime rate is not to demonstrate causality, and is certainly not to show that reducing inequality will reduce crime. There is no graceful movement from criminological research to policy implications. The solution is to build an evaluation strategy into the social-change strategy — a learning system to continually feed back information about the repercussions of the change on the society.

The agenda for future research

Needless to say, the foregoing analysis has been undertaken in the face of serious gaps in our knowledge of inequality, crime and public policy. The final function of this summary chapter is to draw together the conclusions reached throughout the book as to which are the most glaring gaps. The following have been isolated at various points in the work as being especially high priority problems which demand further research attention if we are to move toward a more fruitful analysis of inequality and crime.

1 The effect of class bias on self-reports of delinquency. Have we been misled about the social-class distribution of juvenile crime by self-report measures which overestimate the proportion of delinquency committed by the middle class?
2 International comparisons of inequality of wealth and crime. To test the hypothesis that nations with greater inequality have greater crime, there is a need for more recent, more detailed crime data, from a larger sample of nations, for which critical confounding variables can be controlled.
3 Longitudinal evaluations of the effect on crime of intervention programmes which genuinely and directly redistribute wealth and power.

4 Examination of the effect on crime of reductions in poverty, separately for those who are lifted out of poverty, and those who are left behind to remain in poverty. Is the criminality of the former group decreased at the expense of an increase in crime for the latter group?

5 Explorations of the extent and nature of white-collar crime in organizations where power is relatively centralized compared with organizations where power is relatively dispersed.

In addition to these critical gaps in the empirical research evidence, there is a great need for theoretical development to extend, or offer alternatives to the theory of the white-collar crime paradox in chapter 10. The theory presented in chapter 10 is an incursion into an area relatively untouched by theory and hard data alike. As with all new theoretical incursions, it suffers from the sin of oversimplification. If greater power is associated with greater white-collar criminality, how, for example, does this explain one report that it is low-status lawyers in small struggling practices who are most likely to violate the legal and ethical standards of their profession?[20] In the literature on white-collar crime, there are many anecdotal accounts of businessmen who resorted to white-collar crime because they felt relatively deprived at having failed to get the promotion which they felt they deserved. How does the theory in chapter 10 cope with explaining the phenomenon of the businessman who engages in crime, partly because he feels relatively deprived at not achieving the success deserved and expected, and partly because he is in a position of power which gives him the opportunity to commit and cover up a white-collar crime? That is, how does the theory explain an offence arising partly from the fact that the offender had too little power, and partly from the fact that he had too much power?

Such paradoxes arise from situations where an individual has a low degree of power within a subsystem (e.g. the legal profession) but a high degree of power within the wider system (the whole society). The theory could be buttressed by asserting that the solution to crime arising from little power within the subsystem, and great power within the total system, is to ensure that there is a reduction in power differentials both within and between subsystems. If a senior businessman resorts to white-collar crime because he is a failure within his reference group, then one way to attenuate the sense of failure is to minimize objective status differentials between the failures and the successful within the reference group. If he also resorts to white-collar crime because he, like all senior businessmen, has opportunities to do so by virtue of his power, then another solution is to circumscribe the power of businessmen generally.

However, does this solution really resolve the problem of objective versus subjective powerlessness? The theory in chapter 10 leaves many of these more complex questions unanswered. Perhaps such issues are only peripheral. But certainly there is a need to explore them more fully in future theoretical criminology.

Postscript:

The socialist critique of the reformist criminology in this book

The socialist critique

> Individuals in society are seen as playing a gigantic fruit-machine, but the machine is rigged and only some players are consistently rewarded. The deprived ones then resort to kicking the machine or to leaving the fun-palace altogether (e.g. attacks on property or involvement in drug-taking subcultures).
>
> Nobody appears to ask who put the machine there in the first place, and who it is who takes the profits. Criticism of the game is confined to changing the pay-out sequence so that the deprived can get a better deal. What at first sight looks like a major critique of society (that is, 'anomie' theory) ends up by taking the existing society for granted.[1]

The above quote by Taylor and Taylor captures the essence of the Marxist critique of investigating the effect of piecemeal egalitarian reforms within the capitalist system. This critique has been aimed most explicitly at the very kind of reformist criminology undertaken in this book. To ignore it would be indefensible. Before defending the evaluation of egalitarian reforms within the capitalist system, let us develop more fully the Marxist position.

There is much more to Marxist criminology than the assertion that reformist criminology takes the capitalist system for granted. Reformist criminology is also castigated for taking the law for granted. A reply to the argument that the law is an instrument for the satisfaction of ruling-class interests has already been presented in chapters 1 and 2 of this book. This defence will not be repeated here.

Another thread to the socialist critique of piecemeal egalitarian reform is that such reforms are undermined by equilibrium forces in

the capitalist economy. It was conceded in the last chapter that policies
to find jobs for people may only have the effect of leaving fewer jobs
for other unemployed people, since capitalism depends for its survival
on the maintenance of a pool of unemployed labour. It is known that if
an attempt is made to create greater equality by replacing percentage
increases in wages with flat increases, this attempt is often largely
undermined by wage drift under the influence of capitalist market
forces.[2] Rent control on low-income housing results in landlords
proportionately reducing expenditure on maintenance, and in reduced
investment in rental accommodation.[3] Because equilibrium forces in
the competitive market neutralize egalitarian policies in these kinds of
ways, David Gordon asserts that crime problems 'cannot easily be
solved within the context of capitalist institutions because their solution would tend to disrupt the functioning of the capitalist machine'.[4]

However, Marxists typically overstate this argument. Equilibrium
forces rarely *totally* neutralize the effect of egalitarian policies. For
example, it is possible to have a manpower programme which trains
people to occupy unfilled job vacancies, rather than to take jobs which
would otherwise be filled by other unemployed people.

Another dimension of the socialist critique is that it is not so much
inequality *per se* which fosters crime, but inequality in the context of a
capitalist system. This point hardly needs elaboration because it has
already been acknowledged in this book that inequality may have an
especially strong impact on crime when it occurs in a system in which a
propensity to take advantage of the other person is built in (see in particular chapter 10 pp. 188–94). Having conceded partial validity to
some of the Marxist criticisms of policies to redistribute wealth and
power within the capitalist system, in the next section we will lead into
the Marxist critique of the class-mix policies discussed in Part II.

Class-mix and capitalism

Inequality of wealth and lower-class residential segregation are highly
interrelated problems. Segregation exacerbates inequality, and inequality
exacerbates segregation.

Segregation contributes to inequality because slums heighten the
visibility of deprived groups, making them easier targets for discrimination.[5] 'Exploitation flourishes [in slums] because "captive" markets
can be forced to pay exorbitant prices for inferior merchandise and
services.'[6] When people are forced to live in slums, they are forced to

forego the opportunity to live in an area where their chances of getting the kind of job they would like are maximized. For example, in most American cities there are thousands of unemployed workers in the inner city, yet almost all of the job vacancies are in the suburbs.[7] The formation of a ghetto in an area can even chase industry away from the area.[8] Segregation has the effect of confining networks of informal communication about job contacts upon which lower-class people rely to other lower-class people who are similarly ignorant about job contacts.[9]

Marshall and Jiobu[10] and Jiobu and Marshall[11] have shown, using path analyses, that the extent of the residential segregation of blacks in United States cities is causally dependent on the size of black–white income differentials. My own analysis of data on United States cities, while not providing a test of causality, did establish a correlation of ·47 between the income gap separating the poor from the average-income earner, and the extent to which cities segregate their poor into slums.[12]

Marshall and Jiobu concluded that attitudinal factors are less critical in determining segregation than is normally assumed.[13] What seems more critical is the relative ability of blacks and whites to compete for certain housing sites. As the income differential decreases, this competition is between groups of more nearly equal economic power, so that it becomes increasingly difficult to contain blacks within well-defined ghettos.

In the words of Sandercock, 'Our urban problems are the spatial expression of the inequalities of a capitalist economy.'[14] In a city with limited suitable housing sites, it is useful to conceive of the bidding for housing stock as analogous to filling up seats sequentially in an empty theatre.[15] The first to enter has n choices, the second $n - 1$, and so on, with the last having no choice. If those who enter do so in order of their bidding power, then those with most money have the widest range of choices, while the poor take up whatever is left after all others have exercised their choice. To the extent that the poor have less bidding power than the rest of the population, then to that extent will the poor have no choice but to occupy only those areas of the city deemed by the market as least desirable. Therefore greater equality should create greater class-mix in a capitalist housing market.

However, Harvey has counterposed a socialist critique, by arguing that if urban land use is determined by competitive bidding for the use of land, then the way genuinely to alter urban land use is to abolish competitive bidding — that is, to destroy capitalism. In the following quotation, Harvey refers to the von Thunen theory, which is one of a number of variants of theories which explain slum formation in terms of the competitive bidding for housing stock.

> Our objective is to eliminate ghettos. Therefore, the only valid policy with respect to this objective is to eliminate the conditions which give rise to the truth of the theory. In other words, we wish the von Thunen theory of the urban land market to become *not* true. The simplest approach here is to eliminate those mechanisms which serve to generate the theory. The mechanism in this case is very simple — competitive bidding for the use of land. If we eliminate this mechanism, we will presumably eliminate the result. This is immediately suggestive of a policy for eliminating ghettos, which would presumably supplant competitive bidding with a socially controlled urban land market and socialized control of the housing sector.[16]

There exists some empirical evidence which Harvey could have used to support his prediction. Musil[17] has compared segregation indices for blue-collar and white-collar workers in Prague prior to socialism (1930) and post-socialism (1950). He found a clear tendency for residential segregation on the basis of class to decrease over the twenty-year period. Czechoslovakia, like Cuba and some other socialist countries, has a totally socialized housing industry, whereby private ownership is abolished and the state bureaucracy attempts to allocate housing on the basis of need.

The socialist solution to slums is not a new one. It was first proposed by Engels in a set of essays entitled *The Housing Question*.[18]

> As long as the capitalist mode of production continues to exist, it is folly to hope for an isolated solution of the housing question or of any other social question affecting the fate of the workers. The solution lies in the abolition of the capitalist mode of production and the appropriation of all the means of life and labour by the working class itself.[19]

To illustrate this, Harvey points out that urban renewal simply moves the slum from one part of the city to another, and that to prevent blockbusting would be to prevent blacks from getting housing. On the basis of this shallow analysis of the range of policy options available to those who would work within the capitalist system, he concludes:

> The point I am working towards is that although all serious analysts

concede the seriousness of the ghetto problem, few call into question the forces which rule the very heart of our economic system. Thus we discuss everything except the basic characteristics of a capitalist market economy. We devise all manner of solutions except those which might challenge the continuance of that economy. Such discussions and solutions serve only to make us look foolish, since they eventually lead us to discover what Engels was only too aware of in 1872 — that capitalist solutions provide no foundation for dealing with deteriorated social conditions.[20]

However, Harvey's conclusion is based on a very selective review of the policy options available within the capitalist system. He ignores the rich diversity of policies to reduce class segregation reviewed in the Appendix to this book. In the light of this review, it is hardly necessary to answer Harvey's assertion that the only viable way to overcome the slum problem is to overthrow capitalism.

It is undoubtedly true that competitive bidding for housing stock in a capitalist market contributes to forcing lower-class people to live in slums. It is also undoubtedly true that housing developers find that there is maximum profit in developing 'exclusive' estates aimed solely at the middle-class market.[21] However, while the Marxists are quick to point to the limitations of solutions within the capitalist system, they are often blind to the limitations of the socialist solution. The choices of people to live in homogeneous class areas are not totally conditioned by market forces; there is also evidence of a social preference for living with people of a similar background to one's own.[22] Musil's[23] data show that there is still considerable residential segregation of manual workers from white-collar workers in Prague's totally socialized housing market.

Why not study limited reforms?

Whether one considers the overthrow of capitalism to be desirable or not will be decided by far more important considerations than crime reduction. Irrespective of where one stands on this question, one can only accept the Marxist criticism that working within the capitalist system places structural limitations upon what is likely to be achieved in crime reduction through egalitarian policies. In turn, the overthrow of capitalism is not a panacea for crime which knows no limitations. The overthrow of capitalism creates merely the potential for a more equal and less segregated society. Gross inequalities in wealth and power persist in existing socialist societies, and what evidence we have seems to suggest that in these societies, as in ours, the lower class have the highest delinquency rate.[24]

To ignore socialism is to ignore the most far-reaching policy available for reducing class segregation and inequalities in wealth and power. Is socialism the ultimate egalitarian policy for crime reduction? There is clearly insufficient evidence to enable an answer to this question. Although two recent studies cite evidence that crime rates dropped following the revolutions in Cuba and Russia respectively,[25] it is doubtful whether much trust can be placed in official statistics which prove that the regimes which compiled them have been successful in reducing crime.

Certainly, reform within the capitalist system has its limitations (what approach does not!). But why should this preclude an analysis of the effect on crime of those limited reforms which can be achieved. Indeed, there has been ample demonstration in this book that such limited reforms are capable of having limited effects on crime. Must we wait for the socialist millenium before any thorough empirical investigation of the effect of egalitarian policies on crime can be undertaken? If we do, it will be a long time before we know just how much efficacy egalitarian policies do have for crime reduction.

Appendix:

Class-mix policies

Introduction

This appendix presents a preliminary survey of the range of policies available to the social planner who in future may wish to reduce crime by increasing class-mix. Are there really any feasible policies which would be available to him? It is futile to suggest that there is a need for more policy-oriented research on the question of whether class segregation encourages crime, if in fact there exist no practicable policies to reduce class segregation.

This appendix does not attempt a systematic evaluation of class-mix policies. The purpose is merely to show that there are a rich variety of policies which could be used to encourage class-mix. And this is done simply to establish that further investigation of whether class-mix discourages crime is important, because public policy decisions which have consequences for class-mix are being made all of the time. Which class-mix policies are more effective, which are most easily implemented, and which have undesirable consequences for other goals of public policy besides crime reduction are issues beyond the scope of this book.

Some might contend that even if greater class-mix would reduce crime, there are no feasible ways of achieving greater mix other than by forcibly uprooting lower-class people from slum environments. But slum clearance is not the only way of fostering mix by encouraging middle-class people to come back to the central city. Forced residential mobility can itself be a cause of crime.[1] However, it can be argued that the factors which maintain lower-class residential segregation involve much more force and limitation of free residential choice for lower-class people than do class-mix policies. This argument is developed in the sections that follow.

Examples of policies will be taken from several countries. While

245

there are unique features in urban structure and housing from nation to nation, each can learn from the policy experience of others.

Housing policy in the US and class-mix

Rainwater speaks of the existence in the United States of a 'general political preference for concentrating and warehousing lower-class people'.[2] He suggests that by hiding them away in shunned areas of the city we can sweep their problems under the mat. The solution is all too simple – reverse this conscious political preference for lower-class segregation and the situation will change. It is not only the preferences of policy-makers that determine the degree of segregation, but also the preferences of millions of individual property owners and tenants conditioned by the market forces at work in real estate and housing.

Nevertheless, there are grounds for believing that the reversal of a political preference for class segregation can have an effect. Grier and Grier point out how the preferences of policy-makers in the United States prior to 1950 were segregationist, and how these preferences filtered down into specific policies.[3]

Federal policies and practices in housing reinforced and increased the separation between the 'Negro' cities and the white suburbs. In part, this was intentional. From 1935 to 1950 – a period in which about 15 million new dwellings were constructed – the power of the national government was explicitly used to prevent integrated housing. Federal policies were based upon the premise that economic and social stability could best be achieved through keeping neighbourhood populations as homogeneous as possible. Thus, the *Underwriting Manual* of the Federal Housing Administration (oldest and largest of the federal housing agencies, established by the Housing Act of 1934) warned that 'if a neighbourhood is to retain stability, it is necessary that properties shall continue to be occupied by the same social and racial group.' It advised appraisers to lower their valuation of properties in mixed neighbourhoods, 'often to the point of rejection'. FHA actually drove out of business some developers who insisted upon open policies.

The Griers also point out how the FHA mortgate-insurance programme and its post-Second World War counterpart for returned servicemen, the Veteran Administration's loan-guarantee programme, tended to pull upwardly mobile white families out into the suburbs and away from the central cities. These were programmes for the middle-income earner, since evidence of reasonable earnings and faithful repayment of past obligations were required.

Many middle-income families benefiting from these programmes, given free choice, would have chosen to live or remain in the cities, perhaps to be close to work or relatives. But this option was effectively closed off because the FHA and VA programmes did not provide nearly so liberal terms on the mortgages of older homes in the central cities. Lower down-payments, longer repayment periods, and lower monthly installments, enticed the upwardly mobile into new homes in the suburbs. The FHA and VA programmes in this way encouraged the middle-class desertion of the central cities, creating even more desperate centres of deprivation. This might be the reason for the surprising finding from the multiple-regression analysis by Cho that US cities with high FHA expenditure per capita were cities with higher homicide and burglary rates.[4]

Jane Jacobs[5] is one who has suggested that the best way to attack the problems of the slum is to attract the large numbers of slum dwellers who become upwardly mobile into the middle class to stay. She suggests that one way to do this is to convince (or legally impel) banks and lending institutions to finance such people for improvements to dwellings within slums. At the moment, the credit blacklisting of areas, and similar practices, make it impossible for the middle-class person to build a middle-class home in a slum. Jacobs argues that in a whole range of ways the slum must be made an attractive and interesting place for upwardly mobile people to stay in. 'Unslumming' is then fostered by the stability and sense of respectability that such people lend to the area.

While the FHA and VA programmes encouraged middle class out-migration from the slums, the other major US housing programme of this century — the subsidized low-income public housing of the Public Housing Administration — encouraged lower-class people to stay in the central city, and even lower-class inmigration. Subsidized low-income housing was provided mainly in the lower-class inner city, because one of its objectives was to overcome blighted housing in these areas. It is clear, then, how federal government housing policy in the United States has historically discouraged class-mix.

The differences between the two programs thus reinforce each other in their effects upon patterns of residence. While the FHA and VA have helped promote white dominance in the suburbs, public housing has helped enhance Negro dominance in the cities.[6]

Land-use barriers to class-mix

Zoning, because it is generally based on the existing characteristics of areas, tends to widen the gap between 'rich' and 'poor' areas. Thus, residentially attractive neighbourhoods are safeguarded from developments which might reduce their attractiveness while less attractive areas are given no such safeguards. In this way, zoning increases the degree of intra-metropolitan segregation.[7]

The residents of wealthy suburbs use their power to maintain the exclusiveness of their neighbourhood, and to keep noxious, noisy or unaesthetic industries, or other undesirable land uses, away from their homes. Undesirable land uses are located instead in lower-class areas, thereby making lower-class areas even more undesirable to middle-class people.

Local government has the power to have a substantial impact on class-mix, simply by rezoning exclusive middle-class residential areas to allow flats or high-rise development. Indeed every zoning decision that a local authority makes in its town plan has some implications for class-mix. This is not to say that town plans should be designed with optimization of class-mix as a major consideration. Metropolitan zoning is simply pointed to as one area of public policy which could be manipulated to create greater class-mix, should that be considered a desirable policy goal after other possible consequences besides reduced crime are taken into account.

Real-estate developers and suburban governments in many Western nations have used a variety of devices to exclude lower-class people from middle-class suburbs. These include minimum-lot-size requirements, minimum-house-size requirements, a requirement that houses built be above a certain value, restrictive subdivision regulations, and unduly expensive building standards.[8] It is possible to legislate for the banning of these exclusionary practices. Some of the legislation in the United States, to prohibit discrimination against Negroes in the housing market, is a guide to how this can be done.

The Griers report that in testimony before the Commissioners of the District of Columbia, the president of the Mortgage Bankers Association of Metropolitan Washington stated bluntly that 'applications from minority groups are not generally considered in areas that are not recognized as being racially mixed'.[9] The Griers conclude that the evidence from a number of such testimonies and from research surveys indicates that the same practice is followed by most lending sources in the United States. This is the kind of exclusionary practice which has been the target for anti-discrimination laws in that country.

Public-housing policy in Australia

A variety of public-housing policies in Australia have had effects, positive and negative, upon class-mix. During the decade following the Second World War most state housing authorities segregated their problem tenants into poor-quality dwellings called 'emergency dwellings'. This practice of segregating the people one would expect to be most prone to crime and delinquency has particularly important implications for the present analysis, in terms of the creation of illegitimate opportunity. Such segregation of problem tenants has been justified in countries such as the United Kingdom and Sweden, because it facilitates the close supervision of multiproblem families by social workers.

State-housing commissions in Australia today seem to be agreed that scattered-site low-income housing is socially preferable, but economically unrealistic. Perhaps the compromise solution which will ultimately be settled on is Wilson's[10] suggestion that while infill public housing in middle-class areas is prohibitively expensive, housing commissions should at least avoid the past mistakes of vast public-housing wildernesses containing many tens of thousands of uniformly lower-class residents. The nature of the compromise decided upon between scatter-site and large public-housing developments will have dramatic implications for the urban mosaic in states such as South Australia, where over a third of all housing is public.

One policy which has (perhaps unintentionally) served to foster greater class-mix than occurs in public housing in most other countries is the Queensland Housing Commission's policy of integrating purchase housing with rental housing. Moreover, upwardly mobile people who have been renting Queensland Housing Commission houses are able to count a substantial proportion of the rent they have paid over the years towards the purchase of their formerly rented home. This provides a direct incentive for upwardly mobile people with aspirations for home ownership to stay in public-housing areas.

Jones[11] has pointed out how the application in different states of means tests of differing stringencies has resulted in public housing in some states being more lower class than in others. States with virtually no means tests have moderate concentrations of higher- and medium-income people sprinkled among the more commonly lower-class public-housing recipients.

The South Australian Housing Trust has a subsidy programme for middle-income home purchasers in addition to its provision of low-income public housing. The Housing Trust explicitly sets out to create class-mix by intermingling recipients under the middle- and low-income programmes in its estates. In the development of the new town of Elizabeth, the South Australian Housing Trust made an additional effort to foster class-mix by leaving 10 per cent of available lots vacant, so that private builders could construct dwellings for those requiring higher-quality housing. However, few builders were interested, and most of the building sites were eventually turned over for Trust dwellings.

Jones[12] also suggests that the New South Wales Housing Commission's policy at Campbelltown of interspersing housing-commission areas of 5,000–6,000 people with private developments of similar size creates difficulties in the supply of amenities, since the private areas take much longer to develop than the commission estates. So, often, programmes to promote class-mix do not look so attractive when confronted with the hard realities of economic rationality.

A variety of housing policies in Australia, such as the sale of slum clearance land to private developers at a subsidized price by the Victorian Housing Commission, have been justified on the grounds of fostering class-mix. The Australian government's programme to restore and preserve the inner-city Sydney suburb of Glebe seeks to encourage class-mix by setting aside a proportion of the terraced houses for private rather than public restoration, and by providing a diversity of housing types — family dwellings, one-bedroom flats, hostels, and pensioner units.[13]

Some state-housing authorities are now toying with the idea used by the United States Housing Allowance Program whereby low-income people are given subsidies to rent on the private-housing market. This proposal avoids the stigma of housing specifically set aside for the poor. It facilitates maximum choice of neighbourhood. Evidence from the United States indicates that the Housing Allowance Program has achieved a certain amount of slum dispersal through recipients of the benefit choosing to rent private accommodation outside the slum.[14]

The indirect approach

Michelson[15] points out that a popular viewpoint amongst planners in recent years has been that while neighbourhoods can be kept homogeneous, they should be articulated in such a way that there are centres or facilities that all groups *have* to use. This approach probably has only limited relevance to the crime question. If middle-class and lower-class people are forced to rub shoulders at a shopping centre, for example, it is hard to imagine how this fairly fleeting form of contact would have substantial effects upon the structure of illegitimate opportunities, upon norm-conflict, or upon other fundamental variables that are hypothesized to intervene between class-mix and crime.

One central community facility which is the focus of sustained interaction among various groups is the school. For young people, class-mix in schools is probably more fundamental with regard to illegitimate opportunity or norm-conflict to which they are exposed than is class-mix in the neighbourhood. The school is where most of their peer-group interaction takes place. Schools can be made less homogeneous by the simple device of locating them near the boundaries separating homogeneous neighbourhoods rather than in the centre of homogeneous neighbourhoods.

Simply to locate schools so as to encourage class-mix within schools is hardly enough. Evidence from a Brisbane study indicates that no matter how conveniently situated is the local school, many middle-class parents living in lower-class areas will send their children long distances to attend a predominantly middle-class high school.[16] This tendency has been exacerbated in Brisbane by principals who visit primary schools outside their own area to recruit new high-school students. By increasing their enrolments in this way they push their school into a higher administrative category, which entitles them to more in the way of staff, equipment and salaries. The upshot of this policy has been that almost all the middle-class students from certain lower-class suburbs are lured away to middle-class state high schools up to ten miles away.

The Education Department is now taking steps to delimit which primary schools can be visited by 'recruiting officers' from given high schools. Other steps which could be taken to discourage this middle-class drift away from lower-class schools are the cancelling of free rail tickets and bus concessions for those who travel such distances, or the outright insistence by the Education Department that children attend their local school.

Hauser *et al.*[17] in their report on Chicago public schools, demonstrated that, if students were assigned to schools in terms of proximity and with full use of seating capacities, many underutilized all-white public schools would be desegregated, and many mainly Negro over-crowded schools in Chicago would be integrated and thinned out. Rationally planned assignment of pupils could reduce racial segregation in schools by some 15 to 20 per cent.

Officers of the Juvenile Aid Bureau in Brisbane point out that another way in which 'good' state high schools in middle-class areas maintain their exclusiveness is by expelling 'bad' pupils. These schools have a reputation to maintain, and they fear complaints from middle-class parents — so problem pupils are handled by suspension. Suspended students then go to predominantly lower-class schools which cannot suspend them lest they have nowhere else to go.

This is but the most dramatic way in which problem pupils are eased out of 'good' schools and dumped together in problem schools. Indeed, the whole educational system in Australia seems to be geared to keeping lower-class and middle-class children apart. An elite private-school system functions for the children of the wealthy. Within schools, children who do not perform well (mainly lower-class children) are segregated by a process of streaming or tracking classes. All of these factors maximize that juxtaposition of lower-class youth which creates the conditions for the formation of lower-class delinquent subcultures.[18]

Glazer[19] has suggested that it may be possible 'to deliberately use schools as a tool for reshaping residential neighbourhoods'.[20] He pointed out that if a neighbourhood is becoming increasingly lower class, the neighbourhood school will tend to become increasingly unsatisfactory to middle-class parents as 'standards' are perceived to be dropping. In response, middle-class people will either move to another neighbourhood or transport their children long distances to another school. Part of the solution to this source of class concentration may be to provide disproportionate funds for schools in lower-class areas, so that they are more likely to be perceived by middle-class parents as 'good' schools with high 'standards'.

An interesting case study of how a community attempts to use the school and other indirect techniques for shaping residential patterns is the case of Oak Park in Chicago. This white middle-class area is threatened with block-by-block resegregation into an all-black area. Lauber[21] has discussed how the white community considered a wide range of strategies to stop the community from going all-black, while encouraging an integrated black and white community. These strategies include legal prohibitions against 'steering' by real-estate agents and lending institutions (directing white home-seekers only to all-white areas and blacks to all-black areas). Another strategy being investigated is an 'equity assurance plan' to guarantee the resale value of homes and thereby allay the fears of whites about racial invasion. An Oak Park Housing Center has been opened to practise a kind of 'reverse steering' to guide blacks into white areas and whites into areas going black.

Plans are being considered for the replacement of local neighbourhood schools (which might become all-white or all-black) with grade centres which draw students from throughout Oak Park. The most controversial of the suggestions to avoid black resegregation in Oak Park has been an amendment to the village's fair-housing ordinance to establish a portion of Oak Park as a 'designated area' in danger of 'becoming a black segregated area'. The amendment would make it unlawful to sell or rent accommodation to a black person in the designated area if more than 30 per cent of the block concerned were already black. Any black person refused housing under this ordinance would be assisted to find comparable housing elsewhere in Oak Park.

Oak Park is a fascinating example of how the racism, the financial self-interest, and the idealism of a community have all been harnessed to serve the purpose of racial integration as an alternative to rapid resegregation of an all-white area into all-black. Grass-roots community organization has thrown up a variety of local indirect approaches for creating integration. Some will work and some will fail, but the richness and variety of the solutions posited illustrates that in creating mix there are likely to be many possible local solutions.

Class-mix and the planning of new towns

It would seem easier to plan for class-mix in towns which are being developed from scratch than in cities where powerful inertia in urban structure already exists. In most cases, planners of new towns strive for class-mix, but this is not always the case. Williams, in her study of the large new Australian coal-mining town of Moranbah, established by the Utah Development Co. in 1970, found that the Moranbah Town Plan has been contrived so that residents in top managerial positions have been designated housing on a particular hill.[22] This has become known as 'snob hill'.

The US government is reported to have given $200,000 in 1966 to a private developer to find some way to work lower-income residents into his new town.[23] The optimism about the value of incorporating class-mix into the planning of new towns may not be justified. A follow-up of the British new towns built on class-mix principles shows that local neighbourhoods became progressively less integrated through time. Localities began to take on the coloration of one class level or another.[24]

Idealistic advocates of class-mix must confront the possibility that their policies will never have the impact on class-mix which they expect, because in the final analysis many people choose to live with those of their own kind. Gans[25] instanced cases in which a cost differential of around 20 per cent for adjacent homes was successfully maintained, but emphasized that developers have been stuck with unsaleable homes when differences were greater. Whether people choose to live with those of their own kind because of a preference for having neighbours similar to themselves, or because of the market forces of real-estate capitalism, is an issue which is taken up in the postscript to this book.

The range of policies

Governments are continually framing a multitude of policies which have implications for class-mix. And governments frequently act on the assumption that removing lower-class people from lower-class areas will reduce crime. A recent example in Brisbane was the decision to close down the 'Born Free Club'. This club was a sleeping place and living quarters for down-and-out Aborigines in South Brisbane — the locality with the highest rate of violent crime in the city. The police requested that the club be closed because they claimed it was being used as a base for muggings and assaults. It was decided that a new hostel for Aborigines would be built in a more 'respectable' area of the city where corrupting influences would be reduced.

Similar principles are applied even to individual offenders. The former director of children's services in Queensland once told the author that when his department had to deal with a delinquent boy under the influence of a 'bad local area' or of a local delinquent gang, they would often encourage him to get away from it by joining the navy.

The above discussion clearly refutes the argument that the class-mix question has no implications for practical government policies. Moreover, in a diverse range of areas, the actions of policy-makers are already influenced by notions of fostering class-mix.

Conclusion

This appendix has demonstrated that there exist a considerable number
of policies that could be used to increase class-mix without forcibly
dislocating people or increasing residential mobility. In fact, it has been
shown that class-mix policies do not necessarily involve force or limitation of choice, nor more residential mobility than would otherwise have
occurred. If, for example, we are considering whether new housing
estates or new towns should be constructed on a class-mixed basis, we
are dealing with new occupants who are going to change their residence
anyway.

However, to show that feasible, non-disruptive, class-mix policies do
exist, is not to show that these policies are desirable. This book does
not attempt to assess the global desirability of class-mix policies.

Notes

Chapter 1 Defining the problem

1 Wolfgang, M. E. and Ferracuti, F. (1967), *The Subculture of Violence: Towards an Integrated Theory in Criminology*, London: Social Science Paperbacks, p. 299.
2 For example, see Rothenberg, J. (1972), 'Elimination of Blight and Slums', in M. Stewart, ed., *The City: Problems of Planning*, Harmondsworth, Penguin, pp.130–54.
3 Baldwin, J., Bottoms, A. E. and Walker, M. A. (1976), *The Urban Criminal: A Study in Sheffield*, London: Tavistock, pp. 146–9.
4 Sullenger, T. E. (1936), *Social Determinants in Juvenile Delinquency*, New York: Wiley, pp. 170–80. Longmoor, E. S. and Young, E. F. (1936), 'Ecological Interrelationships of Juvenile Delinquency, Dependency, and Population Movements: A Cartographic Analysis of Data from Long Beach, California', *American Journal of Sociology*, 41, 598–610. Porterfield, A. L. (1948), 'A Dread of Serious Crime in the United States: Some Trends and Hypotheses', *American Sociological Review*, 13, 44–54. Reiss, A. J. (1951), 'Delinquency and the Failure of Personal and Social Controls', *American Sociological Review*, 16, 196-207. Nye, I. F. (1958), *Family Relationships and Delinquent Behaviour*, New York: Wiley. Eaton, J. W. and Polk, K. (1961), *Measuring Delinquency: A Study of Probation Department Referrals*, Pittsburgh: University of Pittsburgh Press. Clinard, M. B. (1964), 'The Relation of Urbanization and Urbanism to Criminal Behaviour', in E. W. Burgess and D. Bogue, eds, *Contributions to Urban Sociology*, Chicago: University of Chicago Press, 541-58. Lunden, W. A. (1964), *Statistics on Delinquents and Delinquency*, Springfield, Illinois: Charles C. Thomas, 152–4. Shaw, C. R. and McKay, H. D. (1969), *Juvenile Delinquency and Urban Areas*, Chicago: University of Chicago Press.
5 Rodman, H. and Grams, P. (1967), 'Juvenile Delinquency and the Family: A Review and Discussion', in The President's Commission on Law Enforcement and Administration of Justice, *Task Force Report: Juvenile Delinquency and Youth Crime*, Washington: US Govt Printing Office, p. 214.
6 Australian Institute of Criminology (1975), *Planning a Low Crime Social Environment for Albury-Wodonga*, Canberra, mimeographed.
7 National Advisory Commission on Criminal Justice Standards and Goals (1973), *Community Crime Prevention*, Washington: US Govt Printing Office, p. 139.
8 Moynihan, D. P. (1969), 'Towards a National Urban Policy', an introduction to the report of the National Commission on the Causes and Prevention of

Violence, *Violent Crime: The Challenge to Our Cities,* New York: George Braziller, p. 10.

9 Burgess, E. W. (1952), 'The Economic Factor in Juvenile Delinquency', *Journal of Criminal Law, Criminology and Police Science,* 43, 29-42.

10 Jordan, V. E. (1974), 'The System Propagates Crime', *Crime and Delinquency,* 3, p. 233.

11 The President's Commission on Law Enforcement and Administration of Justice (1967), *The Challenge of Crime in a Free Society,* Washington: US Govt Printing Office.

12 Brady, J. P. (1975), 'The Talking Stone: Evolution and Action of People's Criminology', *The Insurgent Sociologist,* V, p. 76.

13 Gordon, D. M. (1973), 'Capitalism, Class and Crime in America', *Crime and Delinquency,* 19, p. 163.

14 Rein, M. (1970), *Social Policy: Issues of Choice and Change,* New York: Random House, 417-18.

15 Hoult, T. F. (1969), *Dictionary of Modern Sociology,* Totowa, New Jersey: Littlefield, Adams, p. 348.

16 See Wrong, D. H. (1972), 'Social Inequality Without Social Stratification', in D. W. Theilbar and S. D. Feldman, eds, *Issues in Social Inequality,* Boston: Little, Brown, 91-104. Rodman, H. (1968), 'Class Culture', in *International Encyclopaedia of the Social Sciences,* New York: Macmillan, 15.

17 Tawney, R. H. (1931), *Equality,* London: Allen & Unwin.

18 Hoult, op. cit., p. 165.

19 Weber, M. (1957), *The Theory of Social and Economic Organization,* translated by T. Parsons, Glencoe, Ill.: Free Press, p. 152.

20 As the book progresses it will become clear that to limit the definition of crime to offences punishable under the Criminal Code would be to adopt a very class-biased definition of crime which would invalidate any analysis of inequality and crime. On normally very arbitrary grounds, the law decides to punish most 'white-collar crimes' under civil codes. See chapter 10 for a more detailed discussion of this argument.

21 For a more detailed outline of the arguments of the opponents of official statistics see Braithwaite, J. B. (1977), 'Australian Delinquency: Research and Practical Considerations', in P. R. Wilson, ed., *Delinquency in Australia,* Brisbane: University of Queensland Press.

22 Proveda, T. G. (1970), 'The Image of the Criminal: A Critique of Crime and Delinquency Theories', *Issues in Criminology,* 5, p. 62. See also Clemente, F. and Kleiman, J. (1977), 'Fear of Crime in the United States: A Multivariate Analysis', *Social Forces,* 56, 519-31.

23 Gordon, op. cit., p. 179.

24 Chambliss, W. J. and Seidman, R. B. (1971), *Law, Order and Power,* New York: Addison-Wesley.

25 Ibid., p. 66.

26 Quoted in Lenski, G. (1966), *Power and Privilege,* New York: McGraw-Hill, p. 52.

27 For the most notable exposition of the argument see Taylor, I., Walton, P. and Young, J. (1973), *The New Criminology: For a Social Theory of Deviance,* London: Routledge & Kegan Paul. See also Quinney, R. (1974), *Critique of Legal Order: Crime Control in Capitalist Society,* Boston: Little, Brown. Krisberg, B. (1975), *Crime and Privilege: Toward a New Criminology,* Englewood Cliffs: Prentice-Hall. Pearce, F. (1976), *Crimes of the Powerful: Marxism, Crime and Deviance,* London: Pluto Press. Hepburn, J. (1977), 'Social Control and Legal Order: Legitimated Repression in a Capitalist State', *Contemporary Crises,* 1, 77-90.

28 Hagan, J. and Leon, J. (1977), 'Rediscovering Delinquency: Social-History, Political-Ideology and Sociology of Law', *American Sociological Review*, 42, 587–98.

29 Greenber, D. F. (1976), 'One Dimensional Marxist Criminology', *Theory and Society*, 3, 611–21.

30 Morris, N. and Hawkins, G. (1970), *The Honest Politician's Guide to Crime Control*, Chicago: University of Chicago Press, p. 2.

31 Another consequence of the limitation of the scope of the book to offences against persons or property is that most studies of female delinquency are excluded from consideration. This is because most measures of female delinquency in the literature are dominated by sexual offences. Moreover, most of the theory on class and crime has been concerned more with explaining the behaviour of male rather than female offenders. These two factors combine to make this book more relevant to male than to female criminality.

32 Braithwaite, J. B. and Law, H. G. (1978), 'The Structure of Self-Reported Delinquency', *Applied Psychological Measurement*, 2, 221–38.

33 Kraus, J. (1973), 'Judicial Labels as a Typology of Offences Committed by Male Juveniles', *British Journal of Criminology*, 13, 269–74.

34 See Taylor *et al.*, op. cit.

35 Wilson and Brown found that while large numbers of respondents in an Australian national sample felt that various offences without victims should not be a crime, there were virtually no dissenters from the legal *status quo* for all of the offences against persons and property. See Wilson, P. R. and Brown, J. W. (1973), *Crime and the Community*, Brisbane: University of Queensland Press, 53–4. Similarly, the New South Wales Bureau of Crime Statistics and Research found on a Sydney sample of 1,183 that there were substantial numbers of people who felt that 'public drunkenness', 'prostitution', and 'vagrancy' should not be punished, but practically no respondents felt that the offences with victims should not be punished. See New South Wales Bureau of Crime Statistics and Research (1974), *Crime, Correction and the Public*, Statistical Report 17, Sydney. Chilton and DeAmicis also found recently that the level of agreement over seriousness ratings for offences was very low for crimes without victims when compared to crimes with victims. See Chilton, R. and DeAmicis, J. (1975), 'Overcriminalization and the Measurement of Consensus', *Sociology and Social Research*, 15, 318–29. See also Rossi, P. H., Waite, E., Bose, C. E. and Berk, R. E. (1974), 'The Seriousness of Crimes: Normative Structure and Individual Differences', *American Sociological Review*, 39, 224–37. The most thorough exploration of this question has been Newman's cross-national study of perceptions of deviance in six cultures. While there was some evidence of the applicability of a conflict model for victimless crimes, a clear social consensus between cultures emerged over traditional crimes against persons and property. See Newman, G. (1976), *Comparative Deviance: Perception and Law in Six Cultures*, New York: Elsevier. Thomas *et al.* found rank order correlations of over ·9 between the ranking of the seriousness of criminal offences provided by males compared with females, blacks with whites, under 45s with over 45s, and high compared with low socio-economic status. See Thomas, C. W., Cage, R. and Foster, S. (1976), 'Public Opinion on Criminal Law and Legal Sanctions: An Examination of Two Conceptual Models', *Journal of Criminal Law and Criminology*, 67, 110–16. On a sample of 2,278 adolescents, Wright and Cox found considerable consensus concerning offences relating to property and the rights of others. See Wright, D. and Cox, E. (1967), 'Religious Belief and Co-education in a Sample of 6th Form Boys and Girls', *British Journal of Social and Clinical Psychology*, 9, 23–31. Wright, D. and Cox, E. (1967),

'A Study of the Relationship Between Moral Judgment and Religious Belief in a Sample of English Adolescents', *Journal of Social Psychology*, 72, 135–44.

36 Young, J. (1975), 'Working Class Criminology', in I. Taylor, P. Walton and J. Young, eds, *Critical Criminology*, London: Routledge & Kegan Paul, p. 71.

37 Sellin, T. (1938), *Culture Conflict and Crime*, New York: Social Science Research Council Bulletin no. 41, 19–32.

38 Schwendinger, H. and Schwendinger, J. (1975), 'Defenders of Order or Guardians of Human Rights', in I. Taylor *et al.*, op. cit., 113–46.

39 For some more recent critiques of the use of official statistics see Cicourel, A. V. (1968), *The Social Organization of Juvenile Justice*, New York: Wiley. Chambliss, W. J. and Nagasawa, R. H. (1969), 'On the Validity of Official Statistics', *Journal of Research in Crime and Delinquency*, 6, 71–7. Box, S. (1971), *Deviance, Reality and Society*, London: Holt, Rinehart & Winston. Chapters 3 and 6 Taylor *et al.* (1973), op. cit.

40 Murphy, F. J. (1946), 'Delinquency off the Record', in *Yearbook of the National Probation Association*, New York: National Probation Association, 178–95.

41 Sellin, T. and Wolfgang, M. (1964), *The Measurement of Delinquency*, New York: Wiley.

42 Ibid., p. 122.

43 Op. cit., p. 29.

44 Nye, F. I. and Short, J. F. (1957), 'Scaling Delinquent Behaviour', *American Sociological Review*, 22, 326–31. Erickson, M. and Empey, L. (1963), 'Court Records, Undetected Delinquency and Decision Making', *Journal of Criminal Law, Criminology and Police Science*, 54, 458–9. Voss, H. (1963), 'Ethnic Differentials in Delinquency in Honolulu', *Journal of Criminal Law, Criminology and Police Science*, 54, 325–6. Robins, L. N. (1963), 'The Reluctant Respondent', *Public Opinion Quarterly*, 27, 276–86. Christie, N., Andenaes, J. and Skirbekk, S. (1965), 'A Study of Self-Reported Crime', in *Scandinavian Studies in Criminology*, vol. 1, London: Tavistock, 55–85. Elmhorn, K. (1965), 'Study in Self-Reported Delinquency Among School Children in Stockholm', in *Scandinavian Studies in Criminology*, vol. 1, London: Tavistock, 117–46. Hirschi, T. and Selvin, H. (1967), *Delinquent Research: An Appraisal of Analytic Methods*, New York: Free Press. Sherwin, R. C. (1968), *Social Class Values and Deviant Behaviour: An Empirical Test of Some Theories of Delinquency*, PhD dissertation, University of Connecticut, 83–6. Gould, L. (1969), 'Who Defines Delinquency: A Comparison of Self-Reported and Officially Reported Delinquency for Three Racial Groups', *Social Problems*, 17, 325–36. Gold, M. (1970), *Delinquent Behaviour in an American City*, Belmont, Calif.: Brooks-Cole. Fisher, R. (1970), 'Borstal Recall Delinquency and the Cloward–Ohlin Theory of Criminal Subcultures', *British Journal of Criminology*, 10, 52–63. Gibson, H., Morrison, S. and West, D. J. (1970), 'The Confession of Known Offences in Response to a Self-Reported Delinquency Schedule', *British Journal of Criminology*, 10, 277–80. Williams, J. R. and Gold, M. (1972), 'From Delinquent Behaviour to Official Delinquency', *Social Problems*, 20, 209–29. McCandless, B. R., Persons, W. S. and Roberts, A. (1972), 'Perceived Opportunity, Delinquency, Race, and Body Build Among Delinquent Youth', *Journal of Consulting and Clinical Psychology*, 38, 281–7. Farrington, D. P. (1973), 'Self-Reports of Deviant Behaviour: Predictive and Stable?', *Journal of Criminal Law and Criminology*, 64, 99–100. Blackmore, J. (1974), 'The Relationship between Self-Reported Delinquency and Official Convictions among Adolescent Boys', *British Journal of Criminology*, 14, 172–6. Hardt, R. H. and Peterson-Hardt, S. J. (1977), 'On Determining the Quality of the Delinquency Self-Report Method', *Journal of*

Research in Crime and Delinquency, 14, 247–61.

45 Nettler, G. (1974), *Explaining Crime*, New York: McGraw-Hill, p. 94.

46 Gold (1970), op. cit., 19–24.

47 Jessor, R., Graves, T., Hanson, R. and Jessor, S. (1968), *Society, Personality and Deviant Behaviour*, New York: Holt, Rinehart and Winston, p. 216. Gould (1969), op. cit.

48 Clark, J. and Tifft, L. (1966), 'Polygraph and Interview Validity of Self-Reported Deviant Behaviour', *American Sociological Review*, 31, 516–23.

49 Ball, J. (1967), 'The Reliability and Validity of Interview Data Obtained from 59 Narcotic Drug Addicts', *American Journal of Sociology*, 72, 650–4. Of course this ingenious validation study is not concerned with behaviour which fits the definition of crime being applied in this book.

50 Farrington, op. cit.

51 McCandless *et al.*, op. cit.

52 For example, Williams and Gold, op. cit. could only account for 9 per cent of the variance in officially recorded delinquency with self-reported delinquency. Gould, op. cit., p. 332, obtained a gamma of only ·16 between a self-report measure and juvenile court and police records. For McCandless *et al.*, op. cit., the rank order correlation between admitted and committed delinquency was ·12.

53 Clark, J. P. reported in R. Hardt and G. Bodine (1965), *Development of Self-Report Instruments in Delinquency Research: A Conference Report*, Youth Development Center, Syracuse University, p. 16.

54 Dentler, R. and Monroe, L. (1961), 'Social Correlates of Early Adolescent Theft', *American Sociological Review*, 26, 733–43.

55 Belson, T. (1969), 'The Extent of Stealing by London Boys and Some of Its Origins', Survey Research Centre, London School of Economics.

56 Kulik, J. A. and Sabin, T. R. (1968), 'Disclosure of Delinquent Behaviour under Conditions of Anonymity and Non-Anonymity', *Journal of Consulting and Clinical Psychology*, 32, 506–9.

57 Farrington, op. cit.

58 Coleman, J. S. (1961), *The Adolescent Society*, New York: The Free Press of Glencoe, footnote 4, p. 16.

59 Braithwaite and Law, op. cit.

60 Ibid.

61 Farrington, op. cit., Nettler, op. cit., 93–4. Hardt and Bodine, op. cit. Gould, op. cit. Phillips, D. L. (1971), *Knowledge From What? Theories and Methods in Social Research*, Chicago: Rand McNally, chapter 2.

62 Gould, op. cit., 329–31.

63 Gold (1970), op. cit., p. 23.

64 Nettler, op. cit., 85–6.

65 Sheehan, P. W. (1974), *A Neoclassical Account of Experimental Method: Some Dilemmas for the Social Scientist*, University of Queensland, University of Queensland Inaugural Lectures, p. 25.

66 Webb, E. J., Campbell, D. T., Schwartz, R. D. and Sechrest, L. (1972), *Unobtrusive Measures: Nonreactive Research in the Social Sciences*, Chicago: Rand McNally, p. 3.

Chapter 2 The class–crime relationship

1 Ray, J. S. (1971), 'The Questionnaire Measurement of Social Class', *Australian and New Zealand Journal of Sociology*, 7, 58–64.

2 For an argument for the salience of occupation as an index of wealth and power, see Barber, B. (1957), *Social Stratification: A Comparative Analysis of*

Structure and Process, New York: Harcourt, Brace & World. See especially chapter 8, 'Indices of Social Class Position'.

3 These studies have been thoroughly reviewed by Duncan Timms. Timms also presents a theory to explain this pattern of ecological differentiation which so consistently emerges. See Timms, D. (1971), *The Urban Mosaic: Towards a Theory of Residential Differentiation*, Cambridge: University of Cambridge Press.

4 Sweetster, F. L. (1965), 'Factorial Ecology: Helsinki, 1960', *Demography*, 2, 372–86.

5 Schmid, C. F. and Tagashira, K. (1964), 'Ecological and Demographic Indices: A Methodological Analysis', *Demography*, 1, 195–211.

6 Clinard, M. B. and Abbott, D. J. (1973), *Crime in Developing Countries: A Comparative Perspective*, New York: Wiley.

7 Chambliss, W. J. (1969), *Crime and the Legal Process*, New York: McGraw-Hill, 84–6.

8 Box, S. (1971), *Deviance, Reality and Society*, New York: Holt, Rinehart and Winston, p. 172.

9 Myerhoff, H. L. and Myerhoff, B. G. (1964), 'Field Observations of Middle Class "Gangs"', *Social Forces*, 42, 328–36.

10 Bayley, D. H. and Mendelsohn, H. (1969), *Minorities and the Police*, New York: Free Press, p. 102.

11 West, D. J. (1967), *The Young Offender*, Harmondsworth: Penguin, p. 59.

12 Gibbens, T. C. N. and Ahrenfeldt, R. H. (1966), *Cultural Factors in Delinquency*, London: Tavistock, p. 45.

13 Ashpole, R. E. (1970), *Parental Strategies and Social Class in the Adjudication of Delinquency*, unpublished PhD dissertation, University of Utah.

14 Cicourel, A. V. (1968), *The Social Organization of Juvenile Justice*, New York: Wiley.

15 Ibid., p. 67.

16 Wilson, J. Q. (1968), *Varieties of Police Behaviour: The Management of Law and Order in Eight Communities*, Cambridge, Mass.: Harvard University Press.

17 O'Connor, G. W. and Watson, N. A. (1964), *Juvenile Delinquency and Youth Crime: The Police Role*, Washington: International Association of Chiefs of Police, p. 134.

18 See ibid., p. 134. Bayley and Mendelsohn, op. cit. Westley, W. A. (1970), *Violence and the Police: A Sociological Study of Law, Custom and Morality*, Massachusetts: MIT Press. Garrett, M. and Short, J. F. (1975), 'Social Class and Delinquency: Predictions and Outcomes of Police-Juvenile Encounters', *Social Problems*, 22, 368–82. A study by Cameron found that department-store detectives had theories about who were the most likely types of people to offend. They were keen to observe and follow Negroes, but were less suspicious of white middle-class shoppers. See Cameron, M. A. (1964), *The Booster and the Snitch*, New York: Free Press.

19 Chapman, D. (1968), *Sociology and the Stereotype of the Criminal*, London: Tavistock.

20 Box, S. and Russell, K. (1975), 'The Politics of Discreditability: Disarming Complaints Against the Police', *The Sociological Review*, 23, 315–46.

21 Black, D. J. (1970), 'Production of Crime Rates', *American Sociological Review*, 35, 722–48.

22 Black, D. J. and Reiss, A. J. (1970), 'Police Control of Juveniles', *American Sociological Review*, 35, 63–77.

23 See Wolfgang, M. E. (1958), *Patterns in Criminal Homicide*, Philadelphia: University of Pennsylvania Press.

24 Wilson, J. Q., op. cit., p. 43.

25 Terry, R. M. (1967), 'Discrimination in the Handling of Juvenile Offenders by Social-Control Agencies', *Journal of Research in Crime and Delinquency*, 4, p. 218.
26 For example see, Axelrad, S. (1952), 'Negro and White Institutionalized Delinquents', *American Journal of Sociology*, 57, 569–74. Black and Reiss, op. cit. However, Williams and Gold found *no* tendency for blacks to receive more severe dispositions than whites. See Williams, J. R. and Gold, M. (1972), 'From Delinquent Behaviour to Official Delinquency', *Social Problems*, 20, 223–4.
27 For example see Gold, M. (1963), *Status Forces in Delinquent Boys*, Ann Arbor, Michigan: Institute for Social Research, 9–10. Cicourel, op. cit. Wolfgang, M. E., Figlio, R. M. and Sellin, T. (1972), *Delinquency in a Birth Cohort*, Chicago: University of Chicago Press. Bodine, summarized in Box, op. cit., p. 195. For a study which has failed to confirm this, see Pine, G. J. (1965), 'Social Class, Social Mobility and Delinquent Behaviour', *Personnel and Guidance Journal*, 43, 770–4.
28 Wolfgang *et al.*, op. cit.
29 Goldman, N. (1963), *The Differential Selection of Juvenile Offenders for Court Appearance*, New York: National Council on Crime and Delinquency.
30 McEachern, A. W. and Bauzer, R. (1967), 'Factors Related to Disposition in Juvenile-Police Contacts', in M. W. Klein, ed., *Juvenile Gangs in Context: Theory, Research and Action*, Englewood Cliffs: Prentice-Hall, 148–60.
31 Hohenstein, W. H. (1969), 'Factors Influencing the Police Disposition of Juvenile Offenders', in T. Sellin and M. Wolfgang, eds, *Delinquency*, New York: Wiley, 138–49.
32 Arnold, W. R. (1971), 'Race and Ethnicity Relative to Other Factors in Juvenile Court Dispositions', *American Journal of Sociology*, 77, 211–27.
33 Ferdinand, T. N. and Luchterhand, E. G. (1970), 'Inner-City Youth, the Police, the Juvenile Court, and Justice', *Social Problems*, 17, 510–27.
34 Thornberry, T. P. (1973), 'Race, Socioeconomic Status and Sentencing in the Juvenile Justice System', *Journal of Criminal Law and Criminology*, 64, 90–9.
35 Terry, R. M. (1967), 'Discrimination in the Handling of Juvenile Offenders by Social-Control Agencies', *Journal of Research in Crime and Delinquency*, 4, 218–30.
36 Weiner, N. L. and Willie, C. V. (1971), 'Decisions by Juvenile Officers', *American Journal of Sociology*, 77, 199–210.
37 Terry, op. cit.
38 Weiner and Willie, op. cit.
39 Shannon, L. W. (1963), 'Types and Patterns of Delinquency Referral in a Middle-Sized City', *British Journal of Delinquency*, 24, 24–36.
40 Bordua, D. J. (1967), 'Recent Trends: Deviant Behaviour and Social Control', *Annals*, 57, 149–63.
41 Thornberry, op. cit.
42 Black and Reiss, op. cit. Lundman, R. J., Sykes, R. E., and Clark, J. P. (1978), 'Police Control of Juveniles: A Replication', *Journal of Research in Crime and Delinquency*, 15, 74–91.
43 White, G. F. (1975), 'Public Responses to Hypothetical Crimes: Effect of Offender and Victim Status and Seriousness of the Offence on Punitive Reactions', *Social Forces*, 53, 449–59.
44 Piliavin, I. and Briar, S. (1964), 'Police Encounters with Juveniles', *American Journal of Sociology*, 70, 206–14.
45 Matza, D. (1969), *Becoming Deviant*, Englewood Cliffs: Prentice-Hall, p. 183.
46 Whyte, W. F. (1943), *Street Corner Society: The Social Structure of an Italian*

Slum, Chicago: University of Chicago Press.
47 Suttles, G. D. (1968), *The Social Order of the Slum*, Chicago: University of Chicago Press. Suttles, G. D. (1972), *The Social Construction of Communities*, Chicago: University of Chicago Press.
48 Evidence for this is also to be found in Shaw, M. and Williamson, W. (1972), 'Public Attitudes to the Police', *The Criminologist*, 26, 18–32. People from lower-class areas were found to have less 'co-operative' attitudes towards helping the police to catch criminals, when compared with people from middle-class areas.
49 Box, op. cit., p. 196.
50 Jongman, R. W. and Smale, G. J. (1973), 'Factors Relating to the Public Prosecutor's Policy of Case Dismissal', *Nederlands Tijdschrift Voor Criminologie*, 15, 55–65.
51 Cameron, op. cit.
52 Bullock, H. A. (1961), 'Significance of the Racial Factor in the Length of Prison Sentence', *Journal of Criminal Law, Criminology and Police Science*, 52, 411–17.
53 Marshall, H. and Purdy, R. (1972), 'Hidden Deviance and the Labelling Approach: The Case for Drinking and Driving', *Social Problems*, 19, 541–53.
54 Robin, G. D. (1970), 'The Corporate and Judicial Disposition of Employee Thieves', in E. O. Smigel and H. L. Ross, eds, *Crimes Against Bureaucracy*, New York: Van Nostrand, 124–6.
55 Nagel, S. S. (1970), 'The Tipped Scales of American Justice', in A. S. Blumberg, ed., *The Scales of Justice*, Chicago: Aldine, 31–49.
56 Green, E. (1961), *Judicial Attributes in Sentencing*, London: Macmillan. Green, E. (1964), 'Inter- and Intra-Racial Crime Relative to Sentencing', *Journal of Criminal Law, Criminology and Police Science*, 55, 348–58.
57 Wolfgang, M. and Riedel, M. (1975), 'Rape, Race and the Death Penalty in Georgia', *American Journal of Orthopsychiatry*, 45, 658–67.
58 Garfinkel's study was a replication of an earlier study by Johnson which reached the same conclusion on North Carolina homicide data. See Johnson, G. (1941), 'The Negro and Crime', *American Academy of Political and Social Sciences*, 271, 93–104. Garfinkel, H. (1949), 'Research Note on Inter- and Intra-Racial Homicides', *Social Forces*, 27, 369–81.
59 Newman, D. J. (1956), 'Pleading Guilty for Considerations: A Study of Bargain Justice', *Journal of Criminal Law, Criminology and Police Science*, 46, 780–90.
60 Wolfgang, M., Kelly, A. and Nolde, H. C. (1962), 'Comparison of the Executed and Commuted among Admissions to Death Row', in N. Johnston *et al.*, *The Sociology of Punishment and Correction*, New York: Wiley, 63–8.
61 Eggleston, E. M. (1976), *Fear, Favour or Affection*, Canberra: Australian National University Press.
62 Oaks, D. H. and Lehman, W. (1970), 'Lawyers for the Poor', in A. S. Blumberg, ed., *The Scales of Justice*, Chicago: Aldine, 91–122.
63 Bensing, R. C. and Schroeder, O. (1960), *Homicide in an Urban Community*, Springfield, Ill.: Charles C. Thomas.
64 Pope, C. E. (1975), *Sentencing of California Felony Offenders*, Utilization of criminal justice statistics, Analytic Report 6, US Dept of Justice, Law Enforcement Assistance Administration.
65 Cameron, op. cit.
66 Hindelang, M. J. (1974), 'Decisions of Shoplifting Victims to Invoke the Criminal Justice Process', *Social Problems*, 21, 580–93.
67 Cohen, L. E. and Stark, R. (1974), 'Discriminatory Labelling and the Five-Finger Discount', *Journal of Research in Crime and Delinquency*, 11, 25–39.

68 Chiricos, T. G. and Waldo, G. P. (1975), 'Socioeconomic Status and Criminal Sentencing: An Empirical Assessment of a Conflict Proposition', *American Sociological Review*, 40, 753–72.

69 Willick, D. H., Gehlker, G. and Watts, A. M. (1975), 'Social Class as a Factor Affecting Judicial Disposition: Defendants Charged with Criminal Homosexual Acts', *Criminology*, 13, 57–77.

70 Lotz, R. and Hewitt, J. D. (1977), 'The Influence of Legally Irrelevant Factors on Felony Sentencing', *Sociological Inquiry*, 47, 39–48.

71 Hagan, J. (1974), 'Extra-Legal Attributes and Criminal Sentencing: An Assessment of a Sociological Viewpoint', *Law and Society Review*, 8, 357–83. See also another study by Hagan which, after controlling for legal variables, found no evidence of sentencing discrimination against Indians. Hagan, J. (1974), 'Criminal Justice and Native People: A Study of Incarceration in a Canadian Province', *Canadian Review of Sociology and Anthropology*, special issue (August), 220–36.

72 In an interesting experimental demonstration of Matza's point, Stewart and Cannon simulated the stealing of a shopper's bag by a thief dressed as a worker, a businessman or a priest. The experiment showed that the probability of an ambiguous act being interpreted as criminal by bystanders is lower when the offender is of higher status. Stewart, J. and Cannon, D. (1977), 'Effects of Perpetrator Status and Bystander Commitment on Responses to a Simulated Crime', *Journal of Police Science and Administration*, 5, 318–23.

73 Quinney, R. (1974), *Critique of Legal Order: Crime Control in Capitalist Society*, Boston: Little, Brown, p. 52. For a more recent exposition of this position see Manders, D. (1975), 'Labelling Theory and Social Reality: A Marxist Critique', *The Insurgent Sociologist*, VI, 53–66. Also see Spitzer, D. (1975), 'Toward a Marxian Theory of Deviance', *Social Problems*, 22, 638–51. Pearce, F. (1976), *Crimes of the Powerful: Marxism, Crime and Deviance*, London: Pluto Press.

74 Hirschi, T. (1972), 'Social Class and Crime', in D. W. Theilbar and S. D. Feldman, eds, *Issues in Social Inequality*, Boston: Little, Brown, p. 507.

75 Congalton, A. A. and Najman, J. M. (1974), *Safety in the Suburbs*, Sydney: New South Wales Bureau of Crime Statistics and Research, Statistical Report No. 14.

76 Wheeler, S. (1960), 'Sex Offences: A Sociological Critique', *Law and Contemporary Problems*, 25, p. 267.

77 See Faust, F. L. (1970), 'Dimensions of Delinquency Tolerance: Differential Tolerance of Juvenile Delinquent Behaviour by Adult Members of Different Socio-Economic Classes and Racial Groups', PhD dissertation, Ohio State University.

78 Young, J. (1975), 'Working-Class Criminology', in I. Taylor, P. Walton and J. Young, eds, *Critical Criminology*, London: Routledge & Kegan Paul, p. 72.

79 Tittle, C. R. and Villemez, W. J. (1977), 'Social Class and Criminality', *Social Forces*, 56, 475–502.

80 In cases in which tests of statistical significance were not calculated, studies are classified as 'Yes' only if the data trend was reasonably strong or has been regarded as strong by other researchers in the area.

81 Pine, G. J. (1965), 'Social Class, Social Mobility and Delinquent Behaviour', *Personnel and Guidance Journal*, 43, 770–4.

82 Box, S. and Ford, J. (1971), 'The Facts Don't Fit: On the Relationship Between Social Class and Criminal Behaviour', *The Sociological Review*, 19, 31–52. Cohen, A. K. and Short, J. F. (1971), 'Crime and Juvenile Delinquency', in R. K. Merton and R. Nisbet, eds, *Contemporary Social Problems*, 3rd edition, New York: Harcourt, Brace, Jovanovitch, 110–11.

83 Box and Ford, op. cit., p. 39.

84 Hirschi, T. and Selvin, H. (1967), *Delinquency Research: An Appraisal of Analytic Methods*, New York: Free Press, 108–9. Hirschi, T. (1969), *Causes of Delinquency*, Berkeley and Los Angeles: University of California Press.

85 Gold, M. (1963), *Status Forces in Delinquent Boys*, Ann Arbor, Michigan: University of Michigan, Institute for Social Research, 5–7.

86 See Braithwaite and Law for a discussion of the use of inappropriate scaling techniques in the measurement of self-reported delinquency. Braithwaite, J. B. and Law, H. G. (1978), 'The Structure of Self-Reported Delinquency', *Applied Psychological Measurement*, 2, 221–38.

87 Box and Ford, op. cit., p. 39, state in their review that 'Akers's research hardly provides any enlightenment on the relationship between social class and strictly delinquent (that is law-breaking) behaviour.'

88 McDonald, L. (1968), *Social Class and Delinquency*, London: Faber & Faber, 136–42.

89 Hirschi (1969), op. cit., 70–5.

90 Ibid., p. 71.

91 Ibid., p. 69.

92 Ibid., p. 72.

93 Spady, D. R. (1972), *Socio-economic Status and the Ecology of Juvenile Delinquency: Some Methodological Considerations*, PhD dissertation, University of Oregon.

94 Clark, J. P. and Tifft, L. L. (1966), 'Polygraph and Interview Validation of Self-Reported Deviant Behaviour', *American Sociological Review*, 31, 516–23.

95 The present author has recalculated χ^2 on these two studies, treating those who admit to only one offence as non-delinquents. Both studies then support a statistically significant tendency for the lower class to admit to more delinquency.

96 Gold, op. cit., 4–7.

97 Clark, J. P. and Wenninger, E. P. (1962), 'Socio-economic Class and Area as Correlates of Illegal Behaviour Among Juveniles', *American Sociological Review*, 27, 833.

98 Box, S. (1971), *Deviance, Reality and Society*, London: Holt, Rinehart & Winston, p. 87.

99 Bytheway, B. (1975), 'The Statistical Association between Social Class and Self-Reported Delinquency', *International Journal of Criminology and Penology*, 3, 243–51.

100 Gold (1963), op. cit., 4–5.

101 Christie, N., Andenaes, J. and Skirbekk, S. (1965), 'A Study of Self-Reported Crime', in *Scandinavian Studies in Criminology*, vol. 1, London: Tavistock, p. 107.

102 Box (1971), op. cit., 72–3.

103 Carter, D. (1974), 'An Exploratory Study of the Personal Networks of Convicted Juvenile Offenders', unpublished BA honours thesis, University of Queensland.

104 Braithwaite, J. B. and Braithwaite, V. A., unpublished data, some of which will be published in a forthcoming article entitled, 'An Exploratory Study of Delinquency and the Nature of Schooling'.

105 Hardt, R. H. (1968), 'Delinquency and Social Class: Bad Kids or Good Cops?' in I. Deutscher and E. Thompson, eds, *Among the People: Encounters with the Poor*, New York: Basic Books.

106 However, variations by social class of area did appear in the self-reporting of being 'ticketed'.

107 Smith, G. (1975), 'Leisure, Recreation and Delinquency', unpublished MA thesis, University of Queensland.

108 Hackler, J. C. and Lautt, M. (1969), 'Systematic Bias in Self-Reported Delinquency', *Canadian Review of Sociology and Anthropology*, 6, 92–106.

109 Gold, M. (1970), *Delinquent Behaviour in an American City*, Belmont, California: Brooks-Cole.

110 Ibid., p. 13.

111 Hardt, R. H. and Peterson-Hardt, S. J. (1977), 'On Determining the Quality of the Delinquency Self-Report Method', *Journal of Research in Crime and Delinquency*, 14, 247–61.

112 See Elliott, D. S. and Voss, H. L. (1974), *Delinquency and Dropout*, Lexington, Mass.: Lexington Books.

113 Hirschi, T. (1969), *Causes of Delinquency*, Berkeley and Los Angeles: University of California Press.

114 Hindelang, M. J. (1978), 'Race and Involvement in Common-Law Personal Crimes', *American Sociological Review*, 43, 93–109.

115 Woods, G. D. (1972), 'Some Aspects of Pack Rape in Sydney', in D. Chappell and P. R. Wilson, eds, *The Australian Criminal Justice System*, Melbourne: Butterworth, 109–14.

116 Congalton, A. A. and Najman, J. M. (1974), *Safety in the Suburbs*, Statistical Report 14, New South Wales Bureau of Crime Statistics and Research, Sydney, p. 15.

117 Smith, G., op. cit.

118 Schmitt, R. C. (1956), 'Intercorrelations of Social Problem Rates in Honolulu', *American Sociological Review*, 21, 617–19. Schmid, C. F. (1960), 'Urban Crime Areas', *American Sociological Review*, 25, 527–42, 655–78. Boggs, S. L. (1965), 'Urban Crime Patterns', *American Sociological Review*, 30, 899–908. Allison, J. P. (1972), 'Economic Factors and the Rate of Crime', *Land Economics*, 68, 193–6. In the latter study, the important exception to a negative correlation between social class of area and crime-occurrence rates was for burglary.

119 Thrasher, F. M. (1927), *The Gang*, Chicago: University of Chicago Press. Wattenberg, W. W. and Balistrieri, J. J. (1950), 'Gang Membership and Juvenile Misconduct', *American Sociological Review*, XV, p. 749. Cartwright, D. S. and Howard, K. I. (1966), 'Multivariate Analysis of Gang Delinquency: I. Ecologic Influences', *Multivariate Behavioural Research*, 1, 321–72.

120 Won, G. and Yamamoto, G. (1968), 'Social Structure and Deviant Behaviour: A Study of Shoplifting', *Sociology and Social Research*, 53, 44–55.

121 Hartshorne, H. and May, M. A. (1928), *Studies in the Nature of Character*, New York: Macmillan. For a re-examination of Hartshorne and May's data see also Burton, R. V. (1963), 'Generality of Honesty Reconsidered', *Psychological Review*, 70, 481–99.

122 West, D. J. (1969), *Present Conduct and Future Delinquency*, London: Heinemann.

123 Stinchcombe, A. L. (1964), *Rebellion in a High School*, Chicago: Quadrangle Books.

124 Lerman, P. (1965), reported in R. H. Hardt and G. E. Bodine, *Development of Self-Report Instruments in Delinquency Research: A Conference Report*, Syracuse, New York: Youth Development Center, Syracuse University, p. 10.

125 Lovegrove, S. A. (1973), 'The Significance of Three Scales Identifying a Delinquent Orientation among Young Australian Males', *The Australian and New Zealand Journal of Criminology*, 6, 93–106.

126 Glueck, S. and Glueck, E. (1966), *Juvenile Delinquents Grown Up*, New York: Kraus Reprints.

127 Miller, D. R. and Swanson, G. E. (1958), *The Changing American Parent*, New York: Wiley.
128 Stark, R. and McEvoy, J. (1970), 'Middle-Class Violence', *Psychology Today*, 4, 52–4.
129 Short, J. F. and Strodtbeck, F. L. (1965), *Group Process and Gang Delinquency*, Chicago: University of Chicago Press.
130 Miller, W. B. (1967), 'Theft Behaviour in City Gangs', in M. W. Klein, ed., *Juvenile Gangs in Context: Theory, Research and Action*, Englewood Cliffs: Prentice-Hall, 25–37.
131 Tittle, C. R. and Villemez, W. J. (1977), 'Social Class and Criminality', *Social Forces*, 56, 475–502.

Chapter 3 Theories of lower-class criminality

1 Engels, F. (1969), *The Condition of the Working Class in England in 1844*, Harmondsworth: Penguin.
2 Ibid., 144–5.
3 Young, J. (1975), 'Working-Class Criminology', in I. Taylor, P. Walton and J. Young, eds, *Critical Criminology*, London: Routledge & Kegan Paul, p. 79.
4 Engels, op. cit., p. 145.
5 Ibid., p. 240.
6 Ibid., p. 161.
7 Bonger, W. (1916), *Criminality and Economic Conditions*, Boston: Little, Brown.
8 Ibid., p. 37.
9 Ibid., p. 40.
10 Dollard, J., Miller, N. E., Doob, L. W., Mowrer, O. H. and Sears, R. R. (1939), *Frustration and Aggression*, New Haven: Yale University Press.
11 Ibid., p. 114.
12 Examples are Schiller's explanation of Negro crime as a response to repression by whites and the white system, and Guttmacher's observations on the responses of murderers to the economic privations of their infancy. Guttmacher says, 'Almost without exception one finds in their early backgrounds not only economic want, but cruelties and miseries of every kind. Such early conditioning predisposes to a marked under-valuation of life. To these individuals people are objects to be manipulated for predatory purposes. The Gluecks, in their important studies on juvenile delinquency, have found that the seriously delinquent child was involved in accidents far more frequently than the non-delinquent child. Disregard for their own safety came early and paralleled their disregard for the welfare of others. One can safely hypothesize that the amount of satisfying nurture that the child receives in its earliest years must be a fundamental element in the formation of its attitudes on the value of human life.' See Schiller, B. (1969), 'Racial Conflict and Delinquency: A Theoretical Approach', *Phylon*, 30, 261–71. Guttmacher, M. S. (1972), 'The Normal Murderer', in D. Dressler, ed., *Readings in Criminology and Penology*, New York: Colombia University Press, 99–100.
13 Feldman, R. and Weisfeld, G. (1973), 'An Interdisciplinary Study of Crime', *Crime and Delinquency*, 19, p. 156.
14 One exception is a totally inadequate study by Reiss and Rhodes which found virtually no relationship between 'status deprivation' and delinquency. The measure of 'status deprivation' used was the single item, 'Would you say

that most of the students in your school have better clothes and a better home to live in than you have?' See Reiss, A. J. and Rhodes, A. L. (1963), 'Status Deprivation and Delinquent Behaviour', *Sociological Quarterly*, 4, 135–49.

15 Adams, J. S. (1965), 'Inequity in Social Exchange', in L. Berkowitz, ed., *Advances in Experimental Social Psychology*, vol. 2, New York: Academic Press, p. 273.

16 For an insightful analysis of the limited awareness of inequity among British manual workers see Runciman, W. G. (1966), *Relative Deprivation and Social Justice*, London: Routledge & Kegan Paul.

17 National Advisory Commission on Criminal Justice Standards and Goals (1973), *Community Crime Prevention*, Washington DC, p. 45.

18 Ibid., p. 45.

19 Blanch, K. (1975), 'Women in Crime: Equal Rights, Equal Wrongs', *Cleo* (Australian edn), August, p. 25.

20 Matza, D. (1964), *Delinquency and Drift*, New York: Wiley, p. 89.

21 Ibid., p. 102.

22 Taylor, I., Walton, P. and Young, J. (1973), *The New Criminology: For a Social Theory of Deviance*, London: Routledge & Kegan Paul, p. 182.

23 Rainwater, L. (1966), 'Work and Identity in the Lower Class', in S. B. Warner, ed., *Planning for a Nation of Cities*, Cambridge, Mass.: MIT Press, 105–23.

24 See Shipee-Blum, E. V. (1959), 'The Young Rebel: Self-Regard and Ego-Ideal', *Journal of Consulting Psychology*, 23, 44–50. Scarpitti, F. R., Murray, E., Dinitz, S. and Reckless, W. (1960), 'The Good Boy in a High Delinquency Area', *American Sociological Review*, 25, 555–8. Massimo, J. L. and Shore, M. F. (1963), 'A Comprehensive Vocationally Oriented Psychotherapeutic Program for Delinquent Boys', *American Journal of Orthopsychiatry*, 33, 634–42. Dorn, D. S. (1968), 'Self-Concept, Alienation, and Anxiety in a Contraculture and Sub-Culture: A Research Report', *Journal of Criminal Law, Criminology and Police Science*, 59, 531–5. Lanphier, C. M. and Faulkner, J. E. (1970), 'Deviance in a Middle-Class Community', *International Journal of Comparative Sociology*, 11, 146–56. Kelly, D. H. (1971), 'School Failure, Academic Self-Evaluation, and School Avoidance and Deviant Behaviour', *Youth and Society*, 2, 489–503. Gold, M. and Mann, D. (1973), 'Delinquency as Defense', *American Journal of Orthopsychiatry*, 42, 463–79. Siegel, L. J., Rathus, S. A. and Ruppert, C. A. (1973), 'Values and Delinquent Youth: An Empirical Re-examination of Theories of Delinquency', *British Journal of Criminology*, 13, 237–44.

25 See Hill, T. J. (1957), 'Attitudes Toward Self: An Experimental Study', *Journal of Educational Sociology*, 30, 395–7. McDonald, R. L. and Gynther, M. D. (1963), 'MMPI Differences Associated with Sex, Race, and Social Class in Two Adolescent Samples', *Journal of Consulting Psychology*, 27, 112–16. Silverman, M. I. (1964), 'The Relationship Between Self-Esteem and Aggression in Two Classes', *Dissertation Abstracts*, 25, 2,616. McDonald, R. L. and Gynther, M. D. (1965), 'Relationship of Self and Ideal-Self Descriptions with Sex, Race and Class in Southern Adolescents', *Journal of Personality and Social Psychology*, 1, 85–8. Soares, A. T. and Soares, L. M. (1968), *Self-Perceptions of Culturally Disadvantaged and Non-Disadvantaged Children*, paper presented at the Eastern Psychological Convention, Boston. Coward, B. E., Feagin, J. R. and Williams, J. A. Jr (1974), 'The Culture of Poverty Debate: Some Additional Data', *Social Problems*, 21, 621–34.

26 Havighurst, R. J. and Taba, H. (1949), *Adolescent Character and Personality*, New York: Wiley. Bieri, J. and Loback, R. (1961), 'Self-Concept Differences in Relation to Identification, Religion, and Social Class', *Journal of Abnormal and Social Psychology*, 62, 94–8. Rosenberg, M. (1965), *Society and the*

Adolescent Self-Image, Princeton: Princeton University Press. Coopersmith, S. (1967), *The Antecedents of Self-Esteem*, San Francisco, VA: Freeman. For a review of a number of studies in this and the previous footnote, plus a number of additional studies which reached more ambiguous conclusions, see Allen, V. L. (1970), 'Personality Correlates of Poverty', in V. L. Allen, ed., *Psychological Factors in Poverty*, Chicago: Markham, 256–8.

27 Allen, op. cit., 251–2. For further evidence see the article by Sarbin, T. R. in the same book, 34–5.

28 Jaffe, L. D. (1963), 'Delinquency Proneness and Family Anomie', *Journal of Criminal Law, Criminology and Police Science*, 54, 146–54.

29 Gold, M. (1969), 'Juvenile Delinquency as a Symptom of Alienation', *Journal of Social Issues*, 25, p. 131.

30 Engstad, P. and Hackler, J. C. (1971), 'The Impact of Alienation on Delinquency Rates', *Canadian Journal of Criminology and Corrections*, 13, 147–54.

31 Dorn, D. S. (1968), 'Self-Concept, Alienation, and Anxiety in a Contra-Culture and Subculture: A Research Report', *Journal of Criminal Law, Criminology and Police Science*, 59, 531–5.

32 Merton, R. K. (1957), *Social Theory and Social Structure*, Glencoe, Ill.: Free Press, chapters 4 and 5.

33 Ibid., p. 146.

34 Adams, P. (1968), *The Australian* (newspaper), 12 September, p. 10.

35 Box, S. (1971), *Deviance, Reality and Society*, London: Holt, Rinehart & Winston, p. 104.

36 Cloward, R. A. and Ohlin, L. E. (1960), *Delinquency and Opportunity: A Theory of Delinquent Gangs*, Glencoe, Ill.: Free Press.

37 For a reaffirmation of Cloward's advocacy of equality of opportunity see Cloward, R. A. (1972), 'The Prevention of Delinquent Subcultures', in D. Palmer and A. S. Linsky, eds, *Rebellion and Retreat*, Columbus, Ohio: Merrill.

38 Of course, greater equality of results will promote greater equality of opportunity because so much inequality of opportunity arises from the financial incapacity of the poor to build opportunity through paying for education, cultural stimulation for children, good clothes to impress the prospective employer, and so on.

39 Rosenberg, B. and Silverstein, H. (1969), *The Varieties of Delinquent Experience*, Waltham, Mass.: Blaisdell, 130–3.

40 Gold, M. (1963), *Status Forces in Delinquent Boys*, Ann Arbor: Institute for Social Research, University of Michigan, 159–60.

41 Quicker, J. C. (1973), 'A Consideration of the Relationship of "Punitiveness" to Delinquency as Developed in Opportunity Theory', *The Journal of Criminal Law and Criminology*, 64, 333–8.

42 Picou, J. S., Cosley, A. J., Lemke, A. W. and Azuma, H. T. (1974), 'Occupational Choice and Perception of Attainment Blockage: A Study of Lower Class Delinquent and Non-Delinquent Black Males', *Adolescence*, 9, 289–98.

43 Elliott, D. S. and Voss, H. L. (1974), *Delinquency and Dropout*, Lexington, Mass.: Lexington Books, 30–1.

44 Elliott, D. S. (1961), *Delinquency, Opportunity and Patterns of Orientations*, Ph D dissertation, University of Washington. Landis, J. R. (1962), *Social Class Differentials in Self, Value, and Opportunity Structure as Related to Delinquency Potential*, Ph D dissertation, Ohio State University (Landis study reported in Reckless, W. C. (1961), *The Crime Problem*, 3rd edn, New York: Appleton-Century-Crofts, 452–3). Elliott, D. S. (1962), 'Delinquency and Perceived Opportunity', *Sociological Inquiry*, XXXII, 216–22. Short, J. F. (1964), 'Gang Delinquency and Anomie', in M. B. Clinard (1964), *Anomie and Deviant Behaviour*, New York: Free Press, 98–127. Landis, J. R. and

Scarpitti, F. R. (1965), 'Perceptions Regarding Value Orientation and Legitimate Opportunity: Delinquents and Non-Delinquents', *Social Forces*, 44, 83–91. Polk, K. (1965), 'An Exploration of Rural Delinquency', in L. Burchinal, ed., *Youth in Crisis: Facts, Myths and Social Change*, Washington DC: US Govt Printing Office, 221–32. Luchterhand, E. and Weller, L. (1966), 'Delinquency Theory and the Middle-Size City: A Study of Problem and Promising Youth', *Sociological Quarterly*, 7, 413–23. Wilcox, L. D. (1969), *Social Class, Anomie and Delinquency*, Ph D dissertation, Colorado State University. McCandless, B. R., Persons, W. S. and Roberts, A. (1972), 'Perceived Opportunity, Delinquency, Race, and Body Build Among Delinquent Youth', *Journal of Consulting and Clinical Psychology*, 38, 281–7. Datesman, D. K., Scarpitti, F. R. and Stephenson, R. M. (1975), 'Female Delinquency: An Application of Self and Opportunity Theories', *Journal of Research in Crime and Delinquency*, 12, 107–23. Cernkovich, S. A. (1978), 'Value Orientations and Delinquency Involvement', *Criminology*, 15, 443–58. For partial support for this hypothesis see Picou *et al.*, op. cit. Participant observation studies such as that by Cumming and Cumming also report findings consistent with this hypothesis. See Cumming, D. and Cumming, F. (1968), 'The Everyday Life of Delinquent Boys', in I. Deutcher and E. J. Thompson, eds, *Among the People: Encounters with the Poor*, New York: Basic Books. Elliott and Voss, op. cit., have reached conclusions contrary to those of all of the above studies. They found very few youths to anticipate failure in their efforts to achieve long-range goals, and that the few juveniles who did anticipate failure were no more likely to engage in delinquency than those who anticipated success.

45 Short, J. F. and Strodtbeck, F. L. (1965), *Group Process and Gang Delinquency*, Chicago: University of Chicago Press, 268–9.
46 Tallman, I. (1966), 'Adaptation to Blocked Opportunity: An Experimental Study', *Sociometry*, 29, 121–34.
47 See the review of evidence to this effect in Schafer, W. E. and Polk, K. (1967), 'Delinquency and the Schools', in The President's Commission on Law Enforcement and Administration of Justice, *Task Force Report: Juvenile Delinquency and Youth Crime*, Washington DC: US Govt Printing Office, 228–9.
48 By relative aspiration is meant, for example, the percentage of youth in various classes who aspire to better-paid occupations than their fathers. Cloward and Ohlin review some evidence that lower-class people aspire to a larger proportionate increase in income than do middle-class people. See Cloward and Ohlin, op. cit., 89–90.
49 See Nagasawa, R. H. (1971), 'Social Class Differentials in Success Striving', *Pacific Sociological Review*, 14, 215–33.
50 Picou *et al.*, op. cit.
51 Studies by Spergel (1961), Wood, Elliott and Spergel (1967), Fredericks and Molnar (1969) and Kelly (1971) have established a clear correlation between delinquency and the gap between aspirations and expectations for success. A relationship in this direction, but a fairly weak one, was found by Short. See Spergel, I. (1961), 'An Exploratory Research in Delinquent Subcultures', *Social Service Review*, 35, 33–47. Wood, A. L. (1961), 'A Socio-Structural Analysis: Murder, Suicide and Economics', *American Sociological Review*, 26, 744–52. Elliott, D. S. (1962), 'Delinquency and Perceived Opportunity', *Sociological Inquiry*, XXXII, 216–22. Spergel, I. (1967), 'Deviant Patterns and Opportunities of Pre-Adolescent Negro Boys in Three Chicago Neighbourhoods', in M. W. Klein, ed., *Juvenile Gangs in Context: Theory, Research and Action*, Englewood Cliffs: Prentice-Hall, 38–54. Fredericks, M. A. and Molnar, M. (1969), 'Relative Occupational Anticipations of Delinquents and Non-Delinquents', *Journal of Research in Crime and Delinquency*, 6, 1–7.

270

Kelly, D. H. (1971), 'School Failure, Academic Self-Evaluation, and School Avoidance and Deviant Behaviour', *Youth and Society*, 2, 489–503. Short, J. F. (1964), 'Gang Delinquency and Anomie', in M. B. Clinard, ed., *Anomie and Deviant Behaviour*, New York: Free Press, 98–127. Studies by Gold, Hirschi, and Rosenberg and Silverstein failed to establish such a relationship. Gold concluded on the basis of his interviews that the relationship did not emerge because many of his lower-class delinquents, when confronted with poor school performance, lowered their aspirations. See Gold (1963), op. cit., 162–73. Hirschi, T. (1969), *Causes of Delinquency*, Berkeley: University of California Press, p. 83. Rosenberg and Silverstein, op. cit., 135–7. For a review and discussion of alternative interpretations of the discrepancy between aspirations and expectations and delinquency see Liska, A. E. (1971), 'Aspirations, Expectations and Delinquency: Stress and Additive Models', *Sociological Quarterly*, 12, 99–107.

52 Mizruchi, E. H. (1967), 'Aspiration and Poverty: A Neglected Aspect of Merton's Anomie', *Sociological Quarterly*, 8, 439–47.

53 Winslow, R. W. (1967), 'Anomie and its Alternatives: A Self-Report Study of Delinquency', *Sociological Quarterly*, 8, 468–80.

54 Merton, op. cit., p. 171.

55 Cohen, A. K. (1955), *Delinquent Boys: The Culture of the Gang*, Glencoe, Ill.: Free Press.

56 See the review in Deutsch, M. (1967), *The Disadvantaged Child*, New York: Basic Books.

57 This has been unanimously concluded by the following studies. Sullenger, T. E. (1936), *Social Determinants in Juvenile Delinquency*, New York: Wiley. Kvaraceus, W. C. (1945), *Juvenile Delinquency and the School*, New York: World Book Co. Gold, M. (1963), op. cit., p. 44. Lunden, W. A. (1964), *Statistics on Delinquents and Delinquency*, Springfield, Ill.: Charles C. Thomas. Polk, K. (1965), *Those Who Fail*, Eugene, Oregon: Lane County Youth Project. Polk, K. and Halferty, D. S. (1966), 'Adolescence, Commitment and Delinquency', *Journal of Research in Crime and Delinquency*, 3, 82–96. Schafer, W. E. and Polk, K. (1967), 'Delinquency and the Schools', in The President's Commission on Law Enforcement and Administration of Justice, *Task Force Report: Juvenile Delinquency and Youth Crime*, Washington DC: US Govt Printing Office, 222–7. Rhodes, A. L. and Reiss, A. J. (1969), 'Apathy, Truancy and Delinquency as Adaptations in School', *Social Forces*, 48, 12–22. Fisher, R. (1970), 'Borstal Recall Delinquency and the Cloward–Ohlin Theory of Criminal Subcultures', *British Journal of Criminology*, 10, 52–63. Lanphier, C. M. and Faulkner, J. E., op. cit. Burns, J. L. (1971), 'Delinquents Failed by the System', *Special Education*, 60, 13–16. Empey, L. T. and Lubeck, S. G. with Laporte, R. L. (1971), *Explaining Delinquency: Construction, Test, and Reformulation of a Sociological Theory*, Lexington: Heath Lexington Books. Kelly, D. H. (1971), 'School Failure, Academic Self-Evaluation, and School Avoidance and Deviant Behaviour', *Youth and Society*, 2, 489–503. Kelly, D. H. and Balch, R. W. (1971), 'Social Origins and School Failure: A Reexamination of Cohen's Theory of Working-Class Delinquency', *Pacific Sociological Review*, 14, 413–30. Farrington, D. P. (1973), 'Self-Reports of Deviant Behaviour: Predictive and Stable?', *The Journal of Criminal Law and Criminology*, 64, 99–110. Frease, D. E. (1973), 'Delinquency, Social Class and the Schools', *Sociology and Social Research*, 57, 443–59. Gold, M. and Mann, D. (1973), 'Delinquency as Defense', *American Journal of Orthopsychiatry*, 42, 463–79. Mugishima, F. and Matsumoto, Y. (1973), 'An Analysis of Delinquent Differentiation Related to Boys' Social Origin and Educational Attainment', *Report of the*

Japanese Research Institute of Police Science, 14. Hassall, P. (1974), *Schools and Delinquency: A Self-Report Study of Delinquency in Christchurch, New Zealand*, Paper to Sociological Association of Australia and New Zealand Conference, University of New England. Phillips, J. C. (1974), *The Creation of Deviant Behaviour in High Schools: An Examination of Cohen's General Theory of Subcultures*, Ph D dissertation, University of Oregon.

58 Toby, E. J. and Toby, M. L. (1957), *Low School Status as a Predisposing Factor in Subcultural Delinquency*, US Office of Education and Rutgers University. Another longitudinal study by Elliott and Voss found a considerably weaker association between school failure and delinquency. See Elliott and Voss, op. cit.

59 Downes, D. (1966), *The Delinquent Solution*, London: Routledge & Kegan Paul, 236–9.

60 Box, S. (1971), *Deviance, Reality and Society*, London: Holt, Rinehart & Winston, 107–8.

61 This question has been dealt with in the theory testing of Empey and Lubeck (1971), op. cit.

62 This argument is developed more fully in Braithwaite, J. B. (1975), 'Competitiveness in Schools and Delinquency', *Australian Journal of Social Issues*, 10, 107–10.

63 Polk, K. (1965), *Those Who Fail*, Eugene, Oregon: Lane County Youth Project. Polk, K. and Halferty, D. S. (1966), 'Adolescence, Commitment, and Delinquency', *Journal of Research in Crime and Delinquency*, 3, 82–96. Kelly, D. H. and Balch, R. W. (1971), 'Social Origins and School Failure: A Reexamination of Cohen's Theory of Working Class Delinquency', *Pacific Sociological Review*, 14, 413–30. Phillips, J. C. (1974), *The Creation of Deviant Behaviour in High Schools: An Examination of Cohen's General Theory of Subcultures*, Ph D dissertation, University of Oregon.

64 In the McDonald study, school performance was indexed by what stream a student was in. See McDonald, L. (1968), *Social Class and Delinquency*, London: Faber & Faber.

65 Rodman has offered a resolution with his lower-class 'value stretch'. He argues that lower-class people are committed to both distinctly middle-class and distinctively lower-class values. They accept a wider range of values but are less strongly committed to all values in the range. They allow their values to 'stretch' to fit the situation. Pragmatism thus allows them to act in the light of circumstances, and values become somewhat role-specific. See Rodman, H. (1963), 'The Lower Class Value Stretch', *Social Forces*, 42, 205–15. A partial test of this theory has been undertaken by Della Fave. Della Fave found that the success values of lower-class adolescents generally were not more 'stretched' than the success values of middle-class adolescents. But within the lower class, students in terminal curricula showed greater evidence of value stretching. Della Fave, L. R. (1977), 'Aspirations Through Four Years of High School: An Inquiry Into the Value Stretching Process', *Pacific Sociological Review*, 20, 371–88.

66 Miller, W. B. (1958), 'Lower-Class Culture as a Generating Milieu of Gang Delinquency', *Journal of Social Issues*, XIV, 5–9.

67 This criticism is developed by Bordua. See Bordua, D. J. (1961), 'Delinquent Subcultures: Sociological Interpretations of Gang Delinquency', *Annals*, 338, 119–36.

68 Matza, D. and Sykes, G. M. (1961), 'Delinquency and Subterranean Values', *American Sociological Review*, 26, 712–19.

69 Sutherland, E. H. and Cressey, D. R. (1966), *Principles of Criminology*, 7th edn, Philadelphia: Lippincott, p. 82.

70 Sherwin, R. C. (1968), *Social Class Values and Deviant Behaviour: An Empirical Test of Some Theories of Delinquency*, Ph D dissertation, University of Connecticut.

71 Ibid., p. 209.

72 Short, J. F. and Strodtbeck, F. L. (1965), *Group Process and Gang Delinquency*, Chicago: University of Chicago Press. See also Gordon, R. A., Short, J. F., Cartwright, D. S. and Strodtbeck, F. L. (1963), 'Values and Gang Delinquency: A Study of Street Corner Groups', *American Journal of Sociology*, 69, 109–28.

73 Landis, J., Dinitz, S. and Reckless, W. (1963), 'Implementing Two Theories of Delinquency: Value Orientation and Awareness of Limited Opportunity', *Sociology and Social Research*, XLVII, p. 145.

74 Fannin, L. T. and Clinard, M. B. (1965), 'Differences in the Conception of Self as Male Among Lower and Middle Class Adolescents', *Social Problems*, 13, 205–14.

75 Erlanger, H. S. (1974), 'The Empirical Status of the Subculture of Violence Thesis', *Social Problems*, 22, 280–91.

76 Barron, M. L. (1951), 'Juvenile Delinquency and American Values', *American Sociological Review*, 16, 208–14.

77 Feather, N. T. (1975), *Values in Education and Society*, New York: Free Press, 181–3.

78 Cochrane, R. (1974), 'Values as Correlates of Deviance', *British Journal of Social and Clinical Psychology*, 13, 257–67.

79 Op. cit., 147–50.

80 Ball-Rokeach, S. J. (1973), 'Values and Violence: A Test of the Subculture of Violence Thesis', *American Sociological Review*, 38, 736–49.

81 Cernkovich, S. A. (1978), 'Value Orientations and Delinquency Involvement', *Criminology*, 15, 443–58.

82 Their general conclusion is that 'The findings of the present study suggest the existence of a delinquency subculture which values many conventional ideals, practices, and institutions highly, but not so highly as do non-delinquents.' See Siegel, L. J., Rathus, S. A. and Ruppert, C. A. (1973), 'Values and Delinquent Youth: An Empirical Re-Examination of Theories of Delinquency', *British Journal of Criminology*, 13, 237–44.

83 Chapman, J. (1966), 'Role and Self-Concept Assessments of Delinquents and Non-Delinquents', *Sociological Quarterly*, 7, 373–9.

84 Hindelang, M. J. (1969), 'The Commitment of Delinquents to their Misdeeds: Do Delinquents Drift?', *Social Problems*, 17, 502–9.

85 Hackler, J. C. (1970), 'Testing a Causal Model of Delinquency', *Sociological Quarterly*, 11, 511–22. Liska, A. E. (1973), 'Causal Structures Underlying the Relationship Between Delinquent Involvement and Delinquent Peers', *Sociology and Social Research*, 58, 23–36.

86 Sykes, G. and Matza, D. (1957), 'Techniques of Neutralization: A Theory of Delinquency', *American Sociological Review*, 22, 664–70.

87 Ball, R. A. (1968), 'An Empirical Exploration of Neutralization Theory', in M. Lefton, J. K. Skipper and C. H. McCashy, eds, *Approaches to Deviance*, New York: Appleton–Century–Crofts, 255–65.

88 Although Short and Strodtbeck (op. cit.) found lower-class boys to be more tolerant of infractions of proscriptive norms than middle-class boys, Faust found lower-class adults to be *less* tolerant of delinquent behaviour than middle-class adults, and blacks to be less tolerant than whites. Hackler found that low-prestige boys were not more inclined to endorse delinquent behaviour. See Faust, F. L. (1970), *Dimensions of Delinquency Tolerance: Differential Tolerance of Juvenile Delinquent Behaviour by Adult Members of*

Different Socio-Economic Classes and Racial Groups, Ph D dissertation, Ohio State University. Hackler, op. cit.

89 Gordon, D. M. (1973), 'Capitalism, Class and Crime in America', *Crime and Delinquency*, 19, 163–86.

90 Ibid., p. 175.

91 Although this is the case for traditional crime (crimes handled by the police), it is not the case for white-collar crime. In addition to the rewards of white-collar crime being great, even by middle-class standards, the costs are minimal because prosecution is almost non-existent.

92 Ehrlich, I. (1972), 'The Deterrent Effect of Criminal Law Enforcement', *Journal of Legal Studies*, 1, 259–77.

93 Toby, J. (1957), 'Social Disorganization and Stake in Conformity: Complementary Factors in the Predatory Behaviour of Hoodlums', *Journal of Criminal Law, Criminology and Police Science*, 48, 12–17.

94 Gold, M. (1963), *Status Forces in Delinquent Boys*, Ann Arbor: Institute for Social Research, University of Michigan, p. 168.

95 Miller, H. S. (1972), *The Closed Door*, prepared for the Manpower Administration, US Department of Labor, February.

96 Buikhuisen, W. and Dijksterhuis, P. H. (1972), 'Delinquency and Stigmatization', *British Journal of Criminology*, 11, 185–7.

97 Boshier, R. and Johnson, D. (1974), 'Does Conviction Affect Employment Opportunities?', *British Journal of Criminology*, 14, 264–8.

98 Robins, L. N., Gyman, H. and O'Neal, P. (1962), 'The Interaction of Social Class and Deviant Behaviour', *American Sociological Review*, 27, 480–92.

99 Ibid., p. 480.

100 Noblit, G. W. (1973), *Delinquency and Access to Success: A Study of the Consequences of the Delinquency Label*, Ph D dissertation, University of Oregon.

101 For a review of some empirical evidence that deviant labelling intensifies deviance see Scheff and Sundstrom, Duncan Hackler and Gove. Scheff, T. and Sundstrom, E. (1970), 'The Stability of Deviant Behaviour Over Time: A Reassessment', *Journal of Health and Social Behaviour*, 11, 37–43. Duncan, D. F. (1969), 'Stigma and Delinquency', *Cornell Journal of Social Relations*, 4, 41–8. Hackler, J. C. (1970), 'Testing a Causal Model of Delinquency', *Sociological Quarterly*, 11, 511–22. W. Gove, ed. (1975), *The Labelling of Deviance*, New York: Halsted Press.

102 Schur, E. M. (1969), *Our Criminal Society*, Englewood Cliffs: Prentice-Hall, p. 17.

103 Frease, D. E. (1973), 'Delinquency, Social Class and the Schools', *Sociology and Social Research*, 57, 443–59.

104 Hackler, op. cit.

105 Chiricos, T. G., Jackson, P. D. and Waldo, G. P. (1972), 'Inequality in the Imposition of a Criminal Label', *Social Problems*, 19, 553–71.

106 Gordon, D. M., op. cit., p. 182.

107 Wilkins, L. T. (1971), 'The Deviance-Amplifying System', in W. G. Carson and P. Wiles, eds, *Crime and Delinquency in Britain*, London: Martin Robertson, 219–25.

108 Gordon, D. M., op. cit., p. 182.

109 Morris, T. (1957), *The Criminal Area: A Study in Social Ecology*, London: Routledge & Kegan Paul, p. 173.

110 Schuessler, K. F. and Cressey, D. (1950), 'Personality Characteristics of Criminals', *American Journal of Sociology*, 55, 476–84. See also an updating of Schuessler and Cressey's work by Anderson, and a review by Waldo and Dinitz which draws somewhat more favourable conclusions for the

effect of personality on crime. See Anderson, K. G. (1961), *Applications of Objective Tests of Personality to Criminal Populations, 1950-1959: A Review and Appraisal*, MA thesis, Indiana University. Waldo, G. P. and Dinitz, S. (1967), 'Personality Attributes of the Criminal: An Analysis of Research Studies, 1950-65', *Journal of Research in Crime and Delinquency*, 4, 185-202.

111 Allen, V. L. (1970), 'Theoretical Issues in Poverty Research', *Journal of Social Issues*, 26, p. 161. Allen is here referring to his earlier review 'Personality Correlates of Poverty', in V. L. Allen, ed., *Psychological Factors in Poverty*, Chicago: Markham.

112 Conger, J. J. and Miller, W. C. (1966), *Personality, Social Class and Delinquency*, New York: Wiley.

113 Reiss, A. J. and Rhodes, A. L. (1961), 'The Distribution of Juvenile Delinquency in the Social Class Structure', *American Sociological Review*, 26, 730-2. Lunden, W. A. (1964), *Statistics on Delinquents and Delinquency*, Springfield, Ill.: Charles C. Thomas, p. 89. Short, J. F. and Strodtbeck, F. L. (1965), *Group Process and Gang Delinquency*, Chicago: University of Chicago Press. Slatin, G. T. (1969), 'Ecological Analysis of Delinquency: Aggregation Effects', *American Sociological Review*, 34, 894-906. Gibson, H. B. and West, D. J. (1970), 'Social and Intellectual Handicaps as Precursors of Early Delinquency', *British Journal of Criminology*, 10, 21-32. McQuaid, J. (1970), 'A Personality Profile of Delinquent Boys in Scottish Approved Schools', *British Journal of Criminology*, 10, 147-57. Farrington, D. P., op. cit. See also the recent review by Hirschi and Hindelang. Hirschi, T. and Hindelang, M. J. (1977), 'Intelligence and Delinquency: A Revisionist Review', *American Sociological Review*, 42, 571-87.

114 Cohen, op. cit., p. 103.

115 See Ginsberg, H. (1972), *The Myth of the Deprived Child*, Englewood Cliffs: Prentice-Hall. Bowles, S. and Gintis, H. (1972), 'I.Q. in the U.S. Class Structure', *Social Policy*, 3, 65-96. Broadhurst, P. L. and Fulker, D. W. (1974), 'Behavioural Genetics', *Annual Review of Psychology*, 25, 389-416.

116 Allen, 'Theoretical Issues in Poverty Research', op. cit., p. 161.

117 Rodman, H. (1968), 'Family and Social Pathology in the Ghetto', *Science*, 161, 756-62. Valentine, C. A. (1968), *Culture and Poverty*, Chicago: University of Chicago Press. Roach, J. L. and Gursslin, O. R. (1967), 'An Evaluation of the Concept "Culture of Poverty"', *Social Forces*, 45, 383-92. E. B. Leacock, ed. (1971), *The Culture of Poverty: A Critique*, New York: Simon & Schuster.

118 Reference is made to many such studies in the critiques in footnote 117. See also Schwartz, A. J. (1975), 'A Further Look at "Culture and Poverty": Ten Caracas Barrios', *Sociology and Social Research*, 59, 362-86.

119 Allen, 'Theoretical Issues in Poverty Research', op. cit., 161-2, summarizing his earlier review 'Personality Correlates of Poverty', op. cit.

120 Of two subsequent studies, one by Johnson and Sanday and one by O'Rand and Ellis, the former is consistent with Allen's conclusion on time perspective, and the latter is inconsistent. See Johnson, N. J. and Sanday, P. R. (1971), 'Subculture Variations in an Urban Poor Population', *American Anthropologist*, 73, 128-43. O'Rand, A. and Ellis, R. A. (1974), 'Social Class and Social Time Perspective', *Social Forces*, 53, 53-62.

121 The review by Miller *et al.* reaches this same conclusion on delayed gratification. See Miller, S. M., Riessman, F. and Seagull, A. A. (1965), 'Poverty and Self-Indulgence: A Critique of the Non-Deferred Gratification Pattern', in L. A. Ferman, J. L. Hornbluh and A. Haber, eds, *Poverty in America*, Ann Arbor: University of Michigan Press, 285-302.

122 Johnson and Sanday, op. cit.
123 Liebow, E. (1966), *Tally's Corner: A Study of Negro Streetcorner Men*, London: Routledge & Kegan Paul, p. 66.
124 Saunders *et al.* report the results of two empirical studies which, taken together, contradict the hypothesis that delinquency is related to impulsivity. See Saunders, J. T., Reppucci, N. D. and Sarata, B. P. (1973), 'An Examination of Impulsivity as a Trait Characterizing Delinquent Youth', *American Journal of Orthopsychiatry*, 43, 789-95.
125 In fact there is evidence that the poor exhibit attitudes and behaviour which are just as work-oriented as the non-poor. See Davidson, C. and Gartz, C. A. (1974), 'Are the Poor Different? A Comparison of Work Behaviour and Attitudes Among the Urban Poor and Non-Poor', *Social Problems*, 22, 229-45.
126 For the best review of evidence see Burkhardt, W. R. (1973), *The Application of Opportunity Theory to Delinquency Prevention: Evaluation of a Case Study and Critique of the Literature*, Ph D dissertation, Wayne State University. Miller, W. B. (1962), 'The Impact of a Total Community Delinquency Control Project', *Social Problems*, 10, 168-91. Jones, H. (1969), 'From Reform School to Society', in H. H. Weissman, ed., *Individual and Group Services in the Mobilization for Youth Experience*, New York: Association Press. Schur, E. M. (1973), *Radical Non-Intervention*, Englewood Cliffs: Prentice-Hall.
127 Weeks, H. A. and Smith, M. G. (1939), 'Juvenile Delinquency and Broken Homes in Spokane, Washington', *Social Forces*, 18, 48-59. Carr-Saunders, A. M. (1942), *Young Offenders*, Cambridge: Cambridge University Press. Kvaraceus, W. C. (1945), *Juvenile Delinquency and the School*, New York: World Book Co. Schulman, H. M. (1949), 'The Family and Juvenile Delinquency', *Annals of the American Academy of Political and Social Science*, 261, 21-31. Glueck, S. and Glueck, E. (1950), *Unravelling Juvenile Delinquency*, New York: Commonwealth Fund. Ferguson, T. (1952), *The Young Delinquent in His Social Setting*, London: Oxford University Press. Monahan, T. P. (1957), 'Family Status and the Delinquent Child: A Reappraisal and Some New Findings', *Social Forces*, 35, p. 257. Toby, J. (1957), 'The Differential Impact of Family Disorganization', *American Sociological Review*, 22, 505-12. Nye, F. I. (1958), *Family Relationships and Delinquent Behaviour*, New York: Wiley. McCord, W. and McCord, J. (1959), *Origins of Crime*, New York: Columbia University Press. Gold (1963), op. cit., p. 149. Slocum, W. L. and Stone, C. (1963), 'Family Culture and Patterns of Delinquent Type Behaviour', *Marriage and Family Living*, 25, 202-8. Lunden, op. cit., p. 98. Banks, C. (1965), 'Boys in Detention Centres', in C. Broadhurst and P. L. Broadhurst, eds, *Studies in Psychology*, London: London University Press. West, D. J. (1967), *The Young Offender*, London: Duckworth, p. 70. Douglas, J. W. B., Ross, J. M. and Simpson, H. R. (1968), *All Our Future*, London: Peter Davies. Bruce, N. (1970), 'Delinquent and Non-Delinquent Reactions to Parental Deprivation', *British Journal of Criminology*, 10, 270-6. Chilton, R. J. and Markle, G. E. (1972), 'Family Deprivation, Delinquent Conduct and the Effect of Subclassification', *American Sociological Review*, 37, 93-9. West, D. J. (1973), *Who Becomes Delinquent?*, London: Heinemann, p. 70.
128 Goode, W. J. (1951), 'Economic Factors and Marital Stability', *American Sociological Review*, 16, 802-12. Cloward *et al.*, op. cit., p. 627. Gibson, C. (1974), 'The Association between Divorce and Social Class in England and Wales', *British Journal of Sociology*, 25, 79-93.
129 Wilkinson, K. (1974), 'The Broken Family and Juvenile Delinquency: Scien-

tific Explanation or Ideology?', *Social Problems*, 21, 726–39.
130 Willie, C. V. (1967), 'The Relative Contribution of Family Status and Economic Status to Juvenile Delinquency', *Social Problems*, 14, 326–35.
131 Cavan, R. S. and Ranck, K. H. (1938), *The Family and the Depression: A Study of One Hundred Chicago Families*, Chicago: University of Chicago Press. Komarovsky, M. (1940), *The Unemployed Man and His Family*, New York: Dryden Press.
132 Gold (1963), op. cit., p. 43.
133 McKinley, D. G. (1964), *Social Class and Family Life*, New York: Free Press, 92-3, 156-7.
134 Bronfenbrenner, U. (1958), 'Socialization and Social Class Through Time and Space', in E. E. Maccoby, T. M. Newcomb and E. L. Hartley, eds, *Readings in Social Psychology*, New York: Henry Holt, 400–25.
135 Rodman, H. and Grams, P. (1967), 'Juvenile Delinquency and the Family: A Review and Discussion', in The President's Commission on Law Enforcement and Administration of Justice (1967), *Task Force Report: Juvenile Delinquency and Youth Crime*, Washington DC: US Govt Printing Office, p. 194.
136 Erlanger, H. S. (1974), 'Social Class and Corporal Punishment in Child-Rearing: A Reassessment', *American Sociological Review*, 39, 68–85.
137 Rainwater, L. (1974), 'The Slum and Its Problems', in L. Rainwater, ed., *Inequality and Justice*, Chicago: Aldine, p. 153.
138 Density refers to population per unit area, and crowding to persons per room.
139 Calhoun, J. B. (1962), 'Population Density and Social Pathology', *Scientific American*, 206, 139–48.
140 Mays, J. B. (1963), *Crime and the Social Structure*, London: Faber & Faber, p. 158.
141 Roncek, D. W. (1975), 'Density and Crime: A Methodological Critique', *American Behavioral Scientist*, 18, 843–60. The results of a recent study by Spector are also consistent with this conclusion. See Spector, P. E. (1975), 'Population Density and Unemployment: The Effects on the Incidence of Violent Crime in the American City', *Criminology*, 12, 399–401.
142 Kvalseth, T. O. (1977), 'Note on the Effects of Population Density and Unemployment on Urban Crime', *Criminology*, 15, 105–10.
143 Roncek ignored in his review the following four studies which have also found a positive association between overcrowding and crime. Glueck, S. and Glueck, E. T. (1950), *Unravelling Juvenile Delinquency*, New York: The Commonwealth Fund. Davies, M. (1969), 'Offence Behaviour and the Classification of Offences', *British Journal of Criminology*, 9, 39–50. McCarthy, J. D., Galle, O. R. and Zimmern, W. (1975), 'Population Density, Social Structure, and Interpersonal Violence', *American Behavioural Scientist*, 18, 771–89. Booth, A., Welch, S. and Johnson, D. R. (1976), 'Crowding and Urban Crime Rates', *Urban Affairs Quarterly*, 11, 291–308.
144 Mintburn, L. and Lambert, W. W. (1964), *Mothers of Six Cultures*, New York: Wiley.
145 Shaw, C. R. and McKay, H. D. (1969), *Juvenile Delinquency and Urban Areas*, Chicago: University of Chicago Press.
146 Jacobs, J. (1965), *The Death and Life of Great American Cities*, Harmondsworth: Pelican, p. 41.
147 Shaw and McKay, op. cit., p. 185.
148 See footnote 88.
149 Maccoby, E. E., Johnson, J. P. and Church, R. M. (1958), 'Community Integration and the Social Control of Juvenile Delinquency', *Journal of Social Issues*, 14, 38–51.

150 Mays, J. B. (1959), *On the Threshold of Delinquency*, Liverpool: Liverpool University Press.
151 Whyte, W. F. (1943), *Street Corner Society: The Social Structure of an Italian Slum*, Chicago: University of Chicago Press, 140–6.
152 Kobrin, S. (1951), 'The Conflict of Values in Delinquency Areas', *American Sociological Review*, 16, 653–61.
153 Cohen, op. cit.
154 Lander, B. (1954), *Towards an Understanding of Juvenile Delinquency*, New York: Columbia University Press.
155 See Gordon, R. A. (1967), 'Issues in the Ecological Study of Delinquency', *American Sociological Review*, 32, 927–44. Rosen, L. and Turner, S. (1967), 'An Evaluation of the Lander Approach to the Ecology of Delinquency', *Social Problems*, 15, 189–200.
156 Gordon (1967), op. cit.
157 Campbell, D. T. and Fiske, D. W. (1959), 'Convergent and Discriminant Validation by the Multitrait-Multimethod Matrix', *Psychological Bulletin*, 56, 81–105.
158 Parker, H. (1974), *View from the Boys*, Newton Abbot: David & Charles, p. 107.
159 Gold (1963), op. cit., p. 43.
160 See Smith, G. (1975), *Leisure, Recreation and Delinquency*, MA thesis, University of Queensland.
161 Armston, G. and Wilson, M. (1973), 'City Politics and Deviancy Amplification', in I. Taylor and L. Taylor, eds, *Politics and Deviance: Papers From the National Deviancy Conference*, Harmondsworth: Penguin.
162 Suttles, G. D. (1972), *The Social Construction of Communities*, Chicago: University of Chicago Press, 192–3.
163 Suttles, G. D. (1968), *The Social Order of the Slum*, Chicago: University of Chicago Press.
164 Ibid., p. 26.
165 Suttles (1972), op. cit.

Chapter 4 The class-mix hypothesis

1 Morris, T. (1957), *The Criminal Area: A Study in Social Ecology*, London: Routledge & Kegan Paul.
2 For a discussion of various versions of this kind of theory see Etherington, W. (1975), *The Idea of Planned Residential Social Mix: An Historical Analysis*, Paper to Conference of Australian and New Zealand Academy for the Advancement of Science, Canberra.
3 Wolfgang, M. E. and Ferracuti, F. (1967), *The Subculture of Violence: Towards an Integrated Theory in Criminology*, London: Social Science Paperbacks, p. 299.
4 Cloward, R. A. and Ohlin, L. E. (1960), *Delinquency and Opportunity*, Glencoe, Ill.: Free Press.
5 See chapter 3 of this book.
6 McDonald, L. (1968), *Social Class and Delinquency*, London: Faber & Faber.
7 Ibid., p. 42.
8 Palmore, E. and Hammond, P. E. (1964), 'Interacting Factors in Juvenile Delinquency', *American Sociological Review*, 29, 848–54. There is also a detailed discussion of this paper along the lines followed in this chapter by Blalock. See Blalock, H. M. (1969), *Theory Construction: From Verbal to*

Mathematical Formulations, Englewood Cliffs: Prentice-Hall, 159–62.

9 These two versions of the first prediction are corollaries one of the other. If we have four cells as in Table 4.1, the fact that the difference between A and B is greater than the difference between C and D logically implies that the difference between A and C is greater than the difference between B and D. This can be shown mathematically. If $A - B > C - D$, then adding B and subtracting C from both sides of the inequality, $A - C > B - D$.

10 Bohlke, R. H. (1961), 'Social Mobility, Stratification Inconsistency and Middle Class Delinquency', *Social Problems*, 8, 351–63.

11 Greenbie, B. B. (1974), 'Social Territory, Community Health and Urban Planning', *Journal of the American Institute of Planners*, 40, 74–82.

12 Goldthorpe, J. H., Lockwood, D., Beckhofer, F. and Platt, J. (1969), *The Affluent Worker in the Class Structure*, Cambridge: Cambridge University Press.

13 Gans, H. (1967), *The Levittowners*, New York: Pantheon Books, p. 170.

14 Gutman, R. (1963), 'Population Mobility in the American Middle Class', in L. Duhl, ed., *The Urban Condition*, New York: Basic Books, 172–84.

15 Morris, R. N. and Mogey, J. (1965), *The Sociology of Housing: Studies at Berinsfield*, London: Routledge & Kegan Paul.

16 Keller, S. (1966), 'Social Class in Physical Planning', *International Social Science Journal*, 18, p. 504. Keller's footnotes are eliminated from this quotation.

17 See Deutsch, M. and Collins, M. E. (1965), 'Interracial Housing', in W. Peterson, ed., *American Social Patterns*, Garden City, NY: Doubleday, 7–62. Wilner, D. M., Walkley, R. P. and Cook, S. W. (1955), *Human Relations in Interracial Housing*, Minneapolis: University of Minnesota Press. Haggstrom, W. C. (1963), 'Self-Esteem and Other Characteristics of Residentially Desegregated Negroes', *Dissertation Abstracts*, 23, 3007–3008. Mayer, R. M. (1972), *Social Planning and Social Change*, Englewood Cliffs: Prentice-Hall, chapter 3.

18 Sennett, R. (1970), *The Uses of Disorder: Personal Identity and City Life*, Harmondsworth: Penguin.

19 Ibid., p. 45.

20 Ibid., p. 120.

21 Ibid., p. 156.

22 Nettler, G. (1974), *Explaining Crime*, New York: McGraw-Hill, 129–30.

23 Ibid., p. 129.

24 Hooker, E. L. (1945), *The Houston Delinquent in his Community Setting*, Houston: Research Bureau, Council of Social Agencies. Also reported in Neumeyer, M. H. (1949), *Juvenile Delinquency in Modern Society*, New York: Van Nostrand, p. 31.

25 Lander, B. (1954), *Towards an Understanding of Juvenile Delinquency*, New York: Columbia University Press, 32–4.

26 Willie, C. V. and Gershenovitz, A. (1964), 'Juvenile Delinquency in Racially Mixed Areas', *American Sociological Review*, 29, 740–4.

27 Ibid., p. 743.

28 Bordua, D. J. (1958), 'Juvenile Delinquency and "Anomie": An Attempt at Replication', *Social Problems*, 6, 230–8.

29 Chilton, R. J. (1964), 'Delinquency Area Research in Baltimore, Detroit and Indianapolis', *American Sociological Review*, 29, 71–83.

30 Conlen, J. J. (1971), *An Area Study of Juvenile Delinquency in Baltimore, Maryland: A Retest of Lander's Thesis and a Test of Cohen's Hypothesis*, Ph D dissertation, St Louis University.

31 Tobias, J. (1967), *Crime and Industrial Society in the Nineteenth Century*, London: Batsford, 198–200.

32 Fleisher, B. M. (1966), *The Economics of Delinquency*, Chicago: Quadrangle Books.

Chapter 5 Testing the class-mix hypothesis on data in the literature

1 McDonald, L. (1968), *Social Class and Delinquency*, London: Faber & Faber, 126–32.
2 Actually, the present author counts from McDonald's text nineteen significant differences by area for lower-class boys, and ten for middle-class boys. It is perplexing that McDonald claimed on p. 132 that it is 17 versus 10. Either way, the trend is quite clear.
3 Baldwin, J., Bottoms, A. E. and Walker, M. A. (1976), *The Urban Criminal: A Study in Sheffield*, London: Tavistock, p. 125.
4 Reiss, A. J. and Rhodes, A. L. (1961), 'The Distribution of Juvenile Delinquency in the Social Class Structure', *American Sociological Review*, 26, 720–32.
5 In the original Reiss and Rhodes study there were seven categories. For this re-analysis it is necessary to collapse down to three groups, which are as equal in numbers of subjects as possible, so that sample sizes for within group comparisons are adequate. 'Upper and upper middle', 'balanced middle', and 'crosscut top', are collapsed into the 'high' category; 'crosscut center', and 'representative of all' into 'medium'; and 'crosscut bottom', and 'lower' into 'low'. Without such a collapsing of categories, it would have been impossible to calculate χ^2 because of empty cells.
6 Lancaster, H. O. (1951), 'Complex Contingency Tables Treated by the Partition of χ^2', *Journal of the Royal Statistical Society*, B, 13, 242–9.
7 Lewis, B. N. (1962), 'Interaction in Multi-Dimensional Contingency Tables', *Journal of the Royal Statistical Society*, A, 125, 99–103.
8 Or, the complementary relevant hypothesis, that the relationship between school status and delinquency was different for different levels of class.
9 Matsumoto, Y. (1970), 'The Distribution of Juvenile Delinquency in the Social Class Structure – A Comparative Analysis of Delinquency Rate Between Tokyo and Nashville', *Japanese Sociological Review*, 20, 2–18.
10 Clark and Wenninger have conducted something approaching a replication of the Reiss and Rhodes study. However, their published data are inadequate to enable a test of the class-mix hypothesis. Even with further details of the original data, a satisfactory test of the hypothesis would be unlikely because of the small numbers of subjects in certain class groups within certain areas. See Clark, J. P. and Wenninger, E. P. (1962), 'Socio-Economic Class and Area as Correlates of Illegal Behaviour Among Juveniles', *American Sociological Review*, 27, 826–34.

Chapter 6 Testing the class-mix hypothesis on self-report data

1 See, for example, Erikson, K. T. (1962), 'Notes on the Sociology of Deviance', *Social Problems*, 9, p. 308. Becker, H. S. (1963), *Outsiders: Studies in the Sociology of Deviance*, New York: Free Press.
2 See the author's Ph D dissertation, chapter 6, and also Braithwaite, J. B. and Law, H. G. (1978), 'The Structure of Self-Reported Delinquency', *Applied Psychological Measurement*, 2, 221–38.
3 See Carroll, J. B. (1961), 'The Nature of the Data, Or How to Choose a Correlation Coefficient', *Psychometrika*, 26, 347–72.

4 Braithwaite and Law, op. cit.
5 See Moser, C. A. (1958), *Survey Methods in Social Investigation*, London: Heinemann.
6 Elmhorn, J. (1965), 'Study in Self-Reported Delinquency among School Children in Stockholm', in *Scandinavian Studies in Criminology*, vol. 1, London: Tavistock, 117–46.
7 There is some evidence that anonymity has some (though not great) effect in increasing the candour of self-reports of delinquency. See Christie, N., Andenaes, J. and Skirbekk, S. (1965), 'A Study of Self-Reported Crime', in *Scandinavian Studies in Criminology*, vol. 1, London: Tavistock, 55–85. Elmhorn, op. cit. Kulik, J. A. and Sabin, T. R. (1968), 'Disclosure of Delinquent Behaviour Under Conditions of Anonymity and Non-Anonymity', *Journal of Consulting and Clinical Psychology*, 32, 506–9.
8 Except for the marijuana item (17) which was 'yes/no'; the beer drinking item (15) which was open-ended and coded 'none', 'one', 'two', 'three or four', 'five or six'; and the spirit-drinking item (16) which was coded 'never', 'only two or three times a year', 'only about once a month', 'at least once a week'.
9 Braithwaite and Law, op. cit.
10 Broom, L., Jones, F. L. and Zubrzycki, J. (1965), 'An Occupational Classification of the Australian Workforce', *Australian and New Zealand Journal of Sociology*, 1, 1–13.
11 Semi-skilled and unskilled as operationalized in the ANU code. These data were from the 1971 Census, which was the most recent census. The interviews were conducted in late 1972.
12 MacDonald, G. T. (1974), *Factorial Ecology of the Brisbane Urban Area*, Brisbane, report to the Department of Urban and Regional Development, mimeographed.
13 See Appendix III of the author's Ph D thesis.
14 See Moore, E. G. (1966), *Residential Mobility in an Urban Context*, Ph D dissertation, University of Queensland. See also Stilwell, F. J. and Hardwick, J. M. (1973), 'Social Inequality in Australian Cities', *Australian Quarterly*, 45, 18–36.

Chapter 7 Testing the class-mix hypothesis on official delinquency data

1 Of course, they include cases which are never handled by the police but are referred directly by agencies such as school authorities, social agencies, or even the security agencies of private companies.
2 Phillips, D. K. (1971), *Knowledge from What?*, Chicago: Rand McNally.

Chapter 8 Testing the class-mix hypothesis on inter-city comparisons

1 When one is investigating the effect of the ecology of residential environments on behaviour, problems arise with adults which are less significant with juveniles. Most adults will not have lived in the same residential environment for all of their lives: so that a person who now lives in a small class-mixed middle-class city may have lived in a big-city slum for most of his youth. Thus, for example, if the association between criminality and the urban environment in which people *at present* live is only moderate, it might be much stronger

281

were it possible to take account of the urban environments people have experienced for the remainder of their preceding years.

2 Cho, Y. H. (1974), *Public Policy and Urban Crime*, Cambridge, Mass.: Ballinger Publishing Co., chapter 9.

3 For a clear discussion of the problems of including too many predictors in regressions, see Gordon, R. A. (1968), 'Issues in Multiple Regression', *American Journal of Sociology*, 73, 592–616. See also the argument by Kerlinger and Pedhazur that any multiple regression analysis should include at least 100 cases. Kerlinger, F. N. and Pedhazur, E. J. (1973), *Multiple Regression in Behavioural Research*, New York: Holt, Rinehart & Winston.

4 A National Opinion Research Center study for the President's Commission on Law Enforcement and Administration of Justice found that the main reasons for the non-reporting of offences by victims were lack of confidence in the police, belief that the offence was a private matter or a desire not to harm the offender. Somewhat less important reasons were fear of reprisal, no desire to take time, and lack of knowledge on reporting methods. See The President's Commission on Law Enforcement and Administration of Justice (1971), *The Challenge of Crime in a Free Society*, Washington DC: US Govt Printing Office, p. 21.

5 Police may underreport because police effectiveness is often measured by the number of offences which are reported, and by the percentage of reported offences which are cleared by arrest. Police can improve the image of their own efficiency in both of these regards by reporting fewer uncleared offences.

6 For a discussion of the latter three points, see Robison, S. M. (1966), 'A Critical View of the Uniform Crime Reports', *Michigan Law Review*, 64, 1,031–54. See also Cho, op. cit.

7 See President's Commission, op. cit. Congalton and Najman also found auto theft to have a high reportability compared to other offences. See Congalton, A. A. and Najman, J. M. (1973), *Who Are the Victims: A Study of the Victims of Reported and Unreported Crimes*, Sydney, mimeographed: University of New South Wales, p. 24.

8 Heller, N. B. and McEwan, J. T. (1973), 'Applications of Crime Seriousness Information in Police Departments', *Journal of Criminal Justice*, 1, 241–53.

9 Blumstein, A. (1974), 'Seriousness Weights in an Index of Crime', *American Sociological Review*, 39, 854–64.

10 Skogan, W. G. (1974), 'The Validity of Official Crime Statistics: An Empirical Investigation', *Social Science Quarterly*, 55, 52–64. Further support for Skogan's conclusions can be found in the work of Decker. See Decker, S. (1977), 'Official Crime Rates and Victim Surveys: An Empiricist Comparison', *Journal of Criminal Justice*, 5, 47–54.

11 Skogan, op. cit., p. 25.

12 Pyle found a theft factor which loaded strongly on larceny and auto theft, and a general factor which loaded on the other five. Harries also found such a two-factor structure. But the two crimes loading on a specific factor, distinguished from the general factor, were homicide and aggravated assault. He called this a violent crime factor. See Pyle, G. F. with others (1974), *The Spatial Dynamics of Crime*, Department of Geography, University of Chicago, Research Paper No. 159. Harries, K. D. (1974), *The Geography of Crime and Justice*, New York: McGraw-Hill, p. 118.

13 For discussion of a number of indices, see Alker, H. R. and Russel, B. M. (1964), 'On Measuring Inequality', *Behavioural Science*, 9, 207–18. See also Duncan, O. T. and Duncan, E. (1955), 'Residential Distribution and Occupational Stratification', *American Journal of Sociology*, 60, 493–503.

14 For details of this definition, see United States Census Population and Hous-

ing of 1970, *Current Population Reports*, Series P-23, no. 28, 'Revision in Poverty Statistics, 1959 to 1968'.

15 These calculations were made from the United States Census of Population and Housing of 1970, *Census Tract Reports*, PHC (1), vols 1-243.

16 Lopez-Rey, M. (1970), *Crime: An Analytical Appraisal*, London: Routledge & Kegan Paul.

17 That is, for the year of the census and for three years on each side of 1970. These were calculated from Federal Bureau of Investigation (1967-73), *Uniform Crime Reports for the United States*, Table 5.

18 Morgan, B. S. (1975), 'Segregation of Socioeconomic Groups in Urban Areas: A Comparative Analysis', *Urban Studies*, 12, 47-60.

19 An intercorrelation matrix for all variables included in the UCR analysis is presented in Appendix V of the author's PhD dissertation.

20 See Braithwaite, J. B. (1975), 'Population Growth and Crime', *Australian and New Zealand Journal of Criminology*, 8, 57-61. From Appendix V of the author's PhD dissertation it is also clear that city size is positively correlated with all index crime rates.

21 A number of studies which have found more violent crime in Southern states are mentioned by McCarthy, J. D., Galle, O. R. and Zimmern, W. (1975), 'Population Density, Social Structure, and Interpersonal Violence', *American Behavioral Scientist*, 18, 771-89. See also Gastil, R. D. (1971), 'Homicide and a Regional Culture of Violence', *American Sociological Review*, 36, 412-27.

22 See Schuessler, K. and Slatin, G. (1964), 'Sources of Variation in U.S. City Crime, 1950 and 1960', *Journal of Research in Crime and Delinquency*, 1, 127-48. Cho, op. cit. Harries, op. cit. McCarthy *et al.*, op. cit.

23 See chapter 11 for a discussion of these studies.

24 Goldberger, A. S. (1964), *Econometric Theory*, New York: Wiley, p. 201.

Chapter 9 Class-mix: conclusions and policies

1 See the discussion of this point in chapters 1 and 3.

2 The evidence for this is both cross-sectional and time-series in nature. Cross-sectional evidence, including the data analysed in chapter 8, indicates that larger cities are characterised by greater lower-class segregation. (See Morgan, B. S. (1975), 'Segregation of Socioeconomic Groups in Urban Areas: A Comparative Analysis', *Urban Studies*, 12, 47-60. Stillwell, F. J. and Hardwick, J. M. (1973), 'Social Inequality in Australian Cities', *Australian Quarterly*, 45, 18-36.) Therefore, with time and population growth, as cities become larger, class-mix might be expected to decrease. Moore has demonstrated a decrease in class-mix for south Brisbane between 1954 and 1961. (See Moore, E. G. (1966), *Residential Mobility in an Urban Context*, PhD dissertation, University of Queensland.) Stillwell *et al.*, op. cit., point out that time-series data between 1933 and 1966 for Sydney, Melbourne, Adelaide, and Perth indicate a decline in class-mix. Hermalin and Farley show that during the period 1950 to 1970 blacks in the United States have become increasingly overrepresented in the central cities, and increasingly underrepresented in the suburbs. (See Hermalin, A. I. and Farley, R. (1973), 'The Potential for Residential Integration in Cities and Suburbs: Implications for the Busing Controversy', *American Sociological Review*, 38, 595-610.)

3 Grier, E. and Grier, G. (1968), 'Equality and Beyond: Housing Segregation in the Great Society', in B. J. Frieden and R. Morris, *Urban Planning and Social Policy*, New York: Basic Books, p. 128.

4 Bailey, R. M. (1974), 'South Austin: The Cutting Edge of the City's Expanding Ghetto', *Planning*, 14, 10–13.
5 Jones, M. A. (1972), *Housing and Poverty in Australia*, Melbourne: Melbourne
University Press.
6 For a discussion of the problems in making policy inferences from delinquency research, see Braithwaite, J. B. (1977), 'Australian Delinquency:
Research and Practical Considerations', in P. R. Wilson, ed., *Delinquency in
Australia*, Brisbane: University of Queensland Press.
7 Gibbens, T. C. N. and Ahrenfeldt, R. H. (1966), *Cultural Factors in Delinquency*, London: Tavistock, 46–7.

Chapter 10 Rethinking the distribution of crime among classes

1 Dubos, R. (1974), quoted in Y. H. Cho, *Public Policy and Urban Crime*,
Cambridge, Mass.: Ballinger Publishing Co., p. 203.
2 Sutherland, E. H. (1949), *White Collar Crime*, New York: Holt, Rinehart &
Winston.
3 Ibid., 121–2.
4 Barrett, A. R. (1895), *The Era of Fraud and Embezzlement*, Boston.
5 The President's Commission on Law Enforcement and Administration of
Justice (1970), 'Crime and Victims in a Free Society', in C. A. Bersani, ed.,
Crime and Delinquency, London: Macmillan, p. 8.
6 Braithwaite, J. (1978), 'An Exploratory Study of Used Car Fraud', in P. R.
Wilson and J. Braithwaite, eds, *Two Faces of Deviance: Crimes of the Powerless and Powerful*, Brisbane: University of Queensland Press.
7 Including various offences which are not against persons and property (e.g.
drug offences), but excluding offences against public order (vagrancy, public
drunkenness).
8 Pearce, F. (1976), *Crimes of the Powerful: Marxism, Crime and Deviance*,
London: Pluto Press, p. 79.
9 Ibid., p. 93.
10 Jeffery, W. J. (1970), 'The Forty Thieves', *FBI Law Enforcement Bulletin*,
39, p. 17.
11 See Sutherland, op. cit. Jaspan, N. and Black, H. (1960), *The Thief in the
White Collar*, Philadelphia: Lippincott. Monteino, J. B. (1966), *Corruption:
Control of Maladministration*, Bombay: Manaktala. Caplovitz, D. (1968), *The
Poor Pay More*, New York: Free Press. G. Geis, ed. (1968), *White-Collar Criminal:
The Offender in Business and the Professions*, New York: Atherton Press.
Magnuson, W. G. and Carper, J. (1968), *The Dark Side of the Marketplace*,
Englewood Cliffs: Prentice-Hall. T. L. Becker and V. G. Murray, eds, *Govern-
ment Lawlessness in America*, New York: Oxford University Press. Oughton,
F. (1971), *Fraud and White-Collar Crime*, London: Elek Books. Lieberman,
J. K. (1973), *How the Government Breaks the Law*, Baltimore: Penguin.
Pearce, F. (1973), 'Crime, Corporations and the American Social Order', in I.
Taylor and L. Taylor, eds, *Politics and Deviance*, Harmondsworth: Pelican, 13–
42. Krisberg, B. (1975), *Crime and Privilege: Toward a New Criminology*, Englewood Cliffs: Prentice-Hall. Pearce, F. (1976), op. cit.
12 Magnuson and Carper, op. cit. give the best account of the extent of this
problem. They point out that every year the following fatalities occur in the
United States: 'One hundred thousand persons will be mangled or killed
while operating power mowers, countless others by tools in the workshop.
About 100,000 persons will be cut, disfigured or fatally injured while walking
through glass doors. Twelve thousand persons will die, and 150,000 will suffer

excruciating pain and often lifelong scars from fires, resulting from a match or lighted cigarette dropped on flammable clothing or upholstery. At least 1,000 will be electrocuted and many more burned and injured by faulty electrical equipment. Babies will strangle in ill-designed cribs; women will be poisoned by the noxious fumes of cleaning fluids; whole families will be asphyxiated by carbon monoxide from faulty heaters; youngsters will be cut, blinded and killed by dangerously designed toys. The list could go on almost endlessly' (p. 125).

13 Hills, S. L. (1971), *Crime, Power and Morality: The Criminal Law Process in the United States*, Scranton: Chandler Publishing Co., p. 169.

14 Swartz, J. (1975), 'Silent Killers at Work', *Crime and Social Justice*, 3, 15–20.

15 Carson, W. G. (1970), 'White-Collar Crime and the Enforcement of Factory Legislation', *British Journal of Criminology*, 10, 383–98.

16 See Young, J. H. (1967), *The Medical Messiah*, Princeton: Princeton University Press.

17 Geis, G. (1973), 'Victimization Patterns in White-Collar Crime', in I. Drapkin and E. Viano, eds, *Victimology: A New Focus*, vol. V, Lexington, Mass.: Lexington Books, p. 95.

18 Certainly these are offences punishable by law, and therefore crimes according to the definition of this book.

19 International law enjoys varying degrees of formal legitimation in the legal and quasi-legal codes of individual nations. The US Army Field Manual, *The Law of Land Warfare, 1956*, (chapter 8, section 498), states 'Any person, whether a member of the armed forces or a civilian, who commits an act which constitutes a crime under international law is responsible therefore and liable to punishment.' Yet dum-dum bullets, illegal under international law, were used with impunity during the police invasion of Attica State Prison in the United States.

20 See Fenwick, C. G. (1965), *International Law*, 4th edn, New York: Appleton-Century-Crofts.

21 See Horowitz, D. (1971), *From Yalta to Vietnam: American Foreign Policy in the Cold War*, Harmondsworth: Penguin, chapter 10.

22 Bloch, H. A. and Geis, G. (1967), *Man, Crime and Society*, New York: Random House.

23 For more thorough critiques of the definition of white-collar crime than the brief presentation here see Bloch and Geis, op. cit., 399–403, and Newman, D. J. (1958), 'White-Collar Crime', *Law and Contemporary Problems*, 23, 735–53.

24 However, quite often for conviction under regulatory laws, demonstration of wilful intent will increase punishment.

25 Newman, op. cit.

26 Braithwaite, op. cit.

27 Sutherland, op. cit.

28 Newman, op. cit., p. 743.

29 Wilson, P. R. and Brown, J. W. (1973), *Crime and the Community*, Brisbane: University of Queensland Press.

30 Reed, J. P. and Reed, R. S. (1974), 'Doctor, Lawyer, Indian Chief: Old Rhymes and New on White Collar Crime', *Australian and New Zealand Journal of Criminology*, 7, 145–56.

31 Geis has also concluded after briefly discussing some studies of public attitudes toward crime that attitudes to white-collar crime are tougher than is generally believed. See Geis (1973), op. cit., p. 100.

32 Burgess, E. W. (1950), comment on F. E. Hartung, 'White-Collar Offences in the Wholesale Meat Industry in Detroit', *American Journal of Sociology*, 56, p. 34.

33 Sutherland, op. cit., p. 9.
34 Nice, R. (1965), *Dictionary of Criminology*, London: Vision Press, p. 204.
35 Jeffery, op. cit., p. 18.
36 Taylor, I., Walton, P. and Young, J. (1975), *Critical Criminology*, London: Routledge & Kegan Paul, p. 30.
37 Sorokin, P. A. and Lunden, W. A. (1950), *Power and Morality*, Boston: Porter Sargent, p. 44.
38 Ibid., p. 40.
39 Ibid., p. 42.
40 Ibid., p. 46.
41 Geis, G. (1967), 'White-Collar Crime: The Heavy Electrical Equipment Antitrust Cases of 1961', in M. B. Clinard and R. Quinney, eds, *Criminal Behaviour Systems: A Typology*, New York: Holt, Rinehart & Winston.
42 Braithwaite, op. cit.
43 Maccoby, M. (1976), *The Gamesman: The New Corporate Leaders*, New York: Simon & Schuster.
44 Mills, C. W. (1956), *The Power Elite*, New York: Oxford University Press.
45 Lane, R. E. (1953), 'Why Businessmen Violate the Law?', *Journal of Criminal Law, Criminology and Police Science*, 44, 151–65.
46 Quinney, E. R. (1963), 'Occupational Structure and Criminal Behaviour: Prescription Violation by Retail Pharmacists', *Social Problems*, 11, 179–85.
47 Rosenberg, M. assisted by Scuhman, E. A. and Goldsen, R. K. (1957), *Occupations and Values*, New York: Free Press, chapter 8.
48 Spencer, J. C. (1968), 'A Study of Incarcerated White-Collar Offenders', in G. Geis, ed., *White-collar Criminal: The Offender in Business and the Professions*, New York: Atherton Press, p. 343.
49 Cressey, D. (1971), *Other People's Money*, Calif.: Wadsworth Publishing Co.
50 Interview in *Pix People*, 1974.
51 These blurred distinctions were also found to be important in the study of used-car fraud. Braithwaite, op. cit.
52 Martin, J. P. (1962), *Offenders as Employees*, London: Macmillan.
53 Robin, G. D. (1970), 'The Corporate and Judicial Disposition of Employee Thieves', in E. O. Smigel and H. L. Ross, eds, *Crimes against Bureaucracy*, New York: Van Nostrand, 124–46.
54 Feest, J. B. (1971), '"Betriebsjustiz": Internal Administration at the Place of Work', *Abstracts on Criminology and Penology*, 11, 6–14.
55 Campanis, P. (1970), 'Normlessness in Management', in J. D. Douglas, ed., *Deviance and Respectability: The Social Construction of Moral Meanings*, New York: Basic Books, 291–325.
56 Ibid., 322–3.
57 Ibid., p. 316.
58 Ibid., p. 316.
59 Blau, P. M. (1964), *Exchange and Power in Social Life*, New York: Wiley.
60 Ibid., p. 229.
61 The nature of the latter function is not explicitly specified by any of the theories in chapter 3. However, it is often implicit that the function is accelerating. That is, the more powerless people are, the greater will be the effect on non-power crime of further increasing their powerlessness.
62 Lieberman, J. K. (1973), *How the Government Breaks the Law*, Baltimore: Penguin.
63 Ibid., p. 235.
64 Ibid., p. 259.
65 Maddox, G. (1973), 'Federalism: Or Government Frustration', *Australian Quarterly*, 45, 92–100.

66 Jeffery, op. cit., p. 19.
67 Jaspan, N. and Black, H. (1960), *The Thief in the White Collar*, Philadelphia: Lippincott, p. 248.
68 See for example the results of the Liberty Mutual Insurance study reported in Jaspan and Black, op. cit., 51–2.
69 Drew, D., quoted in Sutherland, op. cit., 51–2.
70 Sharpston, M. J. (1970), 'The Economics of Corruption', *New Society*, 16, 944–6.
71 Coates, K. (1970), 'Open the Books', in K. Coates and T. Topham, eds, *Workers' Control*, London: Panther, p. 375.
72 Schur, E. M. (1969), *Our Criminal Society*, Englewood Cliffs: Prentice-Hall, p. 187.
73 Lane, op. cit.

Chapter 11 Alternative levels of analysis for determining whether inequality contributes to crime

1 Hirschi, T. (1972), 'Social Class and Crime', in D. W. Theilbar and S. D. Feldman, eds, *Issues in Social Inequality*, Boston: Little, Brown, 513–14.
2 Stinchcombe, A. (1964), *Rebellion in a High School*, Chicago: Quadrangle.
3 Kelly, D. H. and Balch, R. W. (1971), 'Social Origins and School Failure: A Reexamination of Cohen's Theory of Working-Class Delinquency', *Pacific Sociological Review*, 14, 413–30.
4 Kelly, D. H. (1971), 'School Failure, Academic Self-Evaluation, and School Avoidance and Deviant Behaviour', *Youth and Society*, 2, 489–503.
5 Frease, D. E. (1973), 'Delinquency, Social Class and the Schools', *Sociology and Social Research*, 57, 443–59.
6 Polk, K., Frease, D. and Richmond, F. L. (1974), 'Social Class, School Experience, and Delinquency', *Criminology*, 12, 84–96.
7 Several of these studies also investigated the relationship for other forms of deviance besides delinquency against persons and property.
8 Polk, K. (1969), 'Class, Strain and Rebellion Among Adolescents', *Social Problems*, 17, 214–24.
9 See the summary of evidence on this question in chapter 3, footnote 51, pp. 270–1.
10 Mizruchi has reported that middle-class respondents experienced greater stress than lower-class respondents when confronted with limited opportunities to realise their occupational aspirations. See Mizruchi, E. H. (1964), *Success and Opportunity*, New York: Free Press, p. 127.
11 Pavin, M. (1973), 'Economic Determinants of Political Unrest: An Economic Approach', *Journal of Conflict Resolution*, 17, 271–96.
12 The source of data for the homicide rates in this analysis was the *United Nations Demographic Yearbook*, New York: United Nations Publications, 1956 to 1970.
13 Wolfgang and Ferracuti, and Clinard and Abbott have been guilty of failing to take this precaution. See Wolfgang, M. E. and Ferracuti, F. (1967), *The Subculture of Violence: Towards an Integrated Theory in Criminology*, London: Social Science Paperbacks, 273–6. Clinard, M. B. and Abbott, D. J. (1973), *Crime in Developing Countries: A Comparative Perspective*, New York: Wiley.
14 Lydall, H. (1968), *The Structure of Earnings*, Oxford: Clarendon Press.
15 United States Social Security Administration (1965), *International Comparisons of Ratios of Social Security Expenditures to Gross National Product*, Research and Statistics Note No. 5, Washington DC: US Govt Printing Office, February 23.

16 Cutwright, P. (1967), 'Income Redistribution: A Cross-National Analysis', *Social Forces*, 46, 180–90.

17 Krohn, M. D. (1976), 'Inequality, Unemployment and Crime: A Cross-National Analysis', *Sociological Quarterly*, 17, 303–13. Another recent international comparison by McDonald mirrored Krohn's findings. Intersectoral income inequality was significantly positively associated with homicide rates, but showed non-significant negative relationships with Interpol crime rates. Interestingly, there was no significant relationship between unemployment rates and homicide in McDonald's cross-national regressions. See McDonald, L. (1976), *The Sociology of Law and Order*, Boulder, Colorado: Westview Press, chapter 5.

18 Wiers, P. (1944), *Economic Factors in Michigan Delinquency*, New York: Columbia University Press.

19 Fleisher, B. M. (1966), *The Economics of Delinquency*, Chicago: Quadrangle Books. See also Fleisher, B. M. (1966), 'The Effect of Income on Delinquency', *American Economic Review*, 56, 118–37.

20 Schuessler, K. and Slatin, G. (1964), 'Sources of Variation in US City Crime, 1950 and 1960', *Journal of Research in Crime and Delinquency*, 1, 127–48.

21 Singell, L. D. (1968), 'Economic Causes of Delinquency: National Versus Local Control', *Urban Affairs Quarterly*, 4, 225–33.

22 Spector, P. E. (1975), 'Population Density and Unemployment: The Effects on the Incidence of Violent Crime in the American City', *Criminology*, 12, 399–401.

23 Danziger, S. (1976), 'Explaining Urban Crime Rates', *Criminology*, 14, 291–5.

24 Danziger, S. and Wheeler, D. (1975), 'The Economics of Crime: Punishment or Income Redistribution', *Review of Social Economy*, 33, 113–31.

25 Hemley, D. D. and McPheters, L. R. (1974), 'Crime as an Externality of Regional Economic Growth', *Review of Regional Studies*, 4, 73–84.

26 Cho, Y. H. (1974), *Public Policy and Urban Crime*, Cambridge, Mass.: Ballinger Publishing Co., 146–55.

27 McCarthy, J. D., Galle, O. R. and Zimmern, W. (1975), 'Population Density, Social Structure and Interpersonal Violence', *American Behavioral Scientist*, 18, 771–89.

28 Flango, V. E. and Sherbenou, E. L. (1976), 'Poverty, Urbanization and Crime', *Criminology*, 14, 331–46.

29 Booth, A., Welch, S. and Johnson, D. R. (1976), 'Crowding and Urban Crime Rates', *Urban Affairs Quarterly*, 11, 291–308.

30 Angell, R. C. (1974), 'The Moral Integration of American Cities: Part II', *American Journal of Sociology*, 80, 607–29.

31 Ehrlich, I. (1974), 'Participation in Illegitimate Activities: An Economic Analysis', in G. S. Becker and W. M. Landes, eds, *Essays in the Economics of Crime and Punishment*, New York: Columbia University Press.

32 Marlin, J. T. (1973), 'City Crime: Report of Council on Municipal Performance', *Criminal Law Bulletin*, 9, 557–604. This kind of finding has also been made in a study of property crime in Canada in which time-series and cross-section observations at the provincial level were pooled. In this study Avio and Clark found that income inequality was a good predictor of rates for theft, fraud, and break and enter; whereas unemployment rate was less consistent in showing positive elasticities in the regression equations. Avio, K. L. and Clark, C. S. (1976), *Property Crime in Canada: An Econometric Study*, Toronto: University of Toronto Press.

33 Loftin, C. and Hill, R. H. (1974), 'Regional Subculture and Homicide: An Examination of the "Gastil-Hackney Thesis"', *American Sociological Review*, 39, 714–24.

34 Eberts, P. and Schwirian, K. P. (1970), 'Metropolitan Crime Rates and Rela-

tive Deprivation', in D. Glaser, ed., *Crime in the City*, New York: Harper & Row, 90–8.

35 Dunstan, J. A. P. and Roberts, S. F. (1977), *Delinquency and Socioeconomic Status: An Ecological Analysis of Melbourne*, Melbourne: Caulfield Institute of Technology, Occasional Monograph No. 1.

36 For details of this definition see United States Census of Population and Housing of 1970, *Current Population Reports*, Series P-23, no. 28, 'Revisions in Poverty Statistics, 1959 to 1968'.

37 Fuchs, V. R. (1967), 'Redefining Poverty and Redistributing Income', *The Public Interest*, 8, p. 89.

38 This, and the above indices, were calculated from the data in the United States Census of Population and Housing of 1970, *Census Tract Reports*, PHC (1), vols 1–243. It is interesting to note that there is a tendency for the cities with the smallest proportions of poor people to be the cities for which there is the biggest income gap between the poor and the average income earner. The latter variable is correlated −·62 with the percentage below the poverty line, and −·16 with the percentage earning less than half the median income.

39 The full stepwise multiple-linear-regression results for the control and other models are presented in Appendix X of the author's PhD thesis.

40 The full stepwise multiple-linear-regression results for the new control and income-inequality models are presented in Appendix XI and Appendix VI of the author's PhD thesis.

41 National Advisory Commission on Criminal Justice Standards and Goals (1973), *Community Crime Prevention*, Washington DC: US Govt Printing Office, p. 116.

42 Morgan and Clark have found that cities with high levels of job inequality between blacks and whites are less likely to have racial disorders; and Jiobu found that black deprivation, as indexed by the percentage of blacks poor and the percentage in low-status occupations, was negatively associated with the incidence of racial violence by blacks against whites. See Morgan, W. R. and Clark, T. N. (1973), 'The Causes of Racial Disorders: A Grievance-Level Explanation', *American Sociological Review*, 38, 611–24. Jiobu, R. M. (1974), 'City Characteristics and Racial Violence', *Social Science Quarterly*, 55, 52–64.

43 Boven, R. and O'Neill, D. P. (1975), *A Regional Analysis of Juvenile Offending in New Zealand*, Research Section, Department of Social Welfare, New Zealand: General Research Report No. 7.

44 Ross, M. (1974), 'Economic Conditions and Crime – Metropolitan Toronto 1965–1972', *Criminology Made in Canada*, 2, 27–41.

45 Singell, L. D. (1967), 'Examination of the Empirical Relationships Between Unemployment and Juvenile Delinquency', *American Journal of Economics and Sociology*, 26, 377–86.

46 Fleisher, op. cit.

47 Phillips, L., Votey, H. L. and Maxwell, D. (1972), 'Crime, Youth and the Labor Market', *Journal of Political Economy*, May/June, 491–504.

48 Brenner, H. (1976a), *Estimating the Social Costs of National Economic Policy: Implications for Mental and Physical Health, and Criminal Aggression*, a study prepared for the Joint Economic Committee, Congress of the United States, Washington DC: US Govt Printing Office. Brenner, H. (1976b), 'Time-Series Analysis: Effects of the Economy on Criminal Behaviour and the Administration of Criminal Justice', in United Nations Social Defence Research Institute, *Economic Crises and Crime*, Rome: UN Publication No. 15, 25–68.

49 Bonger, W. A. (1916), *Criminality and Economic Conditions*, Boston: Little, Brown.

50 Thomas, D. S. (1927), *Social Aspects of the Business Cycle*, New York: Knopf.

51 Winslow, E. (1931), *Relationship Between Employment and Crime as Shown by Massachusetts Statistics*, Report of US National Commission on Law Observance and Enforcement, vol. I, part IV, Washington DC: US Govt Printing Office.

52 Van Kleek, M. (1931), *Notes on Fluctuations in Employment and in Crime in New York State*, Report of U.S. National Commission on Law Observance and Enforcement, vol. I, part V, Washington DC: US Govt Printing Office.

53 Warner, S. B. (1934), *Crime and Criminal Statistics in Boston*, Cambridge: Harvard University Press.

54 Wiers, op. cit.

55 Phelps, H. A. (1929), 'Cycles of Crime', *Journal of Criminal Law, Criminology and Police Science*, XX, 107–21.

56 Parent, F. J. (1974), *A Community Level, Time-Series Analysis of Concomitant Variation in Economic and Crime Indices: Sanford-Springvale, Maine, 1951–1970*, PhD dissertation, University of New Hampshire.

57 Henry, A. F. and Short, J. F. (1954), *Suicide and Homicide: Some Economic, Sociological and Psychological Aspects of Aggression*, New York: Free Press.

58 Bogen, D. (1944), 'Juvenile Delinquency and Economic Trends', *American Sociological Review*, 9, 178–84.

59 Glaser, D. and Rice, K. (1959), 'Crime, Age and Employment', *American Sociological Review*, XXIV, 679–86. The clear deficiencies and misinterpretations of this study have been described by Gibbs and Guttentag. See Gibbs, J. P. (1966), 'Crime, Unemployment and Status Integration', *British Journal of Criminology*, 6, 49–58. Guttentag, M. (1968), 'The Relationship of Unemployment to Crime and Delinquency', *Journal of Social Issues*, 24, 105–14.

60 Carr, L. J. (1950), *Delinquency Control*, New York: Harper & Row, 86–9. An interesting inversion of this trend is the study by Evans of crime in Japan between 1955 and 1970. Evans found that during periods when income inequality went up reported crime decreased, but juvenile arrest rates increased. Evans, R. (1977), 'Changing Labor Markets and Criminal Behaviour in Japan', *Journal of Asian Studies*, 36, 477–89.

61 Gold, M. (1963), *Status Forces in Delinquent Boys*, Ann Arbor: Institute for Social Research, University of Michigan, p. 41.

62 The most thorough reviews of studies on crime and the business cycle are still probably those of Sellin and Vold, and these reviews make it clear what a vast volume of conflicting evidence there is. See Sellin, T. (1937), *Research Memorandum on Crime in the Depression*, New York: Social Science Research Council Bulletin No. 27. Vold, G. B. (1958), *Theoretical Criminology*, New York: Oxford University Press, 164–81.

63 Mendershausen, H. (1946), *Changes in Income Distribution During the Great Depression*, New York: National Bureau of Economic Research.

64 Gurr, T. R., Grabosky, P. N. and Hula, R. C. (1977), *The Politics of Crime and Conflict: A Comparative History of Four Cities*, Beverly Hills: Sage.

65 Ibid., 211–12. This conclusion is replicated by Zehr in his work on crime trends in nineteenth-century Germany and France: 'Concurrently, a change occurred in the economic determinants of crime: the relationship between basic subsistence costs and both violent and property crimes loosened as the century progressed due, seemingly, to rising standards of living.' Zehr, H. (1976), *Crime and the Development of Modern Society: Patterns of Criminality in Nineteenth Century Germany and France*, London: Croom Helm, p. 138.

66 Danziger and Wheeler, op. cit.

67 Short, J. F. (1952), 'A Note on Relief Programs and Crimes during the depression of the 1930s', *American Sociological Review*, 17, 226–9.

68 Burkhardt, W. R. (1973), *The Application of Opportunity Theory to Delinquency Prevention: Evaluation of a Case Study and Critique of the Literature*, PhD dissertation, Wayne State University.

69 This programme, which consisted of community organization, social case-work, and gang work, also showed no impact on delinquency. See Miller, W. B. (1962), 'The Impact of a Total Community Delinquency Control Project', *Social Problems*, 10, 168–91.

70 Cho, op. cit., 182–97.

71 Hackler, J. C. (1966), 'Boys, Blisters and Behaviour: The Impact of a Work Program in an Urban Central Area', *Journal of Research in Crime and Delinquency*, 3, 155–64.

72 Hackler, J. C. and Hagan, J. L. (1975), 'Work and Teaching Machines as Delinquency Prevention Tools: A Four-Year Follow-Up', *Social Service Review*, 49, 92–106.

73 Robin, G. D. (1969), 'Anti-Poverty Programs and Delinquency', *Journal of Criminal Law, Criminology and Police Science*, 60, 323–31.

74 Lane Human Resources Inc. (1967), *Orientation to Youth Problems: A Community Training Program*, Eugene, Oregon: Lane Human Resources Inc., 130–2. See also Wilkins, L. T. and Gottfredson, D. M. (1969), *Research Demonstration and Social Action*, Davis, California: National Council on Crime and Delinquency Research Center.

75 San Francisco Youth Opportunities Center (1966), *An Evaluation of the San Francisco Youth Opportunities Center*, San Francisco: San Francisco Youth Opportunities Center, p. 77.

76 Jones, H. (1969), 'From Reform School to Society', in H. H. Weissman, ed., *Individual and Group Services in the Mobilization for Youth Experience*, New York: Association Press, p. 90.

77 Odell, B. N. (1974), 'Accelerating Entry Into the Opportunity Structure', *Sociology and Social Research*, 58, 312–17.

78 Zivan, M. (1966), *Youth in Trouble: A Vocational Approach*, Final report of a research and demonstration project, May 31, 1961–August 31, 1966, Dobbs Ferry, New York: Children's Village.

79 Kovacs, F. W. (1967), *Evaluation and Final Report of the New Start Demonstration Project*, Colorado Department of Employment.

80 Richert, J. P. (1975), 'The Court Employment Project in New York', *American Bar Association Journal*, 17, 35–44.

81 Rovner-Pieczenik, R. (1970), *Project Crossroads and Pre-Trial Intervention: A Program Evaluation*, National Committee for Children and Youth. Holahan, J. F. (1970), *A Benefit–Cost Analysis of Project Crossroads*, National Committee for Children and Youth. Holahan, J. F. (1971), *Benefit–Cost Analysis of Programs in the Criminal Justice System*, PhD dissertation, Georgetown University.

82 Ibid.

83 Reitzes, D. C. (1955), 'The Effect of Social Environment upon Former Felons', *Journal of Criminal Law, Criminology and Police Science*, 46, 226–31. Glaser, D. (1964), *The Effectiveness of a Prison and Parole System*, New York: Bobbs-Merrill, 232–59. Blackler, C. (1968), 'Primary Recidivism in Adult Men', *British Journal of Criminology*, 8, 130–69. Evans, R. (1968), 'The Labor Market and Parole Success', *Journal of Human Resources*, 3, 201–12. Taggart, R. (1972), *The Prison of Unemployment: Manpower Programmes for Offenders*, Baltimore, Johns Hopkins.

84 Taggart, op. cit., 40–4.
85 Ibid.
86 ABT Associates Inc. (1971), *An Evaluation of MDTA Training in Correctional Institutions*, vols 1, 2, 3, and final summary, Washington DC. See also Taggart, op. cit., 44–9.
87 See Taggart, op. cit., 66–8.
88 Ibid., p. 67.
89 Gearhart, W. J., Keith, H. L. and Clemmons, G. (1967), *An Analysis of the Vocational Training Program in the Washington State Adult Correctional Institutions*, Research Review No. 23, State of Washington, Department of Institutions.
90 Taggart, op. cit.
91 Martinson, R. (1974), 'What Works? – Questions and Answers about Prison Reform', *The Public Interest*, 35, 22–54.
92 Lipton, D., Martinson, R. and Wilks, J. (1975), *The Effectiveness of Correctional Treatment: A Survey of Evaluation Studies*, New York: Praeger.
93 Pownall, G. (1969), *Employment Problems of Released Prisoners*, College Park, Md: University of Maryland, mimeographed.
94 Lipton *et al.*, chapter 3, 340–6.
95 Rein, M. (1970), *Social Policy: Issues of Choice and Change*, New York: Random House, p. 238.

Chapter 12 Inequality: conclusions and policies

1 This point of view has been expressed by Wheeler *et al.* See Wheeler, S., Cottrell, L. and Romasco, A. (1970), 'Juvenile Delinquency – Its Prevention and Control', in P. Lerman, ed., *Delinquency and Social Policy*, New York: Praeger.
2 Oughton, F. (1971), *Fraud and White-Collar Crime*, London: Elek Books.
3 Ibid., p. 84.
4 See Appendix IX of the author's PhD dissertation.
5 Pavin, M. (1973), 'Economic Determinants of Political Unrest: An Economic Approach', *Journal of Conflict Resolution*, 17, 271–96.
6 In a game simulation with the properties of a 'real' society (SIMSOC), Silver found some support for this formulation. He found that feelings of status threat among those incumbent in positions of high status were increased by greater openness of classes. Thus, Silver argues, variations in the extent of social mobility change the point of origin of conflict in the class structure. Increased openness of classes reduce conflict arising from the frustration of blocked mobility for the lower class, but increases conflict arising from feelings of threat by those in high positions. See Silver, B. B. (1973), 'Social Mobility and Intergroup Antagonism: A Simulation', *Journal of Conflict Resolution*, 17, 605–23.
7 This is a special case of Sorokin's 'principal of limits' that 'in practically all causally connected sociocultural variables there are limits beyond which the causal-functional relationship ceases or else assumes another character'. See Sorokin, P. (1967), 'Reasons for Sociocultural Change and Variably Recurrent Processes', in W. E. Moore and R. M. Cook, eds, *Readings on Social Change*, Englewood Cliffs: Prentice-Hall, p. 73.
8 Rosenfeld, E. (1968), 'Social Research and Social Action in Prevention of Juvenile Delinquency', in J. Stratton and R. Terry, eds, *Prevention of Delinquency: Problems and Programs*, London: Macmillan, p. 37.
9 Lemert, E. M. (1967), *Human Deviance, Social Problems and Social Control*, New Jersey: Prentice-Hall, 17–26, 40–64.

10 Box, S. (1971), *Deviance, Reality and Society*, New York: Holt, Rinehart & Winston.
11 Ibid., p. 99.
12 De Tocqueville, A. (1856), *The Old Regime and the French Revolution*, New York: Harper & Row, p. 214. For a discussion of this argument, see Coser, L. A. (1967), *Continuities in the Study of Social Conflict*, London: Macmillan.
13 Adler, F. (1975), *Sisters in Crime: The Rise of the New Female Criminal*, New York: McGraw-Hill.
14 A comparable example arises in McDonald's research on the relationship between civil rights activity and violent crime. Does civil rights activity aggravate frustrations among Negroes, or does it alleviate frustrations? In choosing which of these two propositions is more consistent with his data, McDonald opts for the former. See McDonald, T. D. (1972), *Correlates of Civil Rights Activity and Negro Intra-racial Violence*, PhD dissertation, Southern Illinois University. See also the study by Scase which found that Swedish workers expressed greater relative deprivation than English workers, even though they had objectively better conditions than the English. Scase concludes that this is because 'in presenting itself as the champion of social justice, the [Swedish] Social Democratic Party has generated a sense of relative deprivation among manual workers'. See Scase, R. (1974), 'Relative Deprivation: A Comparison of English and Swedish Manual Workers', in D. Wedderburn, ed., *Poverty, Inequality and Class Structure*, Cambridge: Cambridge University Press.
15 Davies, J. C. (1962), 'Toward a Theory of Revolution', *American Sociological Review*, 27, 5–8, 15–18.
16 Ibid., p. 6. Pettigrew has conducted a study which concluded that Davies's theory is consistent with evidence on black unrest in the United States. See Pettigrew, T. F. (1974), 'Black Unrest in the 1960s', in L. Rainwater, ed., *Inequality and Justice*, Chicago: Aldine, 216–24. See also Gurr, T. R. (1972), 'Sources of Rebellion in Western Societies: Some Quantitative Evidence', in J. F. Short and M. E. Wolfgang, eds, *Collective Violence*, Chicago: Aldine-Atherton, 132–49.
17 In short, Adler's theory starts from the fact that during infancy and childhood human beings are weak and inferior to adults. A sense of inferiority leads to efforts to remedy or compensate, and herein is engendered the pervasive motive of longing to establish superiority over others. See Ansbacher, H. and Ansbacher, R. (1956), *The Individual Psychology of Alfred Adler*, New York: Basic Books.
18 Dahrendorf, R. (1969), 'On the Origin of Inequality Among Men', in A. Beteille, ed., *Social Inequality*, Harmondsworth: Penguin, 16–44.
19 Merton, R. K. (1936), 'The Unanticipated Consequences of Purposive Social Action', *American Sociological Review*, 1, 894–904.
20 Carlin, J. E. (1966), *Lawyers' Ethics: A Survey of the New York City Bar*, New York: Russel Sage Foundation.

Postscript: The socialist critique of the reformist criminology in this book

1 Taylor, L. and Taylor, I. (1968), 'We are all Deviants now — Some Comments on Crime', *International Socialism*, 34, 28–32.
2 For example, see Isaac, J. E. (1967), 'Wage Drift in the Australian Metal Industries', in J. E. Isaac and G. W. Ford, eds, *Australian Labour Economics: Readings*, Melbourne: Sun Books, 214–21.

3 Jones, M. A. (1972), *Housing and Poverty in Australia*, Melbourne: Melbourne University Press, p. 77.

4 Gordon, D. M. (1973), 'Capitalism, Class and Crime in America', *Crime and Delinquency*, 19, 163–86.

5 See Jiobu, R. M. and Marshall, H. H. (1971), 'Urban Structure and the Differentiation Between Blacks and Whites', *American Sociological Review*, 36, 638–49.

6 Grier, E. and Grier, G. (1968), 'Equality and Beyond: Housing Segregation in the Great Society', in B. J. Frieden and R. Morris, eds, *Urban Planning and Social Policy*, New York: Basic Books, 124–47.

7 See Harvey, D. (1973), *Social Justice and the City*, London: Edward Arnold. See also Davidoff, P., Davidoff, L. and Gold, N. N. (1967), 'Suburban Action: Advocate Planning for an Open Society', *Journal of the American Institute of Planners*, 36, 12–21.

8 Jiobu and Marshall, op. cit.

9 See Rein, M. (1970), *Social Policy: Issues of Choice and Change*, New York: Random House, p. 384.

10 Marshall, H. and Jiobu, R. (1975), 'Residential Segregation in United States Cities: A Causal Analysis', *Social Forces*, 53, 449–59.

11 Jiobu and Marshall, op. cit.

12 There was, in fact also a negative correlation of − ·44 between the income gap and the percentage below the poverty line in the poorest 20 per cent of the city. However, this is a spurious relationship because cities with few people below the poverty line were cities with large income gaps between the poor and the average income-earner.

13 A dissenting view is Michelson's. He suggests, with absolutely no evidence to back it up, that 'when the ideology supporting formal acknowledgement of class differences in society breaks down, then class differences are supported by other means, one of which is residential segregation.' See Michelson, W. (1970), *Man and his Urban Environment: A Sociological Approach*, Reading, Mass.: Addison-Wesley, p. 119.

14 Sandercock, L. (1975), *Cities for Sale: Property, Politics and Urban Planning in Australia*, Melbourne: Melbourne University Press, p. 1.

15 This analogy has been used by Harvey, op. cit., p. 164.

16 Ibid., p. 137.

17 Musil, J. (1968), 'The Development of Prague's Ecological Structure', in R. Pahl, ed., *Readings in Urban Sociology*, Oxford: Pergamon Press.

18 Engels, F. (1935), *The Housing Question*, New York: Lawrence & Wishart.

19 Ibid., p. 77.

20 Harvey, op. cit., p. 144.

21 Grier and Grier claim that 'the decision to let private enterprise satisfy the housing need carried with it unfortunate consequences for future residential patterns. It meant that the great majority of the new postwar suburban housing was built for those who could afford to pay the full economic price. Thus the basic mechanisms of the private enterprise system, successful as they were in meeting overall housing needs, selectively operated to reinforce existing trends which concentrated low-income families in the cities. At the same time, they encouraged the centrifugal movement of those who were more wealthy to the outskirts of the city.' See Grier and Grier, op. cit., p. 127.

22 See Lieberson, S. (1963), *Ethnic Patterns in American Cities*, New York: Free Press. See also the discussion of the norm-conflict prediction in chapter 4 of this book.

23 Musil, op. cit.

24 Spadijir-Dzinic, J. (1968), 'Socioloski Pristup Istrazivanju Maloletñicke Delinkvencijo' (a sociological approach to the investigation of juvenile delinquency), *Sociologija*, 10, 269–80. Connor, W. D. (1970), 'Juvenile Delinquency in the U.S.S.R.: Some Quantitative and Qualitative Indicators', *American Sociological Review*, 35, 283–97.

25 Cantor, R. (1974), 'New Laws for a New Society', *Crime and Social Justice*, 2, 12–23. Djekebaev, U.S. (1975), 'The Overcoming of Social Alienation and Problems of Rooting Out Criminal Behaviour under the Conditions of the Transition of Formerly Backward Peoples to Socialism Skipping the Capitalist Stage', *Soviet Sociology*, XIII, 60–95.

Appendix: Class-mix policies

1 See the discussion of this point in chapters 1 and 3.

2 Rainwater, L. (1974), 'The Slum and its Problems', in L. Rainwater, ed., *Inequality and Justice*, Chicago: Aldine, p. 149.

3 Grier, E. and Grier, G. (1968), 'Equality and Beyond: Housing Segregation in The Great Society', in B. J. Frieden and R. Morris, eds, *Urban Planning and Social Policy*, New York: Basic Books, p. 128.

4 Cho, Y. H. (1974), *Public Policy and Urban Crime*, Cambridge, Mass.: Ballinger Publishing Co., 182–90.

5 Jacobs, J. (1965), *The Death and Life of Great American Cities: The Failure of Town Planning*, Harmondsworth: Penguin.

6 Grier and Grier, op. cit., 129–30.

7 Stillwell, F. J. and Hardwick, J. M. (1973), 'Social Inequality in Australian Cities', *Australian Quarterly*, 45, p. 28.

8 For a discussion of these practices, see Davidoff, P., Davidoff, L. and Gold, N. N. (1970), 'Suburban Planning: Advocate Planning for an Open Society', *Journal of the American Institute of Planners*, 36, 12–21.

9 Grier and Grier, op. cit., p. 131.

10 Wilson, P. R. (1976), *Public Housing: Pragmatics and Policies*, Brisbane: University of Queensland Press.

11 Jones, M. A. (1972), *Housing and Poverty in Australia*, Melbourne: Melbourne University Press.

12 Ibid., p. 193.

13 Jackson Teece Chesterman Willis (1973), *The Church of England Lands, Glebe*, Report to Department of Urban and Regional Development.

14 See Wilson, P. R., op. cit. Also see *Report to the Congress: Observations on Housing Allowances and Experimental Housing Allowance Program*, Comptroller General Report, Washington.

15 Michelson, W. (1970), *Man and His Urban Environment: A Sociological Approach*, Reading, Mass.: Addison-Wesley, p. 123.

16 Stehbens, I. H., undergraduate assignment, Department of Geography, University of Queensland.

17 Hauser, P., *et al.* (1964), *Report to the Board of Education, City of Chicago*, by the advisory panel on integration of the public schools, Chicago. (Reported in Dentler, R. A., 'Barriers to Northern School Desegregation', in Frieden and Morris, op. cit., p. 169.)

18 For a discussion of how streaming facilitates the formation of delinquent subcultures see Wilson, P. R., Braithwaite, J. B., Guthrie, A. and Smith, G. (1975), *Truancy*, Report to the Education Section of the Poverty Commission, Canberra.

19 Glazer, N. (1959), 'The School as an Instrument of Planning', *Journal of the American Institute of Planners*, 25, 191–9.
20 Ibid., p. 193.
21 Lauber, D. (1974), 'Integration Takes More Than a Racial Quota', *Planning*, 14, 14–17.
22 Williams, C., forthcoming PhD dissertation, University of Queensland.
23 Michelson, op. cit., p. 120.
24 See Heraud, B. J. (1968), 'Social Class and the New Towns', *Urban Studies*, 5, 33–58.
25 Gans, H. (1967), *The Levittowners*, New York: Pantheon Books, p. 281.

Select bibliography

Many of the works cited in footnotes throughout the text are not included in this select bibliography. The bibliography includes only those works that directly discuss the relationship between class and crime.

ABT Associates Inc. (1971), *An Evaluation of MDTA Training in Correctional Institutions*, vols 1, 2, 3 and Final Summary, Washington DC.

Adler, F. (1975), *Sisters in Crime: The Rise of the New Female Criminal*, New York: McGraw-Hill.

Akers, R. L. (1964), 'Socioeconomic Status and Delinquent Behaviour: A Retest', *Journal of Research in Crime and Delinquency*, 1, 38–46.

Allen, D. E. and Sandhu, H. S. (1968), 'A Comparative Study of Delinquents and Non-Delinquents: Family Affect, Religion and Personal Income', *Social Forces*, 46, 263–8.

Allen, V. L. (1970), *Psychological Factors in Poverty*, Chicago: Markham.

Allison, J. P. (1972), 'Economic Factors and the Rate of Crime', *Land Economics*, 68, 193–6.

Amir, M. (1971), *Patterns of Forcible Rape*, Chicago: University of Chicago Press.

Anderson, K. G. (1961), *Applications of Objective Tests of Personality to Criminal Populations, 1950-1959: A Review and Appraisal*, MA thesis, Indiana University.

Angell, R. C. (1974), 'The Moral Integration of American Cities: Part II', *American Journal of Sociology*, 80, 607–29.

Armston, G. and Wilson, M. (1973), 'City Politics and Deviancy Amplification', in I. Taylor and L. Taylor, eds, *Politics and Deviance: Papers from the National Deviancy Conference*, Harmondsworth: Penguin.

Arnold, W. R. (1965), 'Continuities in Research: Scaling Delinquent Behaviour', *Social Problems*, 13, 59–66.

Arnold, W. R. (1971), 'Race and Ethnicity Relative to other Factors in Juvenile Court Dispositions', *American Journal of Sociology*, 77, 211–27.

Ashpole, R. E. (1970), 'Parental Strategies and Social Class in the Adjudication of Delinquency', unpublished PhD dissertation, University of Utah.

Asunti, T. (1969), 'Homicide in Western Nigeria', *British Journal of Psychiatry*, 115, 1,105–13.

Axelrad, S. (1952), 'Negro and White Institutionalized Delinquents', *American Journal of Sociology*, 57, 569–74.

Baldwin, J., Bottoms, A. E. and Walker, M. A. (1976), *The Urban Criminal: A*

Study in Sheffield, London: Tavistock.

Ball, R. A. (1968), 'An Empirical Exploration of Neutralization Theory', in M. Lefton, J. K. Skipper and C. H. McCashy, eds, *Approaches to Deviance*, New York: Appleton, 255-65.

Ball-Rokeach, S. J. (1973), 'Values and Violence: A Test of the Subculture of Violence Thesis', *American Sociological Review*, 38, 736-49.

Bankowski, Z. and Mungham, G. (1976), *Images of Law*, London: Routledge & Kegan Paul.

Bannister, S. (1976), 'Education and Employment Histories of a Group of Young Offenders', in United Nations Social Defense Research Institute, *Economic Crises and Crime*, Rome: UN Publication No. 15, 129-40.

Barber, R. (1973), 'An Investigation into Rape and Attempted Rape Cases in Queensland', *Australian and New Zealand Journal of Criminology*, 6, 214-30.

Barron, M. L. (1951), 'Juvenile Delinquency and American Values', *American Sociological Review*, 16, 208-14.

Bates, W. (1962), 'Caste, Class, and Vandalism', *Social Problems*, 9, 349-58.

Bayley, D. H. and Mendelsohn, H. (1969), *Minorities and the Police*, New York: Free Press.

Bechdolt, B. V. (1975), 'Cross-Sectional Analysis of Socioeconomic Determinants of Urban Crime', *Review of Social Economy*, 33, 132-40.

Becker, T. L. and Murray, V. G., eds, *Government Lawlessness in America*, New York: Oxford University Press.

Belson, W. A. (1969), 'The Extent of Stealing by London Boys and some of its Origins', Survey Research Centre, London School of Economics.

Belson, W. A. (1975), *Juvenile Theft: The Causal Factors*, London: Harper & Row.

Belson, W. A. (1978), personal communication. As yet unpublished data from a large-scale study on the effects of television violence on self-reported violent behaviour among London boys.

Bensing, R. C. and Schroeder, O. (1960), *Homicide in an Urban Community*, Springfield, Ill.: Charles C. Thomas.

Black, D. J. (1970), 'Production of Crime Rates', *American Sociological Review*, 35, 722-48.

Black, D. J. and Reiss, A. J. (1970), 'Police Control of Juveniles', *American Sociological Review*, 35, 63-77.

Blackler, C. (1968), 'Primary Recidivism in Adult Men', *British Journal of Criminology*, 8, 130-69.

Blackmore, J. (1974), 'The Relationship between Self-Reported Delinquency and Official Convictions among Adolescent Boys', *British Journal of Criminology*, 14, 172-6.

Bloch, H. A. and Geis, G. (1967), *Man, Crime and Society*, New York: Random House.

Bloom, B. L. (1966), 'A Census Tract Analysis of Socially Deviant Behaviour', *Multivariate Behavioural Research*, 1, 307-20.

Bogen, D. (1944), 'Juvenile Delinquency and Economic Trends', *American Sociological Review*, 9, 178-84.

Boggs, S. L. (1965), 'Urban Crime Patterns', *American Sociological Review*, 30, 899-908.

Bohlke, R. H. (1961), 'Social Mobility, Stratification Inconsistency and Middle Class Delinquency', *Social Problems*, 8, 351-63.

Bonger, W. A. (1916), *Criminality and Economic Conditions*, Boston: Little, Brown.

Booth, A., Welch, S. and Johnson, D. R. (1976), 'Crowding and Urban Crime Rates', *Urban Affairs Quarterly*, 11, 291-308.

Bordua, D. J. (1958), 'Juvenile Delinquency and "Anomie": An Attempt at Replication', *Social Problems*, 6, 230–8.

Bordua, D. J. (1961), 'Delinquent Subcultures: Sociological Interpretations of Gang Delinquency', *Annals*, 338, 119–36.

Bordua, D. J. (1967), 'Recent Trends: Deviant Behaviour and Social Control', *Annals*, 57, 149–63.

Boshier, R. and Johnson, D. (1974), 'Does Conviction Affect Employment Opportunities ?' *British Journal of Criminology*, 14, 264–8.

Boven, R. and O'Neill, D. P. (1975), *A Regional Analysis of Juvenile Offending in New Zealand*, Research Section, Department of Social Welfare, New Zealand: General Research Report No. 7.

Box, S. (1971), *Deviance, Reality and Society*, London: Holt, Rinehart & Winston.

Box, S. and Ford, J. (1971), 'The Facts Don't Fit: On the Relationship between Social Class and Criminal Behaviour', *The Sociological Review*, 19, 31–52.

Box, S. and Russell, K. (1975), 'The Politics of Discreditability: Disarming Complaints against the Police', *The Sociological Review*, 23, 315–46.

Brady, J. P. (1975), 'The Talking Stone: Evolution and Action of People's Criminology', *The Insurgent Sociologist*, V, 76–9.

Braithwaite, J. B. (1975), 'Competitiveness in Schools and Delinquency', *Australian Journal of Social Issues*, 10, 107–10.

Braithwaite, J. B. (1975), 'Population Growth and Crime', *Australian and New Zealand Journal of Criminology*, 8, 57–61.

Braithwaite, J. B. (1977), 'Australian Delinquency: Research and Practical Considerations', in P. R. Wilson, ed., *Delinquency in Australia*, Brisbane; University of Queensland Press.

Braithwaite, J. B. (1978), 'An Exploratory Study of Used Car Fraud', in P. R. Wilson and J. B. Braithwaite, eds, *Two Faces of Deviance: Crimes of the Powerless and Powerful*, Brisbane: University of Queensland Press.

Braithwaite, J. B. and Braithwaite, V. A., unpublished finding, based on data to be published in a forthcoming article entitled 'An Exploratory Study of Delinquency and the Nature of Schooling'.

Braithwaite, J. B. and Condon, B. (1978), 'On the Class Basis of Criminal Violence', in P. R. Wilson and J. B. Braithwaite, eds, *Two Faces of Deviance: Crimes of the Powerless and Powerful*, Brisbane: University of Queensland Press.

Brenner, H. (1976a), *Estimating the Social Costs of National Economic Policy: Implications for Mental and Physical Health, and Criminal Aggression*, a study prepared for the Joint Economic Committee, Congress of the United States, Washington DC: US Govt Printing Office.

Brenner, H. (1976b), 'Time-Series Analysis: Effects of the Economy on Criminal Behaviour and the Administration of Criminal Justice', in United Nations Social Defence Research Institute, *Economic Crises and Crime*, Rome: UN Publication No. 15, 25–68.

Brown, M. J., McCulloch, J. W. and Hiscox, J. (1972), 'Criminal Offences in an Urban Area and their Associated Social Variables', *British Journal of Criminology*, 12, 250–68.

Bruce, N. (1970), 'Delinquent and Non-Delinquent Reactions to Parental Deprivation', *British Journal of Criminology*, 10, 270–6.

Buikhuisen, W. and Dijksterhuis, P. H. (1972), 'Delinquency and Stigmatization', *British Journal of Criminology*, 11, 185–7.

Bullock, H. A. (1961), 'Significance of the Racial Factor in the Length of Prison Sentence', *Journal of Criminal Law, Criminology and Police Science*, 52, 411–17.

Burgess, E. W. (1952), 'The Economic Factor in Juvenile Delinquency', *Journal of Criminal Law, Criminology and Police Science*, 43, 29–42.

Burkhardt, W. R. (1973), *The Application of Opportunity Theory to Delinquency Prevention: Evaluation of a Case Study and Critique of the Literature*, PhD dissertation, Wayne State University.

Burns, J. L. (1971), 'Delinquents Failed by the System', *Special Education*, 60, 13–16.

Burt, C. (1944), *The Young Delinquent*, New York: D. Appleton and Co., 4th edn.

Bytheway, B. (1975), 'The Statistical Association Between Social Class and Self-Reported Delinquency', *International Journal of Criminology and Penology*, 3, 243–51.

Cameron, M. A. (1964), *The Booster and the Snitch: Department Store Shop-Lifting*, Glencoe, Ill.: Free Press, 92–4.

Campanis, P. (1970), 'Normlessness in Management', in J. D. Douglas, ed., *Deviance and Respectability: The Social Construction of Moral Meanings*, New York: Basic Books, 291–325.

Canadian Government (1951), *Statistics of Criminal and Other Offences*, 74th Annual Report, Part III, Ottawa, 60–1.

Cantor, R. (1974), 'New Laws for a New Society', *Crime and Social Justice*, 2, 12–23.

Cardarelli, A. P. (1974), 'Socio-Economic Status and Delinquency and Adult Criminality in a Birth Cohort', unpublished PhD dissertation, University of Pennsylvania.

Carlin, J. E. (1966), *Lawyers' Ethics: A Survey of the New York City Bar*, New York: Russel Sage Foundation.

Carr, L. J. (1950), *Delinquency Control*, New York: Harper & Row.

Carr-Saunders, A. M. (1942), *Young Offenders*, Cambridge: Cambridge University Press.

Carson, W. G. (1970), 'White-Collar Crime and the Enforcement of Factory Legislation', *British Journal of Criminology*, 10, 383–98.

Cartwright, D. S. and Howard, K. I. (1966), 'Multivariate Analysis of Gang Delinquency: I. Ecological Influences', *Multivariate Behavioural Research*, 1, 321–72.

Casparis, J. and Vaz, E. W. (1973), 'Social Class and Self-Reported Delinquent Acts Among Swiss Boys', *International Journal of Comparative Sociology*, 14, 47–58.

Cernkovich, S. A. (1978), 'Value Orientations and Delinquency Involvement', *Criminology*, 15, 443–57.

Chambliss, W. J. (1969), *Crime and the Legal Process*, New York: McGraw-Hill.

Chambliss, W. J. and Seidman, R. B. (1971), *Law, Order and Power*, New York: Addison-Wesley.

Chapman, D. (1968), *Sociology and the Stereotype of the Criminal*, London: Tavistock.

Cherchi, A., Pankoff, A., Frau, R. and Piras, F. (1972), 'Course, Distribution and Nature of Juvenile Maladjustment in Sardinia', *Quaderni di Criminologia Clinica*, 14, 454–527.

Chester, C. R. (1976), 'Perceived Relative Deprivation as a Cause of Property Crime', *Crime and Delinquency*, 22, 17–30.

Chilton, R. J. (1964), 'Continuity in Delinquency Area Research: A Comparison of Studies for Baltimore, Detroit and Indianapolis', *American Sociological Review*, 29, 71–83.

Chilton, R. J. (1967), 'Middle Class Delinquency and Specific Offence Analysis', in E. W. Vaz, ed., *Middle-Class Juvenile Delinquency*, New York: Harper & Row, 91-101.

Chilton, R. and DeAmicis, J. (1975), 'Overcriminalization and the Measurement of Consensus', *Sociology and Social Research*, 15, 318-29.

Chilton, R. J. and Markle, G. E. (1972), 'Family Deprivation, Delinquent Conduct and the Effect of Subclassification', *American Sociological Review*, 37, 93-9.

Chimbos, P. D. (1973), 'A Study of Breaking and Entering Offences in "Northern City" Ontario', *Canadian Journal of Criminology and Corrections*, 15, 316-25.

Chiricos, T. G., Jackson, P. D. and Waldo, G. P. (1972), 'Inequality in the Imposition of a Criminal Label', *Social Problems*, 19, 553-71.

Chiricos, T. G. and Waldo, G. P. (1975), 'Socioeconomic Status and Criminal Sentencing: An Empirical Assessment of a Conflict Proposition', *American Sociological Review*, 40, 753-72.

Cho, Y. H. (1974), *Public Policy and Urban Crime*, Cambridge, Mass.: Ballinger Publishing Co.

Christie, N., Andenaes, J. and Skirbekk, S. (1965), 'A Study of Self-Reported Crime', in *Scandinavian Studies in Criminology*, vol. 1, London: Tavistock, 55-85.

Cicourel, A. V. (1968), *The Social Organization of Juvenile Justice*, New York: Wiley.

Clark, J. P. and Wenninger, E. P. (1962), 'Socio-Economic Class and Area as Correlates of Illegal Behaviour Among Juveniles', *American Sociological Review*, 27, 826-34.

Clemente, F. and Kleiman, J. (1977), 'Fear of Crime in the United States: A Multivariate Analysis', *Social Forces*, 56, 519-31.

Clinard, M. B. and Abbott, D. J. (1973), *Crime in Developing Countries: A Comparative Perspective*, New York: Wiley.

Cloward, R. A. (1972), 'The Prevention of Delinquent Subcultures', in D. Palmer and A. S. Linsky, eds, *Rebellion and Retreat*, Columbus, Ohio: Merrill.

Cloward, R. A. and Ohlin, L. E. (1960), *Delinquency and Opportunity: A Theory of Delinquent Gangs*, Glencoe, Ill.: Free Press.

Cochrane, R. (1974), 'Values as Correlates of Deviance', *British Journal of Social and Clinical Psychology*, 13, 257-67.

Cohen, A. K. (1955), *Delinquent Boys: The Culture of the Gang*, Glencoe, Ill.: Free Press.

Cohen, A. K. and Short, J. F. (1971), 'Crime and Juvenile Delinquency' in R. K. Merton and R. Nisbet, eds, *Contemporary Social Problems*, 3rd edn, New York: Harcourt, Brace, Jovanovitch.

Cohen, L. E. and Stark, R. (1974), 'Discriminatory Labelling and the Five-Finger Discount', *Journal of Research in Crime and Delinquency*, 11, 25-39.

Conger, J. J. and Miller, W. C. (1966), *Personality, Social Class and Delinquency*, New York: Wiley.

Conlen, J. J. (1971), *An Area Study of Juvenile Delinquency in Baltimore, Maryland: A Retest of Lander's Thesis and a Test of Cohen's Hypothesis*, PhD dissertation, St Louis University.

Connor, W. D. (1970), 'Juvenile Delinquency in the U.S.S.R.: Some Quantitative and Qualitative Indicators', *American Sociological Review*, 35, 283-97.

Cormack, M. (1976), 'The Association between Crime and Unemployment: A Pilot Study in Scotland', in United Nations Social Defence Research Institute, *Economic Crises and Crime*, Rome: UN Publication No. 15, 85-101.

Cressey, D. (1971), *Other People's Money*, Belmont, Calif.: Wadsworth Publishing Co.

Select bibliography

Danziger, S. (1976), 'Explaining Urban Crime Rates', *Criminology*, 14, 291–5.

Danziger, S. and Wheeler, D. (1975), 'The Economics of Crime: Punishment or Income Redistribution', *Review of Social Economy*, 33, 113–31.

Datesman, D. K., Scarpitti, F. R. and Stephenson, R. M. (1975), 'Female Delinquency: An Application of Self and Opportunity Theories', *Journal of Research in Crime and Delinquency*, 12, 107–23.

Davidson, C. and Gartz, C. A. (1974), 'Are the Poor Different? A Comparison of Work Behaviour and Attitudes among the Urban Poor and Non-Poor', *Social Problems*, 22, 229–45.

De Fleur, L. B. (1969), 'Alternative Strategies for the Development of Delinquency Theories Applicable to Other Cultures', *Social Problems*, 17, 30–9.

De Fleur, L. B. (1971), 'Ecological Variables in the Cross-Cultural Study of Delinquency', in H. Voss and D. Peterson, eds, *Ecology, Crime and Delinquency*, New York: Appleton, Century, Crofts.

Dembo, R. (1973), 'A Measure of Aggression among Working Class Youth', *British Journal of Criminology*, 13, 245–52.

Dentler, R. A. and Monroe, L. J. (1961), 'Social Correlates of Early Adolescent Theft', *American Sociological Review*, 26, 733–43.

Dirksen, C. (1948), *Economic Factors in Delinquency*, Milwaukee: Bruce Publishing Co.

District of Columbia Crime Commission (1969), Findings reported in Report of the Nation of Commission on Causes and Prevention of Violence, *Violent Crime: The Challenge to Our Cities*, New York: Brazilier.

Djekabaev, U. S. (1975), 'The Overcoming of Social Alienation and Problems of Rooting Out Criminal Behaviour under the Conditions of the Transition of Formerly Backward Peoples to Socialism Skipping the Capitalist Stage', *Soviet Sociology*, XIII, 60–95.

Dorn, D. S. (1968), 'Self-Concept, Alienation, and Anxiety in a Contra-Culture and Subculture: A Research Report', *Journal of Criminal Law, Criminology and Police Science*, 59, 531–5.

Douglas, J. W. B., Ross, J. M., Hammond, W. A. and Mulligan, D. G. (1966), 'Delinquency and Social Class', *The British Journal of Criminology*, 6, 294–302.

Downes, D. (1966), *The Delinquent Solution*, London: Routledge & Kegan Paul, 236–9.

Dunlop, A. B. and McCabe, S. (1965), *Young Men in Detention Centres*, London: Routledge & Kegan Paul, p. 38.

Dunstan, J. A. P. and Roberts, S. F. (1977), *Delinquency and Socioeconomic Status: An Ecological Analysis of Melbourne*, Melbourne, Caulfield Institute of Technology, Occasional Monograph No. 1.

Eaton, J. W. and Polk, K. (1961), *Measuring Delinquency: A Study of Probation Department Referrals*, Pittsburgh: University of Pittsburgh Press.

Eberts, P. and Schwirian, K. P. (1970), 'Metropolitan Crime Rates and Relative Deprivation', in D. Glaser, ed., *Crime in the City*, New York: Harper & Row, 90–8.

Ehrlich, I. (1972), 'The Deterrent Effect of Criminal Law Enforcement', *Journal of Legal Studies*, 1, 259–77.

Ehrlich, I. (1974), 'Participation in Illegitimate Activities: An Economic Analysis', in G. S. Becker and W. M. Landes, eds, *Essays in the Economics of Crime and Punishment*, New York: Columbia University Press.

Elliott, D. S. (1961), *Delinquency, Opportunity, and Patterns of Orientations*, PhD dissertation, University of Washington.

Elliott, D. S. (1962), 'Delinquency and Perceived Opportunity', *Sociological Inquiry*, XXXII, 216–22.

Elliott, D. S. and Voss, H. L. (1974), *Delinquency and Dropout*, Lexington, Mass.: Lexington Books.

Elmhorn, K. (1965), 'Study in Self-Reported Delinquency Among School Children in Stockholm', *Scandinavian Studies in Criminology*, vol. 1, London: Tavistock, 86–116.

Empey, L. T. and Erickson, M. L. (1966), 'Hidden Delinquency and Social Status', *Social Forces*, 44, 546–54.

Empey, L. T. and Lubeck, S. G. with Laporte, R. L. (1971), *Explaining Delinquency: Construction, Test, and Reformulation of a Sociological Theory*, Lexington, Mass.: Heath Lexington Books.

Empey, L. T. and Lubeck, S. G. (1971), *The Silverlake Experiment: Testing Delinquency Theory and Community Intervention*, Chicago: Aldine.

Engels, F. (1969), *The Condition of the Working Class in England in 1844*, Harmondsworth: Penguin.

Engstad, P. and Hackler, J. C. (1971), 'The Impact of Alienation on Delinquency Rates', *Canadian Journal of Criminology and Corrections*, 13, 147–54.

Epps, E. G. (1950), *Socio-Economic Status, Level of Aspiration and Juvenile Delinquency*, PhD dissertation, Washington State University.

Epps, E. G. (1967), 'Socioeconomic Status, Race, Level of Aspiration and Juvenile Delinquency: A Limited Empirical Test of Merton's Conception of Deviation', *Phylon*, 28, 16–27.

Erickson, M. (1973), 'Group Violations, Socio-Economic Status and Official Delinquency', *Social Forces*, 52, 41–52.

Erickson, M. and Empey, L. (1963), 'Court Records, Undetected Delinquency and Decision Making', *Journal of Criminal Law, Criminology and Police Science*, 54, 458–9.

Erlanger, H. S. (1974), 'Social Class and Corporal Punishment in Child-Rearing: A Reassessment', *American Sociological Review*, 39, 68–85.

Erlanger, H. S. (1974), 'The Empirical Status of the Subculture of Violence Thesis', *Social Problems*, 22, 280–91.

Evans, R. (1968), 'The Labor Market and Parole Success', *Journal of Human Resources*, 3, 201–12.

Evans, R. (1977), 'Changing Labor Markets and Criminal Behaviour in Japan', *Journal of Asian Studies*, 36, 477–89.

Faine, J. R. (1974), *A Multi-Dimensional Approach to Understanding Varieties of Delinquent Behaviour*, unpublished PhD dissertation, University of Iowa.

Fannin, L. T. and Clinard, M. B. (1965), 'Differences in the Conception of Self as Male Among Lower and Middle Class Adolescents', *Social Problems*, 13, 205–14.

Farrington, D. P. (1973), 'Self-Reports of Deviant Behaviour: Predictive and Stable?', *Journal of Criminal Law and Criminology*, 64, 99–110.

Faust, F. L. (1970), *Dimensions of Delinquency Tolerance: Differential Tolerance of Juvenile Delinquent Behaviour by Adult Members of Different Socio-Economic Classes and Racial Groups*, PhD dissertation, Ohio State University.

Feather, N. T. (1975), *Values in Education and Society*, New York: Free Press, 181–3.

Feest, J. B. (1971), '"Betriebsjustiz": Internal Administration at the Place of Work', *Abstracts on Criminology and Penology*, 11, 6–14.

Feldman, R. and Weisfeld, G. (1973), 'An Interdisciplinary Study of Crime', *Crime and Delinquency*, 19, 150–62.

Ferdinand, T. N. and Luchterhand, E. G. (1970), 'Inner-City Youth, The Police, The Juvenile Court and Justice', *Social Problems*, 17, 510–27.

Ferguson, T. (1952), *The Young Delinquent in his Social Setting*, Lodon: Oxford University Press.

Fisher, R. (1970), 'Borstal Recall Delinquency and the Cloward–Ohlin Theory of Criminal Subcultures', *British Journal of Criminology*, 10, 52–63.

Flango, V. E. and Sherbenou, E. L. (1976), 'Poverty, Urbanization and Crime', *Criminology*, 14, 331–46.

Fleisher, B. M. (1966), *The Economics of Delinquency*, Chicago: Quadrangle Books.

Fleisher, B. M. (1966), 'The Effect of Income on Delinquency', *American Economic Review*, 56, 118–37.

Frease, D. E. (1973), 'Delinquency, Social Class and the Schools', *Sociology and Social Research*, 57, 443–59.

Fredericks, M. A. and Molnar, M. (1969), 'Relative Occupational Anticipations of Delinquents and Non-Delinquents', *Journal of Research in Crime and Delinquency*, 6, 1–7.

Galle, O. R., Gove, W. and McPherson, J. M. (1972), 'Population Density and Pathology: What are the Relations for Man?', *Science*, 176, 23–30.

Garfinkel, H. (1949), 'Research Note on Inter- and Intra-Racial Homicides', *Social Forces*, 27, 369–81.

Garrett, M. and Short, J. F. (1975), 'Social Class and Delinquency: Predictions and Outcomes of Police-Juvenile Encounters', *Social Problems*, 22, 368–82.

Gastil, R. D. (1971), 'Homicide and a Regional Culture of Violence', *American Sociological Review*, 36, 412–27.

Gearhart, W. J., Keith, H. L. and Clemmons, G. (1967), *An Analysis of the Vocational Training Program in the Washington State Adult Correctional Institutions*, Research Review No. 23, State of Washington, Department of Institutions.

Geis, G., ed. (1968), *White-Collar Criminal: The Offender in Business and the Professions*, New York: Atherton Press.

Geis, G. (1973), 'Victimization Patterns in White-Collar Crime', in I. Drapkin and E. Viano, eds, *Victimology: A New Focus*, vol. V, Lexington, Mass.: Lexington Books.

Gibbens, T. C. N. and Ahrenfeldt, R. H. (1966), *Cultural Factors in Delinquency*, London: Tavistock.

Gibson, H. B. (1971), 'The Factorial Structure of Juvenile Delinquency: A Study of Self-Reported Acts', *British Journal of Social and Clinical Psychology*, 10, 1–9.

Gibson, H. B., Morrison, S. and West, D. J. (1970), 'The Confession of Known Offences in Response to a Self-Reported Delinquency Schedule', *British Journal of Criminology*, 10, 277–80.

Gibson, H. B. and West, D. J. (1970), 'Social and Intellectual Handicaps as Precursors of Early Delinquency', *British Journal of Criminology*, 10, 21–32.

Gil, D. G. (1970), *Violence Against Children: Physical Child Abuse in the United States*, Cambridge, Mass.: Harvard University Press, 110–17.

Glaser, D. (1964), *The Effectiveness of a Prison and Parole System*, New York: Bobbs-Merrill, 232–59.

Glueck, S. and Glueck, E. (1930), *Five Hundred Criminal Careers*, New York: Kraus Reprint Corporation.

Glueck, S. and Glueck, E. (1934), *Five Hundred Delinquent Women*, New York: Kraus Reprint Corporation.

Glueck, S. and Glueck, E. (1950), *Unravelling Juvenile Delinquency*, New York:

The Commonwealth Fund.

Glueck, S. and Glueck, E. (1966), *Juvenile Delinquents Grown Up*, New York: Kraus Reprint Corporation.

Gold, M. (1963), *Status Forces in Delinquent Boys*, Ann Arbor: University of Michigan, Institute for Social Research.

Gold, M. (1969), 'Juvenile Delinquency as a Symptom of Alienation', *Journal of Social Issues*, XXV, p. 131.

Gold, M. (1970), *Delinquent Behavior in an American City*, Belmont, California: Brooks-Cole.

Gold, M. and Mann, D. (1973), 'Delinquency as Defense', *American Journal of Orthopsychiatry*, 42, 463–79.

Goldman, N. (1963), *The Differential Selection of Juvenile Offenders for Court Appearance*, New York: National Council on Crime and Delinquency.

Gordon, D. M. (1973), 'Capitalism, Class and Crime in America', *Crime and Delinquency*, 19, 163–86.

Gordon, R. A. (1967), 'Issues in the Ecological Study of Delinquency', *American Sociological Review*, 32, 927–44.

Gordon, R. A., Short, J. F., Cartwright, D. S. and Strodtbeck, F. L. (1963), 'Values and Gang Delinquency: A Study of Street Corner Groups', *American Journal of Sociology*, 69, 109–28.

Gould, L. C. (1969a), 'Juvenile Entrepreneurs', *American Journal of Sociology*, 74, 710–19.

Gould, L. C. (1969b), 'Who Defines Delinquency: A Comparison of Self-Reported and Officially Reported Delinquency for Three Racial Groups', *Social Problems*, 17, 325–36.

Gove, W., ed. (1975), *The Labelling of Deviance*, New York: Halsted Press.

Green, E. B. (1961), *Judicial Attributes in Sentencing*, London: Macmillan.

Green, E. B. (1964), 'Inter- and Intra-Racial Crime Relative to Sentencing', *Journal of Criminal Law, Criminology and Police Science*, 55, 348–58.

Green, E. B. (1970), 'Race, Social Status and Criminal Arrest', *American Sociological Review*, 35, 476–90.

Greenber, D. F. (1976), 'One-Dimensional Marxist Criminology', *Theory and Society*, 3, 611–21.

Gurr, T. R., Grabosky, P. N. and Hula, R. C. (1977), *The Politics of Crime and Conflict: A Comparative History of Four Cities*, Beverly Hills: Sage.

Hackler, J. C. (1966), 'Boys, Blisters and Behaviour: The Impact of a Work Program in an Urban Central Area', *Journal of Research in Crime and Delinquency*, 3, 155–64.

Hackler, J. C. (1970), 'Testing a Causal Model of Delinquency', *Sociological Quarterly*, 11, 511–22.

Hackler, J. C. and Hagan, J. L. (1975), 'Work and Teaching Machines as Delinquency Prevention Tools: A Four-Year Follow-Up', *Social Service Review*, 49, 92–106.

Hackler, J. C. and Lautt, M. (1969), 'Systematic Bias in Self-Reported Delinquency', *Canadian Review of Sociology and Anthropology*, 6, 92–106.

Hagan, J. (1974), 'Criminal Justice and Native People: A Study of Incarceration in a Canadian Province', *Canadian Review of Anthropology and Sociology*, special issue (August), 220–36.

Hagan, J. (1974), 'Extra-Legal Attributes and Criminal Sentencing: An Assessment of a Sociological Viewpoint', *Law and Society Review*, 8, 357–83.

Hagan, J. and Leon, J. (1977), 'Rediscovering Delinquency: Social History, Political Ideology and Sociology of Law', *American Sociological Review*, 42, 587–98.

Hardt, R. H. (1968), 'Delinquency and Social Class: Bad Kids or Good Cops?' in I. Deutscher and E. Thompson, eds, *Among the People. Encounters with the Poor*, New York: Basic Books.

Hardt, R. H. and Peterson-Hardt, S. (1977), 'On Determining the Quality of the Delinquency Self-Report Method', *Journal of Research in Crime and Delinquency*, 14, 247–61.

Harries, K. D. (1974), *The Geography of Crime and Justice*, New York: McGraw-Hill.

Hassall, P. (1974), 'Schools and Delinquency: A Self-Report Study of Delinquency in Christchurch, New Zealand', a paper at the Sociological Association of Australia and New Zealand 1974 conference, University of New England, Aust.

Havighurst, R. J. (1962), *Growing Up in River City*, New York: Wiley.

Hemley, D. D. and McPheters, L. R. (1974), 'Crime as an Externality of Regional Economic Growth', *Review of Regional Studies*, 4, 73–84.

Henry, A. F. and Short, J. F. (1954), *Suicide and Homicide: Some Economic, Sociological and Psychological Aspects of Aggression*, New York: Free Press.

Hepburn, J. (1977), 'Social Control and Legal Order: Legitimated Repression in a Capitalist State', *Contemporary Crises*, 1, 77–90.

Hills, S. L. (1971), *Crime, Power and Morality: The Criminal Law Process in the United States*, Scranton: Chandler Publishing Co.

Himelhoch, J. (1965), 'Delinquency and Opportunity: an End and a Beginning of Theory', in A. Gouldner and S. M. Miller (eds), *Applied Sociology: Opportunities and Problems*, Glencoe, Ill.: Free Press.

Hindelang, M. J. (1969), 'The Commitment of Delinquents to their Misdeeds: Do Delinquents Drift?', *Social Problems*, 17, 502–9.

Hindelang, M. J. (1971), 'Age, Sex and the Versatility of Delinquent Involvements', *Social Problems*, 18, 522–35.

Hindelang, M. J. (1971), 'Extroversion, Neuroticism, and Self-Reported Delinquent Involvement', *Journal of Research in Crime and Delinquency*, 8, 23–31.

Hindelang, M. J. (1974), 'Decisions of Shoplifting Victims to Invoke the Criminal Justice Process', *Social Problems*, 21, 580–93.

Hindelang, M. J. (1978), 'Race and Involvement in Common Law Personal Crimes', *American Sociological Review*, 43, 93–109.

Hirschi, T. (1969), *Causes of Delinquency*, Berkeley and Los Angeles: University of California Press.

Hirschi, T. (1972), 'Social Class and Crime', in D. W. Theilbar and S. D. Feldman, eds, *Issues in Social Inequality*, Boston: Little, Brown, 503–14.

Hirschi, T. and Selvin, H. (1967), *Delinquent Research: An Appraisal of Analytic Methods*, New York: Free Press.

Hohenstein, W. H. (1969), 'Factors Influencing the Police Disposition of Juvenile Offenders', in T. Sellin and M. Wolfgang, eds, *Delinquency*, New York: Wiley.

Holahan, J. F. (1970), *A Benefit–Cost Analysis of Project Crossroads*, National Committee for Children and Youth.

Holahan, J. F. (1971), *Benefit–Cost Analysis of Programs in the Criminal Justice System*, PhD dissertation, Georgetown University.

Hollingshead, A. B. (1947), 'Selected Characteristics of Classes in a Middle Western Community', *American Sociological Review*, 12, 385–95.

Hooker, E. L. (1945), *The Houston Delinquent in His Community Setting*, Houston: Research Bureau, Council of Social Agencies.

Jaffe, L. D. (1963), 'Delinquency Proneness and Family Anomie', *Journal of Criminal Law, Criminology, and Police Science*, 54, 146–54.

Jaspan, N. and Black, H. (1960), *The Thief in the White Collar*, Philadelphia: Lippincott.

Jessor, R., Graves, T., Hanson, R. and Jessor, S. (1968), *Society, Personality and*

Deviant Behaviour, New York: Holt, Rinehart & Winston.

Jiobu, R. M. and Marshall, H. H. (1971), 'Urban Structure and the Differentiation Between Blacks and Whites', *American Sociological Review*, 36, 638–49.

Johnson, E. M. (1969), *An Empirical Study of Self-Reported Delinquency and Occupational Values*, PhD dissertation, the Louisiana State University and Agricultural and Mechanical College.

Johnson, G. (1941), 'The Negro and Crime', *American Academy of Political and Social Sciences*, 271, 93–104.

Jones, H. (1969), 'From Reform School to Society', in H. H. Weissman, ed., *Individual and Group Services in the Mobilization for Youth Experience*, New York: Association Press.

Jongman, R. W. and Smale, G. J. (1973), 'Factors Relating to the Public Prosecutor's Policy of Case Dismissal', *Nederlands Tijdschrift Voor Criminologie*, 15, 55–65.

Jordan, V. E. (1974), 'The System Propagates Crime', *Crime and Delinquency*, 3, p. 233.

Kelly, D. H. (1971), 'School Failure, Academic Self-Evaluation and School Avoidance and Deviant Behaviour', *Youth and Society*, 2, 489–503.

Kelly, D. H. (1974), 'Track Position and Delinquent Involvement: A Preliminary Analysis', *Sociology and Social Research*, 58, 380–86.

Kelly, D. H. and Balch, R. W. (1971), 'Social Origins and School Failure: A Reexamination of Cohen's Theory of Working-Class Delinquency', *Pacific Sociological Review*, 14, 413–30.

Kelly, D. H. and Pink, W. T. (1975), 'Status Origins, Youth Rebellion and Delinquency: A Reexamination of the Class Issue', *Journal of Youth and Adolescence*, 4, 339–47.

Kobrin, S. (1951), 'The Conflict of Values in Delinquency Areas', *American Sociological Review*, 16, 653–61.

Kovacs, F. W. (1967), *Evaluation and Final Report of the New Start Demonstration Project*, Colorado Department of Employment.

Kratcoski, P. C. and Kratcoski, J. E. (1975), 'Changing Patterns in the Delinquent Activities of Boys and Girls: A Self-Reported Delinquency Analysis', *Adolescence*, X, 83–91.

Krisberg, B. (1975), *Crime and Privilege: Towards a New Criminology*, Englewood Cliffs: Prentice-Hall.

Krohn, M. D. (1976), 'Inequality, Unemployment and Crime: A Cross-National Analysis', *Sociological Quarterly*, 17, 303–13.

Kulik, J. A., Stein, K. B. and Sabin, T. R. (1968), 'Dimensions and Patterns of Adolescent Antisocial Behaviour', *Journal of Consulting and Clinical Psychology*, 32, 375–82.

Kvalseth, T. O. (1977), 'Note on Effects of Population Density and Unemployment on Urban Crime', *Criminology*, 15, 105–10.

Kvaraceus, W. C. (1945), *Juvenile Delinquency and the School*, New York: World Book Co.

Lalli, M. and Turner, S. H. (1968), 'Suicide and Homicide: A Comparative Analysis by Race and Occupational Levels', *Journal of Criminal Law, Criminology and Police Science*, 59, 191–200.

Lander, B. (1954), *Towards an Understanding of Juvenile Delinquency*, New York: Columbia University Press.

Landis, J. R. (1962), *Social Class Differentials in Self, Value and Opportunity Structure as Related to Delinquency Potential*, PhD dissertation, Ohio State University.

Landis, J., Dinitz, S. and Reckless, W. (1963), 'Implementing Two Theories of

307

Delinquency; Value Orientation and Awareness of Limited Opportunity',
Sociology and Social Research, XLVII, p. 415.

Landis, J. R. and Scarpitti, F. R. (1965), 'Perceptions Regarding Value Orientation and Legitimate Opportunity: Delinquents and Non-Delinquents', *Social
Forces*, 44, 83–91.

Lane Human Resources Inc. (1967), *Orientation to Youth Problems: A Community Training Program*, Eugene, Oregon: Lane Human Resources Inc,
130–2.

Lane, R. E. (1953), 'Why Businessmen Violate the Law?', *Journal of Criminal
Law, Criminology and Police Science*, 44, 151–65.

Lanphier, C. M. and Faulkner, J. E. (1970), 'Deviance in a Middle-Class Community', *International Journal of Comparative Sociology*, 11, 146–56.

Levy, C. and Castets, B. (1971), 'Caractères sociaux de jeunes delinquantes d'un
centre d'observation', (social characteristics of young delinquent girls at an
observation centre), *Population*, 26, 319–30.

Lieberman, J. K. (1973), *How the Government Breaks the Law*, Baltimore:
Penguin.

Lipton, D., Martinson, R. and Wilks, J. (1975), *The Effectiveness of Correctional
Treatment: A Survey of Evaluation Studies*, New York: Praeger.

Liska, A. E. (1971), 'Aspirations, Expectations and Delinquency: Stress and
Additive Models', *Sociological Quarterly*, 12, 99–107.

Liska, A. E. (1973), 'Causal Structures Underlying the Relationship Between
Delinquent Involvement and Delinquent Peers', *Sociology and Social
Research*, 58, 23–36.

Little, W. R. and Ntsekhe, V. R. (1959), 'Social Class Background of Young
Offenders from London', *British Journal of Delinquency*, 10, 130–5.

Loftin, C. and Hill, R. H. (1974), 'Regional Subculture and Homicide: An
Examination of the "Gastil-Hackney Thesis"', *American Sociological Review*,
39, 714–24.

Longmoor, E. S. and Young, E. F. (1936), 'Ecological Interrelationships of
Juvenile Delinquency, Dependency and Population Movements: A Carto-
graphic Analysis of Data from Long Beach, California', *American Journal of
Sociology*, 41, 598–610.

Lotz, R. and Hewitt, J. D. (1977), 'The Influence of Legally Irrelevant Factors on
Felony Sentencing', *Sociological Inquiry*, 47, 39–48.

Lovegrove, S. A. (1973), 'The Significance of Three Scales Identifying a Delinquent Orientation among Young Australian Males', *The Australian and New
Zealand Journal of Criminology*, 6, 93–106.

Luchterhand, E. and Weller, L. (1966), 'Delinquency Theory and the Middle-
Size City: A Study of Problem and Promising Youth', *Sociological Quarterly*,
7, 413–23.

Lunden, W. A. (1964), *Statistics on Delinquents and Delinquency*, Springfield.
Ill.: Charles C. Thomas.

Lundman, R. J., Sykes, R. E., and Clark, J. P. (1978), 'Police Control of
Juveniles: A Replication', *Journal of Research in Crime and Delinquency*, 15,
74–91.

McCandless, B. R., Persons, W. S. and Roberts, A. (1972), 'Perceived Opportunity, Delinquency, Race and Body Build Among Delinquent Youth',
Journal of Consulting and Clinical Psychology, 38, 281–7.

McCarthy, J. D., Galle, O. R. and Zimmern, W. (1975), 'Population Density,
Social Structure and Interpersonal Violence', *American Behavioral Scientist*,
18, 771–89.

McClintock, F. H. (1976a), 'The Beeson Report: Delinquency and Unemployment in the North-East of England', in United Nations Social Defence Research Institute, *Economic Crises and Crime*, Rome: UN Publication No. 15, 79-83.

McClintock, F. H. (1976b), 'Employment Problems of Young Offenders Committed to a Closed English Borstal', in United Nations Social Defence Research Institute, *Economic Crises and Crime*, Rome: UN Publication No. 15, 104-25.

Maccoby, E. E., Johnson, J. P. and Church, R. M. (1958), 'Community Integration and the Social Control of Juvenile Delinquency', *Journal of Social Issues*, 14, 38-51.

McDonald, L. (1968), *Social Class and Delinquency*, London: Faber & Faber.

McDonald, L. (1976), *The Sociology of Law and Order*, Boulder, Colorado: Westview Press.

McEachern, A. W. and Bauzer, R. (1967), 'Factors Related to Disposition in Juvenile-Police Contacts', in M. W. Klein, ed., *Juvenile Gangs in Context: Theory, Research and Action*, Englewood Cliffs: Prentice-Hall, 148-60.

Magnuson, W. G. and Carper, J. (1968), *The Dark Side of the Marketplace*, Englewood Cliffs: Prentice-Hall.

Manders, D. (1975), 'Labelling Theory and Social Reality: A Marxist Critique', *The Insurgent Sociologist*, VI, 53-66.

Mannheim, H. (1948), *Juvenile Delinquency in an English Middletown*, London: Kegan Paul, Trench, Trubner.

Mannheim, H., Spencer, J. and Lynch, G. (1957), 'Magisterial Policy in the London Juvenile Courts', *British Journal of Delinquency*, 8, 13-33.

Marlin, J. T. (1973), 'City Crime: Report of Council on Municipal Performance', *Criminal Law Bulletin*, 9, 557-604.

Marshall, H. and Purdy, R. (1972), 'Hidden Deviance and the Labelling Approach: The Case for Drinking and Driving', *Social Problems*, 19, 541-53.

Martin, J. M. (1961), *Juvenile Vandalism: A Study of its Nature and Prevention*, Springfield, Ill.: Charles C. Thomas.

Martin, J. P. (1962), *Offenders as Employees*, London: Macmillan.

Martinson, R. (1974), 'What Works? — Questions and Answers about Prison Reform', *The Public Interest*, 35, 22-54.

Massimo, J. L. and Shore, M. F. (1963), 'A Comprehensive Vocationally Oriented Psychotherapeutic Program for Delinquent Boys', *American Journal of Orthopsychiatry*, 33, 634-42.

Matsumoto, Y. (1970), 'The Distribution of Juvenile Delinquency in the Social Class Structure — A Comparative Analysis of Delinquency Rate between Tokyo and Nashville', *Japanese Sociological Review*, 20, 2-18.

Matza, D. (1964), *Delinquency and Drift*, New York: Wiley.

Matza, D. (1969), *Becoming Deviant*, Englewood Cliffs: Prentice-Hall.

Matza, D. and Sykes, G. M. (1961), 'Delinquency and Subterranean Values', *American Sociological Review*, 26, 712-19.

Mays, J. B. (1959), *On the Threshold of Delinquency*, Liverpool: Liverpool University Press.

Mays, J. B. (1963), *Crime and Social Structure*, London: Faber & Faber.

Meade, A. (1973), 'Seriousness of Delinquency, the Adjudicative Decision and Recidivism — A Longitudinal and Configuration Analysis', *Journal of Criminal Law and Criminology*, 64, 478-85.

Merril, H. A. (1959), *Problems of Child Delinquency*, Boston: Houghton Mifflin.

Merton, R. K. (1957), *Social Theory and Social Structure*, Glencoe, Ill.: Free Press.

Mike, B. (1976), 'Willem Adriaan Bonger's "Criminality and Economic Conditions": A Critical Appraisal', *International Journal of Criminology and Penology*, 4, 211-38.

Miller, W. B. (1958), 'Lower-Class Culture as a Generating Milieu of Gang Delinquency', *Journal of Social Issues*, XIV, 5–9.

Miller, W. B. (1962), 'The Impact of a Total Community Delinquency Control
Project', *Social Problems*, 10, 168–91.

Miller, W. B. (1967), 'Theft Behaviour in City Gangs', in M. W. Klein, ed.,
Juvenile Gangs in Context: Theory, Research and Action, Englewood Cliffs:
Prentice-Hall, 25–37.

Mizruchi, E. H. (1964), *Success and Opportunity*, New York: Free Press.

Mizruchi, E. H. (1967), 'Aspiration and Poverty: A Neglected Aspect of Merton's
Anomie', *Sociological Quarterly*, 8, 439–47.

Monahan, T. P. (1957), 'Family Status and the Delinquent Child: A Reappraisal
and Some New Findings', *Social Forces*, 35, p. 257.

Monteino, J. B. (1966), *Corruption: Control of Maladministration*, Bombay:
Manaktala.

Moran, R. (1971), 'Criminal Homicide: External Restraint and Subculture of
Violence', *Criminology*, 8, 357–74.

Morgan, B. S. (1975), 'Segregation of Socioeconomic Groups in Urban Areas: A
Comparative Analysis', *Urban Studies*, 12, 47–60.

Morris, T. (1957), *The Criminal Area: A Study in Social Ecology*, London:
Routledge & Kegan Paul.

Mugishima, F. and Matsumoto, Y. (1970), 'A Study of Delinquents' Differenti-
ation from 1042 Cohort in Tokyo: Social Position of Boys in their Residential
Communities and Delinquency', *Reports of the National Research Institute of
Police Science*, 11, 1–1.

Mugishima, F. and Matsumoto, Y. (1973), 'An Analysis of Delinquent Differentiation Related to Boys' Social Origin and Educational Attainment', *Report of
the Japanese Research Institute of Police Science*, 14.

Myerhoff, H. L. and Myerhoff, B. G. (1964), 'Field Observations of Middle Class
"Gangs"', *Social Forces*, 42, 328–36.

Nagel, S. S. (1970), 'The Tipped Scales of American Justice', in A. S. Blumberg,
ed., *The Scales of Justice*, Chicago: Aldine, 31–49.

National Advisory Commission on Criminal Justice Standards and Goals (1973),
Community Crime Prevention, Washington DC.

Nettler, G. (1974), *Explaining Crime*, New York: McGraw-Hill.

Newman, D. J. (1956), 'Pleading Guilty for Considerations: A Study of Bargain
Justice', *Journal of Criminal Law, Criminology and Police Science*, 46, 780–
90.

Newman, D. J. (1958), 'White-Collar Crime', *Law and Contemporary Problems*,
23, 735–53.

New South Wales Bureau of Crime Statistics and Research (1974), *A Thousand
Prisoners*, Statistical Report No. 16, Sydney.

Nixon, A. (1974), *A Child's Guide to Crime*, Sydney: Angus & Robertson.

Noblit, G. W. (1973), *Delinquency and Access to Success: A Study of the Consequences of the Delinquency Label*, PhD dissertation, University of Oregon.

Nye, I. F. (1958), *Family Relationships and Delinquent Behaviour*, New York:
Wiley.

Nye, I. F., Short, J. and Olson, V. J. (1958), 'Socioeconomic Status and Delinquent Behaviour', *American Journal of Sociology*, 63, 381–9.

Oaks, D. H. and Lehman, W. (1970), 'Lawyers for the Poor', in A. S. Blumberg,
ed., *The Scales of Justice*, Chicago: Aldine, 91–122.

O'Connor, G. W. and Watson, N. A. (1964), *Juvenile Delinquency and Youth
Crime: The Police Role*, Washington: International Association of Chiefs of
Police.

Odell, B. N. (1974), 'Accelerating Entry into the Opportunity Structure', *Sociology and Social Research*, 58, 312–17.

Olds, E. B. (1941), article in *The Federator*, XVI (3), 221–31.

O'Rand, A. and Ellis, R. A. (1974), 'Social Class and Social Time Perspective', *Social Forces*, 53, 53–62.

Oughton, F. (1971), *Fraud and White-Collar Crime*, London: Elek.

Palmai, G. (1971), 'Crime and Social Class in Juvenile Delinquency', *Juvenile Court Journal*, 22, 16–17.

Palmer, S. (1960), *A Study of Murder*, New York: Thomas Y. Crowell.

Palmore, E. and Hammond, P. E. (1964), 'Interacting Factors in Juvenile Delinquency', *American Sociological Review*, 29, 848–54.

Parent, F. J. (1974), *A Community Level, Time-Series Analysis of Concomitant Variation in Economic and Crime Indices: Sanford Springvale, Maine, 1951–1970*, PhD dissertation, University of New Hampshire.

Parker, H. (1974), *View from the Boys*, Newton Abbot: David & Charles.

Pearce, F. (1973), 'Crime, Corporations and the American Social Order', in I. Taylor and L. Taylor, eds, *Politics and Deviance*, Harmondsworth: Pelican, 13–42.

Pearce, F. (1976), *Crimes of the Powerful: Marxism, Crime and Deviance*, London: Pluto Press.

Phelps, H. A. (1929), 'Cycles of Crime', *Journal of Criminal Law, Criminology and Police Science*, XX, 107–21.

Phillips, J. C. (1974), *The Creation of Deviant Behaviour in High Schools: An Examination of Cohen's General Theory of Subcultures*, PhD dissertation, University of Oregon.

Phillips, L., Votey, H. L. and Maxwell, D. (1972), 'Crime, Youth and the Labor Market', *Journal of Political Economy*, May/June, 491–504.

Picou, J. S., Cosley, A. J., Lemke, A. W. and Azuma, H. T. (1974), 'Occupational Choice and Perception of Attainment Blockage: A Study of Lower Class Delinquent and Non-Delinquent Black Males', *Adolescence*, 9, 289–98.

Piliavin, I. M. (1969), 'Estudio socio-economico de la delinquencia infantil y juvenil' (socio-economic research on child and juvenile delinquency), *Revista Espanola de la Opinion Publica*, 17, 397–430.

Piliavin, I. and Briar, S. (1964), 'Police Encounters with Juveniles', *American Journal of Sociology*, 70, 206–14.

Pine, G. J. (1965), 'Social Class, Social Mobility and Delinquent Behaviour', *Personnel and Guidance Journal*, 43, 770–4.

Polk, K. (1958), 'Juvenile Delinquency and Social Areas', *Social Problems*, 5, 214–17.

Polk, K. (1965), 'An Exploration of Rural Delinquency', in L. Burchinal, ed., *Youth in Crisis: Facts, Myths and Social Change*, Washington DC: US Govt Printing Office, 221–32.

Polk, K. (1965), *Those Who Fail*, Eugene, Oregon: Lane County Youth Project.

Polk, K. (1967), 'Urban Social Areas and Delinquency', *Social Problems*, 14, 320–5.

Polk, K. (1969), 'Class, Strain and Rebellion Among Adolescents', *Social Problems*, 17, 214–24.

Polk, K., Frease, D. and Richmond, F. L. (1974), 'Social Class, School Experience and Delinquency', *Criminology*, 12, 84–96.

Polk, K. and Halferty, D. S. (1966), 'Adolescence, Commitment and Delinquency', *Journal of Research in Crime and Delinquency*, 3, 82–96.

Pope, C. E. (1975), *Sentencing of California Felony Offenders*, Utilization of Criminal Justice Statistics, Analytical Report 6, US Dept of Justice, Law Enforcement Assistance Administration.

Porterfield, A. L. (1952), 'Suicide and Crime in the Social Structure of an Urban Setting', *American Sociological Review*, XVII, 341-9.

Pownall, G. (1969), *Employment Problems of Released Prisoners*, College Park, Md: University of Maryland, mimeographed.

President's Commission on Law Enforcement and Administration of Justice (1967), *Task Force Report: Corrections*, Washington DC: US Govt Printing Office, 2-3.

Proveda, T. G. (1970), 'The Image of the Criminal: A Critique of Crime and Delinquency Theories', *Issues in Criminology*, 5, p. 62.

Pyle, G. F. (1974), *The Spatial Dynamics of Crime*, University of Chicago, Department of Geography Research Paper No. 159.

Quensel, S. (1971), 'Relative Frequency of Delinquent Behaviour and Social Stratum of Non-Penalised Juvenile Males', *Monatschrift fur Kriminologie und Strafrechtsreform*, 54, 236-62.

Quicker, J. C. (1973), 'A Consideration of the Relationship of "Punitiveness" to Delinquency as Developed in Opportunity Theory', *The Journal of Criminal Law and Criminology*, 64, 333-8.

Quinney, E. R. (1963), 'Occupational Structure and Criminal Behaviour: Prescription Violation by Retail Pharmacists', *Social Problems*, 11, 179-85.

Quinney, R. (1971), 'Crime, Delinquency and Social Areas', in H. Voss and D. M. Peterson, eds, *Ecology, Crime and Delinquency*, New York: Appleton-Century-Crofts.

Quinney, R. (1973), 'Crime Control in Capitalist Society: A Critical Philosophy of Legal Order', *Issues in Criminology*, 8, 75-99.

Quinney, R. (1974), *Critique of Legal Order: Crime Control in Capitalist Society*, Boston: Little, Brown.

Quinney, R. (1977), *Class, State and Crime*, New York: David McKay.

Reiss, A. J. (1951), 'Delinquency and the Failure of Personal and Social Controls', *American Sociological Review*, 16, 196-207.

Reiss, A. J. and Rhodes, A. L. (1961), 'The Distribution of Juvenile Delinquency in the Social Class Structure', *American Sociological Review*, 26, 720-32.

Reiss, A. J. and Rhodes, A. L. (1963), 'Status Deprivation and Delinquent Behavior', *Sociological Quarterly*, 4, 135-49.

Reitzes, D. C. (1955), 'The Effect of Social Environment upon Former Felons', *Journal of Criminal Law, Criminology and Police Science*, 46, 226-31.

Renner, K. (1949), *The Institutions of Private Law and their Social Functions*, London: Routledge & Kegan Paul.

Rhodes, A. L. and Reiss, A. J. (1969), 'Apathy, Truancy and Delinquency as Adaptations in School', *Social Forces*, 48, 12-22.

Richert, J. P. (1975), 'The Court Employment Project in New York', *American Bar Association Journal*, 17, 35-44.

Robin, G. D. (1969), 'Anti-Poverty Programs and Delinquency', *Journal of Criminal Law, Criminology and Police Science*, 60, 323-31.

Robin, G. D. (1970), 'The Corporate and Judicial Disposition of Employee Thieves', in E. O. Smigel and H. L. Ross, eds, *Crimes Against Bureaucracy*, New York: Van Nostrand, 124-46.

Robins, L. N., Gyman, H. and O'Neal, P. (1962), 'The Interaction of Social Class and Deviant Behaviour', *American Sociological Review*, 27, 480-92.

Rodman, H. (1963), 'The Lower Class Value Stretch', *Social Forces*, 42, 205-15.

Rodman, H. and Grams, P. (1967), 'Juvenile Delinquency and the Family: A Review and Discussion', in The President's Commission on Law Enforcement and Administration of Justice, *Task Force Report: Juvenile Delinquency and Youth Crime*, Washington DC: US Govt Printing Office.

Roncek, D. W. (1975), 'Density and Crime: A Methodological Critique', *American Behavioral Scientist*, 18, 843–60.

Rosen, L. and Turner, S. (1967), 'An Evaluation of the Lander Approach to the Ecology of Delinquency', *Social Problems*, 15, 189–200.

Rosenberg, B. and Silverstein, H. (1969), *The Varieties of Delinquent Experience*, Waltham, Mass.: Blaisdell, 130–3.

Ross, M. (1974), 'Economic Conditions and Crime – Metropolitan Toronto 1965–1972', *Criminology Made in Canada*, 2, 27–41.

Rovner-Pieczenik, R. (1970), *Project Crossroads and Pre-Trial Intervention: A Program Evaluation*, National Committee for Children and Youth. .

San Francisco Youth Opportunities Center (1966), *An Evaluation of the San Francisco Youth Opportunities Center*, San Francisco Youth Opportunities Center.

Saunders, J. T., Reppucci, N. D. and Sarata, B. P. (1973), 'An Examination of Impulsivity as a Trait Characterizing Delinquent Youth', *American Journal of Orthopsychiatry*, 43, 789–95.

Scarpitti, F. R., Murray, E., Dinitz, S. and Reckless, W. (1960), 'The Good Boy in a High Delinquency Area', *American Sociological Review*, 25, 555–8.

Schafer, W. E. and Polk, K, (1967), 'Delinquency and the Schools', in The President's Commission on Law Enforcement and Administration of Justice, *Task Force Report: Juvenile Delinquency and Youth Crime*, Washington DC: US Govt Printing Office, 222–9.

Schmid, C. F. (1960), 'Urban Crime Areas', *American Sociological Review*, 25, 527–42, 655–78.

Schmitt, R. C. (1956), 'Intercorrelations of Social Problem Rates in Honolulu', *American Sociological Review*, 21, 617–19.

Schuessler, K. F. and Cressey, D. (1950), 'Personality Characteristics of Criminals', *American Journal of Sociology*, 55, 476–84.

Schuessler, K. F. and Slatin, G. (1964), 'Sources of Variation in US City Crime, 1950 and 1960', *Journal of Research in Crime and Delinquency*, 1, 127–48.

Schur, E. M. (1969), *Our Criminal Society*, Englewood Cliffs: Prentice-Hall.

Schur, E. M. (1973), *Radical Non-Intervention*, Englewood Cliffs: Prentice-Hall.

Sellin, T. (1937), *Research Memorandum on Crime in the Depression*, New York: Social Science Research Council Bulletin No. 27.

Sellin, T. (1938), *Culture Conflict and Crime*, New York: Social Science Research Council Bulletin No. 41, 19–32.

Sennett, R. (1970), *The Uses of Disorder: Personal Identity and City Life*, Harmondsworth: Penguin.

Sharpston, M. J. (1970), 'The Economics of Corruption', *New Society*, 16, 944–6.

Shaw, C. R. and McKay, H. D. (1969), *Juvenile Delinquency and Urban Areas*, Chicago: University of Chicago Press.

Shaw, M. and Williamson, W. (1972), 'Public Attitudes to the Police', *The Criminologist*, 26, 18–32.

Sherwin, R. C. (1968), *Social Class Values and Deviant Behaviour: An Empirical Test of some Theories of Delinquency*, PhD dissertation, University of Connecticut.

Sheth, H. (1961), *Juvenile Delinquency in an Indian Setting*, Bombay: Popular Book Depot.

Shipee-Blum, E. V. (1959), 'The Young Rebel: Self-Regard and Ego-Ideal',

Journal of Consulting Psychology, 23, 44–50.

Shoham, S. and Shaskolsky, L. (1960), 'An Analysis of Delinquents and Non-Delinquents in Israel: A Cross-Cultural Perspective', *Sociology and Social Research*, 53, 333–43.

Short, J. F. (1952), 'A Note on Relief Programs and Crimes during the Depression of the 1930s', *American Sociological Review*, XVII, 226–9.

Short, J. F. (1964), 'Gang Delinquency and Anomie', in M. B. Clinard, ed., *Anomie and Deviant Behaviour*, New York: Free Press, 98–127.

Short, J. F. and Strodtbeck, F. L. (1965), *Group Process and Gang Delinquency*, Chicago: University of Chicago Press.

Shulman, H. M. (1949), 'The Family and Juvenile Delinquency', *Annals of the American Academy of Political and Social Science*, 261, 21–31.

Siegel, L. J., Rathus, S. A. and Ruppert, C. A. (1973), 'Values and Delinquent Youth: An Empirical Re-Examination of Theories of Delinquency', *British Journal of Criminology*, 13, 237–44.

Simondi, M. (1970), *Data on Eighty Cases of Homicide*, Dipartimento Statistico-Matematico, Univ. Degli Studi di Firenze, Serie Ricerche Empiriche No. 5.

Singell, L. D. (1967), 'Examination of the Empirical Relationships between Unemployment and Juvenile Delinquency', *American Journal of Economics and Sociology*, 26, 377–86.

Singell, L. D. (1968), 'Economic Causes of Delinquency: National Versus Local Control', *Urban Affairs Quarterly*, 4, 225–33.

Skogan, W. G. (1974), 'The Validity of Official Crime Statistics: An Empirical Investigation', *Social Science Quarterly*, 55, 52–64.

Slocum, W. L. and Stone, C. (1963), 'Family Culture and Patterns of Delinquent Type Behaviour', *Marriage and Family Living*, 25, 202–8.

Smith, G. (1975), *Leisure, Recreation and Delinquency*, MA thesis, University of Queensland.

Smith, S. M., Hanson, R. and Noble, S. (1973), 'Parents of Battered Babies: A Controlled Study', *British Medical Journal*, 4/5889, 388–91.

Sorokin, P. A. and Lunden, W. A. (1959), *Power and Morality*, Boston: Porter Sargent.

Spadijir-Dzinic, J. (1968), 'Socioloski pristup istrazivanju maloletnicke delink-vencijo' (a sociological approach to the investigation of juvenile delinquency), *Sociologija*, 10, 269–80.

Spady, D. R. (1972), 'Socio-Economic Status and the Ecology of Juvenile Delinquency: Some Methodological Considerations', unpublished PhD dissertation, University of Oregon.

Spector, P. E. (1975), 'Population Density and Unemployment: The Effects on the Incidence of Violent Crime in the American City', *Criminology*, 12, 399–401.

Spergel, I. (1961), 'An Exploratory Research in Delinquent Subcultures', *Social Service Review*, 35, 33–47.

Spergel, I. (1967), 'Deviant Patterns and Opportunities of Pre-Adolescent Negro Boys in Three Chicago Neighbourhoods', in M. W. Klein, ed., *Juvenile Gangs in Context: Theory, Research and Action*, Englewood Cliffs: Prentice-Hall, 38–54.

Spitzer, D. (1975), 'Toward a Marxian Theory of Deviance', *Social Problems*, 22, 638–51.

Stark, R. and McEvoy, J. (1970), 'Middle-Class Violence', *Psychology Today*, 4, 52–4.

Stewart, J. and Cannon, D. (1977), 'Effects of Perpetrator Status and Bystander Commitment on Responses to a Simulated Crime', *Journal of Police Science and Administration*, 5, 318–23.

Stinchcombe, A. L. (1964), *Rebellion in a High School*, Chicago: Quadrangle Books.

Sullenger, T. E. (1936), *Social Determinants in Juvenile Delinquency*, New York: Wiley.

Sutherland, E. H. (1949), *White Collar Crime*, New York: Holt, Rinehart & Winston.

Suttles, G. D. (1968), *The Social Order of the Slum*, Chicago: University of Chicago Press.

Suttles, G. D. (1972), *The Social Construction of Communities*, Chicago: University of Chicago Press.

Swartz, J. (1975), 'Silent Killers at Work', *Crime and Social Justice*, 3, 15–20.

Sykes, G. and Matza, D. (1957), 'Techniques of Neutralization: A Theory of Delinquency', *American Sociological Review*, 22, 664–70.

Taggart, R. (1972), *The Prison of Unemployment: Manpower Programs for Offenders*, New York: John Hopkins.

Tallman, I. (1966), 'Adaptation to Blocked Opportunity: An Experimental Study', *Sociometry*, 29, 121–34.

Taylor, I., Walton, P. and Young, J. (1973), *The New Criminology: For a Social Theory of Deviance*, London: Routledge & Kegan Paul.

Taylor, I., Walton, P. and Young, J. (1975), *Critical Criminology*, London: Routledge & Kegan Paul.

Terry, R. M. (1967), 'Discrimination in the Handling of Juvenile Offenders by Social-Control Agencies', *Journal of Research in Crime and Delinquency*, 4, 218–30.

Thio, A. (1973), 'Class Bias in the Sociology of Deviance', *American Sociologist*, 8, 1–12.

Thomas, D. S. (1927), *Social Aspects of the Business Cycle*, New York: Knopf.

Thornberry, T. P. (1973), 'Race, Socioeconomic Status and Sentencing in the Juvenile Justice System', *Journal of Criminal Law and Criminology*, 64, 90–9.

Thrasher, F. M. (1927), *The Gang*, Chicago: University of Chicago Press.

Timms, D. (1971), *The Urban Mosaic: Towards a Theory of Residential Differentiation*, Cambridge: Cambridge University Press.

Tittle, C. R. and Villemez, W. J. (1977), 'Social Class and Criminality', *Social Forces*, 56, 475–502.

Tobias, J. (1967), *Crime and Industrial Society in the Nineteenth Century*, London: Batsford.

Toby, J. (1957), 'Social Disorganization and Stake in Conformity: Complementary Factors in the Predatory Behaviour of Hoodlums', *Journal of Criminal Law, Criminology and Police Science*, 48, 12–17.

Toby, J. (1957), 'The Differential Impact of Family Disorganization', *American Sociological Review*, 22, 505–12.

Toby, E. J. and Toby, M. L. (1957), *Low School Status as a Predisposing Factor in Subcultural Delinquency*, US Office of Education and Rutgers University.

Toro-Calder, J. (1970), 'Algunos hallazgos de un estudio sobre la delincuencia juvenil en Puerto Rico' (some findings from a study of juvenile delinquency in Puerto Rico), *Revista de Ciencias Sociales*, 14, 233–246.

United States Bureau of the Census (1923), *The Prisoners' Antecedents*, Washington DC: US Govt Printer, p. 32.

University of Pennsylvania (1969), a succession of unpublished studies at the University of Pennsylvania reported in *Violent Crime: The Challenge to Our Cities*, Report of the National Commission on Causes and Prevention of Violence, New York: George Braziller, p. 40.

Van Kleek, M. (1931), *Notes on Fluctuations in Employment and in Crime in New York State*, Report of US National Commission on Law Observance and Enforcement, vol. I, Part V, Washington DC: US Govt Printing Office.

Vaz, E. W. (1966), 'Self-Reported Juvenile Delinquency and Socio-Economic Status', *Canadian Journal of Corrections*, 8, 20–7.

Vaz, E. W., ed. (1967), *Middle-Class Juvenile Delinquency*, New York: Harper & Row.

Vedder, C. B. and Somerville, D. B. (1970), *The Delinquent Girl*, Springfield, Ill.: Charles C. Thomas.

Vinson, T. and Homel, R. (1972), *The Coincidence of Medical and Social Problems Throughout a Region*, Sydney, New South Wales Bureau of Crime Statistics and Research.

Vold, G. B. (1958), *Theoretical Criminology*, New York: Oxford University Press, 164–81.

Voss, H. L. (1963), 'Ethnic Differentials in Delinquency in Honolulu', *Journal of Criminal Law, Criminology and Police Science*, 54, 325–6.

Voss, H. L. (1966), 'Socioeconomic Status and Reported Delinquent Behaviour', *Social Problems*, 13, 314–24.

Wadsworth, M. E. J. (1975), 'Delinquency in a National Sample of Children', *British Journal of Criminology*, 15, 167–74.

Walberg, H. J., Yeh, E. G. and Paton, S. M. (1974), 'Family Background, Ethnicity and Urban Delinquency', *Journal of Research in Crime and Delinquency*, 11, 80–7.

Waldo, G. P. and Dinitz, S. (1967), 'Personality Attributes of the Criminal: An Analysis of Research Studies, 1950–65', *Journal of Research in Crime and Delinquency*, 4, 185–202.

Wallis, C. P. and Maliphant, R. (1967), 'Delinquency Areas in the County of London: Ecological Factors', *British Journal of Criminology*, 7, p. 254.

Warner, S. B. (1934), *Crime and Criminal Statistics in Boston*, Cambridge: Harvard University Press.

Warner, W. L. and Lunt, P. S. (1941), *The Social Life of a Modern Community*, New Haven: Yale University Press, p. 376.

Wattenberg, W. W. and Balistrieri, J. J. (1950), 'Gang Membership and Juvenile Misconduct', *American Sociological Review*, XV, p. 749.

Wattenberg, W. W. and Balistrieri, J. (1952), 'Automobile Theft: A Favored-Group Delinquency', *American Journal of Sociology*, 57, 575–9.

Weeks, H. A. and Smith, M. G. (1939), 'Juvenile Delinquency and Broken Homes in Spokane, Washington', *Social Forces*, 18, 48–59.

Weiner, N. L. and Willie, C. V. (1971), 'Decisions by Juvenile Officers', *American Journal of Sociology*, 77, 199–210.

West, D. J. (1967), *The Young Offender*, Harmondsworth: Penguin.

West, D. J. (1973), *Who Becomes Delinquent?*, London: Heinemann.

Westley, W. A. (1970), *Violence and the Police: A Sociological Study of Law, Custom and Morality*, Cambridge, Massachusetts: MIT Press.

White, G. F. (1975), 'Public Responses to Hypothetical Crimes: Effect of Offender and Victim Status and Seriousness of the Offence on Punitive Reactions', *Social Forces*, 53, 449–59.

Whyte, W. F. (1943), *Street Corner Society: The Social Structure of an Italian Slum*, Chicago: University of Chicago Press.

Wiers, P. (1944), *Economic Factors in Michigan Delinquency*, New York: Columbia University Press.

Wilcox, L. D. (1969), *Social Class, Anomie and Delinquency*, PhD dissertation,

Colorado State University.

Wilkins, L. T. (1971), 'The Deviance-Amplifying System', in W. G. Carson and P. Wiles, eds, *Crime and Delinquency in Britain*, London: Martin Robertson, 219–25.

Wilkins, L. T. (1965), *Social Deviance, Social Policy, Action and Research*, London: Tavistock.

Wilkins, L. T. and Gottfredson, D. M. (1969), *Research Demonstration and Social Action*, Davis, California: National Council on Crime and Delinquency Research Center.

Wilkinson, K. (1974), 'The Broken Family and Juvenile Delinquency: Scientific Explanation or Ideology?', *Social Problems*, 21, 726–39.

Willett, T. C. (1971), *Criminal on the Road*, London: Tavistock.

Williams, J. R. and Gold, M. (1972), 'From Delinquent Behaviour to Official Delinquency', *Social Problems*, 20, 209–29.

Willick, D. H., Gehlker, G. and Watts, A. M. (1975), 'Social Class as a Factor Affecting Juridical Disposition: Defendants Charged with Criminal Homosexual Acts', *Criminology*, 13, 57–77.

Willie, C. V. (1967), 'The Relative Contribution of Family Status and Economic Status to Juvenile Delinquency', *Social Problems*, 14, 326–35.

Willie, C. V. and Gershenovitz, A. (1964), 'Juvenile Delinquency in Racially Mixed Areas', *American Sociological Review*, 29, 740–4.

Wilson, J. Q. (1968), *Varieties of Police Behaviour: The Management of Law and Order in Eight Communities*, Cambridge, Mass.: Harvard University Press.

Wilson, P. R., Braithwaite, J. B., Guthrie, A. and Smith, G., unpublished data from a study of truancy for the Australian Poverty Commission. For a report of this study see Wilson, P. R., Braithwaite, J. B., Guthrie, A. and Smith, G. (1975), *Truancy: Report to the Poverty Commission, Education Section*, Canberra.

Winslow, E. (1931), *Relationship Between Employment and Crime as Shown by Massachusetts Statistics*, Report of US National Commission on Law Observance and Enforcement, vol. I, Part IV, Washington DC: US Govt Printing Office.

Winslow, R. W. (1967), 'Anomie and its Alternatives: A Self-Report Study of Delinquency', *Sociological Quarterly*, 8, 468–80.

Wolf, P. (1962), 'Crime and Social Class in Denmark', *British Journal of Criminology*, 3, 5–17.

Wolfgang, M. E. (1958), *Patterns in Criminal Homicide*, Philadelphia: University of Pennsylvania Press.

Wolfgang, M. E. (1967), 'Criminal Homicide and the Subculture of Violence', in M. E. Wolfgang, ed., *Studies in Homicide*, New York: Harper & Row, 5–6.

Wolfgang, M. E. and Ferracuti, F. (1967), *The Subculture of Violence: Towards an Integrated Theory in Criminology*, London: Social Science Paperbacks.

Wolfgang, M. E., Figlio, R. M. and Sellin, T. (1972), *Delinquency in a Birth Cohort*, Chicago: University of Chicago Press.

Wolfgang, M. E., Kelly, A. and Nolde, H. C. (1962), 'Comparison of the Executed and Commuted among Admissions to Death Row', in N. Johnston *et al., The Sociology of Punishment and Correction*, New York: Wiley.

Wolfgang, M. E. and Riedel, M. (1975), 'Rape, Race and the Death Penalty in Georgia', *American Journal of Orthopsychiatry*, 45, 658–67.

Won, G. and Yamamoto, G. (1968), 'Social Structure and Deviant Behaviour: A Study of Shoplifting', *Sociology and Social Research*, 53, 44–55.

Wood, A. L. (1961), 'Socio-Structural Analysis: Murder, Suicide and Economics', *American Sociological Review*, 26, 744–52.

Select bibliography

Woods, G. D. (1972), 'Some Aspects of Pack Rape in Sydney', in D. Chappell and P. R. Wilson, eds, *The Australian Criminal Justice System*, Melbourne: Butterworth, 109–14.

Young, J. (1975), 'Working-Class Criminology', in I. Taylor, P. Walton and J. Young, eds, *Critical Criminology*, London: Routledge & Kegan Paul, 63–94.

Zivan, M. (1966), *Youth in Trouble: A Vocational Approach*, Final Report of a Research and Demonstration Project, May 31, 1961–August 31, 1966, Dobbs Ferry, New York: Children's Village.

Name Index

Name index

Subject Index

Inequality, crime, and public policy

Inequality, crime, and public policy

John Braithwaite

Australian Institute of Criminology

Routledge and Kegan Paul

London, Boston and Henley

First published in 1979
by Routledge & Kegan Paul Ltd
39 Store Street,
London WC1E 7DD,
Broadway House,
Newtown Road,
Henley-on-Thames,
Oxon RG9 1EN and
9, Park Street,
Boston, Mass. 02108, USA
Set in IBM Journal by
Hope Services
Abingdon, Oxon
and printed in Great Britain by
Lowe & Brydone Ltd
Thetford, Norfolk

British Library Cataloguing in Publication Data

Braithwaite, John

Inequality, crime and public policy.
1. Crime and criminals   2. Social classes
3 Capitalism
I. Title
364.2'56   HV6 169   79-40850

ISBN 0 7100 0323 4